Holy GRAMS

past

present

future

through anagrams

Trenét Worlds

PUBLISHED BY: MultipleWorlds Media
Cincinnati, Ohio 45214
https://multipleworlds.net

CONTENTS

ACKNOWLEDGEMENTS

Holy Grams is the much-abridged edition of **If Words Could Talk**, originally published ©2009. Holy Grams ©2018 focuses strictly only on spiritual perspectives, provides updated commentary, and features Bible verses and historical annotations to support the anagrams.

Special thanks to AI software developer William Tunstall-Pedoe for permission to republish anagrams generated from Anagram Genius.™

http://www.anagramgenius.com

How to Read This Book

Holy Grams follows a simple and predictable format. First, the text subjected to anagramming is displayed as shown:

> ANAGRAM

Guiding phrases in small caps are inserted periodically to assist in the flow of the narrative. NARRATIVES WILL APPEAR LIKE THIS.

The actual anagrams are displayed *italicized, like this.*

RELEVANT LONGEST WORDS/PHRASES USING SOME OF THE LETTERS are extremely revealing and found at the end of the anagram story. They add further emphasis to the truth of the narrative. All italicized anagrams are generated just from the text displayed inside the box!

Anagrams relating to Messianic prophecy or alluding to other significant prophetic events in the Old Testament Anagrams section are ***italicized and bolded***. Scripture references supporting the anagrams are tagged with a (†). Observations from the author's research or personal experience display an asterisk (*). References to the works of men's hands are marked by a double dagger (‡). A dictionary may be helpful with definitions.

Anagrams do not replace the revealed word of God as manifested in the Bible, nor add to it. Rather, they fall under the scriptural admonition of Mark 4:22 that "...there is nothing hid, which shall not be manifested; neither was any thing kept secret, but that it should come abroad", and Solomon's observation in Ecclesiastes 1:9 that "The thing that hath been, it is that which shall be; and that which is done is that which shall be done: and there is no new thing under the sun." There is no new revelation provided outside of what the prophets of God have spoken; therefore, the anagrams serve to confirm and validate what has already been articulated and reveal details which have heretofore been hidden; but nevertheless, line up with the program God has declared through his apostles and prophets. The author has trusted in the guidance of the Holy Ghost to interpret the anagrams; and provided supporting scriptures that validate them with uncanny accuracy.

PART I
the past

GENESIS – CREATION AND FALL OF MAN

ON THAT INFAMOUS DAY…

"Faces dismal angel in afternoon."
"Female scandalising afternoon."
"Ill fame as afternoon ascending."

THE EVIL NATURE OF THE WICKED ONE…

"Alarming felonies of ascendant."
"Draconian felon…gleam as finest."
"I'm an angelic - ensnares daft fool."
"Damn-fool if Satan sincere angel."

"Fat, demoniacal felon angriness."
"Affection as snarling lemonade."
"Nonsense! A fang-filled aromatic."
"Ignorant? Felonies scandal fame."
"Ill fame - and ignorances not safe."

THE ENTICEMENT

"An off-center alongside animals."
"Fine, fanatic, amoral goldenness."
"Fatal necromania if goldenness."
"An ill-mannered goof fascinates."
"Infernal of gladsome, nice Satan."
"Gladsome fascinate on infernal."
"So, fascinated on infernal gleam."
"And I am an effortless congenial."
"Flair of congenial and tameness."
"Demoniacal, ornate angel sniffs."
"Meaningless of Radiant of Clean."
"Danger on! Fascinates on ill fame."
"Tone-deaf if angel's on carnalism."
"Fool and menace as self-training."
"Damnations. Nag of self-reliance."

"Satan felon defaming Censorial."
"Infantile goodness?? Carnal fame!"

"Insane fool star defaming Clean."
"Lame Satan offending Censorial."
"Is not malfeasance felon daring?"

THE TRAP IS SPRUNG

"Angel-face and so fine mortal sin."
"An agile offences and mortal sin."
"Offences and alienating morals."
"Damnation! Agile offences snarl."
"Alarming offences idle on Satan."
"Satan sneering – facile, damn fool."
"Fools neat...carnalism deafening."
"Alert! I am a clean son's offending."
"Scandalise of on fair gentleman."
"Angel of eradicant of manliness."
"An ace angel misleads in front of."
"Malfeasant grins. Fine canoodle."
"Fool fine and mean tragicalness."
"Clean goofed! Infernal Satanism."
"Fascinate! Fool! Malign ensnared."
"Alas! Fool magnificent! Ensnared."
"Satan clean domineer in slag-off."
"Lad slag-off Senior maintenance."

THE RESULT OF SIN

"Innocent earn slag-off maladies."
"Offences nail large damnations."
"Moan! Infernal, tangled fiascoes."
"Deafen tragical of on manliness."
"Infernal goof! Nascent maladies."
"Man groans on an ill-effects idea."
"Sad female! Infernal contagions."
"Contagion and female frailness."

SHAME AND BLAME

"Malfeasant. Considering on ...leaf."   †Genesis 3:7
"Malignant ...feared confessional."   †Genesis 3:8

"Fine of an assorted name-calling."
"Name-calling after fine so-and-so."
"Name-calling of so refined Satan."

REMORSE

"Sniffles to an egomaniacal nerd."
"Sniffles and emotional carnage."
"Sniffles and an emotional grace."

THE CURSE UPON THE SERPENT

"Censorial of ending of malfeasant."
"Mean flailing of censored Satan."

PROPHECY OF A FUTURE SAVIOR

"Infant, endearing. Colossal fame." †Isaiah 9:6-7
"Nail offences, large damnations." †Colossians 2:14
"Saintdom's Ace of infernal angel." †Luke 10:18-19

"Offences and angel or 'tis animal."
"Animal. Cleanest or as offending."
"Son's offending. Lacerate animal." †Hebrews 9:22
"Angriness. Cold feet of an animal."

RELEVANT LONGEST WORDS/PHRASES USING SOME OF THE LETTERS

"self-determining" "free association" "aforementioned"
"considerations" "self-condemnation" "conflagrations"
"organic disease" "Renaissance man"
"ill-manneredness"

Therefore as by the offence of one judgment came upon all men to condemnation; even so by the righteousness of one the free gift came upon all men unto justification of life. Romans 5:12

CAIN and ABEL were the first sons born to Adam; Cain being the eldest. Like Adam, Cain was a tiller of the ground. Abel was a keeper of sheep.

A SACRIFICE PLEASING TO GOD

Although many years would pass until the Law was revealed through Moses, it was understood that blood sacrifice for one's individual sin was to be offered to God. This principle was established when God killed an animal to make coats of skin for Adam and Eve after their trespass. This was the only sacrifice acceptable to God – a type of the efficacious offering of the Lamb of God who would one day come to take away the sins of the world. It was God's validation of just such a sacrifice – and refusal to accept anything less–which irritated Cain. The resulting homicide was deliberate and carefully orchestrated.

The Bible tells us that "the LORD had respect unto Abel and to his offering: But unto Cain and to his offering he had not respect," Genesis 4:4-5. Most likely this respect was demonstrated by the fire of God consuming Abel's sacrifice–similar to Gideon's (Judges 6:21), Manoah's (Judges 13:20), and Elijah's experiences (I Kings 18:38). The grain and vegetables Cain carefully arranged and set before the Lord were not even sautéed, no less consumed. In response to that rejection, the first murder was committed.

This murder was pre-meditated, because Genesis 4:8 informs us "...Cain talked with Abel his brother: and it came to pass, when they were in the field, that Cain rose up against Abel his brother, and slew him." Cain's lack of remorse when confronted by God further demonstrates the damage of sin to the human psyche. True to the fallen nature, he has taken a life but fears to lose his own. God in His mercy permits Cain to live; but places a mark upon him (possibly a prominent scar of unusual shape) as a flag – a warning that he was not to be killed. It is interesting to note there is no indication Cain felt compelled to offer sacrifice for his most recent offence; rather he "...went out from the presence of the LORD, and dwelt in the land of Nod, on the east of Eden." It appears he eventually came to take a perverse sort of pride in his action and found a way to transform the notoriety of his act into the stuff legends are made of, based on the boasting of his descendant Lamech, (Genesis 4:16-24.)

Three different anagram texts were examined to uncover the saga behind the first recorded incident of jealousy, murder, and to be precise–

false worship of God demonstrated by self-righteousness and justification by works of the flesh.

Interesting words appearing in this exercise are *grace*, *criminal*, *prideful*, and *scarface*. The use of the word *spermicidal* appears to point to the fact that Cain effectively eliminated his brother's future progeny by murdering him. Also appearing are *braincase* – possibly alluding to Abel's skull and the trauma which caused his death, and *fireball* – relating to the Consuming Fire as divine acceptance of a sacrifice. *Objective* and *cost effective* also appear. *Cost effective* may refer to plant produce being easier for Cain as a time investment than properly preparing a lamb for sacrifice. Words which can be formed from the anagrammed text such as *Fertile Crescent* and *classical genetic code* set the location and point to the inherent sinfulness resident in the carnal nature common to all descendants of Adam and Eve.

A TWIST IN THE MURDER PLOT?

One of the anagrams appears to suggest that Cain prepared a beverage for his brother that incapacitated him in some way prior to murdering him. While there is nothing in the Biblical record to support this as fact, it is reasonable to assume that being a shepherd, Abel was a relatively strong man. He would have had to regularly lift lambs and kids, in addition to restraining larger animals for shearing. And as Cain was a farmer, he was probably well acquainted with the healing and/or poisonous properties of many plants. Since the Bible gives a rather bare-bones account of the event, I cannot prove a spiked drink was given to Abel to disable his ability to defend himself. I can say with certainty, however, that anyone who will go so far as to kill a family member over acceptance or rejection of a sacrifice is definitely not beyond adulterating a beverage for nefarious purposes.

> CAIN'S PRODUCE SACRIFICE
> AND FAMILIAL MURDER

WHO TEMPTED CAIN TO COMMIT SACRILEGE?

"Lucifer's rapid idea man of accursed criminal."
"Lucifer's famed and primordial inaccuracies."

**A FLIPPANT ATTITUDE REGARDING
THE NEED FOR SACRIFICE AND FORGIVENESS**

"Sacrificial imprudences or dreadful maniac."
"Proud criminal menace defrauds sacrificial."

"I am prideful's criminal; accursed of Radiance."
"Merciful Radiance accord impaired, as sinful."

IMPAIRED SENSE OF JUSTICE...GOD IS UNFAIR

"Fair?? Defrauder accursed. Complains inimical."

ABEL MURDERED FOR OBEDIENCE TO GOD

"Farcical maniac sin defrauds purer domicile."
"I'm nefarious, farcical, and crude spermicidal."

THE COST OF HIS ACT?
HE WILL NEVER BE ABLE TO FARM AGAIN

"Cruel premium of farcical. Radiance disdains."
"Dream dried-up if unsocial scarface criminal."
"Merciful Disciplinarian of a accursed dream."

ACCURSED YET PRIDEFUL – NO REPENTANCE

"I'm accursed inferior and despairful acclaim."
"Maniac's accursed criminal if adore prideful."
"If prideful, criminals adore accursed maniac."

THE MARK OF CAIN

"I'm a cruel and scar-faced, perfidious criminal."
"Careful, I'm accursed! Am red of Disciplinarian."
"I am a dried-up scarface if criminal scoundrel."
"Candid ridicule if I am supernormal scarface."
"An impaired. Credulous if scar-faced criminal."
"Informal ridicule. Maniac's dried-up scarface."

RELEVANT LONGEST WORDS/PHRASES USING SOME OF THE LETTERS

"Disciplinarian" "self-proclaimed" "insufficiencies"
"social insurance" "circumincession"

CAIN'S VEGETABLE OFFERING
ABEL'S ANIMAL SACRIFICE

JEALOUSY TO THE POINT OF PSYCHOPATHIC RAGE

"Craggier calamities if off-balance enviableness."
"Craggier off-balance vilifies amicable neatness."
"Fine amiableness aggrieves. Critical off-balance."
"Satanic off-balance aggrieves. As belief crime nil."

CAIN WANTS THE BLESSING APART
FROM THE SACRIFICE WHICH HONORS

"Self favorite? Grace insignificance. Else, baa lamb."   †Hebrews 9:22
"Farcical egomaniac envisages fireball benefits."
"I Am in fireball inaccessible. Offences aggravate."

GOD REMONSTRATES WITH CAIN... SINCE CAIN CAN'T
SEE THE SIGNIFICANCE HE SEES NO NEED TO COMPLY

"Menace. Slag-off beastlier-variable significance."
"Agreeable it is off-balance. Marvels significance."

THE MURDER IS PLOTTED AND COMMITTED

"Beneficent fireball? Aggressive maniacal fiasco!"
"Greenest off-balance. I came. Braincase vigil fails."
"Graceless if I coffin a saint. Grievance. Blameable."

RELEVANT LONGEST WORDS/PHRASES USING SOME OF THE LETTERS

"self-insignificance" "inconceivableness" "incorrigibleness"
"insignificancies" "overgeneralising" "inconsistencies"
"ineffectiveness" "insignificances" "intolerableness"

```
┌─────────────────────────────────┐
│     VEGETABLES: REJECTION       │
│    FLOCK SACRIFICE: ACCEPTED    │
└─────────────────────────────────┘
```

CHEAP GRACE PREFERRED TO
OBEDIENCE AND HEARTFELT WORSHIP

"Speckled objective – clean certificates of grace."
"Gift re a feckless practice concealed objective."
"Scant objective, freckle-faced, poetic sacrilege."
"Angelic joker practice cost-effective debacles."
"Practicable Grace declines cost-effective joke."
"Preface: flock. Scant objective deceit, sacrilege."
"Silence!! Crackpot sacrilege affected objective."

CAIN...FULL OF HIMSELF

"Deceivable jerk. Ecstatic creep. Conceit slag-off."
"Objective – cockiest self-deceit fragrance place."

AN OPPORTUNITY TO OFFER A SACRIFICE PLEASING TO GOD
FLATLY REJECTED ...AND MET WITH MOCKERY AND DISDAIN

"Effective grace topics obedience. Jerk catcalls.
"Special effective grace 'bestial'. Jerk concocted."   †Hebrews 9:22
"Receptive face-to-face scolding? Rejectable, sick."

HATRED OF ABEL ESCALATES TO MURDER

"Objective farcical. Sick of gentle respected ace."
"Fertile Crescent pig-faced ace cloaks objective."   †I John 3:12
"Jerk concocted ill-effects capacities beverage."
"Objective – grace? Offences! A tactic precedes kill."

CONFRONTATION AND ACCOUNTABILITY

"A slick egocentric replaces affected objective."
"Categorical Presence affected slick objective."

CAIN MARKED ...A LIFETIME REMINDER OF THE LIFE HE TOOK
AND A WARNING TO ANY WHO MIGHT ATTEMPT VENGEANCE

"Scarface. Skeptical reflect genocide objective."
"Objective stone-age traffic circle speckled ace."
"Freak objective. Perfect! Classical genetic code."

RELEVANT LONGEST WORDS/PHRASES USING SOME OF THE LETTERS

"self-objectification" "self-glorification" "self-gratification"
"self-preservation" "objectifications" "grains of paradise"
"negative feedback"

By faith Abel offered unto God a more excellent sacrifice than Cain, by which he obtained witness that he was righteous, God testifying of his gifts... Hebrews 9:22

Forasmuch as ye know that ye were not redeemed with corruptible things... But with the precious blood of Christ, as of a lamb without blemish and without spot... I Peter:18-19

THE EARTH WAS CORRUPT
AND FILLED WITH VIOLENCE

This is a description of the condition of the earth just prior to the Flood Judgment. The Lord Jesus warned these same conditions would precede His return. Thus, it should come as no surprise that the anagrams found from this phrase emphasize entrenched witchcraft, blood lust, and love of death – which apparently reached an apex in the hunting of humans for sport, and the phallic worship characteristic of rejection of the one, true Holy God.

HALLMARKS OF A DOOMED CIVILIZATION

A serpent (an archaic term for snake) is a reptile, and in this topic, we will see the word reptilian surface several times – proving that the spirit of the serpent was actively engaged in sabotaging God's plan for a creation bearing His image in the earth, and replacing it with a warped society celebrating power, carnal excess, and death. Also alluded to is the corruption of the human and animal species via scientific tampering (similar to the chimera experimentation taking place today) and the result of intermingling of celestial and terrestrial life forms. A form of punitive electric shock is even mentioned – perhaps along the line of today's taser technology.

FORWARD TO THE PAST

There is no reason to believe the antediluvian world was any less advanced technologically than our present level of technology. In fact, since people lived for hundreds of years, they had much time to perfect their machinations. Therefore, deductive reasoning implies they were vastly more advanced than our current civilization. Myths of a superhuman race from an advanced civilization eradicated by some cataclysmic event inspired many of the comic books we read as children. The anagrams the author has found imply these 'myths' are likely rooted in fact.

Anything that appears to be cutting-edge technology today is merely a rediscovery of what has long been forgotten. Indeed, Ecclesiastes 1:9-11 advises us there is nothing new under the sun – things of antiquity have merely passed from memory. Verse 10 is especially insightful: "Is there anything whereof it may be said, See, this is new? it hath been already of old time, which was before us." As far as the misuse of nuclear technology is concerned, we can only surmise that God – Ruler of heaven and earth, set divine boundaries on the proliferation and application of such technology, or intervened with the Flood Judgment before man was able to complete radioactive destruction of the earth.

BIRD'S EYE VIEW OF THE PRE-FLOOD CULTURE

The line of Cain was absorbed with establishing a dominion over the earth that excluded Jehovah God and His revealed principles. At the same time, the fallen angels left their designated jurisdiction in an attempt to corrupt the human gene pool; a desperate bid to prevent the advent of the predestined Seed of the Woman.

Sandwiched between these two dangerous and insubordinate factions was a godly remnant who clung to the revealed principles of Jehovah, refusing to mix with either the lineage of Cain or the angels who abandoned their original estate. Those who chose to walk this way were the focus of ridicule, hatred, and persecution. Among the many vices worthy of judgment during this era, patricide was rampant. We do not know how many (besides Abel) of the godly line were murdered before the flood. We do know that God supernaturally took the fiery and vocal prophet Enoch before his enemies could kill him, and that godly Methuselah died the year of the Flood (previous to the actual event.)

You will not have to read far in this section to understand why God judged the Old World in such a cataclysmic manner. The descriptions of the evil practiced are graphic and revolting. This is particularly concerning because Jesus Christ specifically warned us that the world would be identical in the days prior to his return. This means these same wicked actions are the rule rather than the exception in the times we currently live.

Galatians 5:19-21 lists the works of the flesh: adultery, fornication, uncleanness, lasciviousness, idolatry, witchcraft, hatred, variance, emulations, wrath, strife, seditions, heresies, envyings, murders, drunkenness, and revellings (partying). Colossians 3:6 and Ephesians 5:6 both warn that the wrath of God is coming on those who endorse and embrace - and by extension - are entertained by these lifestyles. James 4:4 solemnly warns that whosoever ... will be a friend of the world is the enemy of God.

As people enjoy this world and what it has to offer, they fail to realize it is doomed for destruction. Man is still doing the same things that brought the Flood Judgment, so man will reap the same results.

This time, the purgative will be fire. In Noah's day, the ark was the only refuge of safety. In this present age, the refuge of safety is redemption through the righteousness of Christ; sealed with the Spirit of God.

WORSHIP OF PURE EVIL

"Ancient descriptive? Wrathful, hollow-hearted."
"Devil-worship ethical now. Threatful. Recanted." ‡The Baphomet Crowd
"Recanted tactful, healthier. Devil-worship now."

"Powerful white-hot, drastic deviance enthrall."
"White-hot, viperine hatred catcalls flew round."
"White-hot sacred talent in powerful arch-devil."

"Powerful arch-devil white-hot tentacles drain."
"Wealthier technocrat flaunted devil-worship."
"Wrathful devil-worship enchanter to delicate."

"Wrathful lacerate. Hot indecent devil-worship."
"Evil fascinated. Corpulent hatred worthwhile."
"Cruel, advanced white-hot reptilian self-worth."
"Evil flash eradicant. Worthwhile unprotected."

UNCONTROLLED HATRED, MURDERS, AND LOVE OF DEATH

"Reticent clean? Ill-favored. Throw up death wish."

"Necrophilic flaunter devastated worthwhile."
"Desolate wrathful thrive ...wanted necrophilic."　　‡Death Squads
"Thievish hatred wanted all-powerful necrotic."
"Shallower, wrathful, intrepid, choice vendetta."
"Well! Wrathful hinderer. Sociopathic vendetta."　　‡Gang Murders
"Ill caveats prince. Lewd fun or white-hot hatred."
"Swift truth – necrophiliac venerated, hallowed."
"Threatful. Hollower wanted viperish accident."
"Devilish hire heat. Put contract down. Farewell!"　　‡Hit Men
"All superconfident hatred active while wroth."

"While wroth, see vandal uplift necrotic hatred."　　‡Rage-fueled
　　　　　　　　　　　　　　　　　　　　　　Homicides

THE FAMILY UNDER ATTACK

"Cheerful, patricidal vendettas on while wroth."
"Honest! Patricidal. Wretched, wrathful Evil one."
"Dwarfish prenatal unloved. White-hot electric."　　‡ Abortion

COHABITATION WITH HUMANS AND SPECIES TAMPERING

"Untoward chief arch-devil sleep with tolerant."
"Convicted wrathful lionheart sleep with dear."
"Devil-shaped fornicate while reluctant wroth."
"Authentic, cloddish were-wolf thrive prenatal."
"Authentic were-wolf. Advanced trophies thrill."
"Overwritten, clownish, half-hearted duplicate."
"Enthrall wherever this two-faced duplication."
"Hallowed, over-fed, staunch reptilian twitcher."
"Dried-up ill-health of attractive wrenches now."
"Twitcher putrefies now or advanced ill-health."

WORSHIP OF THE SERPENT AND DESCENT INTO WITCHCRAFT

"Wholehearted, unloved witchcraft reptilians."

"Wrathful, wholehearted, convicted reptilians."
"Wholehearted, unsolved, reptilian witchcraft."
"Witchcraft well and healthier superdevotion."
"Hedonist reverential. Hallowed witchcraft up."
"Virulent, openhearted witchcraft is hallowed."
"Witchcraft pollutes. Evil hardhearted one win."
"Renowned, avid, witchcraft pollutes healthier."
"Superlenient hollow hearted. Avid witchcraft."
"A hollower, devilish, unpenetrated witchcraft."
"Hollow hearted in penal witchcraft servitude."
"Hallowed witchcraft plunderer on hesitative."
"Heroine's hallowed, virulent, adept witchcraft."   ‡Idolatry via the
"Shapelier witchcraft. Well thundered ovation."   music industry
"Venereal in hollow hearted. Stupid witchcraft."
"Levelheaded, saintlier throw up on witchcraft."

WITCHES HUNT VICTIMS

"Horrific, paederast witch hunt neat, well loved."   ‡Child Sacrifice
"Hot splendor witch hunt–eradicative farewell."
"Witch hunt. Now coldhearted pilferer salivate."

IDEAL HUNTS – A TRUE SPORTSMAN'S CHALLENGE

"Placed favorite well or dishearten witch hunt."
"Favorite witch hunt? Well-placed, strained hero."
"Witch-hunt favorite: well placed. Senior hatred."
"Well-spaced witch hunt if lionheart over-rated."
"Well-placed, favorite, iron-hearted witch hunts."

EXPECTANT MOTHERS AND CHILDREN IN PERIL

"Witch now hunt all over the place. Sad, terrified."
"Hard-core witch hunt prenatal. Loved wifeliest."
"Hardcore witch-hunt. Loved wifeliest, prenatal."
"Witch hunt hallowed if perverted lacerations."   ‡ Blood Rituals
"Read well. Venereal dictatorship of witch-hunt."
"Witch hunt hallowed ideal – pervert fornicates."
"Witch praise fornicate. Hatred. Hunt well loved."
"Craftier witch hunt pleased hollower deviant."
"Pederastic? Irrelevant of hallowed witch-hunt."
"Self-trained hallowed procreative witch hunt."
"Hollower, depraved, fertile, satanic witch-hunt."

WIDESPREAD DRUG ADDICTION

"Villain's powerful, hot-headed twitcher nectar."
"White-hot nectaries' advanced, powerful thrill."
"Hasteful addiction pervert clean worthwhile."
"Powerful enchant thrilled hesitative coward."

PHALLIC WORSHIP AND STATUARIES

"Wretched, wrathful, valiant, polished erection." ‡Obelisks

HUMANS FOR SALE AND USE

"Wrathful, white-painted, necrotic slaveholder." ‡Child sex
"Paederast flinched not. Lucrative, worthwhile." trafficking

SPIRITUAL DECEPTION AND SPELL CASTING

"White halo distract – deliver powerful enchant." ‡Mind Control
"Hallowed, over-fed, spiritual twitcher enchant."
"Curse It! Adept enchant ill-favored while wroth." ‡Hexing and
"White-hot evil flow under decrepit charlatans." spell casting
"Well-thrown, convicted, spiritual featherhead."
"Well! Throw up vitriolic, fatheaded enchanters."

A PERILOUS TIME TO LIVE

"Perfection! Lavish worthwhile, ultra-decadent." †James 5:4
"Stealthful rich? Veneration. Low-paid? Wretched." †James 5:1-6
"Well-worn, dirt-cheap, unheroic filth devastate."
"Untoward athletic showpiece fervid enthrall." ‡Sports hero
"Sharp-witted, renowned, loathful, catchier evil." worship
"Throw up innovate self-willed, catchier hatred."

DICTATORSHIP, A POWER MAD ELITE,
AND TWISTED TECHNOCRATS IN CONTROL

"Powerful white-hot, clandestine arch-devil rat."
"Swift, arch-villain. Wholehearted unprotected."
"Decadent arch-villain the worthiest, powerful."
"Wrathful, anarchic elite swindled over-the-top."
"Vital. Throw up deafened, technocrat ill-wisher."
"Hated powerful deviant technocrat ill-wisher."
"Worthwhile plundered. Salivate if technocrat."

TECHNOLOGY TO FACILITATE INTERACTION
BETWEEN THE DICTATOR AND POPULACE

†Revelation 13: 14-15 *"Wrathful, interactive, odd showpiece enthrall."*   ‡Cyborgs
"Wrathful dictator envied. Showpiece enthrall."

ALLEGIANCE TO CREATOR GOD DISCOURAGED
... HATRED AND PERSECUTION OF THE LINE OF SETH

"Wretched, wrathful, evil...polished recantation."
"Ill-favored threatens accident up worthwhile."
"Lacerant thrive if put down hallowed heretics."
"Throw up relevant Hallowed? Scientific hatred."   †Romans 1:30
"Threaten hallowed. Feverish, critical put-down."
"Heroic clan law hatred. Filthiest put-down ever."
"Chronicle a law hatred. Filthiest put-down ever."
"Each clown rail. Filthiest put-down hatred ever."

POSSIBLE METHOD OF TORTURE USED

"Wholehearted swift punitive accord enthrall."
"Clear civil traps. Renowned deathful white-hot."
"Two-hundred whiplash of alternative electric."   ‡Tasering

JUDGMENT ON THE EARTH PENDING, AND RESTRAINT
OF THE ANGELS WHO KEPT NOT THEIR FIRST ESTATE

"Accord worthwhile. Rainiest vendetta helpful." †II Peter 2:5
"Worthwhile. Chief deplores. Truncated valiant."
"Ultra catastrophe. White-livered now flinched."
"Throw up swift hellhole. Deviant incarcerated." †Jude 1:6

RELEVANT LONGEST WORDS/PHRASES USING SOME OF THE LETTERS

"under specification" "contact-other-plane" "intellectualities"
"crocodile-infested" "interrelationship" "necrotic enteritis"
"presanctification" "hundred-percenter" "lunitidal interval"
"well-authenticated"

And Enoch also, the seventh from Adam, prophesied of these, saying, Behold, the Lord cometh with ten thousands of his saints, To execute judgment upon all, and to convince all that are ungodly among them of all their ungodly deeds which they have ungodly committed, and of all their hard speeches which ungodly sinners have spoken against him. Jude 1:14-15

NOAHS FLOOD – ANTEDILUVIAN ERA

When God completed Creation, He surveyed His work and noted it was "very good." Yet, in less than a thousand years (or as can be said in God's time-frame – before the day was over) man in collusion with Satan had succeeded in reducing the earth to the condition where only 'removal of surface material and thorough flushing with water' could re-set the earth to a state where God could continue His long range plan – restoring man and creation to full fellowship with Him through the promised Seed of the Woman. With the birth of Adam and Eve's son Seth, a lineage began which clung to obedience of the then known principles of God. The patriarch Noah and his family (eight souls) were what remained of this lineage to bridge the gap between the "old" and "new" worlds. In the Bible, eight represents new beginnings–thus the purpose of the flood.

Forty days and nights of steady rain was not the only source of flooding during the Great Deluge. The Biblical account states that "all the fountains of the great deep were broken up, and the windows of heaven were opened." Words which repeatedly surface are *evaluation*, *foundational*, *favoured*, and *validate*. The term *nine and a half* possibly alludes to unit of measurement of the giants on the earth; *four-handed* may also refer to one of their characteristics. *One and a half* may indicate chromosomal changes brought about by genetic tampering of certain celestial beings with humans, and *univalent* means a single, unpaired chromosome. The anagrams seem to indicate that the entities in the one and a half category were misusing dinosaurs - perhaps by genetically engineering reptiles as weapons against people.

A fascinating find in this exercise is the word *nautilus*, from the Greek nautilos (literally sailor) and *naiad* (nymphs presiding over rivers and springs in Greek mythology). Also intriguing is the mention of *Neanderthaloid* – proof that species tampering via attempts to combine dissimilar created beings was causing the human race to **devolve** from the original image and likeness of the Creator. Most likely the underlying premise of this genetic tampering was to irreversibly alter man's genetic code – and by extension – invalidate the unique stamp of the Creator upon his humanity – the end game being to prevent the prophesied Seed of the Woman from ever manifesting.

Hosanna indicates a heartfelt cry to the Lord from Noah and creation itself for deliverance. *Radio* possibly indicates advanced technology used in an attempt to contact demonic beings for assistance. *Vernalisation* refers to chilling of seeds so they will germinate at the proper time – as would be necessary to replant the earth. *Avian* may refer to birds, aviation technology, or winged fowl-human hybrids. And, because the genetically engineered cross-species breeding and poisoning of the earth today bears an eerie similarity to the conditions the anagrams unveil, we may be much closer to the next prophesied judgment than many think.

IMAGINE YOURSELF AN 'OLD WORLD CITIZEN'

As an inhabitant of the Old World, life is a pleasurable experience – as long as one is flexible. One must be able to assimilate, because technology and sciences are breaking new ground–literally–on a daily basis. The one regret is that the biosphere is not what it was several hundred years ago, due to the mutation of plant and animal species. The star guides, rulers, and those in higher sciences began alerting everyone a few centuries back that the fault of all this was 'Creator' God and His failure to anticipate the surge of technology and man's need to evolve.

Faced with this dismal failure, the star guides are taking the lead in reversing this trend by assisting in the development of new species and generously offering samples of their genetic material. While some of the early attempts resulted in grotesque and dangerous specimens, there have been some notable successes – such as the ability to fly and swim underwater for prolonged periods – although presently these abilities are reserved for the elite class. Most everyone agrees the star sciences are building a much better earth and the technology they have shared has dramatically improved life over the last several centuries.

But not everyone appreciates their intervention, and there continue to be stubborn pockets of resistance – backwards plodders who insist on clinging to 'Creator' God and His antiquated tradition of blood sacrifice for sin. The star guides teach the people there is no such thing as sin – man is god; and promise rewards of special abilities and powers to whoever is willing to kill these "resisters." It is the dream of every child that he or she will earn favor with the star guides by killing at least one resister in their lifetime.

Sparse media attention is given to the fact that neither sunset or sunrise were visible over the past day and a half, or that the air is heavy with moisture. As the precipitation increases, forecasters allay the fears of the people by telling them this new phenomenon of water falling from the sky is an annual event – the brainchild of earth scientists seeking to improve on the Creator's plan of hydrating the earth with a mist.

Occasionally, contingency plans in line with seeking higher ground and stocking up on supplies are broadcast, buried in the usual venue of casual conversation, sports, music and entertainment. Public service announcements assure there is nothing to be concerned about; and encourage commerce and social functions to continue unabated. The Nephilim and those who hold communications with the fallen angels are not worried, either. It is obvious how much time and detail God has invested in the design and production of earth and lower creation, and it is ludicrous to believe he would just destroy it in one fell swoop.

Just about the time people are convinced they can 'weather the storm', the fountains of the deep convulse with a deafening rumble. Sheer terror envelopes the earth's inhabitants as structures are torn from their foundations and the surrounding terrain twisted beyond recognition. The scene is a terrifying kaleidoscope of water, screaming, cursing, carnage, darkness, and drowning. Utter chaos is everywhere ...with no way to escape. As for the ark, it is impermeable: God has shut Noah and his family in. The old resister was telling the truth after all...

CREATOR GOD CONTEMPLATES A RUINED CREATION

"Horn of Ideal and evaluations." †Psalm 18:2
"Handler of on said evaluation." †Luke 1:69
"Arisen and hold evaluation of."
"Of old, heard an evaluations in."
"On revaluations of Ideal Hand."
"An old-fashioned revaluation."
"Oh No! Failed and revaluations."

"Oh No! Evaluations and I flared."
"Oh No! And Evaluator finalised."
"Overhead and a final solution."
"Value to an old-fashioned rain."
"Violation and flushed on area."

RIGHTEOUS JUDGMENT BY A RIGHTEOUS GOD

"Forehead and an all-out vision."
"Hear of Salvation in unloaded."
"Headline of: 'Salvation around!'
"Hosanna! Not ill-favoured idea."

INSTRUCTIONS ON BUILDING THE ARK

"Note of hand or an ideal visual."

SUPPLIES TO RIDE OUT THE CATASTROPHE

"And liaison hoard of eventual."
"Fine lads hoard on evaluation."   †Genesis 6:21
"Hoard and life on evaluations."
"File and hoard on evaluations."
"Ha! Vernalisation of unloaded."

CONTRIBUTING SINS OF BROAD-SPECTRUM JUDGMENT

SATANISM

"Invade loud-hailer of on Satan."   †Revelation 2:24

IDOLATRY

"Hosanna entail favoured idol."   †Deuteronomy 32:17

LYING

"Handed evaluation of on liars."   †Revelation 21:18

REVOLT AGAINST GOD AND THE
DIVINE ORDER OF CREATION

"Aha! And failed on revolutions."   †Psalm 82:5
"Hosanna if dared evolutional."

WIDE SCALE MURDER

"Out-of-hand alive and on serial."   †Romans 3:15

ABUSE/MISUSE OF LOWER CREATION

"Alleviate hand of on dinosaur."   †Romans 1:30

OUTRAGEOUS WICKEDNESS THE NORM

"Reasoned a villain out-of-hand."   †Proverbs 4:17
"Villain or out-of-hand and ease."

PRIDE

"Oh Dear! On vain self-laudation."   †Psalm 52:1

WIDESPREAD SUBSTANCE ABUSE

"Evaluations of heroin and lad."   †Revelation 9:21

GROSS CARNALITY

"Half-nude and violation arose."   †Habakkuk 2:15

FRAUD AND DEVIOUSNESS AS THE NORM

"Handler of a devious national."   †Psalm 10:7
"Oh No! Frauds alone invalidate."

THE ENVIRONMENT AND ALL CREATED
SPECIES CORRUPTED BEYOND REMEDY

"Oh no! Fields and a revaluation."   ‡GMO
"Handles evaluation of on arid."   ‡Depletion of water
"Halve of around desalination."   ‡Pollution of oceans
"Defoliation and an overhauls."   ‡Deforestation
"As foul innovational adhered."   ‡Atmospheric spraying
"Hard evaluations of non-ideal."
"Visual of on a Neanderthaloid."
"Ha! Fooled on via ruined natals."   ‡Genetic tampering
"Eh! A load of viral inundates on."   ‡Bio-engineered disease
"Eh! Load on of an Antivirals due."

ALIEN LIFE FORMS SLATED FOR JUDGMENT

"An aliens overlaid out-of-hand."

THE NINE-AND-A-HALF...POSSIBLY GIANTS, CYBORGS, OR SOME TYPE OF TRANS-HUMANS WHO IMPERILED TRAVELERS OR OTHERS VENTURING OUTSIDE

"Nine-and-a-half as outdoor evil."
"Nine-and-a-half! Alive! Outdoors!"

POSSIBLY THEY WERE PART HUMAN, PART MACHINE

"Nine-and-a-half, various tooled."
"Sure avoid nine-and-a-half tool."

IN ADDITION TO THEIR IMPOSING STATURE, THEY WERE CHARACTERIZED BY LYING, WICKEDNESS, AND HAVOC WREAKING

"Nine-and-a-half or a devious lot."
"Devious oral to nine-and-a-half."
"A nine-and-a-half loved riotous."

THEY POSSESSED THE ABILITY TO COMMUNICATE VIA AIRWAVES TO THEIR HANDLER OR ANGELIC ENTITIES

"Nine-and-a-half loves radio out."
"Nine-and-a-half, audio to solver."
"Is nine-and-a-half, over, to aloud."
"Nine-and-a-half radio solve. Out!"
"Ole! Out! Nine-and-a-half advisor."

THEY HAD TRESPASSED BY VICTIMIZING HUMANS

"Our nine-and-a-half do violates."
"Our nine-and-a-half, violated so."
"So nine-and-a-half violator due."

THEIR INCREASED NUMBERS AND LONGEVITY WERE A THREAT TO HUMANITY

"Out! Is nine-and-a-half overload."　　†Genesis 6:4
"Do, or a nine-and-a-half outlives."

THE ONE-AND-A-HALF…POSSIBLY ANGELIC-HUMANOID
CROSSBREEDS …AN OTHER-RACE SPAWNED FROM
UNLAWFUL LIAISONS AND VOID OF A FULLY HUMAN SOUL

"One-and-a-half, rude violations."
"One-and-a-half soul derivation."   †Jude 6-7

THEIR SKIN WAS NOT AS CREATOR GOD HAD DESIGNED WHEN HE
FORMED ADAM FROM THE SOIL – POSSIBLY A PLOY TO INVALIDATE
THE DECREE MAN WOULD RETURN TO THE DUST OF THE EARTH

"So one-and-a-half, invalid outer."

THEY BILLED THEMSELVES AS AN EVOLUTIONARY
IMPROVEMENT OVER MAN CREATED BY GOD'S DESIGN

"Rid one-and-a-half as evolution."

LIKE THE NINE-AND-A-HALF, THEY HAD AN
ADVISOR – MOST LIKELY A FALLEN ANGEL ENTITY

"Outline one-and-a-half advisor."

TOGETHER, A REVOLT AGAINST GOD WAS BEING PLANNED

"One-and-a-half said revolution."
"One-and-a-half aids revolution."

THEY WERE IN RIVALRY AGAINST GOD, DESIRING
HUMANITY'S WORSHIP FOR THEMSELVES

"One-and-a-half virtue as on idol."
"One-and-a-half, idolatrous vein."

THEY PRACTICED EVIL, CRUELTY, AND FORNICATION

"One-and-a-half or loud vanities."
"One-and-a-half live and riotous."
"One-and-a-half and riotous evil."
"An one-and-a-half, riotous devil."
"Not one-and-a-half!! Devious liar."
"One-and-a-half evil to dinosaur."
"It is one-and-a-half love around."
"Or one-and-a-half invites aloud."

THEIR LONGEVITY INFLUENCED MULTIPLE GENERATIONS

"I, one-and-a-half loves duration."
"So live one-and-a-half duration."
"One-and-a-half, odious interval."
"So one-and-a-half, evil duration."

GOD JUDGES IN FAIRNESS BASED ON THEIR DEEDS

"So load in one-and-a-half. Virtue??"
"So dial on one-and-a-half. Virtue??"
"One-and-a-half ruins! Do violate."
"I solve one-and-a-half duration."
"It is one-and-a-half. Unload over."

NO ONE CAN HELP THEM …THEIR DEMIGOD POWERS ARE WORTHLESS

"I overload one-and-a-half units."
"I one-and-a-half, sad revolution."
"Revulsion to aid one-and-a-half."
"One-and-a-half over as dilution."

THE FOUR-HANDED – AN UNSTABLE VARIATION

"Alleviations on a four-handed."
"Violation as lean four-handed."
"In a four-handed as on volatile."
"Four-handed, so an alleviation."

FUTILE ATTEMPTS TO ESCAPE OR SURVIVE THE DELUGE AND CONTINUE WITH PLANS FOR EVOLUTION: THE GREAT LADDER FIASCO

"An evolution if has a ladder on!"
"Evaluations and hire fool and…"
"Evaluation on ladder fashion."
"Oh! No ladder if an evaluations."
"On evaluation on a fish ladder?"
"Evaluation. Fashion no ladder."

NO RESOURCES FOR WATER OF SUCH DEPTH

"Volatile – and oar unfashioned."

SPECULATION OF SEEKING HIGHER GROUND

"Oh Dear! Evaluations of inland."
"Oh! Leads on of valiant idea. Run!!"

SPECULATION OF SHELTERING IN CAVES
AND BAILING WATER

"Evaluations of hole and drain."
"Validation? Or hole and unsafe."

SPECULATION OF REINFORCING EXISTING STRUCTURES

"Head over, nail foundationals."
"Aha! Nail resolved foundation."
"O Dear! Foundations halve nail."
"Fountainheads overload nail!"
"And I handle roof evaluations."
"Ha! Unloaded. Renovations fail."

SPECULATION OF WATERPROOFING DWELLINGS
AND STOCKING UP ON SUPPLIES

"Evaluations of line and hoard."

LIES, DISINFORMATION, GAMBLING, AND ATTEMPTS
TO CAPITALIZE ON THE IMPENDING CATASTROPHE

"Fool: It is overhead and annual."
"Oh – invalid. A false note around."
"Various loan on life-and-death."
"Out-of-hand, realised loan vain."

PLEAS TO THE FALLEN ANGELS FOR ASSISTANCE

"Natives and on of a loud-hailer."
"And a lot of and even hilarious."
"Foundational. And evil, hoarse."
"Flesh evaluation and on radio."
"A handful radios on elevation."

A NATIONAL EMERGENCY; A WORLDWIDE FLOOD:
FOUNTAINS OF THE DEEP BROKEN UP

"Head do of national, universal."

"I, fountainhead on El Salvador."
"Sound national!! Overhead fail!"
"Oh Dear! Unsolved if a national."

TOO LATE, THE REALIZATION OF DOOM

"A handful reasoned violation."
"And a frivolous national heed."
"Oh No! Dread final evaluations."

**ATTEMPT TO MAKE SUPPLICATION TO GOD WITH
SACRIFICE, BUT GOD WILL NOT REGARD IT**

"Eh! Load on of altar's due in vain."
"Deaf and honours alleviation."

**RIGHTEOUSNESS EXALTS A NATION, BUT
SIN IS A REPROACH TO ANY PEOPLE**

"Ho! I save. Dreadful on national."
"Is foul national and overhead."
"Fluid overheads on a national."
"Oh Dear! Unloved if as national."
"O Dear! Foul national vanished."
"Undo overheads. National fail."
"Overhead fails. Undo national."
"Oh! No validate nefarious land."
"Dual overheads if on national."
"Shoo! Dreadful, naive national."
"Frivolous national end ahead."
"Oh! Adults naive of on rain deal."
"Lad's endeavour of inhalation."
"Eh! Load on of vaunts. Air denial."
"Ideal afternoon. A loud vanish."
"An Oriental of aloud vanished."

GENERATIONS PERISH TOGETHER

"Unloaded. Vanish of a relation."
"A vanished. Undo of relational."
"Oh No! Do invalidate a funerals."

GOD IN CONTROL OF THE PERFECT STORM

"Laid heavens or foundational."   †Isaiah 51:13

"Dial heavens or foundational."
"Slain foundational overhead."
"A Flood One dial. Nature vanish."
"He on a flood valuated in rains."
"Oho! Valuate land foe in drains."
"Oh! Lead on of a navals/air united."
"Oh! Lead on of natural as Divine."

THE PROCESS – THE WINDOWS OF HEAVEN OPENED

"Ah! Flood One din avails nature."
"He on a flood valuated in rains."
"Oho! Valuate land foe in drains."
"Foundational Solver in ahead."
"Foundation alive or as handle!"
"Devaluation or if as handle on!"
"A foundations invade or a hell."
"Foundational and hole varies."
"Overhead all in a foundations."
"Foundation as in all overhead."
"Hello! Foundation as a invader."
"Foul or an additional heavens."
"Ooh! A rain din enfold, valuates."

THE PROCESS CONTINUED:
THE FOUNTAINS OF THE DEEP BROKEN UP

"I, fountainhead on El Salvador."
"A untidier navals hone a flood."
"He untie; load on of naval raids."
"Oh! Deal on of a virulent Naiads."
"Oh! Deal on of Naiads turn alive!"
"In of in and overhead as all-out."
"Is an all-out of in and overhead."

DIVINE JUDGMENT...

"All-out invasion of and adhere."
"Fail and an overhead solution."
"No! And, oh no! Failures validate."
"Ha! Fine or unloaded salvation."
"Found a overload annihilates."

FOR REBELLION AND CARNALITY

"Oh No! Led of a natural vain dies."
"Evaluate foolish and drain on."
"Oh! Leads dilute-on of a nirvana."

FOR HUBRIS AND ARROGANCE

"Oh! Lead on of as ruined valiant."
"Oh! Lead on of as inundate rival."

FOR CORRUPTION OF SPECIES

"Oh! Deal avaunt on of rid aliens!"
"Oh! Lead on of as raid univalent."
"Oh Dear! And an evolution fails."

FOR DESTRUCTION OF THE EARTH

"Oh Dear! Evaluations if on land."
"Oh Dear! No land if evaluations."   †Revelation 11:18

EFFECT ON AVIAN-HUMAN HYBRIDS

"Eh, ideal! Load on of 'turns avian'."
"HE load on of. Avian's ulna tired."
"He load of on dilutes. Avian ran."
"Head on, fool! Avians anti-ruled."
"Oh No! Deal of rein adult avians."
"Oh No! Deal of avians dealt ruin."

NOAH AND HIS FAMILY SAFE

"Shield on a favoured national."
"Alone unshared of validation."
"Notional as I handle favoured."
"Annihilate and solo favoured."   †Genesis 7:1
"Annihilates. Favour loaded on."
"Handle favoured. An isolation."
"Favour. Hole and desalination."
"Favour on a shielded national."   †Genesis 6:8
"An unloaded. Hail! Favorite son."
"Oh! On an allied and favourites!"   †Genesis 6:18

**THE ARK FLOATS, CARRYING NOAH;
WHO IS PERFECT IN HIS GENERATIONS**

"Hoard leaves in foundational."
"Oh! Lead on of dear nautilis van!"
"Oh! Lead on of I, unvaried natals."   †Genesis 6:9

PREPARATION TO DISEMBARK

"And liaison endeavour of halt."
"So unloaded if haven rational."   †Genesis 8:15-19
"Lad and oh so fine revaluation."

GOD GLORIFIED IN JUDGMENT

"Validate fine as an old honour."   †Genesis 8:20-21
"Feels honour and a validation."

THE RAINBOW AS SIGN OF THE COVENANT PROMISE

"Lo, a end of...Oh! Unveils a radiant!"
"Lo! Had one of radiant values in!"   †Genesis 9:8:17

**SCIENTIFIC/ARCHAEOLOGICAL PROOF
OF THE GREAT DELUGE**

"An do hole of – an ruins validate."
"Oh, an lode of data unveil rains."

RELEVANT LONGEST WORDS/PHRASES USING SOME OF THE LETTERS

"revolutionised" "Neanderthaloid" "fountainheads"
"self-laudation" "vernalisation" "nine-and-a-half"
"foundational" "thousand-line" "alleviations"

By faith Noah, being warned of God of things not seen as yet, moved with fear, prepared an ark to the saving of his house; by the which he condemned the world, and became heir of the righteousness which is by faith... Hebrews 11:7

And spared not the old world, but saved Noah the eighth person, a preacher of righteousness, bringing in the flood upon the world of the ungodly... II Peter 2:5

THE TOWER OF BABEL

Imagine a world where everyone speaks the same language! This was the case after Noah's death when his descendants journeyed to the plain of Shinar in what is now modern-day Iraq. It was here they began to form bricks with the intent of building a city, a tower, and 'making a name for themselves'. The logic driving construction of the city and tower – in addition to gaining recognition for themselves – was to prevent themselves from being 'scattered abroad over the face of the earth.' The desire to never again be annihilated by floodwaters may have also been a contributing factor behind building a tower of such immense height.

God did not support this architectural endeavor – reasoning that if they were permitted to continue, nothing would be restrained from them that they desired to do. While this may seem punitive and unnecessary, keep in mind that man's inherent sin nature inevitably leads him on a path away from God, and God's righteous purpose for the earth. He confused their speech, and they left off building the city and tower. The thing they feared – being scattered abroad across the face of the earth – was the very thing they ended up having to do. The name of the place was called "Babel", which means confusion.

Plans to construct a tower also hint that phallic worship may have once again begun to surface among the populace. At any rate, we see no indication of the close walk with God demonstrated by Noah and Enoch. Instead, we see man intent on placing himself on a pedestal and entrenching himself in the place of his choosing.

This subject used three different phrases, "Tower of Babel", "Tower of Babel Confusion of Language", and "Builds City Tower One Language." The name *"Bob"* may allude to the idea of a construction foreman.

TOWER OF BABEL

GOD OBSERVES THE CONSTRUCTION ZONE

"A fort be below."
"Oft bear below."

THE PEOPLE WORK DILIGENTLY

"Oft we belabor."
"Bare elbow oft."
"Few rabble, too."
"Bob to welfare."
"Bob were aloft."

EVEN CHILDREN HELP

"Trowel of babe."

ATTENTION TO DETAIL AND QUALITY

"Beware of blot."
"Beware of bolt."

SONG AND CONVERSATION AMONG THE LABORERS

"Warble befoot."
"Tower foe blab."

THEN, DIVINE INTERDICTION

"Taboo...Ref blew."

CONFUSION AND CHAOS

"Bore blow fate."
"Falter, ebb ...Woo!"
"Aw! Before blot!"
"Woo ...Babel fret."
"Babel woe fort."

**SPEECH AND HEARING DISTORTED
...FRUSTRATION AND ANGER**

"Wobble of tear."
"To bawl before."
"Ear wobble oft."
"Blow of berate."
"Blow of beater."
"Orate flow ebb."

THE WORK GRINDS TO A HALT

"Blew ...foe abort."
"Tar foe wobble."
"A ebb of trowel."
"Oaf trowel ebb."

THE INTEGRITY OF THE STRUCTURE BEGINS TO FAIL

"Fear to wobble."
"Rate of wobble."
"Re oft a wobble."
"A wobblee fort."
"Or wobble fate."
"Ebb... a wet floor."
"Ebb...a roof welt."
"Blew...roof beat."
"A wee fort blob."

THE BUILDERS ARE FORCED TO ACKNOWLEDGE
THE SOVEREIGNITY OF GOD

"Abort. Bow. Flee."
"Boo...bereft law."
"Boo...waft rebel."
"Lo, a bereft bow."
"A rebel bow oft."
"Brew of oblate."
"Bow ...oblate Ref."

THE PEOPLE DISPERSE... SOME WILL
EVENTUALLY CROSS THE OCEANS

"Toe wobble far."
"Bower be float."

RECORDED IN THE BIBLE

"Wrote of Babel."

> TOWER OF BABEL
> CONFUSION OF LANGUAGE

Anagrams from this phrase provide greater insight into the scene at hand once the language of the people was confused. One can practically envision the scenario when the assembly suddenly believed everybody else had either gone crazy or was trying to clown around. The atmosphere of incredulity and name-calling gradually transformed into a sobering reality as people began to seek out and congregate with others they could understand. *Blow off/blow out* describes the genius tactic God exercised in confusing their speech. *Catalogue* and *cataloguing* may refer to attempts to organize based on understanding of speech. *Carnal abuse* may refer to enslavement or forced labor by the weaker while the stronger acted in the capacity of crew foremen and supervisors.

Foul of awful enraging obscene taboo suggests that phallic worship was again becoming prominent in the culture, for when man will not give the Creator pre-eminence, he begins to worship his own creative and procreative abilities. *Foul carnage taboos* hints at the intent to dedicate the completed structure with ceremonial human sacrifices. *Labia* is Latin for lip, and *organ* refers to the tongue as the organ of speech. A reference is also made to *Boolean algebra*, which is used in computer programming and indicates an advanced level of technology. Logic dictates these builders would have had to possess a comprehensive understanding of physics and earth sciences to execute the type of architectural feat they were undertaking: a structure taller than anything known on earth today with implications that caused God himself to intervene. At any rate, the best laid plans of early man were left to dissolve into unrecognizable ruins as the various groups dispersed across the face of the earth.

DIVINE INTERVENTION IN
RESPONSE TO THE WILFULNESS OF MAN

"An off-balance. Fine, gorgeous blow out."
"Clean groaning of beauteous blow off."
"Beauteous Grace baffling now on fool."

**CITY AND TOWER CONSTRUCTION CENTERED AROUND
GREED, CARNALITY, IDOLATRY AND BOASTFULNESS**

"Glowing off-balance of bounteous era."
"Glowing offences of a au naturel boob."
"Foul boob gloating. Unaware offences."
"Foul of awful enraging obscene taboo."
"Blow off genuine foul carnage taboos."
"Encourage blow off of ungenial boast."
"Now able secure gloating of a buffoon."

**THE 'NAME' THEY WERE ATTEMPTING TO ESTABLISH
FOR THEMSELVES WAS DISHONORING TO GOD**

"Logo off-balance. Beauteous frowning."

ALSO, THEIR SPEECH WAS POMPOUS

"Bowel of off-balance tonguing arouse."

**LET US GO DOWN, AND THERE CONFOUND THEIR LANGUAGE,
THAT THEY MAY NOT UNDERSTAND ONE ANOTHER'S SPEECH**

"Blow out gangrenous offence of labia."
"Blow off. Beauteous cleaning of organ."

**LANGUAGE SOUNDS NORMAL TO THE PERSON SPEAKING
BUT IS UNINTELLIGIBLE TO THE HEARER**

"Blow off. Announce goofiest. Arguable."
"Ga-ga of bellower nuisance to buffoon."
"A bellower of a ace buffoon's tonguing."
"Beauteous of clean of garbling of now."
"Able catalogue of buffoon worsening."
"Buffoon's ignorable of new catalogue."
"Ignorable few on buffoon's catalogue."

EVERYONE THINKS EVERYONE ELSE HAS GONE MAD

"Now agreeable buffoon's lunatic goof."

AN ABRUPT CHANGE IN DEMEANOR

"Buffoon's woebegone. Flair coagulant."

"Notable blow off of sanguine courage."
"Now aborting of fabulous of elegance."

**ARCHITECTURAL SKILLS USELESS
IN THE FACE OF LANGUAGE BARRIERS**

"Now, foul stone-age algebraic buffoon."
"Cutoff now of Boolean algebra genius."

**THE INTELLIGENTSIA BEHIND THE CONSTRUCTION
PLANS ARE ENRAGED BUT HELPLESS IN THE FACE
OF DIVINE INTERFERENCE**

"Ciao! Wrongful, able stone-age buffoon."
"Sabotage fool ungenial buffoon crew."
"Blow out ogre of an off-balance genius."
"Off-balance goons argue. Fine blow out."
"Off-balance guile. Now outrage of snob."

**RELIEF FROM FORCED LABOR AS ORDERS
CAN NO LONGER BE UNDERSTOOD**

"Buffoon fool able encouraging sweat."
"Buffoon of glowing abuse on lacerate."
"Blow off fool encouraging neat abuse."
"Genuine blow off to carnal abuse goof."
"Foot on beggar. Unlawful of obeisance."
"A foul aggro offences. Obnubilate now."
"Obnubilate. Encourage of slag-off now."
"Now guarantee flog buffoon sociable."

**PLEAS TO NOT ABANDON THE WORK
IN SPITE OF THE LANGUAGE BARRIER**

"Beaten courage as following buffoon."
"Blow not off of sanguine, able courage."

MAN'S WISDOM IMPOTENT IN THE FACE OF DIVINE DECREE

"Graceful sabotage now lie on buffoon."
"Now genial sabotage of cruel buffoon."
"Beauteous can blow off enraging fool."
"Able   genius goof worn-out. Off-balance."
"Gage of worn-out in. Able of confusable."
"Far-Seeing blow catalogue on buffoon."
"Unbeatable fiasco, on ego of wrongful."

THE PEOPLE REALIZE THE CHANGE IS FROM GOD

"Blow out of as of agreeable of cunning."
"Now obfuscating. Agreeable of on foul."
"Outrageous of Ace now baffling noble."

ALL THE BOASTFUL TALK OVER NOW

"Courageous? Now baffling beaten fool."
"Goofball now fearing bounteous Face."

TEARS AND CURSING

"Water gauge of inconsolable buffoon."
"Noble catalogue of buffoon swearing."
"Buffoons boil now. Outrage. Face Angel."
"Rage of genius blow out on off-balance."

ASSIMILATION INTO GROUPS OF LIKE SPEECH
AND COOPERATION FOR SURVIVAL

"Buffoon feeble now or as cataloguing."
"A buffoons beleaguer of now locating."
"Genial of buffoon. Argue now obstacle."

DISPERSAL

"Blow off. Unreasonable face outgoing."
"Blow out. Sufferable of an ocean-going."
"Neater fabulous blow off: ocean-going."
"Buffoon now globular if stone-age ace."
"Off-balance reusable. Outgoing of now."
"About buffoon's ocean-going farewell."
"Blow off. Unenforceable as a outgoing."
"Wasteful buffoon or ocean-going able."

RELEVANT LONGEST WORDS/PHRASES USING SOME OF THE LETTERS

"unconstrainable" "Boolean algebra" flabbergasting" "unrecognisable"
"unenforceable" "conflagrations" "congregational"
"collaboration" "self-troubling"

The final phrase anagrammed on this topic appears to confirm that the tower was indeed a phallic monument. Not only was man bent on ignoring his Creator and pursuing idolatry, an entire civilization was being influenced by an elite class who made bombastic statements, misguided the people, and engaged in constant foolish talking and boasting. Much like today.

> BUILDS CITY, TOWER –
> ONE LANGUAGE

FOOLISH, IDLE TALK AND RIOTOUS LIFESTYLE

"Worldly beauties ace tonguing."
"Weedy, sociable, ultra tonguing."
"Beauty! Outside, large clowning."
"Beauty! Adore ugliest clowning."
"Below ground, lunatic gayeties."

CRUEL AND SLANDEROUS TALK

"Windbag negotiate ulcerously."
"Unwise bigot cleanly outraged."
"Ugly, crude bigot alienates now."
"Libelous agitated now. Urgency."
"Cowardly elite tonguing abuse."

**IDOLATROUS OBELISK CONSTRUCTION
INTERCEPTED ...THE BUILDERS INCENSED**

"Wittingly end able courageous..."
"Ugly debasing outlaw erection."
"Well! Beauty! So rugged inaction."
"Nice wing...absolutely outraged."
"Well! Incongruity due sabotage."
"Ungodlier cutely win sabotage."

**LET US GO DOWN, AND THERE CONFOUND
THEIR LANGUAGE, THAT THEY MAY NOT
UNDERSTAND ONE ANOTHER'S SPEECH**

"Steady! A nice, grueling blow out."
"Nicely tabulated. Gorgeous win!"
"So Bureau wittingly congealed."

"Ace wisely troubled a tonguing." †Genesis 11:7
"Beauteously wronging dialect."
"Beauteously contain wriggled."
"Now obliterates ugly guidance."
"Cauterise yellow, bad tonguing."
"Warn ugly, tongue-tied sociable."
"Wise doubly lacerate tonguing."
"Absolutely ace wider tonguing."
"Ulcerates ego-building. Not way."
"Glory Be! Casual win tongue-tied."

A CIVILIZATION IN FLUX

"Coward tonguing beauties yell."
"Weary. Able cloudiest tonguing."
"Indicate ugly blow out enrages."
"Weirdo cutely tonguing as able."
"Sweet? Ugly? Condition arguable."
"Low, ugly, tongue-tied braincase."
"Beauteous, large clown dignity."
"Now bug-eyed, outlines tragical."

ROMANTIC PURSUITS INTERRUPTED

"Courting beauty well agonised!"
"Tongue-tied cow really abusing."
"Genuinely disgrace at blow out."
"Good-bye! Wiser, ungallant cutie."
"Gorgeously an ineducable twit."
"Securely datable win outgoing."

ASSOCIATION AND DISPERSION

"Swearingly bulge to education."
"Win grotty, unbiased colleague."
"League now boasting credulity."
"Woebegone as cultural dignity."
"Easy-going, albeit now cultured."
"Easy-going wit on cultured able."
"Win to easy-going, cultured able."
"Sweet guidance on globularity."
"Globular, nice, tongue-tied ways."

RELEVANT LONGEST WORDS/PHRASES USING SOME OF THE LETTERS

"goal-orientated" "congratulations" "indestructible" "inconsiderately"
"insubordinately" "decentralisation" "congregational"
"destroying angel" "renationalised"

**Except the Lord build the house, they labour in vain that build it
... Psalm 127:1**

> ## TWELVE TRIBES – SONS OF JACOB

Anagrams of this phrase allude to events that will be easily recognized by those familiar with the story covered in Genesis chapter 37, and chapters 39-45. The words object and objective are used with great frequency in this exercise. *Object* is used both as a verb–to strongly disagree–and as a noun. *Objective* relates to motive; or, actual individuals.

"...*Bless on of straw*" clearly alludes to Joseph's first dream recounted in Genesis 37:7, and "...*Bless now of star*" points to his second, celestial-themed dream. *Braw* is a Scottish term for being finely dressed in a splendid or gaudy fashion, thus hinting at Joseph's coat. *Observant of twice jobless* refers to his encounter in prison with two of Pharaoh's staff – the chief butler and chief baker. *Blast* is a blight that withers crops. *Snob* refers to the way Joseph's brothers viewed him, and *bowl* is best understood as his silver cup.

JOSEPH IS JACOB'S FAVORITE, CAUSING
JEALOUSY AMONG HIS BROTHERS

"Now bless favorite. Objects!"
"Now bless, or fat objectives."   †Genesis 37:3

HE DISCLOSES TWO DREAMS PREDICTING HIS
FAMILY WILL BOW TO HIM IN HONOR

"Objective? Bless on of straw."   †Genesis 37:7
"Objective? Bless now of star."   †Genesis 37:9
"Son's objective - or best flaw."

JEALOUSY BOILS OVER INTO A PLOT

"Stress of an objective blow."   †Genesis 37:18
"Stern objectives of as blow."
"Favorless objects bite now."   †Genesis 37:19
"Objective: son's worst fable."

THE BROTHERS CONSPIRE TO MURDER
JOSEPH, BUT REUBEN INTERVENES

"Overflows in basest object.   †Genesis 37:20

"Now strives. Objects able of."   †Genesis 37:21
"Few noblest. Savior objects."   †Genesis 37:22
"Objects. Bravest if now lose."
"Safest, or objectives blown."

INSTEAD, JOSEPH IS CAST INTO THE PIT

"Brat's view of object lesson."
"Now, rat objective, boss self!"
"Now aborts self objectives."   †Genesis 37:23-24

"Cover. Sat. Low job benefits."
"Overcast. Jowl info set ebb."
"Overcast. Ebb. Foes jilt own."
"Overcast. Ebb. Lost. Few join."   †Genesis 37:27
"Self star objective now sob."

**SOLD TO THE MIDIANITES FOR TWENTY PIECES
OF SILVER, HE WILL EVENTUALLY ARRIVE IN EGYPT**

"Far job solves. Twice ten. Sob."   †Genesis 37:28

**THE BROTHERS FABRICATE EVIDENCE AND LIE
TO THEIR FATHER JACOB**

"Objective best warn of loss."   †Genesis 37:32
"Fat evils! Now sober objects."
"Beast overflows Object. Sin."
"Objectiveness of lost braw."
"Worn sob. Falsest objective."   †Genesis 37:33

**MEANWHILE, DILIGENTLY AT WORK IN
POTIPHAR'S HOUSE, JOSPEH IS PROMOTED
BASED ON PERFORMANCE**

"Obstacle of new job. Strives."   †Genesis 39:4
"Sweet vertical jobs of snob."   †Genesis 39:5-6

POTIPHAR'S WIFE – A WICKED SEDUCTRESS

"Flower stab son's objective."   †Genesis 39:7
"Slave brews soft objection."
"Job taboo ...swift cleverness."
"Wasn't evil. Rejects of boobs."   †Genesis 39:8-9
"Slave rejects swift on boob."   †Genesis 39:10

"Baboon loves ...rejects swift."
"Now rejects fat boobs evils."
"Slave reject swift on boobs."
"Swift reject a sloven boobs."
"Vast boobs rejections flew."

SCORNED, POTIPHAR'S WIFE GRABS JOSEPH'S GARMENT AS EVIDENCE TO SUPPORT HER FALSE ACCUSATION

"Baboon solve swift rejects."   †Genesis 39:12
"Son's abortive. Objects flew."
"Objects flew so is not brave."
"Objective. Worn falsest sob."   †Genesis 39:14-15
"Brave fools witness object."

POTIPHAR ACTS ON HIS WIFE'S ACCUSATIONS AND CASTS JOSEPH IN PRISON

"Objective tale. Boss frowns."   †Genesis 39:19
"Objective blow of stern ass."
"Best job over now. Facts=lies."   †Genesis 39:20

NOT YOUR AVERAGE INMATE, JOSEPH IS PLACED IN CHARGE OF THE CELL BLOCK

"Vows felon jot scabbier set."   †Genesis 39:21-23
"Objective felon tabs rows."

THE BUTLER AND THE BAKER ARE INCARCERATED; JOSEPH INTERPRETS THEIR DREAMS

"Jabber vices toss two felon."   †Genesis 40:1-3
"Observant of twice jobless."

THE BUTLER WILL BE RESTORED TO HIS POSITION

"Console...brave...swiftest job."   †Genesis 40:9-13

THE BAKER WILL FACE EXECUTION

"Now observe if tactless job."
"Votes job swift censorable."   †Genesis 40:16-19

**PHARAOH'S DREAM TROUBLES HIM AND NO ONE CAN
INTERPRET IT ...THEN, THE BUTLER REMEMBERS JOSEPH**

"Arts of Objective now bless."
"Noble object's of Vast Wiser." †Genesis 41:12-13

JOSEPH INTERPRETS PHARAOH'S DREAM

"Objective best warn of loss."
"Seven blows to fair objects." †Genesis 41:25-32
"Re cows. It blast job of seven."

**HE STRESSES THE IMMEDIATE NEED FOR PHARAOH
TO OBTAIN AN ADMINISTRATOR TO OVERSEE THE
STORAGE AND DISTRIBUTION OF FOOD**

"Forecast evil! Owns best job." †Genesis 41:32-33
"Able to swift converse jobs." †Genesis 41:33-35
"Saw jobs set of convertible."

**PHARAOH FEELS JOSEPH IS MOST QUALIFIED,
AND PROMOTES HIM TO A POSITION
OF GREAT PROMINENCE**

"Select job if now so bravest." †Genesis 41:39
"Now fat, clever, bossiest job." †Genesis 41:40-41
"Cleverest job as wit of snob."
"Sweet vital force jobs snob."
"A fervent object bows silos." †Genesis 41:48-49
"Best job as nicest overflow."

**FAMINE IN THE LAND – JACOB SENDS THE
ELDER SONS TO EGYPT TO PURCHASE FOOD**

"Few. Slobs starve. Objection." †Genesis 42:1-2

**JOSEPH IS THE AUTHORITY THEY MUST APPROACH TO
PURCHASE FOOD – THEY BOW DOWN BEFORE HIM**

"A objector invests; bow self." †Genesis 42:6

**JOSEPH - UNRECOGNIZED BY HIS BROTHERS - ACCUSES
THEM AS SPIES: AN ACCUSATION THEY VEHEMENTLY DENY**

"Vast sober objections flew." †Genesis 42:10-13

JOSEPH INTERROGATES THEM ABOUT THEIR FAMILY; DEMANDING
TO SEE THE YOUNGEST BROTHER WHO DIDN'T ACCOMPANY THEM;
HE DETAINS SIMEON AS A HOSTAGE UNTIL THEY CAN RETURN
WITH BENJAMIN ...FEARFUL, THE BROTHERS REMONSTRATE
WITH EACH OTHER ABOUT THE EVIL THEY DID TO JOSEPH

"Confess over twistable job."   †Genesis 42:21
"A objects leftover sins bows."   †Genesis 42:22

JOSEPH LEAVES THEIR PRESENCE MOMENTARILY
UNTIL HE CAN GET HIS EMOTIONS UNDER CONTROL

"Objective snob's tears flow."   †Genesis 42:24

HE FILLS THEIR SACKS WITH CORN; UNBEKNOWNST TO THEM
HE REFUNDS THEIR MONEY...WHEN THE FOOD IS EXHAUSTED, JACOB
ASKS HIS SONS TO GO TO EGYPT FOR MORE, BUT THEY REMIND HIM
THEY ARE FORBIDDEN TO RETURN WITHOUT BENJAMIN ...JACOB
RESISTS FROM FEAR OF LOSING HIS YOUNGEST SON, BUT THE NEED
FOR FOOD TAKES PRECEDENCE

"Frowns. Sob. Stale objective."
"I bow fervent as object loss."   †Genesis 43:14

THE BROTHERS RETURN WITH BENJAMIN; SIMEON IS
RELEASED, AND A BANQUET PREPARED ...JOSEPH BECOMES
EMOTIONAL AT THE SIGHT OF HIS YOUNGER BROTHER, BUT
RESTRAINS HIMSELF AND DOES NOT YET REVEAL HIS IDENTITY

"Festivals own. Object sober."   †Genesis 43:16
"Objective snob's tears flow."   †Genesis 43:30

COMPLIMENTARY GIFTS FROM JOSEPH ARE SENT TO THE
GUEST QUARTERS OF EACH BROTHER, BUT BENJAMIN'S
GIFT IS FIVE TIMES LARGER THAN THE REST

"Or now fat bless objectives." †Genesis 43:34

AS BEFORE, JOSEPH LADES HIS BRETHREN WITH SUPPLIES;
THIS TIME HOWEVER, HE INSTRUCTS HIS STEWARD TO HIDE
HIS PERSONAL SILVER GOBLET IN BENJAMIN'S SACK

"Now as of best silver object." † Genesis 44:2

JOSEPH INSTRUCTS HIS STEWARD TO OVERTAKE THE DEPARTING
CARAVAN AND BEGIN A CONFRONTATION ABOUT THE SILVER CUP

"Observations objects flew."   †Genesis 44:2
"Stress bowl of an Objective."   †Genesis 44:6
"Silver objects now of beast."

THE BROTHERS DENY TAKING THE CUP

"Vast sober objections flew."   †Genesis 44:8-9

THE SILVER CUP IS FOUND IN BENJAMIN'S SACK

"Least Objective. Frowns. Sob."   †Genesis 44:12

THE BROTHERS MUST RETURN TO FACE JOSEPH

"Objects bow. Rift on a vessel."   †Genesis 44:14
"SOS! Ablest Objective frown."
"Wolf rant! Obsessive object."   †Genesis 44:15

"Objective frowns steal. Sob."   †Genesis 44:16
"Objects bow as if lost nerve."

**JOSEPH SAYS HE MUST TAKE BENJAMIN AS HIS SLAVE;
THEN, EVERYONE ELSE IS FREE TO RETURN**

"Softer blows. An objectives."   †Genesis 44:17

THIS IS NOT AN ACCEPTABLE OPTION

"Objective bless? Frown as to."   †Genesis 44:18

**JUDAH INTERCEDES; TO PREVENT THE GRIEF THAT WILL
SURELY HASTEN JACOB'S DEATH, HE BEGS JOSEPH TO LET
HIM TAKE BENJAMIN'S PLACE**

"Slave objection. Bow. Frets."   †Genesis 44:18
"Braves - if now stole objects."   †Genesis 44:33

**OVERCOME WITH EMOTION, JOSEPH CAN
NO LONGER CONSTRAIN HIMSELF**

"Blows of an Objective rests."   †Genesis 45:1
"Objective snob's tears flow."   †Genesis 45:2

HE REVEALS HIS IDENTITY

"Aborts objective. Owns self."   †Genesis 45:3

AN EMOTIONAL REUNION ENSUES

"Flew on star. Objectives sob."   †Genesis 45:14-15
"Objective star of now bless."   †Genesis 45:17-20
"Or now fat bless objectives."   †Genesis 46:5-6

JOSEPH'S FAMILY IS WELCOMED TO EGYPT
WHERE THERE IS PLENTY

"Lots safe brown objectives."   * True description
                                                         of Hebrews

PHARAOH GENEROUSLY ALLOTS THE LAND OF
GOSHEN FOR JOSEPHS'S FAMILY, PLACING THEM
OVER THE HERDING OF CATTLE

"Fervent Sociable stow jobs."   †Genesis 47:6

RELEVANT LONGEST WORDS/PHRASES USING SOME OF THE LETTERS

"observableness" "objectionable" "object lesson" "colorfastness"
"objectiveness" "self-interest" "self-assertive" "creativeness"
"sociableness" "job-selection" "celebrations"

Seest thou a man diligent in his business? he shall stand before kings; he shall not stand before mean men ...Proverbs 22:29

Behold, how good and how pleasant it is for brethren to dwell together in unity! ...Psalm 133:1

SAMSON AND DELILAH

Have you ever felt life would be easier if you only possessed super- human strength? The story of Samson, a judge from the tribe of Dan – addresses that very question, for with great power comes great responsibility. The Biblical account of his life effectively illustrates that superior physical strength is no substitute for good judgment. But it also poignantly demonstrates II Corinthians 12:9 – that God's strength is made perfect in our weakness.

**GOD TURNS SINFUL ISRAEL OVER TO OPPRESSION
UNDER THE HANDS OF THE PHILISTINES**

"Alas! Land hedonism."
"Land ashames in old."
"I am a son's held land." †Judges 13:1

SAMSON – CALLED BY GOD TO BE A NAZARITE

"Am Holiness ...and lad." †Judges 13:5

**HE GREW, AND THE LORD BLESSED HIM ... AND THE SPIRIT
OF THE LORD BEGAN TO MOVE HIM IN THE CAMP OF DAN**

"Hand smiles on a lad."   †Judges 13:24-25
"Is handsome and all."
"Had load manliness."
"Lad's in a homelands!"

**AGAINST HIS PARENTS WISHES, HE INSISTS
ON MARRYING A PHILISTINE WOMAN OF TIMNATH**

"Maiden - and so shall." †Judges 14:1-3

**ON THE WAY TO FINALIZE THE MARRIAGE ARRANGEMENTS,
A LION ACCOSTS HIM IN THE VINEYARDS OF TIMNATH**

"Lion mad, and hassle." † Judges 14:5

**SAMSON EFFORTLESSLY DISMEMBERS
THE LION WITH HIS BARE HANDS**

"Mass handled a lion."   †Judges 14:6
"Handed a lion - slams." †Judges 14:6

ON A RETURN TRIP TO TIMNATH HE NOTICES BEES
HAVE ESTABLISHED A HIVE INSIDE THE LION'S
CARCASS – APPARENTLY IN THE SKULL

"N' smallish on a dead."   †Judges 14:8
"And small as on hide."
"So small and in head."

SAMSON PRESENTS A RIDDLE ABOUT THE LION AND HIVE
TO THE MALE GUESTS AT THE WEDDING FEAST...THEY COERCE
HIS BRIDE TO OBTAIN THE ANSWER TO AVOID PAYING A STEEP
GRATUITY ...CAUSING THE WEDDING FEAST TO END ON A
DEADLY NOTE FOR THE PHILISTINES

"Aha! No mildness lad."   †Judges 14:19
"Handle in a mad loss."
"Smash non-ideal lad."

TO MAKE MATTERS WORSE, HIS FATHER-IN-LAW GIVES
SAMSON'S WIFE TO ONE OF THE WEDDING GUESTS;
FURTHER ANGERING SAMSON

"Alas! Mishandled on."
"Is mean – and shall do."   †Judges 14:20

AS REVENGE, SAMSON CATCHES THREE HUNDRED FOXES,
TIES THEIR TAILS END TO END, THEN TIES FIREBRANDS
BETWEEN THE TAILS...ONCE IGNITED, HE TURNS THE FOXES
LOOSE THROUGH THE PHILISTINES' FIELDS AND ORCHARDS

"Oh! Sad animals lend."   †Judges 15:4
"And held animals so."
"As hold animals end."   †Judges 15:5
"Hold ends as animal."
"Animal hold as send."
"Oh Man! Land lies sad."
"So handled animals."

HE THEN ENGAGES THE PHILISTINES AS A FORCE OF ONE

"Alas! On laddish men."   †Judges 15:8

**THE PHILISTINES SURROUND JUDAH TO EXACT REVENGE
...RATHER THAN RISK A CONFRONTATION, THE MEN OF
JUDAH BIND SAMSON (THEIR JUDGE! TO TURN HIM OVER
TO THE PHILISTINES ...WHEN THEY REACH LEHI, THE
PHILISTINES SHOUT AGAINST SAMSON**

"Nod. Amass Lehi land."
"Shall. And mad noise."
"Hell adds on manias."   †Judges 15:14

THE SPIRIT OF THE LORD COMES MIGHTILY UPON SAMSON

"A mad Holiness land."   †Judges 5:14

**USING ONLY THE JAWBONE OF AN ASS, SAMSON –
THE JUDGE OUT OF DAN – ANNIHILATES ONE
THOUSAND IN BATTLE AT LEHI**

"O Hell! Dan – an ass dim."
"Hell! Domain and ass."
"Hello! And ass in mad."

"Mind ass-head on all."
"Lehi lands sad moan."
"Add an son slam Lehi."
"Dad an son slam Lehi."   †Judges 15:15
"And an ass mold Lehi."

SAMSON VISITS A HARLOT IN GAZA

"Oh! Ladies' man lands."   †Judges 16:1
"Alas! Hedonism 'n' lad."
"Hedonism and as all."

**THE PHILISTINES PLOT TO KILL HIM AT DAWN ...INSTEAD,
HE PLOWS RIGHT THROUGH THEM WITH THE GATES OF
THEIR OWN CITY -- LEAVING THEM ON A NEARBY HILL**

"O Man! A hill saddens."   †Judges 16:3

SAMSON MEETS DELILAH OF SOREK

"Has mad, insane doll."
"A man handles idols."   †Judges 16:4

**APPROACHED BY THE PHILISTINE LORDS, DELILAH
JOINS THE CONSPIRACY TO UNCOVER THE SECRET
OF SAMSON'S STRENGTH FOR ELEVEN HUNDRED
PIECES OF SILVER**

"She solid land a man?"
"Maiden – and so shall."   †Judges 16:5
"Sad a hellion damns."

**DELILAH PRESSES SAMSON DAILY FOR THE SECRET
OF HIS IMMENSE STRENGTH**

"Lo! Sis handled a man."   †Judges 16:16

**SAMSON TRICKS DELILAH THREE TIMES BEFORE
DIVULGING THE SECRET OF HIS STRENGTH ...SHE
THEN SENDS FOR THE PHILISTINE LORDS**

"A headsman doll sin."
"A handmaid sells on."   †Judges 16:18
"Man sold as I handle."
"Hold 'n' as ladies' man."

SHE LULLS HIM TO SLEEP...

"Lies...a sandman hold."
"A sandman holds lie."   †Judges 16:19

THEN SUMMONS A BARBER...

"A mishandled salon."   †Judges 16:19

SHE BEGINS TO AFFLICT HIM

"Maiden slash on lad."   †Judges 16:19

HIS STRENGTH (JEHOVAH GOD) DEPARTS FROM HIM

"Handle as is old man."   †Judges 16:21

**THE PHILISTINES PUT OUT SAMSON'S EYES, BIND HIM,
AND FORCE HIM TO GRIND GRAIN IN THE PRISON HOUSE
...HE IS THE SOURCE OF REJOICING AND RIDICULE**

"And mill's ahead, son."

"I am an old 'n' slashed."
"Nil as handsome lad."
"O Man! Is sad and hell."
"I, a man, handled loss."   †Judges 16:21
"Lad's on animal shed."
"A handled man silos."
"Ass-head and on mill."

"Shame on and sad ill."

THE PHILISTINES PREPARE A GREAT SACRIFICE IN THE TEMPLE OF DAGON IN HONOR OF SAMSON'S CAPTURE ...SAMSON IS BROUGHT OUT TO ENTERTAIN THE GUESTS – WHICH PROBABLY NUMBER AROUND SEVEN THOUSAND, WITH THREE THOUSAND ON THE ROOF ALONE

"Is a hall and demons."   †Judges 16:23
"Sad in a demon's hall."   †Judges 16:25

SAMSON BEGS THE LORD TO GRANT HIM HIS SUPERHUMAN STRENGTH ONE LAST TIME TO AVENGE HIS EYES

"Dad...mansion...a shell?"   †Judges 16:28

GOD ANSWERS HIS PRAYER–AND GRANTS STRENGTH

"Hands as medallion."   †Judges 16:28

**DOOM IS SEALED FOR EVERYONE PRESENT;
SAMSON WILL TASTE VICTORY EVEN IN DEATH**

"And as Hell's domain..."
"Do madness in a hall."
"Hall is as damned on."
"Do a hall in madness."
"Sad annal...demolish."   †Judges 16:27

MASSIVE CARNAGE ENSUES AS SAMSON EXERTS HIS LAST STRENGTH TO COLLAPSE THE SUPPORTING PILLARS OF THE TEMPLE ...DAGON IS POWERLESS TO SAVE HIS WORSHIPPERS -- HIS IMAGE IS CRUSHED AND MINGLED WITH THEIR BODIES IN A SEA OF BLOOD, BONE, AND STONE

"Slash idol and amen."   †Judges 16:28
"Hall and mad noises."
"Sad all, in handsome."
"Holds in a mean lads."

"Slain handsome lad."
"Smash on an idle lad."
"Sad hall on maidens."
"Shall on sad maiden."
"Dames in hall and so."
"So damned as in hall."
"And domain as shell."
"Sin. Shall moan. Dead."
"Mansion. Shall. Dead."   †Judges 16:30

**HIS BRETHREN AND ALL THE HOUSE OF HIS FATHER
RETRIEVE HIS BODY AND BRING IT HOME FOR BURIAL**

"Oh Man! Land lies sad."   †Judges 16:31

RELEVANT LONGEST WORDS/PHRASES USING SOME OF THE LETTERS

"handmaidens" "animalness" "demand loan" "mishandled"
"ladies'man" "manhandled" "anomalies" "anamnesis"

Better is the sight of the eyes than the wandering of the desire: this is also vanity and vexation of spirit... Ecclesiastes 6:9

Precious in the sight of the LORD is the death of his saints... Psalm 116:15

PART II

the present

SHAPING THE POST-CHRISTIAN ERA

"Gosh! An atheistic partnership."   †II Corinthians 6:14
"This earnest! This approaching!"
"The prophetic saint harassing."   †Ezekiel 3:18
"This neat prophetic harassing."
"Thrashing, as is neat prophetic."
"Higher as honest participants."
"Hierophantic hating trespass."   †Amos 5:10
"Hating as phoniest archpriest."

SHAPING THE POST-CHRISTIAN ERA:
THE CULTURE INCOMPATIBLE WITH THE KINGDOM

The earth abides forever, and the meek and the righteous are destined to inherit it. This is the glorious future awaiting the resurrected saints, which God -who cannot lie- promised before the world began. Yet, over the last fifty or so years, this vision has dwindled to the significance of an archaic fable for many Christians; and the goal in life has transitioned to achieving the maximum in comfort and convenience, while suffering no persecution. Little heed is given to the admonition that we must through much tribulation enter into the kingdom of God, or that strait is the gate, and narrow is the way, which leadeth unto life, and few there be that find it.

What transforms us from blazing light pointing the way to Christ to salt that has lost its savor, branches that bear no fruit, and troubled fountains offering nothing but lukewarm water? The simple answer is succumbing to the carnal mind and becoming conformed to this world. This is because all that is in the world is the lust of the flesh, the lust of the eyes, and the pride of life. None of this is from the Father, but of the world.

Media programming caters to these lusts, and the love of money drives many to act to fulfill them. In contrast, the Kingdom of God is predicated on loving God with all the heart, soul, and strength, and loving ones' neighbor as oneself. Since no man can serve two masters, a divided heart leads to a cold and ineffective witness.

We can avoid the conformation trap by making no provision for the flesh to fulfill the lust thereof. This means relinquishing the streaming media, the episodic dramas, the games, and the dark music. It means to disengage from a mode of thinking which insists you are entitled to a certain lifestyle. It means to crucify yourself to the world and the world to you; and run the race with patience - looking to Jesus and the Kingdom yet to be revealed.

We now turn our attention to one of the obstacles that distract so many from the Kingdom they are commanded to pray for. In the West, this hindrance is defined as The American Dream. Popular culture continues to promote this fallacy, so people still cling to the illusion thereof. The trappings of the dream are now achievable to most only via the double shackles of credit/debt. The character and ethics of the earlier generations who pursued the dream have been replaced with a culture of greed; a mentality of riches for the sake of riches. Words that repeatedly surface in this exercise are *avarice, grievance, rich, chancier, charade, nightmare* and *anathema*.

ACHIEVING THE AMERICAN DREAM

**CHASING THE DREAM IS A TRAP OF AVARICE
(EXTREME GREED FOR MATERIAL WEALTH)**

"Am mightier, enhanced avarice."
"I am the enhanced, grim avarice."
"I'm the arch, demeaning avarice."
"I'm the mega avarice hindrance."

**THIS DREAM WASN'T ALWAYS CONSIDERED THE
APEX OF ACHIEVEMENT IN LIFE**

"Ha Ha! I'm a grim, recent deviance."

THE TRUTH ABOUT ITS ILLUSORY NATURE

"I am a charmer hating evidence."
"Hid avarice menace nightmare."
"I am the grievance chain dream."

IT IS NOT WORTH PURSUING...

"Evade rich, I'm an ace nightmare."
"Evade, I'm a chancier nightmare."   †I Timothy 6:10
"I am a rich achievement danger."
"Vain menace, mightier charade."
"I'm high, mean deviance rat race."
"A grim charade in achievement."

ESPECIALLY WHEN THE FAMILY IS NEVER CONTENT

"I am the receiver and manic hag."   †Proverbs 27:15
"I am the arch grievance maiden."   †Proverbs 30:15

SOME HOPE IN THE LOTTERY

"Game idea man. Chancier. Thrive."   †I Timothy 6:9
"I'm chancier. And I'm the average."

**HIGHER EDUCATION IS PRESENTED AS THE
TRUSTED WAY TO ACHIEVE THE DREAM...**

"An I am reverent high academic."

**IN SPITE OF THE FACT MANY COLLEGE
GRADUATES CAN'T FIND HIGH PAYING POSITIONS**

"Ha ha! Academic meriting? Never!"

AND THEY STILL MUST REPAY THE STUDENT LOANS

"Academic 'n' heavier nightmare."

**SOME FIGURE THEY WILL JUST CHEAT
THEIR WAY TO WEALTH**

"Man! I've charming cheater idea."
"Hammered avarice in cheating."
"Avarice madmen hire cheating."   †Proverbs 22:16
"I'm a cheating. Harm and receive."   †Proverbs 13:11
"Cheating vice harmer idea man."

THEN THERE ARE THE GET RICH QUICK SCHEMES

"Ahem! Venerated, rich magician."
"Hardier magic. An achievement!"
"Enchant. Admire heavier magic."
"Enchant heavier; I'm magic, dear."
"Evade magic... harm inheritance."   †Proverbs 12:11

**INFLUENCED BY WEALTHY POPULAR CULTURE ICONS,
OTHERS WILL RESORT TO VIOLENT CRIME...**

"Anarchic him image venerated."   †I Corinthians 15:33
"Ahem! Avid, rich, manic teenager."
"Eager hit man menace rich diva."
"Eh! Eradicative harm menacing."   †Proverbs 22:24
"Amen! Angrier victim headache."

OR THE LURE OF QUICK CASH VIA THE
SALE OF CONTROLLED SUBSTANCES

"Ahem! Vice nightmare radiance."
"Harmed. I am a vice interchange."   †Revelation 9:21

STILL OTHERS WILL MAKE PLANS TO
STEAL WHAT THEY CANNOT EARN

"Ace thieve-man chair dreaming."   †Proverbs 13:4

DESCENDANTS OF SLAVES STILL STRUGGLE AS
AN AGGREGATE FOR PARITY OF WEALTH

"A ethnic grievance. I am harmed."   †Deuteronomy 28:29,33

MATERIAL TRAPPINGS GIVE THE
ILLUSION OF SUPERIORITY

"Cheerier might. I am an advance."   †James 2:2-4
"Hi! I'm a rich, eager advancement."

AGGRESSIVE WAYS TO CAPTURE THE DREAM
THROUGH THE FILING OF FRIVOLOUS LAWSUITS

"Am the rich grievance idea man."   †Isaiah 58:7
"Charge came in. Idea man thrive."
"Came reaching. Idea man thrive."

THE NEED TO STAY AHEAD MEANS SOME WILL
PLACE THEIR PARENTS IN HOMES FOR THE
ELDERLY WHERE THEY MAY BE ABUSED

"Have enhanced? Maim geriatric."   †Romans 1:30

AVARICE DRIVES PHARMACEUTICAL COMPANIES
TO CONSTANTLY GENERATE NEW DRUGS WHICH
MAY BE INEFFECTIVE OR HAVE BAD SIDE EFFECTS

"Rich anathema grave medicine."
"Aha! Rich ravagement medicine."
"Headache germ in carminative."   †Revelation 9:21
"Ha ha! Magic nerve art medicine."
"Ha ha! Medicine react. Me raving!"

**GREED IS CAPABLE OF INFLUENCING SOME RESEARCHERS
TO CREATE DISEASE WHERE NONE EXISTED BEFORE**

"Idea man... Heavier cancer might."
"Ha ha! I'm nice and creative germ."   †Romans 1:30
"Ha ha! Craven medicine team rig."
"Hi, Cancer! Mega idea man thrive.
"Menace...thrive rich in a damage."   †Revelation 9:21

**CRAZINESS AND DRAMA IN THE CORPORATE AND POLITICAL
ARENAS WHERE PURSUIT OF THE DREAM IS THE SOURCE OF
BACKSTABBING AND SABOTAGE ...THOSE WHO COVET MONEY
OR POWER WILL STOP AT NOTHING TO ACHIEVE IT, AND
THOSE WHO POSSESS IT ARE RELUCTANT TO RELINQUISH IT**

"I'm an aged vice-chairman there!"
"Vice-chairman. Image adherent."
("I gathered vice-chairman mean.")
"Ahead, regiment vice-chairman."
"Ahem! Avid, energetic chairman?"

"Enraged! I am the vice-chairman."
"I'm heated grievance chairman."

"Chairman receiving meathead."
"Craven meathead imagine rich."
"Meathead reign vice-chairman?"
"Heavier, rich, acid management."
"Derange!! I am the vice-chairman."

"I am the angered vice-chairman."
"I am the acid revenge chairman."
"The dire vice-chairman manage?"
"Agree and I'm the vice-chairman."
"Remain the aged vice-chairman."

BUT GODLINESS WITH CONTENTMENT IS GREAT GAIN

"Ahem! I am nice grace; and thrive."   †Philippians 4:19
"I am a rich achievement garden."   †Matthew 6:33

**IN THE END, THE RICHES RUST
AND THE BODY RETURNS TO DUST**

"Grave emaciate...hindrance him."   †I Timothy 6:7
"I am the grave, I'm ace hindrance."   †Luke 12:20

RELEVANT LONGEST WORDS/PHRASES USING SOME OF THE LETTERS

"revaccinating" "degenerative" "heartrending" "anagrammatic"
"materia medica" "merchant marine" "teaching machine"

He that loveth silver shall not be satisfied with silver; nor he that loveth abundance with increase...Ecclesiastes 5:10

Wilt thou set thine eyes upon that which is not? for riches certainly make themselves wings; they fly away as an eagle toward heaven...Proverbs 23:5

TELEVISION PROGRAMMING

Broadcasting media has come a long way from the bulky cathode ray tube models of earlier generations. Today's high definition flat-screens provide a viewing experience our parents could have only imagined, and even this is being eclipsed by emerging developments. But technology aside, we need to truly understand what television is.

TV is a tool: a tool for social engineering. The word itself dissected means distant vision. Tele=distant+vision. The problem is, the majority of the time, it brings you somebody else's distant vision. A vision you perhaps would not normally embrace, but by garnishing the vision with just the right amount of humorous commercials professing empathy for your health, well-being, and peace of mind, television is able to win your confidence. Media icons who present themselves as "your trusted source for news" help cement the impression of television as a friend. Television is predictable – we can follow schedules and episodes – and user friendly – streaming media allows us to capture features we want to view at a more convenient time. In the privacy of our home we can view a variety of action-packed or romantic sagas we could never experience in real life; siding with a hero, villain or even the underdog. Indeed, television provides hours of safe escape from the harsh realities of life. But how safe is it?

We must remember that the other part of the phrase is "programming." Among the definitions of programming (whether broadcast media wants to own up to it or not) are to facilitate automatic responses or attitudes, or condition. Another is to set, regulate, or modify so as to produce a specific response or reaction. Media programming conforms the mind to this world and bends it to be in tune with the prevailing culture. It is well able to accomplish this because the objective is always cloaked in news, sports, commercials, or entertainment; and it caters to the lusts of the eyes, the lusts of the flesh, and the pride of life.

Returning to our definition of television (distant vision) and adding programming (conditioning to generate automatic or specific responses) we begin to see a side of broadcasting media which may not be quite so trustful and friendly. When I was a young woman new in following Jesus, some preachers would preach against watching TV, referring to it as "hell-a-vision". The passage of time has shown them to be on point.

Words repeatedly generated by this phrase are *pig, gorgon, prime,* and *romp.* Pig refers to the overwhelming presence TV has attained in the average household. In Greek mythology, a gorgon was one of three sister monsters who could turn anyone looking at them to stone, just as habitual television viewing deadens viewers to seeking truth on their own or believing anything not endorsed by the 'experts' on the screen. *Aggro* refers to aggressive youth.

LIKE A HOG, TELEVISION AND ITS LESS THAN FAMILY FRIENDLY CONTENT CAN EVOLVE INTO AN IMPOSING PRESENCE IN ANY HOME

"I'm everlasting moron pig."
"Impregnates living room."
"Or, immortal pig evenings."

THE FLICKER RATE IS PROGRAMMED TO HEIGHTEN SUGGESTIBILITY, THEN SUBLIMINALS ARE ADDED

"Imposing; or, mental giver."
"Taping, moreover smiling."
"A prime mover glinting so."   †Proverbs 4:23

TELEVISION POSES AS BENEFICENT

"I'm gentle or as improving..."

ACTUALLY, THE OPPOSITE IS TRUE

"Malign. Poor time serving."
"Improves to malingering."   †Ephesians 5:16-17

TV VIEWING CAN INTERFERE WITH MORALS AND VALUE SYSTEMS PARENTS ATTEMPT TO INSTILL, MOLDING THE CHILD INTO DISTANT VISION'S IMAGE INSTEAD

"Grim mangler on positive."
"Immoral spite governing."
"Molest impair governing."
"Am imperils to governing."   †Proverbs 22:6
"Maggot imperils environ."
"I'm ransoming piglet over."

"Grave moronism in piglet."
"I'm losing over tampering."

**TELEVISION USES ITS POWER TO CONTROL POLITICAL CHOICE
AND REINFORCE THE FALSE LEFT/RIGHT PARADIGM AND
THE MYTH OF AMERICAN SUPERIORITY**

"Vote! Maligner promising."
"Voter-maligner imposing."
"So voting prime maligner."
"Or prime maligning votes."
"Governing - real optimism."
"I'm a loving, strong empire."
"Loving emperor giantism."
"A loving, storming empire."

**FROM MORNING UNTIL ONE DRIFTS OFF TO SLEEP
AT NIGHT, TELEVISION PLAYS ITS ROLE WITHOUT FAIL**

"Mornings pivotal regime."
"Mornings optimal grieve."
"Migraine proving molest."
"Loving, parting memories."

Have you ever considered why anyone would need a "distant vision conditioning" of constant primeval sex, violence, and appeal to insatiable appetite for material things? Or better still, who stands to benefit from your successful "distant vision conditioning"? Prime time programming certainly seems designed to appeal to the baser instincts and desire for immediate gratification.

Animals are guided by their basic instincts. Because of this, they are predictable and easy to control with the proper resources. They can be domesticated or left to become feral. They can be trained, and depending on the species, herded and fleeced. They can be experimented on, bought, sold, traded, and in their prime condition-slaughtered. Additionally, a distinguishing feature of many animals is that they are branded. The animal is concerned with none of these things, however. It cares only that it has food, water, and shelter.

Is this what we are being reduced to as a society? Is there someone, some group, or something with a vested interest in shaping the public to be easily controllable and so engrossed with the daily grind that they can no longer reason or think critically? Perhaps someone distant has a vision for you and me – a vision that requires our acquiescence and cooperation, but never our challenge or debate. Whatever the case, the pervasive influence of television programming has no place in the life of followers of Christ who are prepping for the Kingdom of God.

TELEVISION INTERFERES WITH RELATIONSHIPS …OBSESSION WITH SOAP OPERAS OR OBVIOUS ATTRACTION TO ACTORS AND ACTRESSES CAN CAUSE STRESS IN MARRIAGE

"Romeos tampering living."
"Pig rant loving memories."
"Gremlin's vomiting opera."
"Optimism enraging lover."   †Matthew 19:5

LIKEWISE, OBSESSION WITH SPORTS CAUSES FRUSTRATION

"I am mere sporting loving."
"I'm sporting lover enigma."
"I'm raving simpleton ogre."
"Sporting given memorial."
"Longer, sportive maiming."
"I'm ego in sporting marvel."

VALUES SUCH AS MORAL PURITY ARE MOCKED AND MADE TO APPEAR PASSE: WITH CORRUPTION OF THE YOUNG AS THE OBJECTIVE

"Virgin or mega simpleton."   †Romans 1:24

VIRGINITY IS PORTAYED AS SOMETHING TO BE DEFILED, AND PROMISCUITY IS ADMIRED

"Moron spite virginal gem."
"So prime not gleam virgin."   †I Corinthians 6:9
"Prime gem not so virginal."
"Not promise virginal gem."

THE MORE FREQUENT AND INTENSE THE SEX SCENES, THE HIGHER THE RATINGS

"Prime – loving or steaming."

"More loving, prime giants."
"Is more loving tampering."
"So, mating loving premier."
"Steaming role improving."

**BECAUSE SEX IS SUCH A CRITICAL PART OF THE
PROGRAMMING/CONDITIONING, TEASER
SCENES AIR TO WHET THE VIEWER'S APPETITE**

"Imagine revolting romps."
"Romper gleam so inviting."
"Ton reviling romp images!"   †Matthew 5:28
"Or evil steaming romping."

**THIS IS NOTHING MORE THAN ANCIENT FERTILITY WORSHIP
POWERED BY MODERN TECHNOLOGY: IDOLATRY BROUGHT
TO YOU COURTESY OF 'DISTANT VISION'**

"Immoralist ever ponging."
"Grim. Impersonate loving."
"Vile impregnating rooms."   †I Kings 14:23
"Is loving impregnator me."
"Oversimple groin mating."
"Moron mating privileges."

NUDITY AND PERVERSION ARE PRESENTED AS DESIRABLE

"I'm a vile G-string romp one."
"Glamor poser inviting me."   †Romans 1:24
"Pervert smiling on amigo."

THIS SERVES TO DESENSITIZE VIEWERS TO PORNOGRAPHY

"I'm revolting porn images."
"Vomiting slim eager porn."   †I Timothy 1:10
"Prime or moving genitals."
"Steaming vile, grim porno."

**GRATUITOUS VIOLENCE CAPTIVATES THE YOUTH
IN A SOCIETY WHERE PRISON HAS BECOME AN INDUSTRY**

"Violent images grip. Norm."   †Proverbs 13:2

ASSAULT BY BEATINGS AND CHOKINGS

"Geronimo! Ample striving."

"I'm violent or me grasping."
"Grasping. I'm more violent."   †Psalm 14:3

ROAD RAGE AND VEHICULAR HOMICIDE

"Avenging motor imperils."

CONTRACT AND REVENGE KILLINGS

"I'm vile snoop triggerman."

UNHINGED BLOODLUST

"Violent gore as primming."   †Proverbs 4:17
"Violent pain or grim gems."
"Strong privilege on maim."
"Revolting poser maiming."
"Spoilt? Revenging or maim."

DEMONS vs HUMANS

"Grim impaling overtones."
"Grim empaling is not over."
"Give – or monster impaling."
"Impaling or vomits green."

DISTANT VISION'S IDEA OF TALENT

"I'm poet or singing marvel."
"I'm vile impregnator song."   †Isaiah 23:16
"O man! Grim poets reviling."
"Snigger! Primeval motion."
"Primeval goings-on merit."
"Primeval merits ongoing."
"Is not glamor given prime?"
"Moving or reptilian gems."

WORLDLY CHURCHES OUT OF TOUCH WITH
THE GOSPEL OF THE KINGDOM ...

"Moral poser gem inviting."
"Negative moron pilgrims."   †James 4:4
"Evil pig or storming amen."

AS THEY GLORIFY WAR AND EMPIRE BUILDING

"O Man! I'm strong privilege."
"O Man! Storming privilege."
"Primeval ego in storming."
"I'm armies' revolting pong."
"Moron grasping Evil item."
"Atom imperils governing."
"Imperiling over amongst."

**SLICK ADVERTISING KEEPS CONSUMERS ON
A TREADMILL IN CONSTANT PURSUIT OF
MATERIALISM AND CATERING TO PERSONAL VANITY**

"Grim sloven, I'm an ego-trip."
"Mongrels, I'm vain ego-trip."
"Vain lemmings or ego-trip."
"Groping. Envies immortal."   †Isaiah 40:6-7

**BUY HER THESE DIAMONDS AND SHE
WILL LOVE YOU FOREVER**

"Or VIP on gleaming merits."

LOVE WHICH CAN BE PURCHASED IS NOT LOVE

"Gemstone improving? Liar."

**FAMILIES STRUGGLING TO PUT FOOD ON
THE TABLE WATCH IN FRUSTRATION AS
LAVISH RESTAURANT COMMERCIALS AIR**

"Smiling, over-eating romp."
"O Man! Pig loving merriest."
"So pig loving a merriment."   †Luke 16:21

**THOSE WITH WEAKER CHARACTER WILL STEAL TO OBTAIN
THE THINGS THEY CONSTANLY VIEW ON THE SCREEN**

"Improving stealing more."   †Micah 2:1-2

TACKY COMMERICALS FOR PERSONAL HYGIENE ITEMS

"I'm given to grim personal."   †Proverbs 11:22
"Tampon grime ...so reviling."

**SYNDICATED SHOWS WHERE THE
GUESTS SELL THEIR DIGNITY**

"Glimpse on rare vomiting..."
"Vomiting personal grime."

**LAW ENFORCEMENT SHOWS TO
ACCLIMATE THE PUBLIC TO A POLICE STATE**

"Live aggro imprisonment."

**A STEADY STREAM OF PROPAGANDA DESIGNED TO
ALIGN PUBLIC THOUGHT WITH PRE-PLANNED POLICIES**

"I'm loving enigma reports."
"Smearing, promoting evil."

**A CONSTANT APPEAL TO MEN TO IMPROVE
THEIR SEXUAL PROWESS**

"Simpering. Not male vigor."
"Sample meriting on vigor."
"So nag vigor imperilment."
"Implementors gain vigor."
"Implement as groin vigor."
"Improving ogre ailments."
"Improving manliest goer."
"More improving genitals."
"Stammering...pile on vigor!"
"Premise not malign vigor."

**WHENEVER YOU THINK IT CAN'T GET ANY WORSE,
PROGRAMMING DESCENDS TO NEW DEPTHS**

"Marveling mire stooping."
"Marvel stooping in grime."
"Alert!! Imposing!! Removing??"

OVER TIME, THE BRAIN PASSIVELY ACCEPTS A "FEED"

"Evil impairment gorgons."
"Imperilment via gorgons."
"Gleaming viper monitors."
"Slave moron meriting pig."
"More loving master in pig."

TELEVISION PROGRAMMING ANAGRAMS
ITS OWN NEFARIOUS PURPOSE

"I'm groping, smart Evil one."
"So, tampering on grim evil."

TELEVISION NOW HARBORS TECHNOLOGY THAT
ENABLES IT TO SPY ON HOUSEHOLDS

"Not reveal grim imposing."
"Innovate or grim glimpse."
"Soon grim evil tampering."   †Ecclesiastes 10:20
"Monitoring vipers gleam."

RELEVANT LONGEST WORDS/PHRASES USING SOME OF THE LETTERS

"governmentalism" "neo-imperialist" "pro-government"
"misgovernment" "impersonating" immortalising"
"memorialising" "overmastering" "immoralities"
"improvisation" "interpersonal" "repositioning"

From the anagrams revealed, it is plain to see that television broadcasting exists as the mouthpiece of government institutions, a clearinghouse for corporate advertising, and a propaganda arm for social engineering policies. Seamlessly woven into their agendas is programming which appeals to base carnal instincts, fear, vanity, and humor. Often, this programming contains subliminal messages.

This carefully crafted stratagem is further enhanced by 'news coverage' which tends to gloss over the most important events affecting the public's future; choosing rather to 'spin' selected stories in a manner where the reaction can be predicted and managed. Programming is considered successful when the viewer's thinking is synchronized with the agenda. Or, as has been attributed to a former CIA director, "We'll know our disinformation program is complete when everything the American public believes is false."

And be not conformed to this world: but be ye transformed by the renewing of your mind ...Romans 12:2

SHAPING THE POST-CHRISTIAN ERA...
APOSTASY AND SPIRITUAL DELUSION

A people who feel entitled to pleasure and prosperity in this world will have the same expectations when they gather in a public worship setting. They will expect the edifice where they assemble to have certain amenities. The pastor's wardrobe and the vehicle he drives must reflect a certain level of affluence. This is critical because no one wants to attend a church where it appears people are at best struggling, and at worst, poverty stricken. A full congregation is critical to paying the building loan and operating expenses, and the more seats occupied, the lighter the financial burden.

The congregation won't have a problem with this either, because many of them desire a model of prosperity and perceived success they can aspire to, and they want to be associated with material abundance even if it isn't an accurate depiction of their individual circumstance. So, the excesses and extravagances are tolerated and even welcomed.

Of course, none of this has anything to do with worshiping God in Spirit and truth, such as he seeks. To the angel of the church of Smyrna the risen Lord Jesus exhorted, "I know thy works, and tribulation, and poverty, (but thou art rich")... Revelation 2:9, and James 2:5 advises us that God has "chosen the poor of this world to be rich in faith and to inherit the kingdom He promised those who love Him." As far as a model to imitate, we are to "mark the perfect man," "be followers of God," and look to Jesus - the Author and Finisher of our faith.

One of the most egregious exploitations still taking place in many churches is the extraction of the tithe. Submission of the tithe was mandatory and necessary under the Mosaic law because the tribe of Levi had no inheritance and was tasked with the fulltime duties of the priesthood and temple maintenance. So, the other tribes supported them by bringing the tithe into the storehouse. But when the tithe is collected in modern churches, it is to pay the pastor and staff's salaries, and the operating expenses of the church **building**. The 'church' is a body of baptized believers, not a physical structure with a street address. Therefore, the use of Malachi 3:8-11 to justify demand of the tithe is a misappropriation of scripture. A New Testament assembly can only ask for offerings, and even those must be given with a willing heart and not out of constraint.

Additionally, all blood-washed saints born of the water and the Spirit are part of a **New Covenant royal priesthood** and together, make up the temple of God. If a tithe is desired to be given, it should be strictly voluntary, and the saints should take care of each other's needs; especially the widows and fatherless in their midst.

Never discussed is how the Western monetary system is based on a fiat currency that is constantly devalued by inflation, and how the cost of goods and services are artificially manipulated to control the ability to get and retain wealth. Instead, when the faithful struggle, they are told they are cursed for robbing God of the tenth of their gross income, and to reverse their misfortune they need to pay up.

Anagrams from this next topic feature words such as *beast of prey*, *reprobate*, and *spoofery*. The New Testament speaks extensively about false teachers and personalities who are involved with the church solely for financial gain at the expense of the congregation. And since the post-modern churches have borrowed from the corporate world in implementing growth strategies and slick advertising campaigns, people continue to flock to them – whether God is present or not. At a typical service...

| APOSTASY...
FALSE PROPHETS AND BRETHREN |
| --- |

ALL THE TRAPPINGS OF A TRUE SPIRITUAL EXPERIENCE ARE DISPLAYED

"Prayers and top-of-the-table sharpness."   †Matthew 6:5

THE SPEAKERS ARE CAPTIVATING, BUT DECEPTIVE

"Enthrals. Sharp poets and beast of prey."

THEY KNOW THE TECHNIQUES THAT MESMERIZE THE WORSHIPERS

"Sharp-nosed, sharp beast of prey talent."
"Fatheads personably transport sheep."   †I Peter 2:18

THEY SPEAK GREAT SWELLING WORDS

"A noble of sharpest, sharpest pedantry."
"Daft, transparent hyperboles phase so."   †Jude 1:16

BUT IF YOU CAN SEE PAST THE HYPE...

"Happy? Flash reprobate sad rottenness."   †Matthew 23:27
"Blatant, sharp-set, sharpened spoofery."   †I Peter 5:2

**SCRIPTURE IS WRONGLY DIVIDED TO BULLY THE
PEOPLE INTO TITHING ON THEIR GROSS INCOME**

"Sharp slap and spoofery tenths rebate."
"Sharp spoofery and beater slaps tenth."
"Sharp spoofery and berate. Slaps tenth."

REALLY, THE PEOPLE ARE THE ONES BEING ROBBED

"Happy seat-of-the-pants slanderer robs."   †Matthew 23:4

**PARISHIONERS MAY BE STRUGGLING TO PUT FOOD ON
THE TABLE, BUT THESE APOSTATES DINE LAVISHLY**

"Happy bloatedness of sharpest ranter."   †James 2:15-16

THEY PREACH ANOTHER GOSPEL – THE GOSPEL OF MATERIAL RICHES

"Satan, the sharp beast of prey splendor."
"Notable sharpness property fatheads."

**THEY WEAR A DESIGNER WARDROBE, AND
THEY WILL TELL YOU JESUS HAD ONE TOO**

"Honestly! Best dapper sharper of Satan."   †I Timothy 6:5

**THEY WILL TELL YOU JESUS WAS RICH, HAD A
BIG HOUSE, AND YOU DESERVE ONE TOO**

"Ha Ha! Beasts of prey splendor patterns."   †Matthew 8:20

SOON, THE CONGREGATION IS CONVINCED THAT GAIN IS GODLINESS

"Pleasant hyped of abhorrent trespass."

**NEVER A SERMON OF THE PERSECUTION TO COME, THE
PEOPLE ARE TOLD THEY WILL BE SECRETLY RAPTURED**

"Happy! deftness as transportable hero!
"Happy! Transportable daftness heroes."   †II Timothy 3:12
"Happy! Reprobate daftness enthrals so."
"Happy! Transparent robes of deathless."

BUT A FIERY TRIAL SURPRISE IS WAITING IN THE WINGS

"Happy transportable safeness? Red-hot!!"   †I Thessalonians 5:3

**PEOPLE LEAVE THE SERVICE FEELING GOOD BUT WITH
NOTHING OF SUBSTANCE TO GROW THEM SPIRITUALLY**

"Prattler of best and happy hoarseness."   †Jeremiah 5:31

**THEY HAVE ONLY PERMITTED THE APOSTATE TO
STRENGTHEN THEIR SPIRITUAL BONDAGE**

"Daft reprobate ensnares happy sloths."

**HURTING PEOPLE COME INTO THESE CHURCHES
SEEKING STABILITY AND HEALING ...INSTEAD THEY
ARE OFTEN IGNORED OR FURTHER ALIENATED**

"Top banana oppress freshly shattered."
"To half-shy, aberrant pedant oppresses." †Jeremiah 23:2
"Aberrant pest to an oppressed half-shy."

**SOME GO ELSEWHERE SEEKING FELLOWSHIP
...OTHERS JUST GIVE UP ON GOD**

"Thereafter abandons sloppy sharp-set."   †Ezekiel 34:6

GOD SEES PAST THE HYPE AND STRAIGHT INTO THE HEART

"Top ten prayerless. Bash of rash pedant."
"Sloppy reprobate and the fat rashness."   †Matthew 23:27

**THE WORLD WATCHES AND WANTS NO
PART OF PSEUDO-CHRISTIANITY**

"Harlot's represented as fat happy snob."

**THE CARNALITY AND DECEPTION IS CONCERNING
FOR THOSE EARNESTLY CONTENDING FOR THE FAITH**

"Appeal of sharpness tyrants bothered."   †II Peter 2:2
"Happy? Fears adept abhorrent lostness."   †Titus 2:15

BUT ANY WHO ATTEMPT TO CORRECT THEM WILL PAY DEARLY

"Apply thrashes on reprobate daftness?"
"And potent sharper beast of prey slash."   †II Peter 2:10

DISCREDIT AND SLANDER ARE THE REWARD OF THOSE
WHO ATTEMPT TO CONFRONT THEM ABOUT THEIR ERROR

"An adept, nasty half-brother oppresses."
"Happy fat reprobate slanders the sons."   †II Timothy 4:14-15
"Happy reprobate slanders honest fast."
"Sharp-set beast of prey plans on hatred."

THEY WON'T ACCEPT CORRECTION FROM GOD EITHER...
PER HEBREWS 12:8 THAT MAKES THEM ILLEGITIMATE

"Happy fart nonetheless bastard poser."   †Hebrews 12:8

THEIR DAMNATION SLUMBERETH NOT ...
IT'S JUST BIDING ITS TIME

"Satan thrashes preferably postponed."   †II Peter 2:3

RELEVANT LONGEST WORDS/PHRASES USING SOME OF THE LETTERS

"false-heartedness" "halfheartedness" "treasonableness"
"detestableness" "dress rehearsal" "hypertenseness" "prayerlessness"
"seat-of-the-pants"   "sharp-nosedness" "desperateness"
"heartlessness"

A wonderful and horrible thing is committed in the land; The prophets prophesy falsely, and the priests bear rule by their means; and my people love to have it so: and what will ye do in the end thereof? Jeremiah 5:30-31

Earlier, we noted that people who feel entitled to pleasure and prosperity in this world transfer the same set of expectations to their spiritual experience. This also holds true for the programming that conforms spiritual minds to carnal minds. Two of the anagrams for the phrase 'Shaping the Post-Christian Era' are "Gosh-an atheistic partnership!" and "This earnest! This approaching!" This implies that many who profess trust in Christ will eventually be seduced by the constant barrage of chatter and rhetoric that influence Western culture and policy. Instead of being continually transformed to the mind of Christ, they will become a friend of the world. They will take sides politically, and militarily. Their energies will focus on their safety in this world. Since military forces provide security, fearful sheep will lead the rallying cry for empirical exploits.

Proverbs 21:31 states, "The horse is prepared against the day of battle: but safety is of the LORD." And Psalm 33:17 advises, "An horse is a vain thing for safety: neither shall he deliver any by his great strength." In ancient warfare, horses were used both offensively - in the battle clash with the enemy, and defensively - as a vehicle of escape. Jesus spoke in John 18:36, "My kingdom is not of this world: if my kingdom were of this world, then would my servants fight." These verses indicate the saints should neither lead the charge for wars, nor count on man-made venues for escape from persecution. Rather, they should put their trust in the God they serve.

Since according to Daniel 2:21 it is God who "deposes kings and raises up others", it is futile for Christians to take sides so that their nation or any other can be kept safe or in power. Our directive is to go into all the world and preach the gospel to every creature, making disciples of every nation. The world's directive is to kill and maim to keep the kingdoms of this world in power. These directives are antithetical to each other.

We have forgotten that God is not willing that any should perish, but that all might come to a saving knowledge of Him. People tend not to be open to the gospel you share while they are salvaging the broken pieces of their existence and burying their family members. Since the kingdoms of this world will become the property of our Lord and his Christ at the end of the age, why are Christians still unequally yoking themselves to unbelievers, and partaking in the sins of other men? Churches who endorsed these entanglements, and preachers who manipulated scripture to support it will have to give account before a holy and righteous God who gave his only Son as a ransom for the sins of the entire world. How will they answer the charge?

Connive and its variations repeatedly appear in this topic. *Cloven hoof* refers to the Devil and the satanic spirit which drives the war laden rhetoric preached as prophecy fulfilled. *Halo* references the godly presentation professing Christians should have, and *enchant* speaks to the ease of persuasion in molding the minds of listeners to obey a political agenda rather than being led by the Spirit of God. *Genetic henna land* points both to the people of the Middle East who use the dye in association with weddings and ceremonial events; and other brown-skinned people. *Baa* decodes sheep (of a pastor's flock). *Cedes hat* indicates giving up ones' crown, *solvent* represents salt (salt of the earth; *volt*, light and power. *Honest Bloodstain* points to the blood of Jesus. *Congealed* alludes to frozen; ice cold.

INNOCENT BLOOD ON THE HANDS OF EVANGELICALS

**SOME PREACHERS MANIPULATE SCRIPTURE
TO INFLUENCE THEIR CONGREGATIONS TO
SUPPORT EMPIRICAL AGENDAS...**

"Connivant legend of inconsolable hotheads."
"Cloven hoof attached an ill-boding nonsense."   †II Corinthians 4:2
"Connive falsehood and hell-bent contagions."

**THE DECEPTION HAS BECOME FIRMLY
ENTRENCHED IN MANY CHURCHES**

"And hell-bent connivance foothold agonises."
"Notable foothold and caching evil nonsense."
"Notable foothold convening and leaches sin."

**AT THE ROOT OF THIS FALSE TEACHING IS A SATANIC HATRED
OF GOD AND THOSE WHO EARNESTLY CONTEND FOR THE FAITH**

"An ill-boding. Cloven hoof hates on Ascendent."
"Insolent loathing of noble, advanced chosen."   †Romans 1:30
"Angel's enchant in blood-stained cloven hoof."

**DEPARTING FROM THE FAITH...THE DELIBERATE CHOICE
TO SELL OUT FOR EARTHLY POWER AND INFLUENCE**

"Cloven hoof abandons clean, honest, diligent."   † ITimothy 4:1
"Notable foothold cleave and sinning chosen."
"Satan enabling cloven-hoofed, then con solid."
"I, Satan sold cloven-hoofed. Then able conning."† II Timothy 3:13
"Bet I Satan sold cloven-hoofed on channeling."
"Halo? Nonsense! Table of living death concord."

**THE LONDON CONNECTION VIA SECRET SOCIETIES: THE TIMES OF THE
GENTILES CULMINATE WITH THE RISE OF THE BRITISH EMPIRE, AND
AMERICA AS ITS REBIRTH. OBELISKS - PHALLIC SYMBOLS REPRESENTING
WORSHIP OF FERTILITY AND THE SUN - ARE PLACED AT STRATEGIC POINTS
ACROSS THE EARTH TO SIGNAL AND HERALD THE LUCIFERIAN WORLD ORDER**

"God in Heaven! Notable, old connections flash." ‡Mystery Babylon
"Satanic London-based enlighten cloven hoof."
"Cool Londoner base of living death enchants."

"Violence of London-based loathing enchants."
"London-based, healing loveshaft connection." ‡ Obelisks

HAS FREEMASONRY INFILTRATED THE
CHURCH AT THE HIGHEST LEVELS?

"Cloven hoof hand signals...able non-detection."
"Cloven hoof can't not sin. Bonehead signalled." ‡Masonic hand signs
"Bonehead of living death clean control sons."
"Boneheads clean on controls of living death."
"Soon able controls of enhanced living death."

IF RACISM IS A FACTOR IN THE POLICIES OF THE
GLOBALISTS INVOLVED IN THE SECRET SOCIETIES...

"Insolent cloven hoof. A blond ethnics agenda."   ‡Racial superiority

IS IT POSSIBLE REPROBATES HAVE BEEN CO-OPTED BY
THE GLOBALISTS FOR MORE SINISTER ACTIVITIES?

"Ah! Note fabled connections on slaveholding."   ‡Religion as a cover
"Able. Often had connections on slaveholding."   for criminal activities
"Ah! Oft enabled connections on slaveholding."

BEHIND THE SCENES PLAYERS LEND WHATEVER SUPPORT IS
NEEDED TO MAKE THE REPROBATES CREDIBLE AND INFLUENTIAL

"Enhanced talent of bold hooligans connives."   ‡Handlers and
"Boneheads half-convincing on talented solo."   secular advisors

WARS ARE NEEDED, SO THE WORD OF GOD IS HANDLED
DECEITFULLY... THE MIDDLE EAST IS PRESENTED AS
THOUGH IT WAS STILL IN OLD TESTAMENT TIMES

"Notable cloven hoofing and clean dishonest."   †Jeremiah 22:17
"Goofball dishonest and enchant on violence."
"Connives falsehood and hell-bent contagion."
"God in heaven! Not halo!! Bend lesson! A conflict."
"Loathing on as cloven-hoofed blends ancient."   ‡Fusing Biblical
"God in heaven! Not halo!! Lo, conflict bands seen." history and modern
"Not halo!! A conflict. God in heaven no bless end." empirical exploits

FEAR AND TERROR ARE USED TO GOAD THE FLOCK INTO
TRUSTING IN ARMAMENTS INSTEAD OF THE ARM OF GOD

"Lo! A goon connived; send telethons. Baa flinch."   †Proverbs 29:25
"Lo! Fondling nonviolent Baa. Chosen cedes hat."
"Once fondling enchants loveable sainthood."

**THE PEOPLE ARE MOBILIZED TO SUPPORT
THE 'CORRECT' POLITICAL CANDIDATES**

"Cloven hoof's hell-bent on sign on a candidate."
"Cloven-hoofed snob enchant and legislation."
"Cloven-hoofed legislation. Then, bad cannon."

**SUPPORT FOR WARS MEANS THE DEATH TOLL
WILL CONTINUE UNABATED**

"Cloven hoof entangle hand. Nice bloodstains."
"Cloven-hoofed. Genetic henna land. Bloodstains."

BABIES AND CHILDREN WILL DIE

"Bloodstains. Hence cloven hoof ending natal."

**THE ZEAL FOR THESE MODERN CRUSADES HAS TARNISHED
THE IMAGE OF THE WEST IN THE EYES OF OTHER NATIONS**

"Cloven-hoofed nonsense bad national glitch."

BUT MOSTLY, THE CHRISTIAN FAITH IS MALIGNED

"God in heaven! Halo not noble!! Sends a conflict."

**THOSE WHO SUPPORT OPPRESSION OVERSEAS
WILL ULTIMATELY SUPPORT IT DOMESTICALLY**

"Notable foothold and civil change nonsense."

**THIS DISTORTION OF THE GOSPEL CRUCIFIES
THE SON OF GOD AFRESH**

"Enchanting foothold on voidable cleanness."

**HUGE EDIFICES WITH THOUSANDS OF MEMBERS LEND AN
AIR OF CREDIBILITY TO THIS WARPED VERSION OF CHRISTIANITY**

"Bold sensational cloven-hoofed enchanting."   †II Peter 2:2

**THOSE DESPERATE TO FIND A "CHURCH HOME" ARE
MOST SUSCEPTIBLE TO THIS SNARE**

"Cloven hoof snatching abandoned loneliest."

IDEAL MEMBERS: SINCERE, ZEALOUS, AND UNDISCERNING

"Connivent goofball and honest, ideal chosen."
"An ill-boding cloven hoof and neatest chosen."
"Connivant death-dealing fools noble chosen."
"Bold cloven-hoofed enchants on genial saint."
"Enchanting volcano fooled non-established."
"No dance of death sign is on hell-bent volcano."
"The connivent, all-dancing boneheads fool so."

A VENEER OF RIGHTEOUSNESS AND RESPECTABILITY COVERS MANY OF THESE TEACHERS

"Insolent cloven hoof boasting clean-handed."   †Matthew 23:27
"Goodliness enhanced in blatant cloven hoof."

BUT SOME HAVE BEEN BESET BY SCANDALS

"Cloven hoof cohabits and an insolent legend."   ‡Multiple high-profile
"Novel flash. Decadent hooligan sob innocent."   public disgraces
"Noble cloven hoof hedonist. Neat scandaling."   †I Corinthians 6:9

THERE IS A FORM OF GODLINESS, BUT THE POWER THEREOF IS DENIED

"Cloven hoof notation – clean-handed blessing."   †II Timothy 3:5
"Clean noble godliness of connivant hothead."
"Oh no! Daft lad incensing! Chosen not loveable."
"Clean-handed cloven hoof's an insolent bigot."
*"Violent all-dancing bone heads of **not chosen**."*

THE IDOLATRY OF POWER WORSHIP FILLS THE MEETINGS

"Coldness inhabit – an neat, golden cloven hoof." †Jude 1:16
"Flash on coolheaded, constant non-believing."

THE GOSPEL OF HATE IS PREACHED WITH BOLDNESS

"Connivent, hot-headed, nonsensical goofball."
"An enhanced cloven hoof so-and-so belittling."
"Hedonist goofball and enchants on violence."   †Romans 3:15
"Is not chosen and enhanced goofball violent?"

WORSE, IT IS BROADCAST OVER THE AIRWAVES

"Oh Channel of Dead! Insolent cloven boasting."
"Lovable of oath-intoning. Enhanced coldness."
"Cloven-hoofed channels. Neat bloodstaining."
"Bonehead godliest connivant channels fool."

**RATHER THAN BE KICKED OFF THE NETWORK,
MINISTRY AFTER MINISTRY ECHOES THE PARTY LINE**

"Connivent, notable golden chain falsehoods."

**THE LOVE OF DEATH MASQUERADES
AS RIGHTEOUS INDIGNATION**

"Noble cloven-hoofed and incessant loathing."
"Cloven-hoofed. Genetic henna land bloodstains."

SMUG, SELF RIGHTEOUS, BLIND AND IN ERROR

"Coolheaded connivant snob not healing self."
"Cloven-hoofed bitingness and not clean halo."

**THE SERMONS ARE NOT PREDICATED ON THE
TWO GREAT SCRIPTURAL PILLARS**

"Cloven-hoofed, and not establishing on clean."
"Cloven-hoofed, notional blandness teaching."   †Galatians 5:14

**INSTEAD, THE "US AGAINST THEM BUT GOD IS ON
OUR SIDE" THEME PERMEATES THE SERMON MESSAGES**

"Genial conventions enchant bold falsehood."
"Notable cloven hoof and the insane scolding."
"Hello! Tone-deaf, connivant belching so-and-so."

**THE UNDISCERNING ARE CONVINCED BY
REPETITION AND GREAT DISPLAYS OF EMOTION**

"Connivent goofball enchants. Halo one-sided."   †Acts 8:9-11
"Boldfaced nonetheless connivant hooligan."
"Connivent, hot-headed, nonsensical goofball."

**THE COLLUSION OF DARKNESS QUENCHES THE SPIRIT IN
THE LIVES OF THOSE WHO REALLY WANT TO SERVE GOD;**

**AND THE IDEA THAT SOME PEOPLE ARE WORTHIER
OF LIFE THAN OTHERS APPEALS TO SINFUL PRIDE**

"Noble and chosen. Cloven-hoofed tantalizing."   †Matthew 24:12

**LISTENING TO THIS CARNAL APPEAL
EVENTUALLY TAKES ITS TOLL VIA DECEPTION**

"Bloodstaining leaden cloven hoof enchants."   †Luke 14:11
"Falsehoods and connive hell-bent contagion."
"Flash! Connivent congealed noble sainthood."

**LISTENER'S HEARTS TURN COLD AND DECEPTION
RUSHES TO FILL THE VACUUM CREATED BY SERMONS
OF RHETORIC AND POLICY SHAPING**

"Connivant hateable nonsense fool God-child."   †II Timothy 3:13
"Hot congealed and enchants on self-oblivion."

**ANY NOT ROOTED AND GROUNDED IN THE FAITH ARE
RIPE FOR DECEPTION BY PREACHING, PRINT, AND
DIGITAL MEDIA ENDORSING THE FALSEHOOD**

"Anon catching novel fooled non-established."
"The vocal cannoning fooled non-established."
"Connive a long chant. Fooled non-established."   †II Peter 2:2
"Anglo convict Henna. Fooled non-established."
"Anglo fooled. Than convince non-established."

**USELESS WORSHIP OFFERED BY WORSHIPERS WILLFULLY
IGNORANT OF THE PAIN CAUSED BY POLICIES THEY ENDORSE**

"Half-blind chosen? Congealed! Sonnet vain, too." †Amos 5:23
"The all-dancing conventions fool boneheads."
"Cloven-hoofed hates on innocent. Galas blind."

**THE KINGDOM OF DARKNESS HAS A FIELD DAY AS MANY
IN THE CHURCH EXCHANGE THEIR ALLEGIANCE STILL
CONVINCED THEY ARE SERVING GOD**

"Hell not sob on ascendance on of living death."   †Isaiah 5:14
"Hell-bent loving ascendance on of sainthood."
"Felon clash on Covenant. Sainthood bleeding."

**THE SALT AND BEACON-LIKE LIGHT THAT DEFINES TRUE
CHRISTIANS DIMINISHES BEYOND PERCEPTION...
EVEN THE WORSHIP SONGS ARE NOT ANOINTED**

"A Baa condoning flesh. Then soon volt decline."
"A Baa condoning flesh. Solvent decline. No hot."   †Revelation 3:16
"A Baa condoning flesh. Volts decline. None hot."
"A Baa condoning flesh. Oh, volt sonnet decline."
"Indolence. A Baa condoning flesh. She not volt."
"Indolence. A Baa condoning flesh. He's not volt."

BROTHERLY LOVE BECOMES VIRTUALLY NON-EXISTENT

"A Baa condoning on flesh. Love declines to nth."   †Matthew 24:12

**SOWING TO THE FLESH REAPS CORRUPTION
– AND ALL MUST STAND BEFORE THE ONE WHO
SAID "I AM THE LIGHT OF THE WORLD"**

"Baa indolence. None holds facing the Volt Son."
"A Baa condoning flesh. Incensed oven toll, tho..."
"A Baa condoning flesh. Incensed hot oven toll."   †Matthew 3:12
"Discontent a Baa condoning flesh. Hello oven!"

**IS YOKING WITH UNBELIEVERS TO INFLUENCE GLOBAL
AND NATIONAL POLICY WORTH FORFEITING THE KINGDOM
OF GOD? AS BRANCHES BROKEN OFF FROM THE TRUE
VINE, MANY WILL BE SHUT OUT FROM THE MARRIAGE
SUPPER OF THE LAMB AND THE BRIDE**

"Half-blind chosen? As not onto Vine, congealed."   †Matthew 22:11-13
"Half-blind chosen? Congealed! None toast vino."
"Notable foothold and changes incline ovens."

**THE ANCIENT OF DAYS WHO EXECUTES JUSTICE AND
JUDGMENT FOR THE WIDOW AND ORPHAN OBSERVES
AND WEIGHS IN THE BALANCES**

"A Host of Eons beheld all-dancing convention."
"A Ascendant beholding insolent cloven hoof."   †Hebrews 10:30
"A scandal benighted on insolent cloven hoof."
"A scandal bonding thee, insolent cloven hoof."
"A blotch agenda. Insolent cloven hoof sinned."

"Notable single-handed contains cloven hoof."
"A Ascendant Being hold insolent cloven hoof."
"Nonsense! Cloven-hoofed to git ball and chain."   †Revelation 20: 1-3
"Londoner of living death chosen to balances."
"And I God then balances insolent cloven hoof."   †Daniel 5:27

GREAT WEEPING AND GNASHING OF TEETH AT JUDGMENT

"Clean saddening on this notable cloven hoof."
"A Sancta beholding insolent cloven hoof end."   †Matthew 24:48-51
"Connivent bonehead fondling colossal hate."
"Is connivant. Soon belong dance of death hell."
"Is connivent. Soon belong of death dance hall."
"Half-blind congealed. Notion chosen not save."
"Half-blind chosen? Congealed! Votes no anoint."
"Half-blind chosen? Congealed! An notion stove."   †Matthew 13:41-42
"Half-blind chosen? Congealed! Anon into stove."
"Half-blind chosen? Congealed! Soon titan oven."

THE ECCLESIA MUST KEEP THEMSELVES PURE AND EARNESTLY CONTEND FOR THE TRUE GOSPEL

"Benign, clean handed chosen. So vital not fool."   †I John 5:21
"Enhanced clean of loving, Honest Bloodstain."   †Psalm 125:3
"Notable halo sons concerned of living death."

THOSE WHO EXPOSE RATHER THAN ASSIMILATE LIKE CLONES INTO THIS UNFRUITFUL WORK OF DARKNESS WILL BE PERSECUTED

"Clean bold treason of living death on chosen."
"Bold cloven-hoofed enchant alienating sons."
"Red-hot sons of non-clonable ace living death."
"Non-clonable chastener of living death do so."
"Notable is not loving of clean handed chosen."   †Psalm 37:32
"So, living death hated censor of non-clonable."

RELEVANT LONGEST WORDS/PHRASES USING SOME OF THE LETTERS

"inconceivableness" "conventionalised" "celestial globe"
"Songs of innocence" "long-established" "diabolicalness"
"lighthandedness" "deceivableness" "enchantingness"
"evangelicalness" "boneheadedness"

For there are certain men crept in unawares, who were before of old ordained to this condemnation, ungodly men, turning the grace of our God into lasciviousness, and denying the only Lord God, and our Lord Jesus Christ ...Jude 1:4

THE PERSECUTION OF THE SAINTS:
CHOOSE YE THIS DAY WHOM YOU WILL SERVE

There are always two sides to every coin. We've looked at the way apostasy and programming are affecting those who profess Christ; but live carnally and void of the word and Spirit. Continuing on the theme of the anagrams "Gosh-an atheistic partnership!" and "This earnest! This approaching!" formed from the phrase 'Shaping the Post-Christian Era', we see there is another side - the action taken by the powers of this world against a weak and impotent church.

Much of the horror of the coming persecution of the body of Christ is that it will be led by some of the very personalities people trusted with their spiritual well-being. Just as one of Jesus' disciples betrayed him, the apostates and false brethren will be the Judas goats that lead the undiscerning sheep to their slaughter. Worse, they will use scripture to legitimize their actions. The hatred and disdain sown for people of other lands and ethnicities, and failure to execute The Great Commission will reap a whirlwind of rebuke for a careless and cold-hearted church.

The wise will understand; and use this window of persecution to turn many to righteousness. None of the wicked will understand; and will see *the mark* as their ticket to freedom. This hour will try everyone on the earth; none will be exempt.

MERGER OF CHURCH AND STATE

HAVING LEFT HER FIRST LOVE, THE CHURCH UNEQUALLY YOKES WITH THE FORCES OF WORLDLY POWER ...IN THE STATE SHE FINDS ENFORCEMENT FOR HER AGENDA; IN HER THE STATE FINDS POLITICAL SUPPORT AND MORAL ENDORSEMENT FOR CONQUEST AND DOMINATION

"Armed forces change truth."   †Revelation 2:4
"Furthermore, changed acts."   †II Corinthians 6:14
"Often, sacred thug charmer."
"Net of sacred thug charmer."
"Charmer of changed truest."
"Together, sacred charm fun."

RATHER THAN HUMBLY WAIT BEFORE THE LORD FOR A
WORD IN SEASON TO THE PEOPLE, LUCRE IS ACCEPTED
FROM SECULAR SOURCES TO PREACH A GOSPEL IN LINE
WITH THE GOALS OF THE HATERS OF GOD ...THEY HAVE
CHANGED THE TRUTH OF GOD INTO A LIE, AND WORSHIPPED
AND SERVED THE CREATURE MORE THAN THE CREATOR,
WHO IS BLESSED FOR EVER

"Fund to the grace charmers."
"Menacers of charged truth."   †I Timothy 6:10
"Charmer change of trusted."   †Matthew 7:6
"Charm dense truth of grace."
"Crush. Change. Reformatted."

WELL KNOWN POLITICAL, ENTERTAINMENT, AND MEDIA
PERSONALITIES ARE INVITED INTO THE PULPIT ...PRESTIGE,
POLITICAL CLOUT, AND FINALLY BEING WELCOMED INTO THE
"INNER CIRCLE" ARE MORE IMPORTANT THAN A PURE HEART,
HOLY HANDS, AND FEET SHOD WITH THE PREPARATION OF
THE GOSPEL OF PEACE

"Thug from charades center."
"Gem of retardant churches."   †I Peter 2:18
"Her technocrat fraud gems."

JUNK FOOD 'FEEL GOOD" SERMONS ARE CHOSEN OVER STRONG
MEAT AND THE SINCERE MILK OF THE WORD, LEAVING
CONGREGATIONS TOO WEAK AND CRIPPLED TO LIFT UP JESUS

"Ho-hum! Tender grace crafts."
"Chef grace as modern truth."   †Hebrews 5:14
"Grunt of charmed teachers."   †II Timothy 4:3
"Grr! Unmatched of teachers."
"Teacher forced hamstrung."
"Hamstrung the free accord."
"Dragon fume stretch; reach."
"Dragon fetters reach much."

THE SCRIPTURES ASSUME A SERPENTINE CONTORTION AS
THEY ARE USED TO MAKE THE MEMBERS FEEL COMFORTABLE
ABOUT SHEDDING THE BLOOD OF PEOPLE OVERSEAS

"The fresh argument accord."   †Romans 3:15

**BUT CARE IS TAKEN TO IGNORE THE WARNING THAT
ALL WHO LIVE BY THE SWORD MUST DIE BY THE SWORD**

†Revelation 13:10   *"Her fat argument scorched."*   †Matthew 26:52

**ADDITIONALLY, THE PEOPLE ARE TAUGHT THEY WILL
BE WHISKED AWAY IN A SECRET RAPTURE BEFORE
THE SITUATION EVER DETERIORATES TOO BADLY**

"Accord them huge transfer."   †Revelation 13:7

**THEY HAVE IGNORED THE SPRITURAL ADMONITION TO TRY
THE SPIRITS BY THE SPIRIT, BECAUSE NOT EVERY SPIRIT IS
OF GOD ...THE LITMUS TEST OF FELLOWSHIP IS OBEDIENCE TO
THE COMMANDMENTS OF GOD ...WHERE IS THE DISCERNMENT?**

"Much secret – dragon father."   †I John 4:1
"Dragon father secret chum."

**PEOPLE WHO BLINDLY FOLLOW ALONG WILL SHARE IN
THE GUILT AND ETERNAL PUNISHMENT – DO THEY REALLY
KNOW WHO AND WHAT THEY ARE FOLLOWING?**

"Dragon fuhrer tact scheme."   †I John 5:21
"Further act dragon scheme."   †John 3:20
"Fact: dragon crusher theme."

**IF THEY CAN'T DISCERN THE DECEPTION NOW, WHAT CHANCE
WILL THEY HAVE AGAINST THE LYING WONDERS OF THE FALSE
PROPHET AND THE MARK OF THE BEAST??**

"Furthermore, chanced tags."

**"CHRISTIAN" CONCERTS ARE USED TO RALLY FOLLOWERS; SEARING
THEIR CONSCIENCES TO THE IMPENDING DEATHS RESULTING FROM
MILITANT CHRISTENDOM'S POLICIES ...THEREWITH (THE TONGUE)
BLESS WE GOD, EVEN THE FATHER; AND THEREWITH CURSE WE MEN,
WHICH ARE MADE AFTER THE SIMILITUDE OF GOD**

"Henceforth, megastar. Crud!"   †I John 4:20
"Huge hatred farm concerts."
"Grrr! Count the shamefaced."

**IMPASSIONED SERMONS WILL BE GIVEN TO JUSTIFY HOW THE
DEATH OF THOSE WHO DON'T KNOW JESUS BRINGS GLORY TO
JESUS – BUT IT WILL NOT BE PUT IN THOSE TERMS ...CLASSIC
DOUBLE-SPEAK ...CLOAKED IN THE CHIVALROUS ROBE OF
"PEACE AND SAFETY"**

"Mad fears crunch together."   †I John 4:18
"Mastered gather of crunch."
"Grr! Unmatched of the scare."
"Daft. Or huge harm Crescent."

THE ATTENDEES RETURN IN SELF-RIGHTEOUSNESS...SOON,
ANYONE WHO DISAGREES WILL BE VIEWED AS AN ENEMY
OF GOD AND AN ENEMY OF THE STATE...AND PERSECUTED

"Much face stronger hatred."

"CURSED BE THE MAN THAT TRUSTETH IN MAN, AND MAKETH
FLESH HIS ARM, AND WHOSE HEART DEPARTETH FROM THE LORD"

"Recent charms of dear thug."
"Fact: thug horned screamer."   †Jeremiah 17:5
"Rather, thug enforced scam."

THESE SHEPHERDS SHOULD NEVER HAVE UNEQUALLY YOKED
THEMSELVES, BECAUSE THOSE WHO DO NOT GENUINELY LOVE
JESUS CHRIST ARE DRIVEN BY WISDOM WHICH IS EARTHLY,
SENSUAL, AND DEVILISH

"Toughened craft charmers."
"Strange of the crude charm."   †James 3:15

MASSIVE NUMBERS OF PASTORS ARE RECRUITED TO PREACH A
SCRIPT THE STATE HAS WRESTED FROM THE SCRIPTURES FOR USE
IN TIMES OF UPHEAVAL, RATHER THAN EXHORATION AND COMFORT
FROM THE WORD OF GOD ACCORDING TO PSALM 91 AND ISAIAH 43:2

"Demon furthers chat grace."   †Proverbs 1:10-16
"Gotcha! Referendum charts."
"Chart thug enforces dream."
"Enforced huge smart chart."
"Tough fed charmers recant."
"Huge charts from recanted."

AS A DEAL IS STRUCK WITH THE DEVIL, WATCH FOR MORE
CARNAGE IN THE NEVER-ENDING WARS THE FOOLISH SHEEP
HAVE CO-OPTED THEMSELVES INTO SUPPORTING

"Harm of grace hurts decent."
"Huge contracts freed harm."
"Contracts defer huge harm."

"Ground screech aftermath."
"Harm daughter of Crescent."
"Huge contract harmed serf."
"Dragon cremate serf hutch."
"Great! Deft, human scorcher."
"Crud! Each-other fragments."
"Ha! True, scorched fragment."

**A WATCHMAN'S WORD TO THE CHURCH: TURN FROM
IDOLATRY AND SEEK GOD IN REPENTANCE, FOR THE
HOUR OF REFINEMENT IN THE FIRES OF PERSECUTION IS NIGH**

"Hurrah! Decent gem factors."   †Matthew 5:8
"Gem of rather unscratched."

THE WATCHMAN SPEAKS AS A PROPHET...

"Sacred truth gem n' arch-foe." †Titus 2:15
"Thud from grace chastener."

AND AS A PSALMIST

"Organ screech famed truth."   †Psalm 7:17
"Screech from an aged Truth."

**STUNG BY THE SCRIPTURAL CRITICISM, THEY ATTEMPT TO
DISCREDIT THE WATCHMAN; THE WATCHMAN'S FACE IS SET
LIKE FLINT ...REPEATING THE WARNING WITH ALL URGENCY**

"Chastened. Hurt from grace." †Psalm 141:5
"Thrash defunct grace more."   †Isaiah 50:7

**THE WARNING IS HEEDED BY SOME ...SHEPHERDS PROSTRATE
THEMSELVES IN REPENTANCE BEFORE GOD; EXHORTING THEIR
CONGREGATIONS TO DO LIKEWISE ... FORGIVEN, RESTORED, AND
YIELDED TO THE MASTER, THESE VESSELS NOW BECOME TRUE
SALT AND LIGHT BEARERS WITH A RENEWED ANTICIPATION FOR
THE COMING KINGDOM OF GOD**

"Grr! Ahem! Staunch defector." †Luke 15:7
"The staunch graced reform."   †Luke 15:10

THE WATCHMAN IS MARKED FOR SURVEILLANCE AND DEATH

"Send huge rat from catcher."   †Psalm 37:32
"Henceforth rat mug sacred."   †Revelation 12:11

"Harsh force truncated gem."

EVENTUALLY, MANY ARE SWEPT UP IN THE DRAGNET OF
PERSECUTION AS IT SPREADS ACROSS THE WEST ...THE
TRUE NATURE OF THE BEAST IS REVEALED AS COLD-HEARTED
CHRISTIANS EXPERIENCE THE SAME TYPE OF CRUELTY AND
APATHY THEY SUPPORTED FOR OTHERS AROUND THE WORLD ...
ALTHOUGH THERE ARE GREAT NUMBERS OF THEM TOGETHER,
THEY ARE HELPLESS IN THE FACE OF THEIR PERSECUTORS ...
THE FORMER RALLY BRAVADO IS GONE ...THEIR SUFFERING IS
A FIERY TRIAL TO BRING FORTH THE PURITY OF REPENTANCE

"Ouch! Strength dream farce."
"Face much stronger hatred."

FOR THE WATCHMEN AND THE PURE IN HEART, THEIR SUFFERING
IS FOR RIGHTEOUSNESS SAKE; GREAT IS THEIR REWARD IN THE
KINGDOM OF HEAVEN ...NOW IT BECOMES CLEAR WHO THE
PERSUADERS WERE, AND THAT THEY BEAR THE MARK OF THE BEAST

"The charmers turn dogface."
"Hatred fragment crouches."   †Revelation 13:16
"Than thug screamer forced."
"Earnest thug forced march."
"Scattered of hunger march."
"Thugs forced neater march."

THE CAMPS MEAN TORTURE AND DEATH, AS THE
HORRORS OF THE MIDDLE EAST COME TO MIDDLE AMERICA

"Am arch-foe, crude strength."
"Rude strong-arm fetch each."
"Thenceforth guards cream."
"Ache from a crude strength."

THE MOST HIGH AND ALMIGHTY GOD SHORTENS THE DAYS OF
SUFFERING LEST NO FLESH BE SAVED ...THEN, AS THE LIGHTNING
FLASHES FROM THE EAST TO THE WEST, THE SON OF MAN APPEARS
TO VANQUISH THE HATERS OF GOD AND ESTABLISH HIS REIGN

†Luke 17:24 ***"Face thunderstorm charge."*** †Matthew 24:22

THE WICKED SHEPHERDS AND THEIR OVERSEERS ARE
ABOUT TO MEET THE HORRENDOUS DEMONIC ENTITY
WHO ENTICED THEM TO SELL OUT THEIR FLOCKS TO
STRENGHTEN THE CARNAL KINGDOMS OF MEN

"Furthest grace arch-demon." †Luke 16:28

**THEY REALIZE THE FOOLISHNESS OF THEIR EARTHLY PRIDE ...
THEY BUILT ON A FOUNDATION OTHER THAN JESUS CHRIST AND
HIS RIGHTEOUSNESS AND TRUE HOLINESS ...BEFORE THEM ARE
THE SPIRITS OF THE MILLIONS WHO SUFFERED DUE TO THEIR
ACTIONS...THERE IS NOWHERE TO RUN, AND THEY CANNOT
REPENT ...THEY ARE RUINED**

"Char of unmatched regrets."
"Regret of scratched human." †Revelation 22:15
"Hated farce much stronger."

**THE IMPOSING ARCHITECTURE OF A HELL ENLARGED LOOMS
BEFORE THEM ...AND HELPFUL STAFF AWAIT TO GET THEM
SITUATED IN THEIR QUARTERS**

"Crude gnome. Farthest arch."
"Arch of unmatched regrets." †Isaiah 5:14

**BANNED FROM THE WEDDING SUPPER OF THE LAMB, THERE IS
NOTHING TO LOOK FORWARD TO EXCEPT THIRST, FLAMES, AND
TORMENT ...A PREVIEW OF THE LAKE OF FIRE AWAITING AFTER
THE FINAL JUDGMENT**

"Not fetch sugared charmer."
"Charm get red-hot furnaces." †Revelation 14:11
"Her accursed, hot fragment."

RELEVANT LONGEST WORDS/PHRASES USING SOME OF THE LETTERS

"horned screamer" "catechumenate" "concertmaster" "outer garments"
"remonstrated" "re-consecrated" "Eastern church" "great-hearted"
"recrudescent" "shortchanged" "counteracted" "thunderstorm"

THE PERSECUTION OF THE SAINTS:
PURIFIED AND FAITHFUL UNTO DEATH

Will a day come when followers of Christ are persecuted in the West as they are in other areas of the world? The Bible speaks of a three-and-a-half-year period before the return of the Lord Jesus Christ when this will indeed take place. Anagrams support this prophecy and indicate that those whom believers think they can trust the most during times of upheaval may instead betray them for worldly gain. As persecution is already underway in countries hostile to Christianity, this next topic is included under present day anagrams. Here we examine yet another scenario where 'men of the cloth' depart from the faith and join ranks with the state for prestige and prosperity. Truly, the love of money is a root of all kinds of evil. Early in the discourse *yelper* represents paid citizen spies; and toward the end it refers to the cries of suffering saints. *Gems* are Christians, *greenest* means love of money, and *poetry* is figurative of inspired scripture – the Word of God.

CLERGY RESPONSE TEAMS

ENTITIES HOSTILE TO THE GOSPEL APPROACH CLERGY TO CONVINCE CONGREGATIONS TO GO QUIETLY TO DETAINMENT CAMPS IN THE EVENT OF A NATIONAL EMERGENCY ...NO ONE SEEMS TO CONSIDER DETAINMENT CAMPS ARE DESIGNED TO HOUSE ENEMY PRISONERS OF WAR ...A CONCERNED INDIVIDUAL LEAKS THE MEMO

"Gem alert!! Creepy sons."
"Scary notes repel gem."
"Messenger copy alert."
"Son's creepy telegram."
"E's necropsy telegram."

ONE CANNOT IMAGINE THE ORIGINAL TWELVE APOSTLES DOING SUCH A THING ...THERE IS ALWAYS A NEED FOR MONEY IN THIS PRESENT WORLD, BUT SILVER AND GOLD MUST NOT INFLUENCE THOSE ENTRUSTED TO SHEPHERD THE FLOCK OF GOD

"Greet moneyless. Crap!"   †I Peter 5:2
"Cap moneyless regret."
"Moneyless rage crept."

JESUS WARNED WE CANNOT SERVE GOD AND MAMMON

"Recompenses greatly."
"Greenest ears comply."
"Spelt mercenary egos."
"Steep mercenary logs."
"Sorely greenest camp."
"Select money grasper."
"Greener, classy, top me."
"Or, my greenest places."

A SEARED CONSCIENCE IS THE HALLMARK OF THOSE WHO LEAD THEIR CHARGES TO DESTRUCTION

"Copy mean regretless."
"Amen! Regretless copy."
"Core empty largeness."
"Recant. Sly op emerges."
"Recant. Lo, spy emerges."
"Recant. Egress me ploy."
"On my regretless pace."
"To my graceless preen."

IF THE PRICE IS RIGHT, THE CONSCIENCE CAN BE SILENCED

"Respects large money."   †II Peter 2:15 I
"Copes. Green masterly."   †Timothy 6:10

A BIZARRE THING OCCURS ...THOSE WHO KNOW NOT GOD TRAIN THOSE WHO CLAIM TO KNOW GOD ...THE MEN OF GOD BLINDFOLD THEMSELVES, THEN PERMIT THOSE BORN BLIND TO LEAD THEM!

"Recently posers game."
"Re: Gee, try camp lesson!"   †I Timothy 4:1-2
"Yep, react germ lesson."
"Lesson: Trace prey (gem)."
"Act lesson, merge prey."
"Merge to screenplays."

THE SHEPHERDS DON'T SEEM TO TRULY REALIZE TO WHOM THEY ARE YOKING THEMSELVES

"Employer secrets nag."   †II Corinthians 6:14
"Secret employer snag."

"Sorcery elements gap."
"Glee. Net sorcery maps."
"Steep sorcery mangle."

**THEIR PAYMASTERS ARE LIKE PHARAOH
IN THE DAYS OF SHIPHRAH AND PUAH**

"Sporty glee menacers."
"Necropsy glee master."
"Slyer agreement cops."

**THEY HAVE NO REAL CONCERN FOR THE SHEPHERD,
HIS FLOCK, OR ALLEGIANCE TO THE NATION'S PEOPLE**

"Empty eagle scorners."

**SUPPOSEDLY DETAINMENT CAMPS WILL BE NECESSARY IN THE
EVENT OF A WEAPONIZED BIOLOGICAL EVENT ...ALTHOUGH A
STRICT HOUSE QUARANTINE MAKES MORE SENSE THAN
CONFINING LARGE NUMBERS OF UNRELATED PEOPLE TOGETHER**

"Genteel army process."

A BIOTERRORISM EVENT IS STAGED

"Sleepy germ ancestor."
"Rely germs as potence."
"A slyer potence germs."
"Careless on germ type."
"Creep lose nasty germ."
"Creepy as germ stolen."
"Recent leprosy games."
"Ole! Nasty germs creep."
"Sluyer potence germs."
"Potence layers germs."
"Messy, larger potence."
"Am sores creep gently."
"Lose emergency parts."
"Necropsy merges late."
"Mega leprosy centres."

**FOLLOWING THE SCRIPTING AND ROLE-PLAYING TRAINING,
THEY MAY SAY THAT OTHERS HAVE ALREADY DIED, AND
ALL SHOULD GO TO A CAMP FOR SAFETY**

"Relates gem necropsy."
"Relate necropsy gems."
"Comply – greater sense."

RATHER THAN THE WHOLE COUNSEL OF GOD, THEIR APPEAL IS BUILT ON ONE SET OF SCRIPTURES ALONE

"My page or centerless."   †Romans 13:1-5

ESTABLISHED PRESENCE IN THE COMMUNITY GIVES CREDIBILITY TO THEIR MESSAGE

"Recently a gem posers."
"Recently mega posers."

DO THEY BRING FAITH, OR A FEARSOME FATE? ONCE WORD FILTERS BACK OF THE MISERY IN THE CAMPS, MANY NON-CHRISTIANS WILL FEEL DISDAIN FOR THE GOSPEL, VIEWING THESE CLERGY THROUGH A LENS OF SUSPICION ...THEY WILL SEE THEM AS:

"Elegant mercy posers."
"A gentle mercy posers."
"Poser as gentle mercy."
"Emergency salt poser."
"Mercenary gospel set."
"Mercy eagerness plot."
"Mercy? Transpose glee."
"Sleepy grace monster."
"Steep glory menacers."
"Glory menace pesters."
"Graceless poetry men."
"Pestersome angel cry."
"Some strangely creep."
"Creep mostly enrages."
"Gentle mercy rapes so."
"So spare gentle mercy."
"Serenely. Gem captors."
"Sly gem treason creep."
"Amen! Respect sly ogre."
"Grace? Or spy elements?"
"Sleepy smog recanter."
"Graceless entropy me."
"More glassy pretence."
"Else ape strong mercy."

"Repel on mercy stages."
"Mercy steeples groan."
"Steeply scaremonger."
"So general mercy pest."

**CONVINCING PEOPLE TO VOLUNTARILY
GO TO THEIR DEMISE IS NOT AN EASY TASK ...**

"Try compel eagerness."

**DUE TO THE REPUTATION CAMPS HAVE FOR ASSAULT,
TORTURE, ATTACK DOGS, DEPRIVATION, FILTH AND DEATH**

"Mercenary glee posts."
"Creep 'n' gay molesters."
"Rape censor gem style."
"Poser angry, select me."
"Poser recently gas me."
"Scantly emerge. Poser."
"Creepy mongrel asset."
"Easy! Respect mongrel."
"Gem's cry tone pleaser."
"Germy plate necroses."
"Meets large necropsy."
"Terse necropsy gleam."
"Gray presence molest."
"Gray corpse elements."

**WILL THESE SHEPHERDS BE HONEST AND REVEAL THE
STRONG POSSIBILITY DEATH AWAITS IN THE CAMPS?**

"Comely represent gas."
"Corpse's genteel army."

**OR WILL THEY ACCOMPANY THEIR PARISHIONERS TO
THE CAMPS AND THERE BE GIVEN AUTHORITY TO KEEP
THE "UNRULY" ONES IN LINE? AT SOME POINT, THEY
MAY BE GRANTED POWER TO USE DEADLY FORCE ...**

†Mathew 24:9-10 *"Merry elegance stops."* †Luke 21:12
†Mark 13:11   *"Presently rages come."* †John 16:2

**A WISE PERSON WILL SUSPECT SOMETHING
IS WRONG WITH THE PICTURE**

"Smelt eager necropsy."

"Empty large, necroses."
"Strongly see am creep."   †Proverbs 27:12
"Merely corpse's agent."

**THOSE WHO CAN LEAVE THE AREA MAY BE
ABLE TO AVOID INTERACTION WITH THEM**

"Petrol necessary, gem."
"Merely strong escape."

**BUT IN A SOCIETY WHICH IS CRUMBLING BY THE HOUR,
GETTING AWAY MAY ALSO MEAN MOVING OUT OF RANGE
OF WHAT LITTLE FOOD IS STILL AVAILABLE**

"Meanly steep grocers."
"Type: grocer lameness."

**ELECTED REPRESENTATIVES CANNOT HELP THE
SAINTS AMONG THEIR CONSTITUENTS ...MORE
POWERFUL VOICES HAVE GOTTEN TO THEM FIRST**

"Me yelper at congress."
"Meet congress player."
"Yelper tame Congress."
"Tamely. Congress peer."
"Congress merely tape."   †Psalm 108:12
"Reply scare gemstone."

**SURVEILLANCE IS USED TO IDENTIFY
AND TRACK DOWN BIBLE BELIEVERS**

"Yelper traces on gems."   †Psalm 140:4-5
"Gemstone yelper cars."
"Yelper car notes gems."
"Yelper reacts on gems."
"System creep or angle."
"Selector grasp enemy."

**IN THE CAMPS, LIFE IS PRECARIOUS,
AND DEATH IS A COMMONPLACE EVENT**

"Manly creeps greet so."
"Respect slayer on gem."

ITS SPECTER IS ALWAYS PRESENT

"Necroses. Empty glare."
"Meanly. Corpse's greet."
"Necropsy meal greets."
"Necropsy tale merges."
"Namely, greet corpses."
"Gross cemetery panel."

**THESE CAMPS MAY FEATURE NEW METHODS
OF EXTINGUISHING LIFE...**

"Pea-green mercy slots."
"Salt necropsy emerge."

**AND NOVEL METHODS OF CORPSE
DISPOSAL AND DECONTAMINATION**

"Rays melt corpse gene."
"Compress large teeny."

HERE IS THE PATIENCE OF THE SAINTS

"Sagely censor temper."   †Psalm 141:3

**SOME SHEPHERDS COMPETE TO GET
THE MOST PEOPLE INTO THE CAMPS**

"Sly compare greenest."
"My loser percentages."
"More sly percentages."
"My percentage losers."
"Presently mega score."
"Percentages or sly me."

**BUT A DIFFERENT TYPE OF WAGE AWAITS THEM,
–BASED ON THE LAW OF SOWING AND REAPING**

"Menacer gets leprosy."
"Menacers get leprosy!"
"Not messy grace leper!"
"Screamer openly gets."

**WHAT ABOUT GOD'S PROVEN METHOD OF DEALING
WITH PLAGUE? THE ARM OF THE LORD IS REVEALED
ONLY TO THOSE WHO BELIEVE HIS REPORT: FAITH IN
AND OBEDIENCE TO THE WORD OF GOD!**

†James 5:14-16 *"Poetry cleanses germ."*   †I Peter 2:24
†Psalm 107:20 *"Poetry cleanse germs."*   †Psalm 91:3,6,10
              "Germ potence slayers."

**A CARNAL CHURCH SPIRITUALLY ASLEEP
HAS NOT BELIEVED THIS WAS COMING**

"Sensory grace temple."
"On sleepy grace terms."
"Prayerless, cogent me."   †I Thessalonians 5:3
"Careless entropy gem."
"Sleepy gems or recant."
"Emergency or as slept."
"Or as spelt E-M-E-R-G-E-N-C-Y!!"

THE FIRES OF PERSECUTION BEGIN TO REFINE THE SAINTS

"Gently space remorse."
"Remorse paces gently."
"Mercy gentle, so parse."

**THEY BUILD EACH OTHER UP WITH
SCRIPTURE, LOVE FOR GOD, AND ONE ANOTHER**

"Gentle prose as mercy."   †Ephesians 5:19
"Gem select on prayers."
"Earnest mercy gospel."
"Select on merry pages."
"Gems layer on respect."

**IT IS A TIME OF GREAT SOUL SEARCHING
AND REPENTANCE FOR THOSE INTERNED**

"Sleepy gems n' Creator."   †I Peter 4:1
"Paces gently. Remorse."
"Gems coarsely repent."
"A El gems cry so; repent."
"Lo, gems cry sea; repent."
"Ay! Repent gem's closer."   †Jeremiah 29:13

**MANY DIE IN THESE CAMPS AND THE SAINTS CRY
OUT FOR DELIVERANCE ...THE LORD IN HIS MERCY
SHORTENS THE DAYS SO ALL FLESH DOESN'T PERISH**

"Gem yelpers: Ancestor???!!"
"GENTLE compress year."   †Mark 13:20

**AT THE APPOINTED TIME, THE LORD HIMSELF
DESCENDS WITH A SHOUT, THE VOICE OF THE
ARCHANGEL, AND THE TRUMPET OF GOD**

"Prayers. GENTLE comes."
"Note reply, gems. Cares."
"Relay respect on gems."
"Early respect on gems."
"Presently some Grace!"
"Sense large, top Mercy!!
"O My! <u>Largest Presence!!!</u>" †I Thessalonians 4:16-17

**IN THE BLINK OF AN EYE, THE SAINTS
RECEIVE THEIR RESURRECTED BODIES**

"Greatness reply, Come!"
"Son reply, "Create gems!!" †I Corinthians 15:50-54

**WITH THE SAINTS DELIVERED FROM THEIR GRASP, THEIR
TORMENTORS AND THOSE WHO DELIVERED THEM TO BE
PERSECUTED CAN ONLY WATCH IN SHOCK AND DISMAY**

"Mercenary glee stops."
"My! Crap! Greenest lose."
"Creepy rant. Lose gems!"

**THEY WILL NOW FACE FIERY INDIGNATION ...THEY
ARE SINNERS IN THE HANDS OF AN ANGRY GOD**

"Meets necropsy glare."
"Largest corpse? Enemy."

RELEVANT LONGEST WORDS/PHRASES USING SOME OF THE LETTERS

"scaremongers" "percentages" "garmentless" "screenplays"
"general store" "press agency" "present arms" "replacement"
"regenerates" "compensates" "completeness" "recompenses"

**Then they that feared the LORD spake often one to another: and the LORD
hearkened, and heard it, and a book of remembrance was written before him
for them that feared the LORD, and that thought upon his name ...And they
shall be mine, saith the LORD of hosts, in that day when I make up my jewels;
and I will spare them, as a man spareth his own son that serveth him ...
Malachi 3:16-17**

PART III

the future

UNDERSTANDING THE TIMES

"A determined thing stuns."

LET GOD ARISE

"Lost, dire age." †I John 5:19
"Red Goat lies." †Revelation 20:2-3
"Red Ego's tail." †Revelation 12:3-4
"God see trial." †Revelation 13:10, 14:12
"God rate lies." †John 8:44
"Get, or as lied." †Revelation 21:8
"Lot disagree." †Revelation 16:11
"So large edit." †Isaiah 13:11-12
"So drag elite." †Isaiah 24:21
"So, git leader." †Revelation 20:1-2
"Dealt ego sir." †Revelation 20:3
"Do get serial." †Revelation 20:3
"Rid to eagles." †Revelation 19:17
"Agile strode." †Isaiah 63:1
"To dire gales." †Isaiah 29:6
"Gales or tide." †Isaiah 51:15
"Gloater dies." †Job 40:11-12
"Lots rage, die." †Job 40:11-12
"Godliest era." †Habakkuk 2:14
"Seat godlier." †I Timothy 2:12
"A godlier set." †Revelation 1:5-6
"Ideal go rest." †Hebrews 4:9-11
"I, age old rest." †Mark 2:27-28

WRITING ON THE WALL

"Hallowing written."
"Wow! It enthralling."
"Now, earthling wilt."
"Lethal writing now."
"Till, gather, winnow."
"Twill wear nothing."

DARK CLOUDS OF JUDGMENT:
SOWING TO THE WIND

The anagrams from Writing on the Wall set the stage for divine judgment; those from Mene Mene Tekel Upharsin build further on that theme as evidenced by the appearance of *measurement*, *numerate*, and *numeral*. *Pre-Eminent*, *Super-Eminent*, and *Supreme* all relate to the glory and power of the Most High God; *Keen* speaks to His incomprehensible wisdom and strength. *Sheep* and *sheep-like* are a reference to the children of God, while *humane* is a very Old English word for human, thereby denoting weakness and carnality. *Numen* alludes to commanding Divinity. The anagrams from this phrase show that man's age-old rebellion against God will be forcibly put down, every knee will bow in submission to the Son of Man, and He will rule the nations with a rod of iron.

MENE MENE TEKEL UPHARSIN

GOD KNOWS THE PRECISE NUMBER OF RIGHTEOUS AND UNRIGHTEOUS TO BE JUDGED AT THE END OF THE AGE

"Help! Keen in measurement."
"He, Eminent, keep numerals."   †Isaiah 46:10

HE HAS SEEN THE AFFLICTION OF HIS PEOPLE IN THE FIRES OF PERSECUTION

"Turn Mine meek sheep lean."   †Ezekiel 34:1-6
"Healer: seen Mine unkempt."

THEY HAVE BEEN REFINED IN SUFFERING AND WASHED IN THE BLOOD OF THE LAMB; THEIR ROBES ARE THE WHITE LINEN OF RIGHTEOUSNESS

"Meek sheep men until earn."
"Meek sheep true linen man."   †Revelation 7:14

NOW HE GATHERS TOGETHER THOSE WHO HAVE MADE COVENANT WITH HIM AND SEALS THEM

"Numerate men 'n' sheep-like."
"I'm numerate sheep kennel."   †Psalm 50:5
"Net numeral in meek sheep."
"Hum! Keen Pre-eminent seal."

**THEY WILL NOT BE HURT BY THE WRATH OF GOD
WHICH WILL BE POURED OUT UPON THE EARTH**

"Keen healer 'n' step immune." †Revelation 7:3
"Keen sheep learnt immune."

**THE TESTIMONY HAS GONE OUT FROM THE TWO
WITNESSES: REPENT AND WORSHIP GOD ALONE**

"Keen up, else Eminent harm." †Revelation 11:3-6
"Ahem! Kneel! Super-Eminent."

**THE LAST TRUMP SOUNDS, HERALDING THE FIRST
RESURRECTION AND THE GATHERING OF
LIVING AND DEAD SAINTS**

"Numerate men; liken sheep."
"True Keen helps mean mine."
"An Eminent sure help meek." †I Corinthians 15:52
"Immense Keen help nature."
"Keen risen humane temple!!"

**THAT WHICH WAS SOWN IN A NATURAL, CORRUPTIBLE
BODY IS RAISED AN INCORRUPTIBLE SPIRITUAL BODY**

"Hi! Keen superman element." †I Corinthians 15:53
"Keen theme superman line."

**A WORSHIP SERVICE LIKE NO OTHER AS THOSE WHO OBTAINED
VICTORY OVER THE BEASTS' IMAGE, MARK, AND NAME-NUMBER
SING THE SONG OF MOSES AND THE SONG OF THE LAMB**

"Meantime, sheep run, kneel."
"Hearten up immense kneel."
"Kneel in the Supreme Name."
"Keen Supreme anthem line." †Revelation 15:3-4
"Kneel in the Supreme. Amen!"

**THESE HAVE BEEN WELCOMED INTO THE JOY OF THEIR
LORD AND SERVE HIM NIGHT AND DAY IN HIS TEMPLE**

"I'm the serene kneel up man."†Revelation 7:15
"Hum! Knee Eminent pleaser."

**THIS SENSE OF ADORATION AND LOVE FOR GOD IS
NOT SHARED BY THE EARTH'S RULING ELITE,**

THEIR MILITARY FORCES, AND ALL WHO HAVE RECEIVED
THE BEAST'S MARK AND/OR WORSHIPED HIM ...EVEN AS
HEAVEN RINGS WITH WORSHIP, EARTH HUMS WITH THE
FEVERISH INTENSITY OF A RACE OF REBELS INTENT ON
SINFUL DOMINATION OF THE WORLD

"Sheep kneel. Man mutineer."   †Romans 8:7
"Eh! Me plans keen mutineer."
"MAN: the keen, supreme line."   †II Thessalonians 2:4

THE NEW WORLD ORDER HAS ONLY HAD A FEW YEARS TO EXIST
...A CONSENSUS IS REACHED TO CARRY ON IN SPITE OF ANY
FURTHER SUPERNATURAL CATASTROPHES, LEST THE PAINSTAKING
EFFORTS OF MILLENIA BE LOST ...NEW WEAPONS OF FORMIDABLE
TECHNOLOGY AND SORCERY ITSELF WILL BE DEPLOYED TO SECURE
AND MAINTAIN DOMINATION OF THE EARTH

"Skip El! Mean men tune here."   †Job 21:15
"Like me human seen in repent!" †Revelation 9:20-21
"Human seek repel Eminent."   †Revelation 16:9-11

CONTINUITY OF GOVERNMENT WILL BE MAINTAINED VIA A
NETWORK OF HIGHLY SOPHISTICATED UNDERGROUND CITIES,
POPULATED ONLY BY ARMIES, HEADS OF STATE, ELITE
FINANCIERS, THEIR EMPLOYEES, AND SLAVE LABOR

"Eh! Me tunneler, keeps main."
"Eh! Me keeps a miner tunnel."
"Eh! Me, Marine keeps tunnel."
"Eh! Me, Airmen, keeps tunnel."
"Eh! Me keeps internal menu."   †Revelation 6:15
"Eh! Me keep. Tunnel remains."

THE HATERS OF GOD SHOULD HAVE READ THE BOOK
OF PROVERBS ...THERE IS NO WISDOM NOR
UNDERSTANDING NOR COUNSEL AGAINST THE LORD

"Eh! Keen supreme in mental."   † Proverbs 21:30
"Keen shame tunnel empire."   †Job 28:24

PREPARATION FOR THE SEVEN LAST PLAGUES,
CONTAINING THE FULLNESS OF THE WRATH OF GOD

"The Keen mean perils menu."   †Revelation 16:1

**GOD CLOTHES HIMSELF WITH THE GARMENTS OF VENGEANCE
...THE BREASTPLATE OF RIGHTEOUSNESS, THE HELMET OF
SALVATION, AND THE CLOAK OF ZEAL**

"I, Keener Numen plate mesh." †Ephesians 6:11
"Super! Amen! Keen in helmet." †Ephesians 6:17
"Eh! Keen in supreme mantle." †Isaiah 59:17

**THRUST IN THY SHARP SICKLE, AND GATHER THE CLUSTERS
OF THE VINE OF THE EARTH, FOR HER GRAPES ARE FULLY RIPE**

"Keen: human elements ripe." †Revelation 14:18

**RESISTANCE IS FUTILE, AS THE EMPIRE OF IRON AND CLAY
ATTEMPTS TO OUT-STRATEGIZE AND OVERCOME THE ONE
WHO CREATED BOTH SUBSTANCES**

"Keen; human 'n' steel empire." †Daniel 2:41-43
"Keen pin human, mere steel."

**MAN'S HIGHEST TECH WEAPONS OF MASS DESTRUCTION
ARE AN INSULT TO THE INTELLIGENCE OF A GOD WHO SPOKE
THE HEAVENS AND EARTH INTO EXISTENCE...**

"Ahem! Eminent repel nukes."   †Psalm 46:9-10

**POSSESSING GREATER SENSE THAN THE HUMAN REBELS HIDING
BENEATH THEM, THE MOUNTAINS AND ROCKS OF THE EARTH
HASTILY DEPART AT THE PRESENCE OF THE KING OF KINGS,
EXPOSING THE UNDERGROUND CITIES AND THEIR INHABITANTS**

†Revelation 6:14 *"Let Keen punish mere mean."* †Psalm 33:6
†Revelation 6:17 *"Keen thump. Enemies learn."* †Psalm 110:6
"Keen seen in pummel hater." †Revelation 16:21
"Eh! Keen pummel in earnest."

**IN THE SON OF MAN DWELLS THE FULLNESS OF THE GODHEAD
BODILY ...EVERY KNEE WILL BOW AND EVERY TONGUE
CONFESS THAT JESUS IS LORD TO THE GLORY OF THE FATHER**

"Keen 'n' in the Supreme Male."   †Philippians 2:10
"Am He – Super-eminent. Kneel!!" †Colossians 2:9
"He a sum Pre-Eminent!! Kneel!!" †Ephesians 1:21-22

THE RISEN MESSIAH ASSUMES THE SCEPTER AND THRONE OF EARTHLY GOVERNANCE, RULING THE NATIONS WITH A ROD OF IRON ...THE REBELLIOUS AND THOSE WHO RESENT HIS DOMINION MUST HAIL HIM AND SUBMIT

"I'm the Keen n' lean Supreme."   †Daniel 7:14
"Kneel, tense human empire!"   †Revelation 11:15
"Tense human empire, kneel!"   †Psalm 102:15
"Kneel in the Supreme Name!!"   †Philippians 2:10
("Net humane empires kneel.")
"Mean rump seethe in kneel."

RELEVANT LONGEST WORDS/PHRASES USING SOME OF THE LETTERS

"pre-eminent" "super-eminent" elephantine" "sheep-tamer"
"multi-phase" "timekeepers" "measurement" "enumerates"
"sphere-like" "punishment" "hammer-like" "impalement"
"Lutheranism" "impermanent" "sempiternal"

I saw in the night visions, and, behold, one like the Son of man came with the clouds of heaven, and came to the Ancient of days, and they brought him near before him.

And there was given him dominion, and glory, and a kingdom, that all people, nations, and languages, should serve him: his dominion is an everlasting dominion, which shall not pass away, and his kingdom that which shall not be destroyed.
Daniel 7:13-14

WHEN THE TIMES OF THE
GENTILES ARE FULFILLED

**PROUD AND HAUGHTY SCORNER IS HIS NAME,
WHO DEALETH IN PROUD WRATH...**

"High-flown, stealthful, elite esteemed finer." †Proverbs 21:24
"White-hot, shameful, intelligent self-feeder."
"Well! Heigh-ho! Sneerful, fattiest defilement."

**THE LOFTY LOOKS OF MAN SHALL BE HUMBLED ...
THE HAUGHTINESS OF MEN SHALL BE BOWED DOWN ...
THE LORD ALONE SHALL BE EXALTED IN THAT DAY**

"Honest farewell!! Filthiest, huge, defilement." †Isaiah 2:11

**THE WICKED SHALL BE TURNED INTO HELL,
AND ALL THE NATIONS THAT FORGET GOD...**

"Awful hellhole frighten niftiest esteemed." †Psalm 9:17

RELEVANT LONGEST WORDS/PHRASES USING SOME OF THE LETTERS

"self-determination" "ultra-intelligent" "self-nourishment"
"well-illustrated" "fight-worthiness" "first lieutenant"
"under-estimating" "disenthrallment" "disillusionment"
"self-humiliating" "disintegrations" "self-fulfillment"

REAPING THE WHIRLWIND: THE BRUTAL RECKONING

Don't be deceived by claims that there is no mention of America or the United States in the scriptures. A good Berean will look for clues which identify the nation and those it forges leagues with. Here are pointers that reveal who rules kingdoms, and the times and seasons.

WHO RULES THE WORLD? The god of this present world is Satan.

Luke 4:5-7... And the devil, taking him up into an high mountain, shewed unto him all the kingdoms of the world in a moment of time. And the devil said unto him, All this power will I give thee, and the glory of them: for that is delivered unto me; and to whomsoever I will I give it. If thou therefore wilt worship me, all shall be thine.

WHO IS THE WORLD LOYAL TO? Satan.

Psalm 2:2-3 ...The kings of the earth take their stand and the rulers gather together, against the LORD and against His Anointed One: "Let us break their chains and cast away their cords."

Revelation 17:12-13 ...And the ten horns which thou sawest are ten kings, which have received no kingdom as yet; but receive power as kings one hour with the beast. These have one mind, and shall give their power and strength unto the beast.

WHAT TIME ARE WE LIVING IN?   A period referred to as The Last Days.

Matthew 28:38-39 ...For as in the days that were before the flood they were eating and drinking, marrying and giving in marriage, until the day that Noe entered into the ark, And knew not until the flood came, and took them all away; so shall also the coming of the Son of man be. **Additionally, we are in an era known as the Times of the Gentiles.**

HOW CAN WE KNOW WE ARE IN THE TIMES OF THE GENTILES? World History.

In Luke 21:24 Jesus spoke prophetically ...And they (the people of Judah) shall fall by the edge of the sword and shall be led away captive into all nations: and Jerusalem shall be trodden down of the Gentiles, until the times of the Gentiles be fulfilled. The establishment of the "State of Israel" is not a fulfillment of the restoration of Israel taught in churches, but rather a fulfillment of the prophecy that

Jerusalem would be trodden down of the Gentiles. Based on Jesus' words, when Jerusalem fell, the Hebrew descendants of Abraham, Isaac, and Jacob were killed, or scattered among the nations as slaves; and Gentiles now occupy the land.

WHO ARE THE GENTILES? <u>**Descendants of Noah's son Japheth.**</u>

The Bible identifies Gentiles as the nations occupying the British Isles, Europe, and lands north of the Mediterranean into the Caucasus, Turkey, Russia, and the 'stan' regions of northeast Asia. It also refers to any of these peoples who migrated out of these ancestral lands to settle in other areas of the world. On God's prophetic clock, the times of the Gentiles appear to have begun with the successful military campaigns of the Macedonian ruler Alexander the Great; and will end with the close of this present age.

Analysis of history – and Biblical history in particular - indicates nations appear to have a pre-determined life span. This is difficult to conceive when a culture is riding high on the twin tides of prosperity and military conquest. Those reaping the benefits certainly don't want the honeymoon to end.

Unfortunately, prosperity tends to degenerate to covetousness and greed, and military superiority likewise spirals into hubris and blood lust. These eat away at the spiritual core of a nation and quickly transform it into a useful pawn for the wicked ruler of this age and his faithful circle of earthly cohorts. Proverbs 14:34 tells us, "Righteousness exalts a nation, but sin is a reproach to any people." For the Kingdom of God to be physically established on earth, all nations will be judged, and the ones currently being used as principle pawns of Satan will be destroyed; as no such reproach can be permitted to exist in the Kingdom.

In the anagram subject The Late Great USA, *El* and *Ultra* refer to the Lord God. *Salt* identifies the servants of God, *eagle* refers to America, and *hetaerae* is a high-status woman who uses her physical beauty and wiles to gain social status or power. *True Gate* indicates the Lord Jesus Christ.

God's objective in the demise of the West is not to punish the righteous with the wicked. The righteous suffer persecution from men. It is the wicked who are the targets of God's wrath. Hence, let God arise, and His enemies be scattered!

THE LATE GREAT USA

JUST AS A DOUBLE MINDED MAN IS UNSTABLE IN ALL HIS WAYS,
SO THE PARALLEL UNIVERSE OF AMERICA IS DISINTEGRATING

...A NATION CONCEIVED IN REBELLION, BUILT ON INTRIGUE, EXPANDED
BY GENOCIDE AND ENRICHED BY THE UNPAID LABOR OF OTHERS HAS
HISTORICALLY PRESENTED ITSELF TO ITS PEOPLE AS ALTRUISTIC AND
BENEFICENT ...ACTUALLY IT HAS BEEN A WILLING PAWN IN THE HANDS
OF ENTITIES OPPOSED TO THE KINGDOM OF GOD

... STARTING WITH THE ORDER OF CREATION AND THE ORIGIN OF MAN,
LIE AFTER LIE HAS BEEN CREATED AND PRESENTED AS TRUTH VIA
INDOCTRINATION BY EDUCATION, CULTURE, AND ENTERTAINMENT

...THE END GAME IS TO DESTROY BELIEF IN THE ONE TRUE GOD,
HIS SON JESUS CHRIST, AND GOD'S PLAN FOR HIS KINGDOM ON EARTH

"A eagle eats truth."
"Erase. Taught tale." †Mark 7:8-9
"Treats a huge tale." † I Timothy 6:20-21
"That tale use rage."
"Thus eager at tale."

MANY OF THE PEOPLE ARE TAUGHT THEIR NATION HAS A MANIFEST
DESTINY ...THEY DO NOT CONSIDER WHAT THE FULFILLMENT OF
THIS 'DESTINY' WILL COST IN TERMS OF THE LIVES OF OTHERS

"Ha! Glee at stature."
"Taught are a steel." ‡Manifest Destiny Doctrine
"Taught a steel era."

ANOTHER POPULAR MYTH PROMOTED IS THAT AMERICA IS A
CHRISTIAN NATION, BUT WHY IS THERE A HUGE GRAVEN
IMAGE OF THE GREEK SOLAR DEITY APOLLO AT THE PORT
OF A MAJOR NORTH HARBOR?

"The statue. A large."
"Hate statue glare." †Deuteronomy 5:8-9
"Halt, eager statue!"

THE INDOCTRINATION OF CHILDREN BEGINS EARLY WITH THE MYTH
THAT BETSY ROSS MADE THE FIRST AMERICAN FLAG ...WHEN IN
ACTUALITY IT IS MODELED AFTER THE BRITISH EAST INDIA COMPANY
FLAG ...AN ENTERPRISE HISTORICALLY CONNECTED WITH INTERNATIONAL
DRUG TRADE ...THEIR LEGENDARY COMMANDEERING OF THE HIGH SEAS
IS ALLUDED TO IN A FAMOUS QUOTE:

"WHOSOEVER COMMANDS THE SEA COMMANDS THE TRADE; WHOSOEVER
COMMANDS THE TRADE OF THE WORLD COMMANDS THE RICHES
OF THE WORLD, AND CONSEQUENTLY THE WORLD ITSELF."

‡Sir Walter Raleigh

"The ultra sea gate."
"He sat at regulate."
"Regulate that sea." †Ezekiel 27:3-9, 25-34
"Taught see a alert."
"Alert at the usage."
"Alert sea thug eat."
"Relate as thug eat."

MAMMON IS IMPRINTED WITH A SEAL BEARING IDOLATROUS IMAGES,
HERALDING THE BIRTH OF A NEW ORDER OF THE AGES ...A NEW WORLD
ORDER INDEPENDENT OF GOD AND HIS HOLY STATUTES

"Hate a gutter seal." †Romans 1:28

POWERFUL LEAGUES ARE FORMED WITH OR AGAINST NATIONS,
NEVER FOR ALTRUISTIC PURPOSES BUT FOR CONFISCATION OF
RESOURCES OR CONTROL OF GEOGRAPHICAL AREAS

"Star at the league." †Exodus 23:1
"That league tears."
"League start hate."
"Eager lust at hate."
"Astute, large hate."

A BLIND EYE IS TURNED AGAINST THE DUAL SINS OF COVETOUSNESS
AND VIOLENCE ...AS IN THE MATTER OF AHAB AND NABOTH, GOD
WILL JUDGE RIGHTEOUSLY FOR ALL WHO ARE OPPRESSED

"Argue atlas teeth." †Habakkuk 2:5
"A thug settle area."
"Eager steal at hut."
"Steal at huge rate."

TO WHOM MUCH IS GIVEN, MUCH IS REQUIRED ...THIS LAST DAYS
KINGDOM COULD HAVE BLESSED SO MANY ON THE EARTH ...BUT
PERSONAL POWER AND ENRICHMENT WERE CHOSEN INSTEAD
...THE TIME FOR RECKONING OF STEWARDSHIP DRAWS NIGH

> *"Earth as tutelage."*
> *"A tutelage haters."*   †Hebrews 4:13
> *"Hater as tutelage."*   †Ecclesiastes 11:9

**AS HAS BEEN THE WAY OF EMPIRES THOUGHOUT HISTORY,
AMERICA PRIDES ITSELF ON ITS SURVEILLANCE TECHNOLOGY
AND MILITARY INVINCIBILITY**

> *"A true stealth age."*
> *"True Gaea stealth."*
> *"Argue aet stealth."*

**NUCLEAR ARMAMENTS – DEATH STARS – ARE USED INDISCRIMINATELY
AND THE SOULS OF THOSE DECIMATED CRY OUT FOR DIVINE JUSTICE...**

> *"Theta star league."*   †Romans 1:30
> *"Eager lust at heat."*
> *"Haul. Tease target."*

OFFENCES COMMITTED BOTH FOREIGN...

> *"Huge alert at east."*
> *"Alert at see a thug."*
> *"East relate a thug."*
> *"Ugh! Alert ate east!"*
> *"East tale. Huge rat."*
> *"Aha! True, steal; get."*
> *"Huge rat steal, ate."*
> *"Steal a huge treat."*

AND DOMESTIC...SUCH AS SLAVERY AND RACISM

> *"A guest hater tale."*
> *"Attest eager haul."*
> *"Relate that usage."*
> *"Eat that large use."*
> *"Later hate a guest."*   †I Timothy 1:9-11
> *"Alert! A guest hate."*

JUDGMENT PENDING UPON THOSE WHO INUNDATE
THE NATION WITH WORSHIP OF THE FLESH

"League at the arts."
"Usage? Athlete art."
"At the arts league..."
"Athlete gets aura."
"Tag US athlete era."
"Gut as athlete era."
"Rage at us athlete."
"Rue as tag athlete."
"Gust athlete area."
"A athlete age; rust."   †Isaiah 40:6

JUDGMENT PENDING AGAINST THOSE WHO SUPPRESS THE
TRUTH IN UNRIGHTEOUSNESS, USE THEIR KNOWLEDGE FOR
EVIL INVENTIONS, OR THEIR INFLUENCE TO ORCHESTRATE
DAMNING POLICIES

"Tags the laureate."   †II Corinthians 10:5

JUDGMENT PENDING AGAINST THOSE WHO USE THE MEDIUM OF
MUSIC AND THE POSITION IT EXALTS THEM TO FOR THE PURPOSE
OF LEADING OTHERS IN OPPOSITION TO THE COMMANDMENTS
AND STATUTES OF THE WORD OF GOD

"Hate lute star age." † Ecclesiastes 7:5

JUDGMENT PENDING AGAINST THE WOMEN WHO PRESENT
THEMSELVES TO THE CULTURE AS OBJECTS OF STUMBLING
TO MAKE THE BREAKING OF COMMANDMENTS AND STATUTES
APPEAR OF NO CONSEQUENCE

"Tag hetaerae lust."   †Matthew 5:28

JUDGMENT PENDING AGAINST THE FILTHY TALKERS WHO USE THEIR
PLATFORM TO INCITE HATE AND CLASS WARFARE, ABSOLVING THE
CONSCIENCES OF THOSE WHO ASSENT TO MALTREATMENT OF OTHERS

"Ate lust, hate, rage." †Proverbs 26:28
"Ultra see hate. Tag." †Proverbs 6:19

JUDGMENT PENDING FOR THE DESPISING, PERSECUTION,
AND BLOODSHED OF THE SAINTS AROUND THE WORLD

"Age set. Hate Ultra."†Romans 1:30
"Age hate true salt." †Mark 13:13

**THE EVENTS OF 11 SEPTEMBER 2001 WERE A WAKE-UP
CALL TO THE CHURCH TO LEAD THE WAY IN REPENTANCE**

"Set at a huge alert."
"A huge alert. A test." †Matthew 16:3

**HOWEVER, MUCH OF THE CHURCH ALLOWED ITSELF TO BE
CAUGHT UP IN THE INTRIGUE AND POLITICAL RHETORIC
...WHY SEEK GOD WHEN YOU HAVE HEAT-SEEKING MISSILES?**

"Later taught ease." †Jeremiah 17:5

**AT SOME POINT, TIDINGS OUT OF THE NORTH AND EAST BODE
TROUBLE FOR A NATION BENT ON DOMINATING THE WORLD**

"Huge alert at east." †Revelation 16:12
"Alert thug at ease."
"Tag the ultra ease."
"Tea urge a stealth."
"Tea, tea slaughter."
"East...tea...laughter."

**WILL A DIFFERENT DEADLY LEAGUE EXECUTE A
PINCER GRIP ON AN OVER-EXTENDED MILITARY?**

"Tsar, tea theta league."
"Tsar, tea huge tale."
"Huge late. Tsar, Tea." †Daniel 11:44
"A tsar, tea, lug thee."
"Alter at huge seat."
"Alas! A thug teeter."

**THE MOMENTARY VICTORY OF FOREIGN POWERS IS BUT
A FLASH IN THE PAN COMPARED TO THE IMPENDING
RESTRUCTURING AS POWER OVER ALL NATIONS
REVERTS TO THE RETURNING SON OF MAN**

"Eh! True Gate atlas." †Revelation 11:15

THE ENEMIES OF CHRIST ARE VANQUISHED

"That league stare."
"League threats at."
"Rates that league."
"Shatter at league." †Revelation 18:21-23

"Ha! Tatters league."
"League has tatter."
"Strata the league."
"That league a rest."

NO GRAVEN IMAGES SHALL REMAIN

"A Truth. A steel age."
"Ah! Let True Sage at."
"The stature! A gale." †Jeremiah 30:23-24
"That austere gale."
"Alert! A Heat Guest."
"Truest gale. A heat."
"Utter gale as hate."
"Agree halt statue." †Jeremiah 51:47
"Hear El tag statue."
"Aha! True tag steel." †Isaiah 2:18

**GOD REMEMBERS GREAT BABYLON TO GIVE HER THE FIERCE
CUP OF HIS WRATH ...LIKE A MILLSTONE CAST INTO THE SEA,
SHE WILL SINK TO UTTER OBLIVION**

"Argue halt estate."
"Urge a halt estate."
"Argue let that sea."
"That true sea gale."
"Gale as utter heat."
"Ha! Gut real estate."
"Ugh! At real estate."
"Large estate a hut."
"Rate estate; laugh."
"Hate Ultra? Get sea." †Revelation 18:21

**ALL MANNER OF AVIAN SPECIES ARE SUMMONED BY GOD
TO DEVOUR THE FLESH OF MILITARY FORCES ALIGNED IN
BATTLE AGAINST THE RETURNING KING OF KINGS**

"That eager salute."
"Huge alter a taste."
"Eat! Eat slaughter."
"Ate! Ate slaughter."
"As latter ate huge."

"Greatest haul. Eat." †Revelation 19:17-18
"Greatest haul. Ate."
"Truth as eagle ate."
"Truth as ate Eagle."

DEFEAT BY A GREATER POWER IS JUST THE BEGINNING ...
WHEN THE SHEEP AND GOAT NATIONS ARE JUDGED, THE
DEFENDANTS MUST ANSWER TO THE CHARGES ON THE DOCKET

"Eh! Ultra Gate Seat."
"The Ultra Age Seat." †Psalm 9:19
"Sheet at Ultra age."

INDICTMENT: LIES, HYPOCRISY,
AND DECEIVING THE NATIONS

"Sat. Argue the tale." †Isaiah 47:1-3
"Argues at the tale."
"Aha! Gets true tale."
"The true saga tale."
"Aha! Eagle stutter."

INDICTMENT
VIOLATION OF THE SECOND COMMANDMENT
VIA ADORATION OF GRAVEN IMAGES

"Eh! A large statute."
"Hate large statue." †Exodus 20:4
"Aha! Eagle stutter."

INDICTMENT
ALLEGIANCE WITH THE POWERS OF DARKNESS VIA
OCCULTIC SYMBOLISM ON ARCHITECTURE AND CURRENCY

"Hate a gutter seal."
"True. Seal that age." †Isaiah 24:21-22
"Aha! Eagle stutter."

INDICTMENT
LEAGUES WITH NATIONS AGAINST OTHER NATIONS
CREATING MISERY, CARNAGE, ORPHANS AND WIDOWS

"Sat. League threat." †Proverbs 6:12-19
"League start heat." †Psalm 68:30
"League start hate." †Isaiah 59:3-4, 7-8
"Aha! Eagle stutter."

INDICTMENT
COVETOUSNESS AND GREED

> *"Urge hate at steal."*
> *"Let a huge star eat."* †Isaiah 10:13-14
> *"Argue ate the last."*
> *"Aha! Eagle stutter."*

INDICTMENT
MISUSE OF AND DENIAL OF RESOURCES TO THOSE IN NEED;
DESTRUCTION OF THE EARTH VIA DELIBERATE POLLUTION,
POISONING, AND TAMPERING WITH THE BIOSPHERE

> *"A tutelage haters."*
> *"Thug at a steel era."*
> *"A thug. A steel rate."*
> *"A tale: the true gas."* †Revelation 11:18
> *"Alter at the usage."*
> *"Eat that large use."*
> *"Aha! Eagle stutter."*

INDICTMENT
PRIDE, HUBRIS, AND LIES OF JUSTIFICATION

> *"As eagle, ate truth."* †Psalm 52:3
> *"Ate truth as a glee."* †Revelation 22:15
> *"That's a true eagle."*
> *"Aha! Eagle stutter."*

INDICTMENT
INSTIGATION OF FALSE PRETEXT WARS FOR
PROFIT AND PERSONAL SATISFACTION

> *"That eager US tale."* †Proverbs 26:28
> *"The eager, at a lust."* †Isaiah 14:6
> *"Taught alter a see."*
> *"Aha! Eagle stutter."*

INDICTMENT
A GENERAL DISREGARD FOR THE SANCTITY OF LIFE
EVIDENCED BY THE CONTINUAL PRACTICE OF EUGENICS,
GENOCIDE, ABORTION, FORCED CHEMICAL POISONING
AND DRUGGING

> *"Argue at the least...!!!"* †Revelation 9:21

"Slaughter. Eat, ate."
"Aha! Eagle stutter."

INDICTMENT
PERSECUTION AND MARTYRING OF THE SAINTS OF GOD
FOR REFUSAL TO ACQUIESCE TO THE BEAST, HIS MARK,
HIS NAME, AND THE NUMBER OF HIS NAME

"Argue ate the salt." †Revelation 18:24
"Aha! Eagle stutter."

FOR THE RESURRECTED RIGHTEOUS OF THE AGES, HEBREW
DESCENDANTS REPATRIATED TO THE LAND COVENANTED TO
ABRAHAM, ISAAC, AND JACOB, AND THE SURVIVING POPULACE
PERMITTED TO REMAIN ON THE EARTH, GREAT REJOICING
... ONE THOUSAND YEARS OF PEACE BEGINS ON EARTH

"True. Last hate age." †Habakkuk 2:14
"Halt! True, east age." †Genesis 15:18
"These at Ultra age." † Hebrews 8:10
"Restate! Eat! Laugh!" † Isaiah 14:7
"Eh! Taste Ultra age." †Psalm 34:8
"The true salt. A age." †Revelation 20:6

THEY SHALL ALL BE TAUGHT OF THE LORD, AND THE KNOWLEDGE
OF THE GLORY OF GOD WILL COVER THE EARTH AS THE WATERS
COVER THE SEA ...ALL WILL KNOW THE TRUE GATE AND THE
TRUE PATH ...ALL WILL BE ABLE TO WORSHIP HIM, LEARN OF
HIM, AND KNOW WHAT IT IS TO BE LOVED BY HIM

"Ha! Sage utter tale."
"Has True Gate tale." †John 6:45
"A tutelage hearts."
"Halt! Austere Gate." †John 14:6
"Thee as Ultra Gate." †Isaiah 2:2-3
"Aha! Let's! True Gate."

SATAN HAS BEEN CONFINED IN THE BOTTOMLESS PIT AT THE START
OF THIS NEW 1000 YEAR ERA, BUT AT THE END OF THAT PERIOD HE IS
RELEASED ...HE IMMEDIATELY SETS OUT TO DECEIVE THE NATIONS
ANCESTRALLY LINKED TO THE GENTILE PATRIARCHS GOG AND
MAGOG ...THE CUP OF DISPERSION DRUNK BY ISRAEL HAS BEEN
GIVEN TO THOSE NATIONS AND THEY ARE NOW IN SERVITUDE AND
SCATTERED TO THE FOUR CARDINAL DIRECTIONS AS ISRAEL WAS
DURING THEIR LATTER-DAY CAPTIVITY

...THE ASSAULT IS PLANNED FOR THE RESTORED HEBREW
NATION DWELLING PEACEFULLY IN THE LAND ...MAN HAS
REMAINED A FREEWILL CREATURE AND MANY HAVE BOWED
THE KNEE ONLY UNDER THE MESSIAH'S ROD OF IRON ...NOW
THEIR TRUE SENTIMENTS WILL MANIFEST AS MILITARY
STRATEGIES ARE QUICKLY AND SECRETLY DRAWN UP

"A latest urge hate."
"Argues at let hate."   †Revelation 20:7-8
"A result? Hate Gate."

FIRE COMES DOWN OUT OF HEAVEN AND ANNIHILATES THEM

"Alas! A get the True..." †Revelation 20:9
"Latter Heat usage."

THE FINAL JUDGMENT COMMENCES ...THE COMPLETION OF IT
WILL USHER IN THE NEW HEAVENS AND NEW EARTH, AND THE
GLORIOUS NEW JERUSALEM

"Halt! Seat True age."   †Revelation 21:1-4

RELEVANT LONGEST WORDS/PHRASES USING SOME OF THE LETTERS

"Great Seal" "greatest" "slaughter" "real estate"
"relegates" "regulates" "laureates"
"athletes" "laughter"

WHEN IT GETS REAL:
JUSTICE EXECUTED FOR THE ORPHAN AND WIDOW

Due to the depth of this topic, the anagrams are structured under the following headings: **Feux de Joie**, **The Judicious Expert**, **The Iron-Jawed**, **The Winepress of Wrath**, **Fourteen**, **Adjudication**, **The White-hot Jauntier Chief**, and **Rejoice**. Closing headings are **Conjecture**, **Ecstatic**, and **Hadj Crescendi**. Under these headings, readers will be treated to 'split anagrams' - where a specific phrase within the anagram is repeatedly used to illustrate the riveting saga. Regardless, all anagrams are generated from the phrase 'Justice Executed for the Widow and Orphan'. The reading is intensive, but enough emphasis cannot be placed on this crushing victory over the rebellion of sinful man and an end to the carnage and heartbreak he inflicts on his fellow man!

Anagrams for 'Justice Executed for the Widow and Orphan' open with a direct reference to the flaming fire of Divine judgment at the return of the Messiah Jesus Christ. *Feux de joie*, or fire of joy – is a celebratory gun salute characterized by consecutive firing; but it can also refer to a huge fire kindled to commemorate a joyous occasion. It is best interpreted through the twenty-fourth chapter of Isaiah:

"Wherefore glorify ye the LORD in the fires, even the name of the LORD God of Israel in the isles of the sea."

It is clear Isaiah is referring to the Last Day because two verses prior to this we once again see the imagery of gleaning of grapes–the extraction of which yields the fullness of the wrath of God...

"When thus it shall be in the midst of the land among the people, there shall be as the shaking of an olive tree, and the gleaning grapes when the vintage is done" ...

There are numerous references in both the Old and New Testaments that identify the grapes as representative of the object of God's wrath. The rest of the chapter reaffirms the theme of the Day of the Lord: nowhere to hide, the gathering together of the kings of the earth and the wicked demonic entities that influence them, all in an eerie setting of celestial anomalies.

"Fear, and the pit, and the snare, are upon thee, O inhabitant of the earth...

And it shall come to pass, that he who fleeth from the noise of the fear shall fall into the pit; and he that cometh up out of the midst of the pit shall be taken in the snare: for the windows from on high are open, and the foundations of the earth do shake...

The earth shall reel to and fro like a drunkard, and shall be removed like a cottage; and the transgression thereof shall be heavy upon it; and it shall fall, and not rise again...The earth is utterly broken down, the earth is clean dissolved, the earth is moved exceedingly... And it shall come to pass in that day, that the LORD shall punish the host of the high ones that are on high, and the kings of the earth upon the earth...

And they shall be gathered together, as prisoners are gathered in the pit, and shall be shut up in the prison, and after many days shall they be visited ...Then the moon shall be confounded, and the sun ashamed, when the LORD of hosts shall reign in mount Zion, and in Jerusalem, and before his ancients gloriously."

Judicious alludes to the righteous judgments of God, which overrule all of man's treaties, resolutions, and power broking enforced by military and economic might.

Two-hundred implies two hundred out of three hundred, or the remnant principle expressed as one third remaining.

Expert capitalized points to God's invincibility in battle. Uncapitalized it refers to man, deceived by the technology he wields, and the military force he musters.

Redwood indicates cedars; and by extension, Lebanon.

Jauntier and *jauntiest* speak of the breathtaking beauty, magnificence, and princely demeanor of the rescuing Messiah.

Iron-jawed illustrates His fearsome resolution to root out the wicked from the land and shake them from the ends of the earth.

Juice, juicier, and *juiciest* relate to the treading of the grapes of wrath and the massive bloodshed resulting.

Fourteen is connected to this same sequence, as the actual event of the winepress is detailed beginning at Revelation 14:14.

White-head describes the glorified Messiah as depicted in Revelation 1:14 with head and hair white like wool; as white as snow.

Codex refers to the Holy Scriptures; and *heptad* means seven or seventh, implying those raised at the last trumpet to enter the Sabbath rest.

Hex represents the six-sided occultic symbol known in witchcraft as the Seal of Solomon; and referenced in Amos 5:26 -- "the star of your god, which ye made to yourselves" ...Remphan (Saturn) also mentioned during the martyr Stephen's testimony in Acts 7:43.

Adjudicate and its derivatives represent the final decision made in favor of the saints as handed down by the Highest Judge of the Highest Court.

White-hot capitalized illustrates the blinding glory of the Messiah's majesty and His weapons of warfare which are far superior to man's. Uncapitalized, it represents man's puny attempts to use white phosphorous weaponry against the Messiah and His armies from heaven.

Janus-faced alludes to the ancient Roman deity depicted with one face looking to the past and the other to the future. In the context of this subject, it represents Gentile Zionists – both Anglo and Judaic – foxes – who incorporated the ancient Abrahamic covenant as justification for occupation of Palestine, when the actual desired goal was a World Order independent of God; symbolized by an esoteric pyramid and interlocked triangles. The Roman connection also relates to the papacy, who seeks to establish a permanent presence in Jerusalem.

Pas de deux means dance for two.

Jehad refers to a holy war, and *Crescendi* and *Hadj* represent the Muslim peoples of the Middle East. *Houri* refers to the celestial virgins promised to faithful Muslim men. *Crouched* indicates a fetus in utero, *circuited*, blood vessels and nerves, and *horn*, strength.

> JUSTICE EXECUTED FOR
> THE WIDOW AND ORPHAN

FEUX DE JOIE (Fire of Joy)

GLORIFY GOD IN THE FIRES!!
THE TIMES OF THE GENTILES ARE FUFILLED AND DELIVERANCE
BECOMES A REALITY FOR ALL WHO ARE OPPRESSED BY THE
WICKEDNESS OF POWERFUL MEN ...MEN WHO ARE HATERS OF
GOD AND HIS ANOINTED CHRIST ...MEN WHO BOW TO THE
PRINCIPALITIES, POWERS, RULERS OF THE DARKNESS OF THIS
WORLD, AND SPIRITUAL WICKEDNESS IN HIGH PLACES...

"The sharp-witted feux de joie occur, and now!"
"Oh wow! And feux de joie's Prudent Architect."
"Now watch Sacred input. Red-hot feux de joie!"

JERUSALEM HAS BEEN TRODDEN DOWN OF THE
GENTILES, BUT NOW THE MOST HIGH RECLAIMS IT TO
CONSECRATE IT FOR THE RETURN OF HIS HERITAGE

"Potent Sacred. Ouch! Withdrawn. Feux de joie!"
"Withdrawn!! Consecrated up hot feux de joie!"
"Withdrawn!! Honest adept feux de joie occur."
"Thrown now. Dedicate sharp-cut feux de joie!"

THE FACTS OF THE CASE ARE PRESENTED

"Paced thru town. Rich, so wanted. Feux de joie!"
"Wanted choicest up northward. Feux de joie!"
"Proudest rich. Watch on wanted. Feux de joie."

JUDGMENT IS RULED IN FAVOR OF THE DISPERSED SEED OF
ABRAHAM ... A VERDICT IS HANDED DOWN WHICH CANNOT
BE REVERSED... THERE IS NO HIGHER COURT OF APPEAL

"Top Courts enhanced. Withdraw! Feux de joie!"   †Daniel 7:22
"Withdraw proud. Accent honest. Feux de joie!"
"Withdrawn!! Court chosen adept. Feux de joie!!"
"Withdrawn. A Topnotch secured. Feux de joie!"
"Shutdown and accept worthier. Feux de joie!"
"Withdraw!! Topnotch and secure!! Feux de joie!"
"Counter! Now part had switched. Feux de joie!"
"Feux de joie! Switch! Now proud-hearted can't."

ORDER ISSUED TO VACATE AND REPATRIATE

"Feux de joie!! Now educated which transport."
"Withdraw. Honest adept concur. Feux de joie!"
"Wotcha! Feux de joie! Dispatch now returned." †Ezekiel 37:14

**THE GENTILE MILITARIES HOLD THEIR GROUND,
CHALLENGING THE MOST HIGH**

"Staunch proceed; not withdraw. Feux de joie!" †Psalm 2:2-3

THIS DECISION IS TO THEIR OWN PERIL

"Chose not withdrawn? Captured. Feux de joie!" †Joel 3:2
"Withdrew not? Occupant dasher. Feux de joie!"
"Withdrawn as Topnotch reduce! Feux de joie!"
"Proudest? Not chance. Withdraw. Feux de joie!" †Jeremiah 25:30-33
"And now threw proud. Catchiest feux de joie."
"Withdrew not accounted sharp. Feux de joie!"
"Feux de joie!! Chaos. Withdrawn unprotected."
"Withdraw. Occupant shortened. Feux de joie!!"
"Withdraw captured. Not chosen. Feux de joie!"
"Watch shrewd production. Neat Feux de joie!!"
"Feux de joie!! Shrewd occupant win hot rated."

REBELLION EARNS THEM THE CUP OF GOD'S WRATH

"Feux de joie! Not withdraw= cup, or chastened." †Jeremiah 25:27-29

BODIES PILED UP IN THE ROUTING

"Feux de joie!! Heap constructed on withdraw." †Jeremiah 25:32

**DANCING WITH GREAT REJOICING AS THE LORD OF
TRUTH TRIUMPHS GLORIOUSLY BEFORE HIS ANCIENT ONES**

"Feux de joie when a Sharp-witted Conductor!"
"Sharp-cut feux de joie dance now!! Red-hot wit."
"Wotcha! Prudent win sacred hot feux de joie!"
"Withdraw sure!! Topnotch!! Dance!! Feux de joie!!"
"Now watch dance stir up! Red-hot feux de joie!" † Isaiah 51:11

THE WEALTH OF THE SINNER IS LAID UP FOR THE JUST

"Sharp-cut feux de joie wit. Decent hoard now!!" †Isaiah 33:22-24
"What-ho! Feux de joie! Win reconstructed pad."
"Wotcha! Stun! Rich now departed. Feux de joie!"
"Up-to-date!! Feux de joie! Now shrewd rich can't."
"Each withdraw proud contents. Feux de joie!" †Zechariah 13:8-9

NUMBERING OF THE TWO THIRDS

"Two-hundred, new catastrophic. Feux de joie."
"Two-hundred who can't practice feux de joie."
"Watch practise on two-hundred. Feux de joie!"

ATTEMPTS TO ESCAPE OR HIDE FROM GOD ARE FUTILE

"Feux de joie. Now wanted catch this prouder." †Revelation 6:15
"Now I catch, shut down departer. Feux de joie."
"Catchiest wrap on two-hundred. Feux de joie."
"Proudest not cache. Withdrawn. Feux de joie!" †Isaiah 2:19
"Withdrawn captured. Feux de joie to chosen!"
"Feux de joie! Chastened proud with own cart." †Psalm 9:16

**NO NEED FOR WAR GAMES AND DRILLS FOR AN
OPERATION FORESEEN AND DECREED FROM ETERNITY PAST**

"Watch now. Unpractised. Red-hot feux de joie!"
"Red-hot feux de joie! Now watch a unscripted!"

**TRANSHUMAN CYBORG PERSONNEL ARE LIKE
PLASTIC TOY SOLDIERS BEFORE THE LORD OF HOSTS**

"Watch Word outstrip enhanced. Feux de joie."

**THOSE WHO DID NOT PARTAKE OF THE
WICKEDNESS AND HATRED ARE SPARED**

"Withdraw not encode sharp-cut. Feux de joie." †Acts 10:34-35

THE PEOPLE REJOICE WITH SHOUTS OF PRAISE

"Feux de joie accord win!! Hopes, wanted, truth." †Psalm 58:10
"White-hot feux de joie and upward concerts."

THE RESURRECTED SAINTS RESPOND WITH ALLELUIAS!!

"Patient churches downward to feux de joie."   †Revelation 7:9,13-14

**JUST AS THE LEVITICAL PRIESTS MARCHED IN THE FOREFRONT
OF BATTLE SINGING PRAISES, SO THE SONS OF GOD ARE MIGHTY IN
BATTLE THROUGH THE SPIRITUAL WEAPON OF HIGH PRAISE TO
EXECUTE VENGEANCE ON THE NATIONS, AND PUNISHMENTS UPON THE
PEOPLE; TO BIND THEIR KINGS WITH CHAINS AND THEIR NOBLES WITH
FETTERS OF IRON; TO EXECUTE UPON THEM THE JUDGMENT WRITTEN:
THIS HONOR HAVE ALL HIS SAINTS**

"The feux de joie concepts around withdraw." †II Chronicles 20:21-22
"Note chant produces withdraw. Feux de joie!"

**WITH THE WICKED GONE, THE LIES THAT BLINDED
SO MANY TO THE PAIN OF OTHERS ARE EXPOSED**

"Accord prudent, not whitewash. Feux de joie!" †Psalm 83:1-5
"Now departed. Now truth as chic. Feux de joie."

**THE EARTH HAS GROANED WITH YEARNING FOR THE REDEMPTION
OF THE SONS OF GOD ...NOW IT REJOICES IN ECSTASY AT THE
PRESENCE OF THE LORD UPON IT ...HE CAUSES THE DESERT TO
BLOOM AND THE WASTE PLACES TO BLOSSOM**

"Red-hot feux de joie! Now watch Sacred put in!"
"Red-hot feux de joie! Now watch cedars put in!"
"Now watch a citrus pend! Red-hot feux de joie!"

**OMINOUS CELESTIAL SIGNS HAD HERALDED THE
IMPENDING RETURN OF THE REDEEMER**

"A sun predict. Now watch red hot! Feux de joie!" †Isaiah 35:1-10
                                            †Joel 2:31

**WITH A TRUMPET BLAST, THE GRAVES OPEN AND THE DEAD SAINTS
RESURRECT; THEN THEIR LIVING BRETHREN TRANSFORM TO MEET
THE LORD AND JOIN HIM IN RECLAMATION OF EARTH FOR HIS GLORY**

"Now watch. Inducts a rep! Red-hot feux de joie!" †Revelation 19:14

**THE CHARGES AGAINST THE ENEMY ARE READ: THE LAND WAS TO
LIE EMPTY, DESOLATE, REST, AND ENJOY HER SABBATHS WHILE THE
DESCENDANTS OF JACOB WERE SCATTERED AMONG THE HEATHEN**

"Cited a spurn. Now watch red hot! Feux de joie!" †Leviticus 26:34-35
"Spurn a Edict. Now watch red hot! Feux de joie!"   38-39, 43

THE TREATMENT OF THE DESCENDANTS OF THE HEBREWS DURING THEIR CENTURIES OF DISPERSEMENT AND CAPTIVITY AMONG THE NATIONS IS BROUGHT INTO RECKONING

"Now watch tundra epics. Red-hot feux de joie!"
"Now watch sand picture. Red-hot feux de joie!"
"Throw up scatter, chained down. Feux de joie!"
"Now throw up scratched, detain. Feux de joie!"
"Throw up a disconnected wrath. Feux de joie!" †Jeremiah 50:7,33
"Throw up wretched actions. And feux de joie!"

THE LORD IS ARMED FOR BATTLE – A FIRE GOES BEFORE HIM

"Now, watch. Incurs Adept! Red-hot feux de joie!"†Isaiah 59:17
"Now watch. I caped; turns red-hot. Feux de joie!"

THOSE WHO HAVE KEPT THEIR GARMENTS WILL BE PROTECTED FROM THE WRATH

"Watch now; spared tunic. Red-hot feux de joie!"†Revelation 16:15

THE KINGS OF THE EARTH ARE GATHERED TOGETHER IN THE VALLEY OF JEHOSHAPHAT

†Joel 3:2
"Now watch. Induces. Trap. Red-hot feux de joie!" †Psalm 50:3

THE HATERS OF GOD RESIST ...WHILE A SOLE ARMY MAY BE NO MATCH FOR HIM, SURELY UNITED AS A WORLDWIDE FORCE THEY CAN OVERTHROW HIS ADVANCE, THUS ELIMINATING THE THREAT OF HIS AUTOCRACY ...AT THE VALLEY OF DECISION FAITH IS PUT IN THE COMBINED MILITARY RESOURCES OF MIGHTY NATIONS

"Insured. Now watch pact. Red-hot feux de joie! " †Psalm 2:2-3
"Pact insured? Now watch. Red-hot feux de joie!"
"Watch! Now pact's ruined. Red-hot feux de joie!" †Psalm 2:4-5

THE CONFEDERATE KINGS OF THE EAST SURGE FORWARD TO FILL THE VACUUM

"Now watch rice stand up. Red-hot feux de joie!"

THEY FIGHT AGAINST GOD TO THEIR OWN PERIL

"Now watch. Rice = dustpan. Red-hot feux de joie!" †Revelation 16:12

MISSILES FIRED AGAINST HIM MIGHT AS WELL BE FOAM TOYS

"Now watch. Pertain scud. Red-hot feux de joie!" † Psalm 46:9

**THE PROPHECY OF ENOCH IS FULFILLED AS THE LORD JUDGES
THOSE WHO HAVE SPOKEN HARD SPEECHES AGAINST HIM**

"Disputer can watch now. Red-hot feux de joie!" †Jude 1:14-15
"Now watch. Pins traduce. Red-hot feux de joie!"

**THEIR MINDS ARE FILLED WITH MADNESS ...JUST AS
THE STARS IN THEIR COURSES FOUGHT AGAINST SISERA
IN ANCIENT TIMES, THE TERRESTRIAL AND CELESTIAL
FORCES ARE FLEXED IN THE HANDS OF THEIR CREATOR**

"Now watch rudest panic. Red-hot feux de joie!"
"Now watch. Inapt cursed. Red-hot feux de joie!"
"Now watch induct spear. Red-hot feux de joie!" †Deuteronomy 32:41-43
"Now watch reaps induct. Red-hot feux de joie!"
"Now watch upend racist. Red-hot feux de joie!"
"Wrath. Technocrat upside-down. Feux de joie!"
"Now daunts...watch price. Red-hot feux de joie!"
"Now watch tips durance. Red-hot feux de joie!"
"Now watch dust a prince! Red-hot feux de joie!"
"Now watch rancid upset! Red-hot feux de joie!"
"Captured sin. Now watch. Red-hot feux de joie!"

**THE LORD, MIGHTY IN BATTLE!! WORLD GOVERNANCE HAS
TRANSFERRED TO HIM AND HIS DOMINION HAS NO END**

"Feux de joie!! Switched. Than put crowns, adore."
"Feux de joie!! Crowns, adore. Taste width punch."
"Feux de joie!! Crowns, adore. Punch width state."

THE CORONATION OF THE KING OF KINGS AND EARTH'S RIGHTFUL RULER

"Now watch Sacred put in. Red-hot feux de joie!"
"Watched that Wondrous Prince! Feux de joie!"
"Feux de joie!! Hint: Watched adore put crowns." †Revelation 11:15
"Feux de joie!! Withstand the cup. Adore, crowns." †Daniel 7:14
"What-ho! Accent Word is prudent! Feux de joie!"
"Handiest throw up, accent Word. Feux de joie!!"
"What-ho! New, strident accord up feux de joie."

**A SYNOPSIS OF THE FINAL HOURS OF THIS ERA ...CELESTIAL
OMENS, THE SEVENTH AND LAST TRUMPET, JUDGMENT EXECUTED
BY THE KING ...HIS ASCENSION TO THE THRONE, AND REVERENTIAL
OBEISANCE FROM HIS LOYAL CONSTITUENCY**

"Feux de joie!! Sun twitch. Heptad. Crowns. Adore." †Revelation 19:12

THE JUDICIOUS EXPERT

**THE PERSECUTED ON THE EARTH CRY OUT FOR DIVINE DELIVERANCE,
AND THE SOULS OF THOSE SLAIN FOR THE TESTIMONY OF JESUS
PETITION GOD TO AVENGE THEIR DEATHS ...THEY MUST WAIT UNTIL
THEIR FELLOW SERVANTS AND THEIR BRETHREN ARE ALSO MARTRYED**

"Down-hearted now expect Judicious Father."
"Rejected. Worn-out. Fix stupid headache now!" †Psalm 13:1
"The honored Perfect Judicious wax wanted."
"What-ho! Now Judicious deferred expectant."   †Revelation 6:10
"Wonder of when Judicious Expert attached."
"Oh Dear! Wanted fetch Judicious Expert now!"

**ONLY THE FATHER KNOWS THE DAY AND HOUR, BUT AT THE DECREED
TIME THE MOTION IS GRANTED IN FAVOR OF THE SAINTS ...THE SON
WHO IS FAITHFUL, TRUE, AND KING OF KINGS WILL OPEN THE VEIL BETWEEN
HEAVEN AND EARTH TO JUDGE AND MAKE WAR IN RIGHTEOUSNESS**

"Wotcha! The Judicious Expert and now defer."
"Now! Now Judicious Expert Father detached."   †Revelation 19:11

**THE LORD JESUS CHRIST HAS A NAME WRITTEN ON HIM
THAT NO MAN KNOWS BUT HIMSELF**

"Judicious hath text; now wondered preface."   †Revelation 19:12
"Oh Wow! Expert, deft, Judicious, art enhanced." †Revelation 19:15
"Read now! Oh! When deft, Judicious Expert act!"

**THE ARMIES OF HEAVEN FOLLOW HIM,
CLOTHED IN CLEAN WHITE LINEN**

"What detach of renowned Expert Judicious!"   †Revelation 19:14
"What-ho! An extended, perfect, Judicious row."
"Perfect! What-ho! Judicious on extended war."

**THE RIGHTEOUS PROPHETS THROUGHOUT THE AGES
HAVE WARNED THIS DAY OF RECKONING WAS COMING**

"What-ho! Decent warned of Judicious Expert."   †Jude 1:14-15
                                                  †Psalm 50:3
NOW THE DAY OF THE LORD HAS ARRIVED

"Dear Judicious Expert who then faced town."
"What-ho! Judicious Expert wanted enforced."   †Isaiah 46:10

"What-ho! Perfect! Now dear Judicious extend."
"Perfect! What-ho! And now exerted judicious."† Jeremiah 25:31-32
"Judicious Expert of renowned watch death."

**CHAOS AND CONFUSION; BUT THE LORD PROVIDES A
HIDING PLACE FOR HIS OWN UNTIL THE INDIGNATION IS PAST**

"What-ho! Decent of Judicious Expert wander." † Ezekiel 34:6
"What-ho! Now Judicious Expert faced, tender." †Psalm 50:5
"What-ho! Judicious Expert warden of decent."
"Oh Wow! Decent Father and Judicious Expert." †Isaiah 26:20
"Now adherent of Judicious Expert watched." †Psalm 91:8

**FEAR TAKES HOLD OF THE WICKED …BOLD IN THEIR CRUELTY TO
THEIR FELLOW MAN – THEY ARE NO MATCH FOR GOD …THEY ARE
PUNISHED FOR THEIR GREED AND LOVE OF WAR**

"How north feared! Expect Judicious wanted."
"Expect Judicious who wanted fade norther." †Isaiah 24:17
"Expect Judicious wanted, and hereof wroth." †Isaiah 34:6-8
"Expect Judicious wanted few honor hatred." †Habakkuk 2:5

**ON BOTH SIDES OF THE OCEAN, WHEREVER THE DISPERSED
GENERATIONS OF THE HEBREWS HAVE BEEN SCATTERED,
GENTILE NATIONS HAVE COMBINED FORCES TO EXERCISE
OPPRESSION, SHED INNOCENT BLOOD AND STEAL RESOURCES**

"Injured. Now hated two-faced executorship." †Jeremiah 50:7
"Injure worthiest. Expanded two-faced ouch."

**THEY HAVE MALIGNED THE DESCENDANTS OF THE CHILDREN OF
ISRAEL IN THEIR CAPTIVITY AS APES, MONKEYS, AND LESS THAN HUMAN**

"I Chief rejected untoward put-down hoaxes." †Deuteronomy 28:37
"Waste chronic hatred put-down. Feux de joie!" †J eremiah 24:9
"Toxic hate of unwashed proud win rejected."
"Red-faced, eh? The neurotoxic jaw stupid now."

**THEY HAVE TWISTED SCRIPTURE AND GONE TO GREAT LENGTHS
TO CONVINCE THE WORLD THE SCATTERED DESCENDANTS OF
HEBREWS ARE THE CURSED SEED OF HAM**

"Wretched injustice wound of adept hoaxer."
"Utopian's wretched wound if hoax rejected."
"Death. Fox now wish repudiate conjectured."

NOW THEY MUST FACE THE WRATH OF THE HOLY ONE OF ISRAEL
WHO MADE AN EVERLASTING COVENANT TO ABRAHAM AND HIS SEED

"Perfect! Judicious wrath. Next woodenhead."
"Wotcha! Injured! Decrepit of now exhausted."
"Expert touchers whine of now adjudicated."

BIOLOGICAL WEAPONS USED ON THE OBJECTS OF THEIR
DESPISING TO GENOCIDALLY ELIMINATE THEM WILL BE JUDGED

"Weird toxic whereupon just dance of death."
"Now hardhearted, expect of juiciest wound."

THE LAW OF SOWING AND REAPING IS EXECUTED

"Untoward expect rejoice; found death wish."
"Judicious Expert throw new dance of death."   †Proverbs 26:27

THE COVENANT WITH THE LAND WILL BE REMEMBERED,
AND THE PEOPLE RESTORED TO IT

"What-ho! Now defeated toxic jurisprudence."

JUDGMENT FOR THE BLASPHEMOUS THINGS SPOKEN OF THE
LORD JESUS CHRIST, THE KINSMAN-REDEEMER OF THE
HEBREW PEOPLE ... HE VINDICATES HIS HOLY NAME

"What-ho! Trend now deface Judicious Expert."   †Revelation 13:6
"What-ho! Now Judicious Expert react; defend.   ‡Talmudic references
                                                                        to Jesus

THE WINEPRESS OF THE GRAPES OF WRATH IS TRODDEN

"Now watched an Expert, Judicious, deft Hero." †Isaiah 63:3
"Wanted export. Henceforth, Judicious wade." †Revelation 14:14-20
"Judicious now expended of cheat thwarter."

THE WINEPRESS IS TRODDEN IN THE FIERCENESS AND WRATH
OF ALMIGHTY GOD ...THE WORD OF GOD WILL EMERGE RULER
OF ALL NATIONS

"Wow! Judicious Expert and deface the north."
"Judicious Expert and watched the foe worn."   †Joel 3:12-14
"Judicious Expert; and who wanted the force?"
"Wow! And the Judicious Expert forced neath."
"Wow! And the Judicious Expert confer death."

**VICTORY AND REJOICING OVER THE VANQUISHING OF THE
HIGH AND LOFTY ONES WHO CHOSE WICKEDNESS AND
OPPRESSION OVER REVERENCE TO GOD**

"Judicious Expert! He won at. We danced forth!" †Proverbs 28:28
"The Judicious Expert won. We danced. Oft rah!!" †Psalm 37:17
"And crown the Judicious Expert who defeat!" †Psalm 37
†Zechariah 14:9

**THE BIBLICAL MIRACLES OF LOAVES AND FISHES ARE RECALLED AS
HE PROVIDES FOR THE STARVING SURVIVORS ON EARTH ENTERING
INTO THE KINGDOM ...TEARS OF JOY AS THE PANGS OF HUNGER FADE**

"Watch Judicious Expert and the newer food!" †Psalm 146:7
"Judicious Expert!!! Oft wheat, herd. Dance now!" †Psalm 144:11-15

**A VISION OF THE REDEEMED OF THE AGES AS A BRIDE WITHOUT SPOT OR
WRINKLE IN CLEAN WHITE LINEN – THE RIGHTEOUSNESS OF THE SAINTS
– AND THE BLESSING OF THE UNION BY THE HEAVENLY FATHER**

"What-ho! Entranced of wed Judicious Expert." †Revelation 21:2
"Expect Judicious Father wanted. Honor wed." †Revelation 19:8

THE IRON-JAWED

**WITHOUT FAITH, IT IS IMPOSSIBLE TO PLEASE GOD, BUT
HIS SAINTS HAVE PATIENTLY ENDURED TO THE END**

"Iron-jawed proud extent how faith succeed."   †Matthew 25:21
†Hebrews 11:6

**NOW, THE RESURRECTED REDEEMED ACCOMPANY
THEIR SAVIOR AND DELIVERER IN THE CONQUEST
FOR RECLAMATION OF THE EARTH**

"Sweet, up-to-date church fixed on Iron-jawed." †Song of Solomon 2:3,10
†Ephesians 5:32

**THOSE WHO HAVE SEARCHED THE SCRIPTURES
HAVE SEEN WARNINGS OF THE CUP OF HIS FURY
IN BOTH THE OLD AND NEW TESTAMENTS**

"Iron-jawed Chief hot cup answered Duo Text."   †Deuteronomy 33:2-3
"Expect shrewd, out-and-out Iron-jawed Chief."

**THOSE WHO HAVE IGNORED, OR NOT CARED TO HEED THE HOLY
SCRIPTURES WILL NOT BE AWARE UNTIL JUDGMENT IS UPON
THEM ...NEVERTHELESS, GOD WILL HONOR HIS WORD – IT
NEVER RETURNS TO HIM VOID BUT ACCOMPLISHES THAT
WHICH HE SENT IT TO DO**

"Iron-jawed, hot Chief unexpected outwards."   †II Thessalonians 1:8
"Iron-jawed Chief texts unread. Owed hot cup."   †Psalm 110:5-6
"Iron-jawed Chief wrote, dated hot cup nexus."   †Isaiah 26:21
"Iron-jawed Chief hot cup asunder. Owed Text."   †Isaiah 48:3
"Iron-jawed Chief Text aroused. Wend hot cup."   †Isaiah 55:11
"What-ho! Proud Iron-jawed succeed fine Text."   †Isaiah 46:10

**THOSE WHO DISTORTED THE WORD OF GOD BY ADDING TO IT OR
TAKING AWAY FROM IT WITH VAIN TRADITION — THEREBY
DECEIVING MANY --RECEIVE THE DECREED JUDGMENT**

"Iron-jawed fetch utopians. We hurted Codex."   ‡Scofield's
margin notes

**THE GENTILES MUST LEAVE THE LAND AND NO MAN-MADE SYMBOLS
OR FLAGS WILL EVER REPRESENT THE LAND AGAIN ...THE
STANDARD OF THE LORD ALONE WILL BE EXALTED**

"Ouch! Now Iron-jawed shift educated expert."   †Psalm 147:6
"Hot Iron-jawed! Now, if such educated expert..." †Isaiah 2:17

"What-ho! Prudent, Iron-jawed succeed of exit."
"Shut now. Iron-jawed export educated chief."
"Iron-jawed fetched utopian; exodus wretch."
"Wroth Iron-jawed fetched utopian; excused."
"Iron-jawed fetched utopian. Excused, throw."   †Psalm 147:6
"Thus, now Iron-jawed export educated chief."
"Iron-jawed hot chop new, educated fixtures."
"Iron-jawed Word fetched utopian. Cut hexes."   †Amos 5:26

THE PROPHET'S WORDS COME TO PASS

"Poet wax of chastened, two-hundred juicier."
"A shrewd expectation of juice two-hundred."
"Iron-jawed Chief who export stun educated."
"What-ho! Iron-jawed spruced deft execution."   †Isaiah 2:17
"I watched expect of thunderous Iron-jawed."
"Watched fine hot dexterous Iron-jawed cup."

THOSE GATHERING TO DO BATTLE IN THE VALLEY OF JEHOSHAPHAT ARE IN FOR AN UNPLEASANT SURPRISE

"Crusade, except found White-hot Iron-jawed."
"White-hot Iron-jawed Expert found, accused."   †Zechariah 13:8
†Joel 3:2

THEY RAGE AND IMAGINE A VAIN THING AGAINST GOD

"Unexpected ouch! Iron-jawed wist of hatred."
"Honoured Iron-jawed Ace. Expect swift thud."   †Deuteronomy 7:10
"Ouch! Unexpected! Is thwarted of Iron-jawed!"   †Psalm 24:8
"Ouch! Unexpected Deaths Writ of Iron-jawed!"
"Ouch! Unexpected death wrist of Iron-jawed."   †Isaiah 30:30
"Ouch! Iron-jawed treads with unexpected of!"
"Ouch! Iron-jawed trades with unexpected of."   †Psalm 104:3
"Ouch! Thwarts Iron-jawed? No feud. Expect die!"
"Ouch! Unexpected wrath tides of Iron-jawed!"   †Isaiah 66:15-16

VICTORY FOR THE LORD IS GUARANTEED, BECAUSE HE JUDGES AND MAKES WAR IN RIGHTEOUSNESS, WHEREAS MAN'S JUSTIFICATION FOR WAR IS ALWAYS LUST, COVETOUSNESS, GREED, HATRED, RACISM; OR A COMBINATION OF SOME OR ALL OF THESE

"Ouch! Dear! Iron-jawed, unexpected, hot swift."
"A swift, Iron-jawed, unexpected, red-hot ouch."   † Malachi 4:1
"Swift ouch! expected around the Iron-jawed."

"Iron-jawed of wise truth, and ouch expected."
"Ouch! Chief Iron-jawed Adept went dextrous."   †Revelation 19:11

THE LORD SHALL LAUGH, AND HAVE THEM IN DERISION

"Iron-jawed: Oho! What's up defunct exec? Tired?"
"Iron-jawed's cup, hence outfoxed. What ...tired?"

HIGH TECHNOLOGY WEAPONRY IS RENDERED USELESS

"Now the Iron-jawed chop educated fixtures."
"Wotcha! Iron-jawed dexterous Chief dent up."   †Psalm 46:9-10

WHITE PHOSPHOROUS MEANS NOTHING TO THE ONE WHO HIMSELF IS THE SOURCE OF ALL ENERGY

"Accord fuse up white-hot; extend Iron-jawed."
"Iron-jawed exceed a white-hot products fun."
"Iron-jawed succeeder and put fox white-hot."   †Proverbs 21:30
"Expect crusade; found White-hot Iron-jawed."

THE LORD HAS HIS WAY IN THE WHIRLWIND

"Ouch! Iron-jawed had twister of unexpected."   †Nahum 1:3

HE FIGHTS WITH SHAFTS OF LIGHTNING

"Iron-jawed Chief shot unexpected outward."   †Isaiah 30:30
"Ouch! Unexpected white darts of Iron-jawed."   †Deuteronomy 32:41
"What-ho! Use conducted if Iron-jawed Expert."
"Ouch of Iron-jawed. It draws the unexpected."

THE MOST DECORATED MILITARY GENERALS ARE UNABLE TO OUT-STRATEGIZE THE HEAVENLY ASSAULT

"Wit of thunderous Iron-jaw exceeded patch."

THE LORD...MIGHTY IN BATTLE...

"Wotcha! Iron-jawed, thunderous if expected."
"Iron-jawed, whose Exact Truth founded Epic."   †Zechariah 9:14
"Wise Iron-jawed founded Exact Truth Epoch."
"Iron-jawed Expert with out-of-hand succeed."

SOME WILL BELIEVE THEY CAN ESCAPE IN THE CHAOS

Oh Dear! Except Iron-jawed, swift untouched.”   †Amos 2:14
“Wotcha! Tend up, Iron-jawed, dexterous Chief!”
“Dexterous, Iron-jawed Adept fetch. Win ouch!”

**OTHERS WILL DELUDE THEMSELVES INTO THINKING THEY CAN
HIDE, BUT DARKNESS TO THE LORD IS THE SAME AS DAYLIGHT**

“Iron-jawed, unexpected house width factor.”
“Iron-jawed, Ace Expert of untouched widths.” †Psalm 139:11-12
“Ace, except Iron-jawed of thunderous width.” †Job 34:22
“Deft chanced Iron-jawed without exposure.”
“Now, Chief Iron-jawed deduct that exposure.” †Jeremiah 23:24

**AS A CONSUMING FIRE, THE LORD STRIDES THROUGH THE LENGTH
AND BREATH OF THE LAND ...HIS ENEMIES SCATTER AND FLEE
BEFORE HIM ...COVERT ATTACKS AND STEALTH TECHNOLOGY
AGAINST HIM ARE FUTILE – INSTEAD, HE IS THE ONE CLOAKED
IN THICK CLOUDS OF DARKNESS...**

“Iron-jawed Chief towards thou unexpected.”   †Habakkuk 3:12-15
“Iron-jawed stature. Which do of unexpected?”
“Iron-jawed Chief shout toward unexpected.”
“Iron-jawed Chief unexpected toward south.”
“Iron-jawed Chief unexpected to southward.”   †Zephaniah 1:15

THE RESURRECTED SAINTS ARE UNHURT BY THE CONSUMING FIRE

“Untouched if so watched Iron-jawed Expert.”
“Watched of Iron-jawed Expert is untouched.” †Psalm 91:8
“Exceed top if watch Thunderous Iron-jawed.”
“I excepted of thunderous Iron-jawed, watch.” †Isaiah 26:20
“Watched dextrous Iron-jawed Chief. Note up.”
“Prefixes to Iron-jawed watched untouched.”   †Ephesians 1:5, 11
“Prefixed to Iron-jawed, watches untouched.”
“I watched Iron-jawed of Experts untouched!”

**THOSE WHO WERE GRIEVED BY THE EVIL AND SPOKE OUT
AGAINST IT OR REFUSED TO PUT FORTH THEIR HANDS WITH
THE WORKERS OF INIQUITY ARE SPARED**

“The Iron-jawed excuse if not watched proud.”
“Iron-jawed except duteous and chief worth.”   †Genesis 18:25

THE HEADQUARTERS OF RULERS AND POLICY MAKERS
WHO LOVED TO PLAN WARS, THEIR WEAPONS SILOS,
AND ARMAMENT CACHES ARE DESTROYED

"Next, watched Pure Iron-jawed fetch odious." †Psalm 68:30
"Iron-jawed fetched utopian exec words hut."
"Thus Iron-jawed fetched utopian exec word."
"Iron-jawed fetched utopian exec. Shut word." †Psalm 33:16
"Iron-jawed fetched utopian – we exhort Scud." †Hosea 7:3
"Iron-jawed fetched utopian who exert Scud."
"Iron-jawed fetched utopian exec sword hut."
"Iron-jawed fetched utopian, thuds exec row."   †Psalm 110:5-6
"Iron-jawed: How cup fits educated hero. Next!"
"Wotcha! Unexpected dust if Iron-jawed hero." †Psalm 76:12

THE COLONIALISM AND SUBJUGATION OF INDIGENOUS PEOPLES
CONSISTENT WITH THE TIMES OF THE GENTILES ARE OVER ...THE
PEOPLE REJOICE, FOR THEIR ENEMIES WERE TOO STRONG FOR THEM

"Hitherto Iron-jawed, fox wanted succeed up." †Proverbs 28:28
"'N' Iron-jawed show educated fox piece truth." †Proverbs 29:16
"Now the Iron-jawed, dextrous Chief acted up!"
"Iron-jawed thud foxed, whereupon ecstatic."

WITH THE CLOSE OF THE TIMES OF THE GENTILES
COMES THE END OF RACISM AND BIGOTRY

"Dexterous Iron-jawed to punch white-faced." †Acts 17:26
"Ouch! Iron-jawed extents proud white-faced."
"Extent of which Iron-jawed educates proud." †I John 3:15

TRUTH HIMSELF REVEALS THE DECEPTION THAT HAS
DECEIVED THE WORLD DURING THE TIMES OF THE GENTILES

"Hoax conjecture if two-hundred wise adept."   †Revelation 2:9
"Perfected a hoax! Two-hundred, now juiciest." †Revelation 3:9

TENT CITIES AND REFUGEE CAMPS ARE SHUT DOWN AND
ABANDONED, NEVER TO BE RETURNED TO ...POVERTY STRICKEN
LIVING CONDITIONS ARE EXCHANGED FOR SECURE DWELLINGS

"Iron-jawed execute shutdown of dirt-cheap."
"Iron-jawed switch hut of dear. Exceed up ton." †Ezekiel 28:25-26
"What-ho! Iron-jawed code up decent fixtures." †Jeremiah 31:12
"Expect Iron-jawed secure width out-of-hand."
"With Iron-jawed, expanded. Fetch courteous." †Jeremiah 31:8-11

"Iron-jawed, Author of unexpected switched."

**JERUSALEM WILL BE DESTROYED AND REBUILT UPON ITS OWN HEAP
...THERE WILL BE NO NEED FOR RESOLUTIONS OR FINANCIAL AID
FROM OTHER NATIONS TO RECOGNIZE IT AND SUPPORT IT**

"Iron-jawed undercut that foxed showpiece."
"Iron-jawed extract thou funded showpiece." †Jeremiah 30:18

**THE LAND WILL BE CEDED TO THE DESCENDANTS OF THE TWELVE
TRIBES OF JACOB AS THEY ARE KNOWN BY GOD IN HONOR OF HIS
COVENANT WITH ABRAHAM, ISAAC, AND JACOB**

"Two-hundred foxes adjacent with our piece." †Isaiah 60:3

**THE CRUEL AND TWISTED SATANIC WORLD ORDER IS ABOLISHED ...
IN ITS PLACE IS A GOVERNMENT BORNE ON THE SHOULDER OF THE
RIDER OF THE CELESTIAL WHITE HORSE ...THE SON OF GOD WHO
GAVE HIS EARTHLY BODY ON THE CROSS AS A SACRIFICIAL OFFERING
FOR THE SINS OF THE WORLD ...THE TRUE PLAN FOR THE WORLD HAS
ALWAYS REVOLVED AROUND THIS RANSOM AND ETERNAL LIFE FOR
THOSE WHO WOULD EMBRACE IT**

"Iron-jawed who crux. Steed. Fetched utopian." † Revelation 19:11
"Iron-jawed fetched utopian. Crux wed ethos." †Revelation 19:7-9

**REAL TALK AMONG THE RESURRECTED SAINTS
AND ANGELIC SERVANTS ABOUT THE
INVINCIBILITY OF THE LION OF JUDAH**

"True chat – if Iron-jawed do, show unexpected." †Romans 11:33
"Watched Iron-jawed touch of expenditures."

**THE INHABITANTS OF THE EARTH FEAR,
AND GOD IS GLORIFIED IN THE FIRES**

"White-hot Iron-jawed. Truce focus expanded."
"White-hot Iron-jawed succeed. Fond up extra."

DIVINE JUSTICE EXECUTED; AND THE WRATH OF GOD ABATED

"What-ho! Decent cup if dexterous Iron-jawed."
"Iron-jawed Chief exert hot cup. Undo. Wasted."
"Iron-jawed Chief hot cup. Sword extenuated." †Isaiah 34:5
"Iron-jawed Chief extrude. Hot cup. Now sated." †Jeremiah 25:29-33

MESSIAH JESUS RULES THE NATIONS WITH A ROD OF IRON ...THE REBELLIOUS FACE SWIFT CORRECTION AND RIGOROUS SANCTIONS

"What-ho! Exceeded instruct up of Iron-jawed."   †Psalm 2:9
"Heard swift, unexpected Ouch! to Iron-jawed."
"Ouch! Sad. The unexpected. Writ of Iron-jawed."   †Revelation 2:27

SORCERY OF ANY MEANS – RATHER BY SPELLS, PHARMACEUTICALS, OR MIND CONTROL – WILL NO LONGER BE PRACTICED

"Iron-jawed update; or exceed of witch-hunts."
"Iron-jawed, whereupon deducts exact hit of."
"Oh Dear! Iron-jawed touch! Unexpected swift."   †Malachi 3:5

EVEN THE FORMER 'HOUSES OF WORSHIP' ARE ABOLISHED ... THE PRESENCE OF THE MESSIAH – EMMANUEL, GOD WITH MAN – SUPERCEDES THE FAULTY PRACTICES OF THE FORMER AGES

"The Iron-jawed chop own educated fixtures."
"Hoaxes occupied. New, deft Iron-jawed Truth."   †Ephesians 2:18-22

THOSE ENTERING INTO THE MILLENNIAL KINGDOM HAVE SURVIVED THE HORRORS OF THE TRIBULATION, BUT MUST ALL BE TAUGHT OF GOD ...THAT THERE IS ONLY ONE DOOR AND ONE SHEPHERD ...THE SAINTS SERVING AS KINGS AND PRIESTS IN THE KINGDOM ARE DELEGATED THIS RESPONSIBILITY

"Iron-jawed Chief cup waxed hot. Need tutors."   † John 6:45
"Iron-jawed: Sweet index of up-to-date church."   †II Timothy 2:15
"Iron-jawed extend of wise, up-to-date church."   †II Timothy 3:16-17

THE PEOPLE ARE TAUGHT TO PURIFY THEIR HEARTS THROUGH REPENTANCE AND OBEDIENCE BASED UPON THE TWO GREATEST COMMANDMENTS – TO LOVE THE LORD WITH ALL THEIR HEART, SOUL, AND STRENGTH, AND THEIR NEIGHBOR AS THEMSELVES

"Wash. I expect deduce on Truth of Iron-jawed."   †Jeremiah 16:19
"Now thou deduct: Iron-jawed as Chief Expert."   †Isaiah 52:13, 15

ALL NATIONS AND PEOPLES WILL BOW BEFORE THE SOVEREIGN LORD, WHO FOREORDAINED KINGS AND PRIESTS UNTO HIMSELF

"Iron-jawed Chief expect that wondrous due."   †Romans14:11
"Thou Iron-jawed that prefixed, now succeed."   †Philippians 2:10

THE WINEPRESS OF WRATH

THE BLOOD OF GRAPES –THE WINEPRESS OF THE WRATH OF GOD IS TRODDEN

"Oh Wow! I defend up. Set hand. Juice extractor." †Isaiah 63:2

"Oh Wow! Defend up. Sad in the juice extractor."
"Profound White-head now extracted juices."
"Oh Wow! Juice extractor. He sit and defend up."

"Oh Wow! Defend up hated sin. Juice extractor." †Revelation 14:19
"Oh Wow! Defend up. Sin = juice extractor = death."
"Oh Wow! Defend up. Death's in juice extractor."

"What-ho! Decent wanted proud, juicier, foxes."
"What-ho! Extend of produces--wanted juicier."
"Now fetched. Wanted proud juiciest hoaxer." †Isaiah 63:4,6

"Oh Wow! Juicier and stun of detached expert."
"Now cut hardheaded of now juiciest expert."
"Juicier hash of educated down-town expert."
"Oh no! Juice of educated experts withdrawn." †Ezekiel 35:6

"Oh Wow! Defter and juiciest and expert ouch."
"Wotcha! Sudden death of now juicier expert."
"What-ho! Win, so defended up juice extractor."
"Oh Wow! As juicier, expanded of Decent Truth."
"Oh Wow! The unexpected standard of juicier."
"Oh Wow! Stone-faced Truth expanded juicier." †Revelation 19:15
"What-ho! Juiciest, and expert reduced of now."

FOURTEEN

**CHAPTER 14 AND THE FOURTEENTH VERSE: THE
HARVEST OF WRATH WHERE A SHARP SICKLE IS
USED TO REAP THE EARTH**

"Codex fourteen. Hewn juiciest. Add wrath op." †Revelation 14:14

**ALL TRACES OF THE INTERLOCKED TRIANGLES ASSOCIATED WITH
THE LAND NAMED "HE WILL RULE AS GOD" REMOVED ...AND THE
STANDARD OF THE LORD ALONE RAISED**

"Fourteen juiciest. A Heptad crowd down hex."
"Fourteen juiciest. Watched a hex drop down!"
"Fourteen juiciest. Oh! Watched Word expand." †Isaiah 2:11
"Fourteen juiciest. How odd warped hex can't."

**THE FAILURE OF THE RULE OF CARNAL MAN WILL BE OBVIOUS UNDER
THE ADMINISTRATION OF MESSIAH -- UPON WHOM RESTS THE HOLY
GHOST, AND THE SPIRIT OF WISDOM, UNDERSTANDING, COUNSEL,
MIGHT, KNOWLEDGE, AND FEAR OF THE LORD**

"Fourteen juiciest chapter. How Dad down hex!" †Isaiah 2:17-18
"Fourteen juiciest. Odd how preach tend wax."   †Habakkuk 2:14

THE NATIONS WILL BE RULED WITH A ROD OF IRON

"Fourteen juiciest. Watch Who expanded rod!" †Revelation 19:15

ADJUDICATION

**THE LORD MAKES GOOD ON HIS PROMISE
TO JUDGE WITH RIGHTEOUSNESS AND EQUITY**

"Oh Wow! Chief Exponents' adjudicated truer."
"The unexpected Adjudicator who's now Fire."
"Now adjudicated. Now Chief Text Super-hero."†Psalm 140:12
"Or now Chief Texts whereupon adjudicated."

**WICKED RULERSHIP OF ALL NATIONS IS VOIDED, FOR
THE GOVERNMENT SHALL BE UPON THE SHOULDER OF
THE ANOINTED ONE – THE MESSIAH JESUS CHRIST**

"Adjudication, wherefore expect shutdown."
"Now adjudicated us. Henceforth, it ex-power." †Isaiah 9:6
"Hurt? Expert Adjudication. News of how cede!"

**THIS SUPERNATURAL DELIVERANCE OF THE WEAK FROM
THOSE WHO WERE TOO STRONG FOR THEM PROVES MESSIAH
JESUS CHRIST IS INDEED THE COMPASSIONATE SON OF GOD,
AND A RIGHTEOUS RULER**

"Now experienced of Truth who adjudicates."
"Experience truth of show now adjudicated."   †Psalm 35:10
"Experiences Truth of Who now adjudicated."

GREAT REJOICING THAT GOD INDEED CARES AND HEARS

"Expert Chief sure won! Adjudicated! Own ton!"
"Chief Expert adjudicated! Shouter! Now own!"†Proverbs 13:22
"Chief Expert adjudicated! Shouter! Won own!"

AND MANY WHO ARE LAST SHALL BE FIRST

"Adjudications of worth where unexpected."   †Matthew 19:30

THE WHITE-HOT JAUNTIER CHIEF

**THE PRESENCE OF THE LORD JESUS CHRIST IN THE LAND
OF ISRAEL COINCIDES WITH THE RESURRECTION OF THE
SAINTS ON A DATE KNOWN ONLY TO THE FATHER IN HEAVEN**

"Date of which expected Jauntier Wondrous?" †Matthew 24:36

**THE SAINTS WILL HEAR THE TRUMPET BLAST AND
THE ARCHANGEL'S SHOUT**

"Wondrous White-hot cue prefixed adjacent." †I Thessalonians 4:16

THEN THEY WILL RISE TO MEET HIM IN THE AIR

"Dear of White-hot exceeds upward junction." †I Corinthians 15:52

**GRACE IS EXTENDED FOR THOSE WHO WILL BE SPARED
TO ENTER THE KINGDOM...**

"Excepted hide; watch Jauntier of Wondrous." †Isaiah 26:20-21

**JUDGMENT BEGINS FOR BLOOD SHED IN THE LAND... THE
TREACHEROUS DEALERS HAVE DEALT VERY TREACHEROUSLY**

"Oh Wow! Jauntier Christ expend of educated."
"Now watch this jauntier of proud exceeded."
"Oh Wow! Jauntier Chief cast extended proud."
"Oh Wow! Unexpected of the Jauntier discard."
"Extend withdrawn of occupied Joshua tree."   †Luke 21:24
"Wotcha! Jauntier shift now exceeded proud."

**MULTITUDES, MULTITUDES IN THE VALLEY OF DECISION:
FOR THE DAY OF THE LORD IS NEAR IN THE VALLEY OF DECISION**

"Oh Wow! Undecided experts chat of Jauntier." †Joel 3:14

**HE BREAKETH THE BOW, AND CUTTETH THE SPEAR IN SUNDER;
HE BURNETH THE CHARIOT IN THE FIRE**

"Jauntier: Now educated experts, which do of?"
"Whoops! Now Jauntier Chief deducted extra." †Psalm 46:9
"Oh Wow! And so Chief Jauntier deduct expert."

THE LORD SHALL UTTER HIS VOICE BEFORE HIS ARMY
"Jauntiest profound echo exceed withdraw."   †Joel 2:11
†Isaiah 30:30

A CALL TO LEBANON TO REPENT, PURIFY THEIR HEARTS AND
HANDS AND SEARCH THE SCRIPTURES IN ANTICIPATION OF THE
COMING KING OF KINGS, AND A HERALD THAT THEY NO LONGER
NEED FEAR THE THREAT OF MILITARY AGGRESSION

"Redwood! Expect Jauntier Chief dawn shout." †Psalm 29:5
"Redwood! Unwrap the Jauntiest Chief Codex." †Isaiah 34:16
"Redwood! Jauntiest Chief Watcher expound."
"Redwood! Jauntiest Chief now captured hex."
"Redwood! Jauntiest Chief capture. Down hex."
"Redwood! Jauntiest Chief upend, hew oxcart."
"South Redwood! Expect Jauntier Chief dawn." †Isaiah 14:8

REJOICE

THOSE WHO WILL GO INTO THE KINGDOM ARE ECSTATIC
...NO LONGER WILL THEY BE IGNORED OR FORGOTTEN

"Rejoice! Adept now watched Thunderous fix."
"Rejoice! Watch thunderous wit of expanded."
"Honest rejoice up! Educated fox withdrawn."
"Rejoice! Unexpected withdraw of thousand."
"Huh! Adept rejoice! Crowds of unwanted exit."

THE PEOPLE OF THE BOOK WILL NOW BE SAFE IN THEIR LAND

"Adept of Codex rejoice!! Unwanted wish hurt." †Obadiah 1:15-21
"Rejoice! Foxes withdrawn. Adept untouched."
"Fixes attached two-hundred. Rejoice up now."

THE LAND WAS DISTURBED FROM REST; THEN DIVIDED

"Fox dude transected. What-ho! Win! Rejoice up."

GOVERNMENTS, CULTURE, AND ENTERTAINMENT ALL WEIGHED
IN TO CREATE AND MAINTAIN THE PREMISE THAT GENTILES OF
EUROPEAN EXTRACT WERE THE INHERITORS OF
THE ABRAHAMIC COVENANT

"Fox trends educated. What-ho! Win! Rejoice up." †Psalm 83:4

AT THE SAME TIME, GOVERNMENTS, CULTURE, AND
ENTERTAINMENT WORKED IN TANDEM TO ENSURE
THE TRUE ISRAEL NEVER BECAME A NATION AGAIN

"Extends of traduced. What-ho! Win! Rejoice up." †Psalm 83:4

THE CONSTANT WARS AND APARTHEID CONDITIONS SHOULD
HAVE BEEN A CLEAR INDICATOR THAT THE OCCUPATION OF
THE LAND WAS NOT A FULFILLMENT OF BIBLE PROPHECY

"Oft extend crusaded. What-ho! Win! Rejoice up."

NEVERTHELESS, MANY CHURCHES AND MINISTRIES FOLLOWED
THE EXAMPLE OF FOREIGN AID AND SENT MUCH MONEY TO
THE LAND FOR ITS ENRICHMENT, INSTEAD OF NOURISHING
 THE ORPHANS, WIDOWS, AND POOR IN THEIR OWN MIDST

"Decades extort fund. What-ho! Win! Rejoice up."
"Extracted so funded. What-ho! Win! Rejoice up."

BUT IS A CURSE ATTACHED TO MONEY THAT WILL
ULTIMATELY BRING GREAT HARM TO OTHERS?

"Execrated dot funds. What-ho! Win! Rejoice up."   †Proverbs 22:16

IT SEEMED AS THOUGH THE RIGHTEOUS JUDGMENT OF GOD
WOULD NEVER COME, UNTIL ONE DAY ...

"Faced Texts. Redound. What-ho! Win! Rejoice up."

ONE IN KINGLY VESTURE ARMED FOR BATTLE APPEARS

"A Fort tux descended. What-ho! Win! Rejoice up."   †Revelation 19:16

NO WEAPON FORMED AGAINST HIM IS ABLE TO PROSPER

"Forecast extend dud. What-ho! Win! Rejoice up."

HE JUDGES AND MAKES WAR IN RIGHTEOUSNESS

"Next dusted a force. What-ho! Win! Rejoiced up."   †Psalm 110:1

FOR, BEHOLD, THE LORD WILL COME WITH FIRE, AND WITH
HIS CHARIOTS LIKE A WHIRLWIND, TO RENDER HIS ANGER
WITH FURY, AND HIS REBUKE WITH FLAMES OF FIRE... FOR
BY FIRE AND BY HIS SWORD WILL THE LORD PLEAD WITH
ALL FLESH: AND THE SLAIN OF THE LORD SHALL BE MANY

"Foxed cadets turned. What-ho! Win! Rejoice up."
"A fox end destructed. What-ho! Win! Rejoice up."
"Destructed a fox den. What-ho! Win! Rejoice up."   †Isaiah 66:15-16
"A destruct ended fox. What-ho! Win! Rejoice up."

"A destruct foxed end. What-ho! Win! Rejoice up."
"A curst tended foxed. What-ho! Win! Rejoice up." †Isaiah 34:5

THE WICKED FLEE

"Win! Crafted tend exodus. What-ho! Rejoice up."   †Psalm 68:1

THEIR FLIGHT IS INTO THE WINEPRESS OF WRATH...

"Dour facts extended. What-ho! Win! Rejoice up."
"Exude trodden facts. What-ho! Win! Rejoice up."
"Crafted exuded tons. What-ho! Win! Rejoice up."
"Facts done. Extruded. What-ho! Win! Rejoice up."
"Facts redden tuxedo. What-ho! Win! Rejoice up."   †Isaiah 63:1-3

THE WEALTH OF THE SINNER IS LAID UP FOR THE JUST
...ENFORCED BY THE WORD OF GOD, A TRANSFER TAKES PLACE

"Text forced a sudden. What-ho! Win! Rejoice up."
"Sudden of extracted. What-ho! Win! Rejoice up."
"A Coded Text refunds. What-ho! Win! Rejoice up."
"Dost exacted refund. What-ho! Win! Rejoice up."
"Exacted funded sort. What-ho! Win! Rejoice up."
"Exacted stored fund. What-ho! Win! Rejoice up."
"Ceded a extort funds. What-ho! Win! Rejoice up." †Proverbs 13:22
"Texts refunded. Coda. What-ho! Win! Rejoice up."

THE RETURNING DESCENDANTS OF ABRAHAM WILL LEAVE
TENEMENTS, SHANTY TOWNS, REFUGEE CAMPS, AND WASTE
PLACES TO INHABIT A LAND TOUCHED AND BLESSED BY THE
ALMIGHTY'S HAND

"A Codex tended turfs. What-ho! Win! Rejoice up." †Isaiah 35:1-2
"Turf detoxed! Dances. What-ho! Win! Rejoice up."
"Ascend detoxed turf. What-ho! Win! Rejoice up."

THE LAND WILL EXTEND TO THE ORIGINAL BOUNDARIES DEEDED
TO ABRAHAM AND HIS SEED: FROM THE RIVER OF EGYPT TO
THE RIVER EUPHRATES

"A Coded extend turfs. What-ho! Win! Rejoice up." †Genesis 15:18
"Extended turfs. Coda. What-ho! Win! Rejoice up."

HE DEFENDS ALL WHO TAKE UP THEIR CROSS AND FOLLOW HIM

"Defends toted a crux. What-ho! Win! Rejoice up." †Luke 9:23

HE IS A DEFENDER OF THE ORPHAN AND FATHERLESS

"A Crux. Defended tots. What-ho! Win! Rejoice up.   †Mark 10:14

**AN EXALTED STATUS FOR THE RETURNED SEED OF
ABRAHAM AS THEY ARE NOW NOURISHED BY RULERS...**

"A context udders fed. What-ho! Win! Rejoice up." †Isaiah 60:16

**THE ETERNAL GOD WHO PLANTED THE CEDARS OF
LEBANON WILL BRING THIS TO PASS**

"Founded Sacred Text. What-ho! Win! Rejoice up."
"Text founded cedars. What-ho! Win! Rejoice up." †Psalm 104:16

**JUST AS THE PROPHETS FORETOLD, GOD WILL INTERVENE IN THE
AFFAIRS OF THE NATIONS TO BRING JUSTICE AND DELIVERANCE**

"Rejoice! Wotcha! Poet undaunted. Fix shrewd."   †Micah 4:3

**AT A TIME WHEN NO ONE EXPECTED IT, THE LORD HAS RETURNED
– NOT ON A MISSION OF PEACE, BUT TO JUDGE AND MAKE WAR**

"Rejoice! Enhanced outputs withdraw foxed."
"Rejoiced! Enhanced output!! Foxes withdraw."

**HE MAKES CLEAR WHO HIS GENEALOGICAL DESCENDANTS
ARE WHOM HE WAS MADE LIKE UNTO IN ALL THINGS, AND
THEREFORE NOT ASHAMED TO CALL THEM BRETHREN**

"Fortunate prejudice. Hoaxed now switched."   †Hebrews 2:17

NO ARGUMENT NOW AS TO WHO STAYS OR GOES

"What-ho! Prudent educates. Now fix. Rejoiced!"

**THOSE WHO MISINTERPRETED PROPHECY AND THOSE DECEIVED
BY IT FACE A STRONG REALITY CHECK, BUT THE WISE REJOICE
AS THEY SEE THE WORD RIGHTLY DIVIDED AND FULFILLED**

"Rejoice! Shout and unexpected withdraw of."
"Rejoice of south and unexpected withdraw."
"What-ho! Stun educated. Prefix rejoiced now."
"Watched Iron-jawed touch of expenditures."
"What-ho! Rejoiced around swift unexpected."
"Thou rejoiced as unexpected of withdrawn."   †Proverbs 28:28
"What-ho! Rejoiced up. Wanted deft excursion."

**THE REGATHERED PEOPLES REJOICE IN THEIR
KINSMAN REDEEMER**

"Oh Wow! As if unexpected. Truth and rejoiced."
"When Dextrous win, rejoiced up of attached."   †Ezekiel 11:17

**THE EXPECTATION OF LIVING WITH DIGNITY AND
PROSPERITY BRINGS SHOUTS AND TEARS OF JOY**

"Watch when expanded. Fortuitous rejoiced."
"Wotcha! Now rejoiced this expanded future."   †Micah 4:4

**BULLDOZED HOMES ARE RECONSTRUCTED AND THE PEOPLE
DANCE TOGETHER IN THE STREETS FOR THE TRUTH WHICH
NOW WALKS AND ABIDES AMONG THEM**

"Now rejoiced! Now attached pushed fixture."
"Wotcha! Fine Truth! Now rejoiced: pas de deux." †Jeremiah 31:13

CONJECTURE

THE FALLACY THAT DESCENDANTS OF HEBREW SLAVES ARE FROM HAM AND GENTILE SETTLERS FROM EUROPE ARE DESCENDED FROM ABRAHAM THE HEBREW IS ACCEPTED BY MANY IN THE WEST

"Conjecture of hardheaded wit exist now up." †Revelation 3:9

BUT WHAT HAPPENS WHEN TRUTH HIMSELF CHALLENGES THAT PREMISE?

"Wondrous interjected up white-faced hoax."
"Wotcha! Red-hot!! Unwise of jaundiced expert."
"Win up-to-date if hoaxed shrewd conjecture."

PEOPLE CAN BE FOOLED AND INTIMIDATED... BUT THESE WEAKNESSES DO NOT APPLY TO GOD

"Exit of proud whitewashed and conjecture."
"Oh Wow! Jauntier accepted of hundreds exit."
"Hardheaded exit. Now wit of conjectures up." †Revelation 2:9

THE PEOPLE REJOICE AND GLORIFY GOD

"True Wondrous, which expedite of adjacent."
"Oh Wow! Adjacent expended. Historic future."

ECSTATIC

HOW WONDERFUL TO ENJOY THE BEAUTY AND BENEFITS OF THE LAND ...THE BORDERS ARE OPENED FOR THE RETURN OF THE DISPERSED

"Unhurried ecstatic of jaw! Extended whoop!!"
"Unhurried ecstatic of jaded oxen who wept."
"Unhurried of ecstatic. How jaded oxen wept."
"Jaded hope. Next, unhurried of ecstatic! Wow!!"
"Jaded. Then, unhurried expo of ecstatic. Wow!!"

LIKE THE DEMISE OF PHARAOH UNWILLING TO RELINQUISH HIS SLAVE FORCE, ALL WHO FIGHT AGAINST CHRIST JESUS TO MAINTAIN THE CURRENT WORLD ORDER WILL MEET A MOST UNPLEASANT FATE: AS GOURMET FOOD FOR ALL TYPES OF BIRDS

"Oh Wow! And expected this fine carte du jour." †Revelation 19:17-18

HADJ CRESCENDI

IMMEDIATELY FOLLOWING GREAT TRIBULATION AND CATACLYSMIC CELESTIAL SIGNS, THE LORD JESUS CHRIST (ISSA TO MUSLIMS) MANIFESTS TO WREST THE EARTH FROM THE GRIP OF THE SATANIC KINGDOM OF DARKNESS

"Extend Jehad op. Ecstatic! Wow! Uh, our Friend!"   †Isaiah 65:1
                                                       †Isaiah 45:22

BECAUSE GOD'S WORD IS FOREVER SETTLED IN HEAVEN, THE CAPSTONE AND APEX OF THE NEW WORLD ORDER PYRAMID ARE DESTROYED, AND THE NATIONS CAN NO LONGER BE DECEIVED

"A Crucified Ones' truth jot hewed down apex."   †Daniel 2:34-35

THE WRITINGS OF THE PROPHETS AND APOSTLES TAKE ON NEW MEANING WITHOUT THE DECEIVER TO DISTORT OR ADD TO GOD'S WORD ... THE NATIONS REALIZE THEY HAVE INHERITED LIES AND VANITIES FROM THEIR FOREBEARS ...THEY MUST NOW CHOOSE BETWEEN THE FALSE REWARDS OF CARNAL PLEASURES AND THE LIGHT OF TRUE RIGHTEOUSNESS

"Wanted sexed-up? Choice of Iron-jawed Truth."   Quran 78:33
"Aft Duo Text, Hadj Crescendi weep won houri."
"Hadj weep. Ecstatic. Detox. Refund own houri."   †Jeremiah 16:19

MUSLIMS IN THE MIDDLE EAST AND AFGHANISTAN HAVE BEEN THE VICTIMS OF GENOCIDE VIA THE USE OF DEPLETED URANIUM MUNITIONS IN THEIR NATIONS ... CAUSING HORRIFIC BIRTH DEFECTS, MISCARRIAGES AND STILLBIRTHS ...NOW, THOSE SERVING THE MESSIAH AS KINGS AND PRIESTS MINISTER OF HIS HEALING VIRTUE TO THE PEOPLE, AND MEDICAL PRACTITIONERS IN THE MILLENNIAL KINGDOM PARTAKE OF THE EXPANDED KNOWLEDGE AVAILABLE BY VIRTUE OF THE PRESENCE OF EMMANUEL, GOD WITH US ...

IN THE FOLLOWING SCENE, ANAGRAMS POIGNANTLY ILLUSTRATE THE STORY OF HEALING AND GENETIC RESTRUCTURING IN THE LIFE OF A MUSLIM COUPLE POISONED BY RADIATION

"First a Hadj weep. Ecocide. Hurt. Won un-detox."
"Hadj weep now. Ecocide rift. A sun hurt. Detox."
"Hadj weep now. Ecocide rift. An hurt us. Detox."
"Hadj weep now. Ecocide rift. An thru us. Detox."
"A Hajd weep now. Science drouth fruit. Detox."

EXPOSURE TO THE NUCLEAR RADIOACTIVITY IN THE
WEAPONRY SYSTEMS USED AGAINST THEM CAUSED THIS

...WITHOUT DETOXIFICATION, THEIR PROGENY IS DOOMED;
THEIR FAMILIES WILL DISAPPEAR FROM THE EARTH ... WHEN
THEIR CHILDREN ARE BORN, THE SKIN IS OFTEN ABNORMAL;
BLEEDING AND ULCEROUS

"Hajd weep now. A fruit hue disconcert. Detox."

MORE OFTEN THAN NOT, PREGNANCIES ARE MISCARRIED

"A Hadj weep. Scorched uteri unfit. Now detox."   ‡Depleted Uranium
"Hajd weep now. A scorched untie fruit. Detox."   Contamination

IF THE BIRTH COMES TO TERM, THE DEFORMITIES
MAY BE SO GREAT THE CHILD CANNOT BE NOURISHED

"Hajd weep now. A crouched is unfitter. Detox."

OR THE BRAIN MAY ONLY BE PARTIALLY FORMED,
LEAVING THE CHILD MENTALLY DISABLED FOR LIFE

"Hajd weep now. If as crouched, nuttier. Detox."

SURVIVING BABIES OFTEN FAIL TO THRIVE

"Hajd weep now. If a crouched, runtiest. Detox."

AND MANY PREGNANCIES RESULT IN STILLBIRTHS

"Hajd weep now. A crouched utter finis. Detox."

THE LORD IS FULL OF GRACIOUS COMPASSION AND
TOUCHED BY THE WEAKNESS OF OUR INFIRMITIES

"Hajd weep now. A Crucifies noted hurt. Detox."

WILL THIS MESSIAH JESUS REALLY HELP THEM? IT WAS SOME OF
THE SAME PEOPLE WHO CLAIMED TO SERVE HIM THAT SUPPORTED
THE USE OF THESE DEADLY WEAPONS IN THE MID-EAST WARS ...NOR
HAVE THE MUSLIMS WORSHIPED HIM, TO EXPECT ANY PETITION
GRANTED ...STILL, HE WHO VANQUISHED THEIR OPPRESSORS
MUST SURELY HOLD HOPE FOR THEM ...

"Thou a stern Crucified? Jaw hoped detox; new."

HE ASSURES THEM IF THEY TRUST HIM HE WILL HEAL THEM,
FOR HE WAS BRUISED FOR THEIR INIQUITIES, AND BY HIS
STRIPES THEY ARE HEALED … FURTHER, HE IS RICH IN MERCY TO
ALL WHO CALL UPON HIM; BUT THEY MUST ASK, BECAUSE
WITHOUT FAITH, IT IS IMPOSSIBLE TO PLEASE GOD

"A hurt set on Crucified. Hajd weep now. Detox." †Isaiah 53:5

THE DECISION IS REACHED TO TRUST MESSIAH ISSA …
THEY NOW HE IS A PROPHET, BUT CAN HE ALSO HEAL
THE DEVASTATION OF THEIR POISONED BODIES?

"Hajd weep now. Oh! Entrust a Crucified detox." †Mark 9:24

THEIR PETITION IS GRANTED … AND THEY WILL LET OTHERS SEE,
THAT JESUS MIGHT BE LIFTED UP AND DRAW ALL MEN UNTO HIMSELF

"Thou a Hadj Crescendi weep. Now detox fruit!" †Isaiah 11:10

A DAY OF BREATHTAKING EXCITEMENT AS NEWS CIRCULATES AMONG THE
WORLDWIDE MEDICAL COMMUNITY OF THE OPPORTUNITY TO OBSERVE
FIRSTHAND THE MASTER HEALER PERFORM MULTIPLE OPERATIONS ON
BEHALF OF THE FAMILY …THE LATEST IN VIRTUAL TECHNOLOGY WILL BE
USED TO BENEFIT OF PRACTITIONERS ACROSS ALL MEDICAL DISCIPLINES
…OBSERVERS WATCH AND TAKE NOTES AT A FEVERISH PACE

"He wowed! A touch-screen ID fruit. Jot expand."   Medical Imaging
Workstations

JAWS DROP IN AMAZEMENT AS THE OPERATION BEGINS WITH NO VISIBLE
FORM OF LIFE SUPPORT FOR EITHER THE MOTHER OR THE BABY…SOME
OBSERVERS RECALL THE DEEP SLEEP GOD CAUSED TO FALL UPON ADAM
AS HE OPENED HIS SIDE TO REMOVE A RIB …THE MALFORMED FETUS IS
GENTLY TAKEN FROM THE WOMB …THE MOTHER DOES NOT HEMORRHAGE,
NOR DOES THE INFANT EXPIRE …THE 'QEREN' RAYS OF LIGHT CONVEYING
THE SUSTAINING POWER OF GOD ENCIRCLE THE LITTLE ONE

"How op!! Jaw extended. Horn circuited a fetus." †Genesis 2:21

A SPECIALIST OF SPECIALISTS, THE MASTERS' HANDS DEFTLY REPAIR AREA
AFTER AREA OF DAMAGED TISSUE …TECHNOLOGY PERMITS THE SCREEN TO
FOCUS BY LAYERS RELATING TO ANY FIELD OF SPECIALTY, MAKING THE
OPERATION AN EQUAL LEARNING EXPERIENCE FOR ALL

"How op!! Jaw extended. First, unite a crouched." †Psalm 139:14

AS AREAS ARE REPAIRED, THE FIELDS OF HEALING VIRTUE CAN
VISIBLY BE SEEN INCREASING ...THE INFANT IS NOT OBSERVED
TO BE IN ANY RESPIRATORY OR CARDIAC DISTRESS BUT RESTS
PEACEFULLY THROUGHOUT EACH PROCEDURE

"How op!! Jaw extended. A circuited often rush."

NEXT, THE MOTHER'S UTERUS MUST BE RESTORED TO OPTIMUM
HEALTH ...THE EFFECTS OF THE RADIOACTIVE CONTAMINATION ARE
REMOVED ...THE TOUCH SCREEN MAGNIFIES THE TISSUE LAYERS,
SO OBSERVERS CAN NOTE THE CELL STRUCTURE BOTH BEFORE AND
AFTER TREATMENT ...OBSERVERS ARE TRANSFIXED IN A MIXTURE
OF AWE AND DISBELIEF

"How op!! Jaw extended. Refits a crouched unit."

SINCE THE MOTHER'S CIRCULATORY SYSTEM WILL ACT AS THE
CONDUIT FOR BOTH NOURISHMENT OF THE BABY AND FILTERING
WASTES, IT IS IMPERATIVE TO RESTORE IT TO PREMIUM HEALTH

"How op!! Jaw extended. A circuited her founts."

THE GREAT PHYSICIAN SPEAKS HEALING TO THE CONTAMINATED
BLOOD ...COMMANDING RESTORATION AND REMOVAL OF ALL
POLLUTANTS ...THE HIGHLY MAGNIFIED SCREENS BEAR WITNESS
... STUNNED CYTOLOGISTS WATCH INTENTLY AS THE MUTATED
BLOOD CELLS SHED CORRUPTED MATERIAL, REFORMING TO A
PRISTINE STATE BEFORE THEIR EYES

"How op!! Jaw extended. Circuited a fresh unto."

AROUND THE WORLD, SILENCE GRIPS EACH OBSERVATION STATION
AS THE MOMENT ALL HAVE WAITED FOR ARRIVES ...JESUS GENTLY
TRANSFERS THE FETUS TO ITS MOTHER'S WOMB, HIS FINGERS DEFTLY
CONNECTING AND SEALING THE UMBILICAL CORD TO ITS TINY ABDOMEN...

THE SCREENS ZOOM IN TO CAPTURE THE BLOOD NOW SHUNTING
THROUGH THE VESSELS NORMALLY...THE FETUS, EVERY WHIT WHOLE,
STRETCHES AND KICKS... ECSTATIC SHOUTS ECHO AROUND THE WORLD
AND TEARS STREAM FROM THE EYES OF EVEN THE MOST RESERVED
PRACTITIONERS ...THE FATHER IS OVERCOME WITH JOY

"Next deed, jaw whoop!! Inset a crouched fruit!"

JESUS CLOSES THE MOTHER'S ABDOMEN AND CALLS HER NAME ...
AS SHE AWAKES FROM SLEEP, SHE SENSES SHE IS WHOLE ...HE
TELLS HER THAT HER PETITION HAS BEEN ANSWERED ...
HER CHILD WILL BE BORN HEALTHY

"Hadj weep! Won a detox! Succored thine fruit."

TEARS ARE ONCE AGAIN SHED, BUT THIS TIME THEY ARE TEARS OF
GREAT JOY...THE PARENTS THANK THE MESSIAH PROFUSELY,
BLESSING AND WORSHIPING HIM

"Hadj weep! Won detox! A Crucifies done truth!!"
"How op!! Jaw extended! A Crucified One's Truth!" †John 12:32

JESUS HOLDS UP HIS NAIL SCARRED HAND ...THERE IS A BLESSING FOR
THE FATHER, TOO: HE WILL BE FRUITFUL, AND HIS PROGENY WILL BE
HEALTHY – FOR THE LORD HIMSELF HAS COMMANDED THE BLESSING

"How op!! A jaw extended! Conduce their fruits."   †Genesis 9:7
"How op!! A jaw extended! He conducts a fruitier."
"How op!! A jaw extended! She a fruitier conduct."

SUBSEQUENT TESTING REVEALS THEIR GENETIC MATERIAL TO BE
FREE FROM ALL DEFECTS ...AS WITH THE CASE OF THE GADARENE
MANY CENTURIES EARLIER, THEY ARE INSTRUCTED TO ...
"RETURN TO THINE OWN HOUSE, AND SHEW HOW GREAT THINGS
GOD HATH DONE UNTO THEE"   †Luke 8:39

RELEVANT LONGEST WORDS/PHRASES USING SOME OF THE LETTERS

"share certificate" "interpretations" "contradictions" "unauthenticated"
"writ of execution" "further education" "act of contrition" "reconsideration"
"reintroductions" "superordination" "superconfidence" "authentic-sender"
"procrastination" "correspondence" "detection-proof"
"north-northwest" "auf wiedersehen"

Surely he hath borne our griefs, and carried our sorrows: yet we
did esteem him stricken, smitten of God, and afflicted. But he was
wounded for our transgressions, he was bruised for our iniquities:
the chastisement of our peace was upon him; and with his stripes
we are healed ...Isaiah 53:4-5

For therefore we both labour and suffer reproach, because we
trust in the living God, who is the Saviour of all men, specially of
those that believe ...I Timothy 4:10

RENOVATION OF THE HEAVENS AND EARTH

The Day of the Lord brings intense fiery judgment upon the earth, and celestial disruption so severe that the powers of heaven are shaken, the sun and moon darkened, and stars fall from their places. Moreover, nuclear exchanges and the plague judgments will have wrought great destruction; therefore, it is necessary that the earth be renovated before the start of the thousand years of peace.

The renovation of the earth (not to be confused with the later creation of the new heavens and new earth) is both fitting for the mighty Messiah-King who will rule and a blessing for the nations which must recover from the ravages of the Tribulation. It is fitting for the King, because with the incineration of the works of the earth and the heavens around it, all vestiges of man's rebellion will be obliterated; greatly limiting distractions during an era when all must be taught of the Lord and learn of Him. Since Death – the last enemy to be destroyed – will be vanquished at the Last Judgment at the end of the Millennium of Peace, each day of that one thousand years will be critical for tutelage. The great works, edifices, and graven tributes to men and gods that humans create have no place in the Kingdom of God. Satellites in the atmosphere which existed to spy on nations and individuals will also be done away with.

The Renovation is also a great benefit to the remaining inhabitants of the earth in that it creates a safe environment where land mines, unexploded ordnance, and radioactive contamination formerly existed. A pristine atmosphere, fresh unpolluted water, and re-energized soil will foster conditions conducive to the support of food production for a population experiencing antediluvian longevity.

The duration of the Tribulation persecution is forty-two months (one- thousand two hundred sixty days), and the book of Daniel alludes to an additional thirty days for a total of one thousand two hundred ninety days. There is also an exhortation of blessing in Daniel 12:12 for the one who waits out an entire one-thousand three hundred thirty-five days. While the author cannot say with certainty what occurs during the forty-five to seventy-five-day span between the shorter and longer periods mentioned, it seems likely that this time frame will cover judging of the nations, separation of the sheep and goats, wheat and chaff, and permit time for the Renovation. All who remain counted as sheep/wheat on the one-thousand three hundred thirty-fifth day will by default enter the Millennial Kingdom – hence, the great blessing.

Repetitive words in this anagram topic are *venerate, innovate,* and their derivatives. *Venerate* denotes worship and adoration; when a derivative of it is capitalized, it refers to the Most High God. *Innovate* describes making something new by altering or introducing new changes. *Hat* refers to crown, and *vitae* means life. *Ornate* refers to lavish adornment, and a *tetrahedron* is a triangular pyramid with four faces. *Antedate* implies to take back to an earlier time.

RENOVATION OF THE HEAVENS AND EARTH

RENOVATION – A DAY DECREED LONG AGO AND A PREPARATORY
STEP TOWARD THE FINAL NEW HEAVENS AND NEW EARTH ...FOR
MESSIAH WILL NOT RULE ON AN EARTH CONTAINING THE GREAT
BUILDINGS AND MONUMENTS ERECTED FOR REMEMBRANCE OF
THE GLORY OF CARNAL MEN OR THE HONOR OF IDOL DEITIES

"*Heaven-sent; or Torah vent info ahead.*"   †Isaiah 24:6
"*Ha Ha! Invented of Heaven-sent Orator.*"   †Isaiah 24:20

THE MYSTERY OF THE SEVENTEENTH DAY REFERS TO THE DAY OF
THE MONTH OF NOAH'S FLOOD WHEN "WHEREBY THE WORLD
THAT THEN WAS, BEING OVERFLOWED WITH WATER, PERISHED..."

"*Ha Ha! Read of seventeenth innovator.*"   †Genesis 7:11
"*Ha Ha! Innovator dare of seventeenth.*"
"*Ha Ha! Afternoon or avid seventeenth.*"

BUT THE HEAVENS AND THE EARTH, WHICH ARE NOW, BY
THE SAME WORD ARE KEPT IN STORE, RESERVED UNTO FIRE
AGAINST THE DAY OF JUDGMENT AND PERDITION OF UNGODLY MEN

"*Ha Ha! Reasoned fervent hot innovate.*"
"*Ha Ha! Fervent Hero innovates on date.*"
"*Shhh! Afternoon on a venerative date.*"
"*Ha! ha! Venerative send hot afternoon.*"
"*Aha! Heaven-sent drive hot afternoon.*"
"*Ha Ha! Venerative afternoon ends hot.*"   †II Peter 3:7
"*A Fervent heat ore hot. Anon vanished.*"   †Psalm 102:25-26
"*Fervent heat. Vanished on a Torah One.*"

**GOD IS ABLE TO DO THIS, FOR HE IS THE ETERNAL,
OMNISCIENT, AND OMNIPOTENT CREATOR**

"Aha! Deft, heaven-sent Innovator Hero."
"Veneration. Hard oath of Heaven-sent." †Deuteronomy 32:40
"Ho Ho! Heaven-sent and attain forever."

**THE WORK WILL BE EXECUTED THROUGH THE AGENCY
OF THE ETERNAL GODHEAD**

†I John 5:7
"Hosanna! The Favored Three innovate!" †Luke 3:21-22
†I Timothy 3:16

GOD THE FATHER ...IN THE BEGINNING, GOD

"Ah ha! Innovate as fervent, red-hot One." †Genesis 1:1
"An Honest Father innovate overhead."

**GOD THE SON... IN THE BEGINNING WAS THE WORD, AND
THE WORD WAS WITH GOD, AND THE WORD WAS GOD ...
THE SAME WAS IN THE BEGINNING WITH GOD...**

"Oh! Heaven-sent and another Favorite." †Isaiah 9:6

ALL THINGS WERE MADE BY HIM ...

"Hah! An Heaven-sent or Noted Favorite." †John 1:1-4
"Ha Ha! Or Heaven-sent Favorite tend on." †John 1:14

**GOD THE HOLY GHOST... THE SPIRIT THAT MOVED
UPON THE FACE OF THE WATERS IN THE CREATION**

"Ho Ho! Radiant Veteran of Heaven-sent." †Genesis1:2

**THE REASON FOR THIS RENOVATION IS FOUND IN
THE 8TH CHAPTER OF ROMANS**

"Ha Ha! Reason do the fervent innovate." †Romans 8:22-23
"Ha Ha! Fervent reason to He innovated."

**...THE WHOLE CREATION GROANETH AND TRAVAILETH IN PAIN
TOGETHER UNTIL NOW...FOR THE CREATURE (CREATION/ ORIGINAL
FORMATION) WAS MADE SUBJECT TO VANITY, NOT WILLINGLY,
BUT BY REASON OF HIM WHO HATH SUBJECTED THE SAME IN HOPE ...**

"Hat Heaven-sent Hero! Atoned for vain." †Romans 8:20

NOW IN ANTICIPATION OF THE LORD OF LIFE REIGNING ON EARTH, AND ANTEDILUVIAN LONGEVITY OF ALL CREATED SPECIES, A FRESH AND UNPOLLUTED ENVIRONMENT IS NECESSARY

"Heaven head or anon sent vitae forth." †Psalm 104: 31
"Oh! Renovate fits on heaven and earth."
"Ho Ho! Fervent and innovate the areas."

THIS GLORIOUS LIBERTY CALLS FOR A BLESSED ENVIRONMENT FOR THE MEEK WHO SHALL INHERIT THE EARTH ...A HABITAT FREE FROM THE ORIGINAL CORRUPTION OF SIN, THE POLLUTION OF MAN'S GENOCIDAL EXPERIMENTS AND VENTURES DURING HIS SINFUL REIGN UPON THE EARTH ...AND PURGING OF THE BLOOD OF BILLIONS SHED DURING FORMER MILLENNIA

"Ah! A harsh eon. Fervent, neat devotion." †Matthew 5:5
"Oh! Ha! Fervent, heaven-sent adoration." †Psalm 126:2
"Ha Ha! Earnest innovate over the fond."
"Heaven-sent or Head; favor the nation."
"Heaven-sent or Head; anoint the favor."
"Hoorah! Heaven-sent. A favored intent."
"Heaven-sent or Head; Oh! A favor intent."
"Ha Ha! Fervent innovate shone to dear."

THEREFORE, THE SAINTS REJOICE IN SONG, AND WORSHIP GOD IN THE BEAUTY OF HOLINESS FOR THE WONDERFUL WORK HE IS COMMENCING

"Ha Ha! Do innovate! Hasten of reverent." †Isaiah 30:29
"Hosanna! Venerated on over the faith."
"Hu Ha! The favored veneration sonnet."
"Hosanna! The Hero and favorite event."
"Ha Ha! Fervent, even, honest adoration."

SHELTERING WILL BE PROVIDED FOR THOSE WHO WILL ENTER THE MILLENNIAL KINGDOM

"Ha Ha! Innovate. Favored, honest, enter." †Psalm 61:4
"Ho! Saint on the neater favored haven."
"Ha Ha! Fervent intonate; save honored."
"Ha Ha! To an environs of the Venerated."
"Heaven sent favorite ahead on north."

"Oho! Safe north and a retentive haven."

**GOD IS ABLE TO DO A QUICK WORK IN PURGING AND
REFASHIONING THE EARTH**

"Ha ha! Venerated shorten of innovate."

AT THE PRECISE MOMENT, THE MASSIVE UNDERTAKING BEGINS

"Hoorah! Radiant event of Heaven-sent."
"Ha Ha! Venerated of Throne innovates."

THE HEAVENS BEING ON FIRE, DISSOLVE

"The Father innovates on an overhead."   †II Peter 3:10,12
"That Heaven-sent in an overhead roof."
"Neat afternoon! The overhead vanish."
"That hosanna of overhead intervene."

**THE EARTH WILL ONCE AGAIN KNOW THE PRISTINE BEAUTY
AND EXTRAVAGANT FRUITFULNESS CHARACTERISTIC OF
THE GENESIS CREATION**

"Ha Ha! Then antedate of over environs."

**PRAISES RING FORTH AS THE ENTIRE CREATION
AWAITS THE COMPLETION**

"Ho! Ha! Fervent adoration, Heaven-sent!"
"And hoorah to fair, heaven-sent event!"
"Ha Ha! Fervent note as Hero innovated."

**THE SURFACE OF THE EARTH IS MOLTEN AS VALLEYS
ARE RAISED AND MOUNTAINS LOWERED**

"Hosanna! Ho Ho! Fervent event radiate."   †Isaiah 40:4

**THE LORD IN HIS WISDOM COOLS THE SURFACE AT
AN ACCELERATED RATE WITHOUT WARPING OR
WEAKENING ITS STRUCTURE**

"Ho Ho! Venerative earnest and fan hot."

**NOW THE SUN, WHICH HAD DARKENED IN REVERENCE AT THE
RETURNING OF THE LORD JESUS CHRIST, IS OVERHAULED TO**

INCREASE IN BRILLIANCE SEVEN-FOLD ...ITS LIGHT
BECOMES AS THE LIGHT OF SEVEN DAYS AND THE
LIGHT OF THE MOON IS AS BRIGHT AS THE SUN

"Then heaven's Hero oft trained a nova." †Isaiah 30:26
"O Radiant of seventh! Another heaven!"
"Or the heaven-sent have on of radiant."

THE FIERY TETRAHEDRON, THOUHT TO APPEAR AT THE
GREAT WHITE THRONE JUDGMENT, UNDERGOES
ENHANCEMENTS IN ANTICIPATION OF ITS FUTURE USE

"Ha Ha! Even innovates of tetrahedron."

THE TIME COMES TO VIEW THE FINISHED WORK ...ALL
STARE IN BREATHTAKING INCREDULITY...IT IS THE
EARTH, BUT THE EARTH AS NONE HAVE EVER SEEN IT...
IT SEEMS TOO GLORIOUS TO BE REAL

"After Heaven-sent innovated...Hoorah!!!" †I Corinthians 2:9
"A honored variant of the Heaven-sent."
"Ho Ho! Defter variant on a heaven-sent."
"Ho Ho! A tender variant of heaven-sent."

GREAT BEAUTY AND VIBRANCY ABOUND ...BOTH
ABOVE THE EARTH AND ON THE SURFACE

"Oh heaven! And native forest on earth!"

THE LAND DEEDED TO ABRAHAM AND HIS DESCENDANTS –
WHERE SO MUCH CARNAGE OCCURRED IN CONJUNCTION
WITH THE HATRED OF MAN – BLOOMS...IT HAS TRULY
BECOME HEPHZIBAH – A DELIGHT, AND BEULAH –
MARRIED TO THE LORD

"Fervent innovate. Ha ha! East honored!" †Isaiah 35:1

THIS IS BEFITTING, AS ALL NATIONS MUST TRAVEL
TO JERUSALEM TO WORSHIP HIM

"Ah Hah! Reason fervent, neat devotion." †Revelation 15:4

IN THE SIX THOUSAND YEARS WHICH TRANSPIRED BETWEEN THE
CREATION OF MAN AND THE RETURN OF THE LORD JESUS CHRIST,
THE EARTH EXPERIENCED PROGRESSIVE DEGENERATION ...NOW ON
THIS SEVENTH DAY, IT IS ALIVE WITH PURITY AND THE VITALITY
FROM THE WISE AND LOVING TOUCH OF ITS CREATOR'S HANDS

"Earth have radiant of on seventh eon.   *Young Earth

**THUNDERING APPLAUSE WHICH ECHOES
THROUGHOUT THE HEAVENS BREAKS FORTH**

"Ah! Fervent Hero end. Ah! Neat ovations!" †Isaiah 44:23

**THERE IS A PERIOD OF REVERENT WORSHIP AND
THANKFULNESS FOR THE GOODNESS OF GOD OVER
HIS CREATION, BOTH SMALL AND GREAT**

"Ho! Had veneration of an earth events."   †I Chronicles 16:28-30
"Ah! He of Torah and veneration events.
"Ha Ha! Sainthood reverent of an event."
"Ha Ha! Then venerated on Favorite Son."
"The favored veneration. The hosanna."

THE WORTHY KING IS CROWNED BY HIS WORSHIPERS

"Hat and on favorite heaven-sent Hero."   †Revelation 19:12
"Favored nation hat heaven-sent Hero."
"Hat. Favor anointed heaven-sent Hero."

**PERHAPS THIS AFTERNOON OF RENOVATION TAKES PLACE
JUST PRIOR TO THE SABBATH, FOR A GREAT CELEBRATORY
FEAST HAS BEEN PREPARED IN HONOR OF THE ADVENT OF
A RESTORED EARTH FOR THE THOUSAND YEARS OF PEACE**

"Hoorah! Ornate advent if Heaven-sent."
"Ho Ho! Fair, heaven-sent, ornate advent."
"Ha Ha! And so reverent of the innovate."
"Ha Ha! After innovate, honored. Events!"
"Aha! He, Fervent. Adoration on seventh." †Mark 2:27-28
"Ha Ha! Fervent adoration on the seven."

**THE CROWNED KING IS PRESENT TO CELEBRATE WITH
HIS REDEEMED BRETHREN ...THE FINEST OF FOOD AND
NEW WINE IS SET ON FOR THE CELEBRANTS**

"Hat heaven-sent Hero. Ornate of viand."
"Ha Ha! Reverent innovated. Ah, festoon!"
"Oh! After heaven and earth, set vino on!"
"Oh! Rev ton fiesta on heaven and earth." †Matthew 8:11
"Oh! Feast trove in heaven and on earth." †Isaiah 49:13
"Aha! Seventh! Fete on honored variant."
"Aahh! Oh! Innovated on! Reverent feast!"

**WHILE THIS HAS INDEED BEEN A TURNING-POINT EVENT,
IT HINTS OF AN EVEN GREATER BLESSING TO COME ONCE
THE THOUSAND YEARS ARE COMPLETED**

"Ha Ha! Footnote and heaven-sent river." †Revelation 22:1
"Shhh! Venerative! Footnote and an era." †Revelation 22:10

RELEVANT LONGEST WORDS/PHRASES USING SOME OF THE LETTERS

"eratosthenian" "deteriorates" "reforestation" "seventh heaven"
"reorientated" arfvedsonite" "reorientates"
"heart-to-heart" "thereinafter"

ON THE THRESHOLD OF GLORY

"Ho! Shortly, the longed-for." †Romans 8:22-23
"Grr! Held to honest of holy." †Revelation 3:11
"Then, Lord re of Holy Ghost." †John 16:13
"He holy, or flood strength." †Luke 24:49
"Shh! Oh! Foretold or gently." †Romans 8:30
"Good! Shh! Entry of the roll." †Revelation 3:5
"Ho! The stronger, holy fold." †John 10:27-28
"Legend forth or holy host." †Psalm 145:10-11
"Eh! Forth or honestly gold." †Job 23:10
"Holy strength of Old Hero." †Daniel 7:9
"Throne held Glory of Host." †Isaiah 6:1-3
"Holy Hero flood strength." †I Corinthians 15:53-54
"Oh! Strength of Older Holy." †Psalm 106:48
"Lord of Host! Lengthy Hero." †Isaiah 43:10
"Eh! Oh! Strongly of the Lord." †I John 3:2
"Ho Ho! Do fly! Strength role." †Matthew 22:30

THE MILLENNIAL REIGN OF CHRIST

The state of affairs in the world where we currently live lends little credence to the fact that a glorious epoch is just over the horizon. However, the author protests it is indeed so, and encourages all readers of this book to likewise entertain the reality of its approach. As we see heads of state, policy makers, and journalistic publications calling for a New World Order, consisting of a standardized financial, communications, and spiritual network, we must recognize it for what it is: the Luciferian design to mold and dominate the world.

While this cannot be done without deception, impoverishment, famine, plagues, catastrophes, and death on an unprecedented scale, the Luciferian program will proceed. It will proceed, but it will not succeed. We can take great comfort in the assurance of God's divine intervention on behalf of those who have pledged themselves to His service, those who will obtain mercy to enter his Kingdom, and the creation itself which is groaning in earnest for the redemption of the sons of God.

HOUSE CONDEMNED
DUE TO A FAULTY FOUNDATION

Psalm 127:1 provides a clear explanation as to why the carefully crafted plans of earth's elite over the millennia will collapse just as they think they have achieved their plan of world-wide domination. They are building on a foundation other than Jesus Christ, the Chief Cornerstone. Thus, the mystery religion with its secret societies, signs, and symbols which have existed since the rebellion of Cain. Instead of humbly building on the Foundation which is superior to all others, they have constructed an agenda characterized by the political and financial control of nations and their resources, subterfuge, massive bloodshed, and genocidal extermination – represented by an esoteric pyramid and a capstone. This capstone coupled with symbolic light and eye represents their joint efforts with the Luciferian Light-Bearer; the god of this world. Their goal is to position the capstone on its pyramid base, thereby signaling the preparation of the earth for their ruler.

Romans 1:28-30 provides further insight into the reason man invents and does evil things that will harm his fellow man. It is because he does not like to retain God in his knowledge. Thus, the prideful machinations of sinful, unregenerate man in collusion with the fallen angel Satan who hates God and His creation have brought the earth to its present condition. In fact, the need to show God as irrelevant is behind much of the destruction of the earth's biosphere, as man uses his creative abilities to install harmful and inferior things, then forces those experiments on the world's population. As if that were not enough, Man creates pathogens as a direct challenge to the One who testified He is our Healer. God states that He knows our every thought and our words even before we speak them, so man tries to imitate and creates electronic and neural technologies that violate and harm his fellow man. God breathed life into Adam, and ingeniously created a companion for him that he (Adam) immediately recognized as his complement, so man creates armaments unprecedented in their cruelty and toxicity to destroy both men and women and the fruit of their unions. God blesses abundantly and gives us richly all things to enjoy, but man orchestrates and controls an unfair monetary system that impoverishes and causes many to have to work into their old age just to be able to eat.

God sets free, man enslaves. God empowers, man exploits. God nurtures, man tortures. It should be abundantly clear why we should urgently pray for the Kingdom of God to manifest on earth.

Technology, wealth, control of the earth's resources, and the ability to dominate and wreak suffering and deprivation among the inhabitants of the world give man the illusion he can be as God, and invincible. The Bible teaches that Satan once felt invincible too, and his ego deluded him into thinking he could usurp God's throne. But Jesus said He watched him fall like lightning from heaven. With the estimated speed of lightning at around 60,000 miles per second, it should not be difficult to ascertain which side is the winning team.

Five times, Satan defiantly said, "I will." But because God is "I AM," "I AM" forcibly removed "I will" from free access to the heavenly realms at a speed incomprehensible to human imagination.

Therefore, if man follows Satan, man will get the same results – stunning defeat and ignominy. However, when man builds on the Solid Rock – the Foundation Stone which becomes a mountain that eventually fills the entire earth, he is building toward an everlasting Kingdom that will never be destroyed. Anything not built on this Foundation Stone is doomed to be crushed by it.

THE ELITE OF TODAY vs THOSE OF TOMORROW

Today's elite are, for the most part, reclusive parties who prefer to work behind the scenes in their quest for domination of the earth. While there may be a few whom the public is familiar with, such as foreign policy consultants, most of these rich men and women of the earth remain out of the limelight of television cameras and media interviews. The author has heard estimates of there being as few as ten to around one hundred of these powerful ruling families. At any rate, they honestly feel as though the earth is their personal game board where they can make strategic moves, pit nations against each other, and partner with bankers to loot economies and hasten the internal disintegration of sovereign countries.

The elite of tomorrow, however, will be very visible as they execute their kingly and priestly duties amongst the world population. As they will represent Messiah Jesus Christ and His justice, righteousness, and abundant blessing, they will have nothing to hide. Their plans will not include wars, impoverishment, hunger, biological warfare, eugenics, and death. Instead, they will use their influence and exalted status to tutor the families of the earth in the ways and commandments of Christ and intercede on their behalf toward Him.

There will be one thousand years for people to learn of Christ, voluntarily seek spiritual rebirth, and adopt the easy yoke of holiness. As wonderful as life will be during the Millennium with Emanuel – God with us – the ultimate goal will be to get as many ready as possible for transition to the New Heavens and New Earth. The words of the Lord that, "Except a man be born again, he cannot see the Kingdom of God," and "He that winneth souls is wise", will still ring true.

Jesus, the "Judicious Expert" will judge the nations with righteous judgment. There is no place in His court for bribery, or partiality due to influence. Neither are prosecutors, defense attorneys, juries, bailiffs, or court reporters needed. He will literally fill every function, and all His rulings will be just and equitable.

Few uncommon words appear in the following subject, excepting *yurt*. A *yurt* is a circular, tent-like dwelling used by the peoples of Central Asia, including Afghanistan. *Enchant* in this context refers to delighting to a high degree, and *fancy* indicates imagining. *Orison* denotes prayers.

THOUSAND YEAR REIGN OF CHRIST

IT IS A BEAUTIFUL TIME TO BE ALIVE

"Thousand nicer years of right." †Habakkuk 2:14
"Fortunate or cherishing days."
"Or cherishing fortunate days."

WITH SATAN IMPRISONED IN THE PIT, AND THE RIGHTEOUS CHRIST PRESENT WITH HIS KINGS AND PRIESTS, THE SCALES OF INFLUENCE OVER THE EARTH FOR THE PAST SIX MILLENIA TIP FROM DARKNESS AND REBELLION TO LIGHT AND TRUTH

"Ton fresh righteous radiancy."

THE RIGHTEOUS SHINE AS THE STARS OF HEAVEN

"Radiancy of right heroes stun." †Daniel 12:3
"Thorough radiancy sets finer."
"Shiniest ray of graced thru on."
"Sunny of straight, heroic dear."
"Sure! Right of honest radiancy."

THEY ARE AT REST; SEALED IN THEIR FOREHEADS

"Fine, thorough radiancy rests."
"Astounding rest of hierarchy." †Revelation 7:3
"Scrutiny as Right on forehead."

MANY WERE CALLED TO BE KINGS AND PRIESTS IN THE KINGDOM...THE FEW CHOSEN GAVE ALL TO GAIN CHRIST

"Chosen as adoring fiery Truth."
"Straight chosen around Fiery."

THESE KINGS AND PRIESTS LEARNED DURING THE TRIAL RIDDEN DAYS IN THEIR EARTHLY BODIES TO CRUCIFY THE FLESH WITH ITS PASSIONS AND DESIRES ...BECAUSE THEY YIELDED THEMSELVES TO LEARN OBEDIENCE THROUGH SUFFERING, THEY ARE NOW THE SPIRITS OF JUST MEN MADE PERFECT AND QUALIFIED TO RULE WITH THE LORD OVER NATIONS ...THEIR OVERSIGHT WILL ALWAYS BE JUST

"Rounding to safest hierarchy."
"So understating of hierarchy!"

**BECAUSE OF THIS RIGHTEOUS ADMINISTRATION,
THE WORLD IS NO LONGER A DANGEROUS PLACE**

"Thorough sincerity and safer."   †Isaiah 11:9

**THE ENTIRE WORLD IS TAUGHT TRUE RIGHTEOUSNESS
AND HOLINESS BASED ON THE TWO GREATEST
COMMANDMENTS ...THOSE WITH OPEN HEARTS FIND
MESSIAH'S YOKE IS EASY**

"Fancy righteous is not harder."
"Uh, infers try sainthood grace."   †John 6:45
"Ha Ha! Trusty of reconsidering."
"Shun fire. Try sainthood grace."

**THEY LEARN THAT TRUE BEAUTY AND
HEROISM IS FOUND IN SERVING OTHERS**

"Fresh radiancy is not thru ego."

MESSIAH RULES THE NATIONS WITH A ROD OF IRON

"Oh Dear! Nifty rigour chastens."   †Revelation 19:15
"Fancy! Dear! This honest rigour."
"Fiery rigour chastens and hot."

**BUT HE ALSO JUDGES THEIR CAUSES WITH EQUITY,
...AND PRESIDES OVER THE CASE OF AFGHANISTAN**

"Afghan's true cry. It is honored."   †Job 34:24-28

**SILENCE AS THE JUDGE ASCENDS TO HIS SEAT...THE LORD IS IN HIS
HOLY TEMPLE: LET ALL THE EARTH KEEP SILENCE BEFORE HIM**

"Shh! Fiery, astounding Creator."   †Habakkuk 2:20
"Fiery, thorough, Ascendant Sir."

THE PARTIES APPEAR, AND THE FACTS OF THE CASE ARE HEARD

"Or hearts hang if countryside."
"Or the Afghan Sir countryside."
"Afghan. Or it's her countryside."
"Afghan. Or 'tis her countryside."
"Afghans. Or their countryside."
"Or re this Afghan countryside."

AS POWERFUL INTERNATIONAL INTERESTS JOCKEYED FOR
CONTROL OF THE STRATEGIC CENTRAL ASIAN TERRAIN, A
TERRIFIED AND HELPLESS POPULATION WAS CAUGHT IN
THE CROSSFIRE ...HUNDREDS OF TONS OF DEPLETED
URANIUM MUNITIONS WERE EXPLODED UPON THE REGION
...WHOLE VILLAGES OBLITERATED

THE RADIATION IS KILLING THOSE WHO SURVIVED ...BABIES
ARE BORN GROTESQUELY DEFORMED ... ALMOST EVERY
HOME HAS LOST SOMEONE ...SOMETIMES MULTIPLE FAMILY
MEMBERS; AND WIDOWS AND ORPHANS FORAGE FOR FOOD
AND FUEL   TO SURVIVE THE HARSH WINTERS

"Crony far outsider haste nigh."
"Yon far haste nigh. Direct ours."
"Nosy far haste; direct our nigh."
"Countryside, or ah, fears night."
"Countryside or an high strafe."
"Or re hits Afghan countryside."
"Countryside, or re hit Afghans."
"Has fight near. Cinder rots you."
"Ah! Fight snare, corrode tiny us."
"A ashen fright. Soon yurt cried."

EVIDENCE CAPTURED AND RETAINED IN THE SPIRITUAL REALM
FOR THIS VERY OCCASION IS REPLAYED TO DETERMINE IF THESE
ACCUSATIONS ARE INDEED TRUE ...IT IS LIKE RELIVING THE EVENT
IN REAL TIME ...THE SENTIMENT OF THE JUDGE DOES NOT BODE
WELL FOR THE ACCUSED REGARDING THE UNPROVOKED AGGRESSION
AND THE POISONOUS CRUELTY OF DEPLETED URANIUM WEAPONRY

"Hath anger if descry into ours."
"Hath anger if descry ruins, too."
"Decrys!! If soot ruins hath anger!"

HE WHOSE FAN IS IN HIS HAND, PURGES HIS FLOOR, AND GATHERS
THE WHEAT INTO HIS GARNER BUT BURNS THE CHAFF WITH
UNQUENCHABLE FIRE RULES IN FAVOR OF THE PLAINTIFFS

"Son: Your credit! Fan; gather His." †Matthew 3:12

THE ACCUSED, WHO ARE COVETOUS, PROTEST THE RULING
– BUT THEY ARE REBUKED IN THE LORD'S WRATH

"Cried, not yours!! Fan; gather His."

**THEY HAVE SCORNED THE LORD BY KILLING THOSE MADE
IN HIS IMAGE AND LIKENESS AND DESTROYING THE EARTH
IN THEIR QUEST FOR RICHES AND POWER**

"Hating tried scorn You afresh."
"Cited: nor yours. Hang if haters."
"Edict: nor yours. Hang if haters."

**THE ROD OF IRON RULE BREAKS THEIR RESISTANCE...
JUDGMENT IS PRONOUNCED; THEY WILL BE CUT DOWN**

"Hah! Anger fist! Or rein custody!"
"Foreordains a scythe hurting."   †Psalm 37:1-2

**TO THE AFGHANIS WHO HAVE SUFFERED SO MUCH LOSS,
PEACE, SAFETY, HEALING, AND THE RESTORATION OF
HOMES IS PROMISED ...THEY NEED NEVER FEAR AGAIN**

"A Father's nigh. Security donor."
"I, Father's a nigh surety cordon."
"Foreordains ceasing thy hurt."
"Foreordains change hit yurts."

**GOING FORWARD THEY MUST ALL BE TAUGHT OF THE LORD ...
HE IS THEIR DELIVERER AND SUCCOURER, BUT HE IS TO BE
WORSHIPED IN THE BEAUTY OF HOLINESS**

"Introduces of Your doctrines."
"Fruit on codes! Your doctrines." †John 15:8

**THE KINGS AND PRIESTS WHICH MESSIAH HAS
PREDESTINATED TO MINISTER IN THAT LAND WILL
TEACH THE PEOPLE THE WAYS OF THE LORD**

"Foreordains teach. Hungry? Sit." †Ephesians 1:4
"Foreordains. Uh, try teachings."

THE TEACHER...
"Docent sir re-hangs Your faith..."

TUTORS THE STUDENTS

"Tyro coursed in re-hangs faith."

**UNTIL THEY CAN PRAY THEMSELVES ACCORDING TO
THE WILL OF GOD AND EXPERIENCE ANSWERED PRAYER**

"Cued try orison; re-hangs faith."

**REPENTANCE FOR HATRED OF CHRIST ...THE PEOPLE WERE
CONFUSED BECAUSE THE NATIONS WHICH WERE BOMBING
THEM CLAIMED TO BE CHRISTIAN**

"Is counted sorry, if hath anger."

**THE TIMES OF REFRESHING BECOME A REALITY IN THE LIFE
OF THESE PRECIOUS PEOPLE AS GOD'S HOLY SPIRIT DIRECTS
THEM AND HIS WORD BECOMES EMBEDDED IN THEIR HEARTS
– BRINGING TRUE LIBERTY**

"A fresh thing ...a credit on yours."
"Foreordains change this yurt."
"Foreordains each yurt things."
"Iron Code. Hurray! Night feasts."
"Iron Code. Hurray! Hasten gifts."

**CONSTRUCTION ASSISTANCE POURS IN FROM OTHER AREAS
OF THE WORLD TO THIS HISTORICALLY ISOLATED GROUP ...FOR
A PEOPLE USED TO FIGHTING OFF EMPIRICAL AGGRESSORS, SUCH
AN OUTPOURING OF LOVE SEEMS TOO GOOD TO BE TRUE ...BUT
IT IS AGAPE LOVE – THE LOVE OF GOD THROUGH CHRIST JESUS**

"As Father nigh, introduce rosy."
"As Father nigh, doctor ye ruins."
"Credit U, Son! R yurt rise condo!"
"Henceforth, a guy insist ardor."

**THE LAND BECOMES FRUITFUL AND STARVATION
FADES TO A DISTANT MEMORY**

"Hah! Sing after Your doctrines."
"Ah! Your credits on safer night."
"Your credits on safe. Hath grin."
"Credit Your Son. Ran high feast."
"Credit Your Son. Feast! Hah! Grin."†Psalm 145:7

**THE LORD'S HOUSE IS A HOUSE OF PRAYER FOR ALL NATIONS ...
ALL ARE EXPECTED TO MAKE PILGRIMAGE TO JERUSALEM AT
THE DESIGNATED TIMES OF WORSHIP**

"Foreordains High Yurt. Enacts."
"Foreordains High Yurt stance."
"Foreordains ascent High Yurt."   †Revelation 15:4

**THERE WILL BE ABUNDANT ASSISTANCE AND PROVISION
TO BUILD THE HIGHWAY SOUTHWEST TO JERUSALEM**

"As Father nigh, so record unity."
"Henceforth, rigs a unity roads."

DURING THE MILLENNIUM, ALL KEEP THE SABBATH DAY

"Huge Hero constraints Friday."
"Fridays enchant or righteous."
"Tough, rich Friday ornateness."
"Father's Day or nicer shouting."

**THE FIRST DAY OF THE WEEK REVERTS BACK TO ITS
ORIGINAL PLACE WITHIN THE CONTEXT OF WORSHIP**

"Heroes fraction Sunday right."
"Oh! Rather satisfy on reducing."
"So rich neater of right Sunday."

SOME WILL HAVE A PROBLEM WITH KEEPING SABBATH

"Or hating Fridays chosen true."

**OBSERVANCE IS MANDATORY AND FAILURE TO COMPLY
RESULTS IN SEVERE SANCTIONS**

"Friday enchants or is tougher."
"Fridays entrance or toughish."
"Tougher of chastens in Friday."
"Rich, ornate Friday toughness."
"Rigour chastens on the Friday."
"Hint: care Friday or toughness."

**IT WILL TAKE SOME A LITTLE LONGER THAN OTHERS
TO ADOPT THE EASY YOKE**

"Heritage drift asynchronous."
"Ordinary if chastens tougher."
"Satisfy or heartrending ouch."

**BUT FOR THOSE WHO LOVE THE LORD AND DESIRE HIS
PRESENCE, THE SABBATH WORSHIP IS A TIME OF GREAT
JOY ...MUSIC OF HEARTFELT WORSHIP, HOLY DANCE,
AND HIGH PRAISE FILLS THE ATMOSPHERE**

"Fiery enthusiast chord organ."

"Fiery song thrush to radiance."†Psalm 149:1-4
"Fiery, thorough saint dancers."†Jeremiah 31:4
"Shouting and fiery orchestra."
"Hardier shouting of Ancestry." †Psalm 150

**THE PRESENCE OF THE LIVING GOD IS TANGIBLY FELT AS
HE ABIDES AMONG HIS PEOPLE IN THE PERSON OF CHRIST**

"It's cherished You; fragrant on!" †Psalm 45:7-8

MESSIAH IS LOVED BECAUSE HE IS KNOWN BY HIS WORKS

"Dear fans thorough sincerity."

**HIS PERSONAL APPEARANCE IN ANY LOCALE
DRAWS THRONGS OF WORSHIPPERS**

"Hurray! if this Good entrances!"
"This generous radiancy forth."
"Farsighted, rich, resonant You."

**HIS GLORIFIED KINGS AND PRIESTS, WHO NEVER AGE –
EMANATE HIS PRESENCE**

"Young heroes find rich attars."
"Ho Ho! Intertissued fragrancy." †Psalm 45:8
"This honored fragrancy suite." †I John 3:2

**THEY ARE ECSTATIC ABOUT THEIR RESURRECTED BODIES:
NO MATTER HOW OLD, DISEASED, OR MANGLED THEY WERE
DUE TO CIRCUMSTANCES IN THE FORMER LIFE, THEY ARE
NOW PERFECTED AND WILL REMAIN YOUNG FOREVER**

"Or fancy this senior daughter!"
"Fancy or shiniest or daughter."
"Hurrah! Intensity of so graced."
"Right! Fashion true secondary." †I Corinthians 15:53-54
"Fresh, true soothing radiancy."
"Honoured as if right ancestry."   †Luke 20:35-36

**AS JESUS PROMISED, HE HAS PREPARED A PLACE
FOR THEM IN HIS FATHER'S HOUSE**

"So rich trendy of Huge Artisan." † John 14:2
"Treasury of to and cherishing."
"Or yard enchants if righteous."

"Arty and generous of this rich."
"This configured, honest array."
"Thundery as range of historic."
"Gosh! Thundery, fair creations."
"Heroic star gains of thundery."
"Gosh! Arty and fruitier chosen."
"Hurray! Fitting. Chosen adores." †Psalm 37:4
"Gracious! Shh! Trendy if ornate."
"Heroine's chatty fairgrounds."
"Henceforth, is touring a yards."
"So cherishing fortunate yard."

A GREAT TIME OF EXCITEMENT AS THE REDEEMED OF THE AGES ARE DELEGATED THEIR ROYAL AND PRIESTLY ROLES IN THE ENDURING KINGDOM

"Hooray! Chief starts enduring."
"Shh! A far-seeing, introductory."
"Foster astounding hierarchy."
"Arrays united chosen of right."
"Hurray! Choosing finest rated." †Revelation 20:4

"Searching if a honored trusty."
"Hooray! Chief entrusts daring..."
"On a cherishing of trusty dear."
"Ahoy! Trustier if grand chosen."
"Fancy sustain to higher-order."
"This hardy, generous fraction."

WORK FOR THE RIGHTEOUS WILL CONSIST OF BUILDING THE KINGDOM BY MINISTERING VIA ADMINISTRATION, TUTORING, AND EXERCISING THE TALENTS VESTED IN THEM AT BIRTH

"Hoorah! Grace=finest industry."

THERE IS STILL PLENTY OF TIME FOR BOTH THE RESURRECTED AND EARTHLY CITIZENS TO ENJOY LIFE AND THE ARTS, FOR THE GIFTS AND CALLINGS OF GOD REMAIN

"Enthusing of adores rich arty."
"So if hero, artistry unchanged."
"Is unchanged artistry of hero." †Romans 11:29

**ABILITIES RESIDENT AT BIRTH ARE FURTHER ENHANCED
BY FREEDOM OF LIMITATIONS IN THE GLORIFIED BODY**

"If honoured, artistry changes."
"Hero and crafty or this genius."
"Is truth, adoring fancy heroes."
"Hurray! Chosen or gifted saint."
"Carry on of shiniest daughter."
"Ho Ho! Faces enduring artistry."

**THE MASTER TAKES DELIGHT IN THE GIFTS
HE HAS BESTOWED ON HIS PEOPLE**

"Chief adores; hung artistry on."
"Hung chosen artistry if adore."
"Find honesty rather gracious."
"Cherishing of adore arty stun."

LOVE FEASTS ARE COMPOSED OF CULINARY DELIGHTS

"Chef as thundery originators."
"Hooray! Chef's enduring artist."
"Hero as enduring of tasty rich."
"Hero's enduring of a tasty rich."

AND THERE IS NEW WINE IN THE KINGDOM OF GOD

"Enduring toasts of hierarchy."
"Hurry! Sainthood in grace fest." †Mark 14:25

**THE OLD AND NEW TESTAMENT SAINTS ARE EAGER TO
MEET EACH OTHER AND TRADE STORIES ...AND EVERYONE
WANTS TO MEET ABRAHAM, WHOSE PROGENY THEY
ARE THROUGH HIS SEED, CHRIST**

"Chosen, it is your grandfather." †Hebrews 12:1-2
†Genesis 13:16

**ABRAHAM SEES HIS DESCENDANTS INNUMERABLE AS THE
STARS IN THE HEAVENS JUST AS GOD PROMISED, AND IS
EAGER TO HEAR THEIR STORIES OF FAITH**

"Grandfather: son – he curiosity." †Galatians 3:26-29
† Genesis 15:5

**THE THOUSAND YEARS OF PEACE USHER IN THE
KNOWLEDGE OF THE GLORY OF GOD COVERING THE
EARTH ...PREVIOUS MISCONCEPTIONS ARE DONE AWAY
WITH AND THE GOSPEL IS PREACHED STRICTLY IN THE
CONTEXT OF GODS LOVE WITHOUT RACIAL BIAS**

"Chief assign thundery orator."
"Hoary, fruitiest, grand chosen."
"Historic ranges of a thundery."
"Thundery sage ran of historic."
"Thundery sage or historic fan."
"Thundery soothing fair races."
"Steady cherishing fun orator."
"Hungry dasher of recitations."
"Saint handy resource of right."   †Habakkuk 2:14
"Fancy! Ho Ho! Trustier readings."   †II Timothy 2:15

**INDEED, FOUR REASONS TO STRIVE FOR THE PRIZE OF THE
HIGH CALLING RULING AND REIGNING IN THE KINGOM OF GOD**

"First, huge or honest radiancy."   †Daniel 12:3
"Second, Hurrah! as of integrity."   †Psalm 112:3,9
"Third, If Creator, ha! youngness."   †IJohn 3:2
†Revelation 1:6 *"Fourth, dignity as rare chosen."*   †Ephesians 1:4

**REUNIFICATION WITH SAVED LOVED ONES IS ALSO A
POWERFUL INCENTIVE TO LIVE KINGDOM-MINDED**

"Right-hearted scans your info."
"Right-hearted. Ay, uncross info."
"Right-hearted fancy is our son."
"Right-hearted fancy on our sis."
"Right-hearted yon far cousins."

**BY AIR, WATER, OR LAND, REUNIFICATION AND REPATRIATION
TAKES PLACE, AS THE SEED OF ABRAHAM IS RETURNS TO THE LAND**

"Right-hearted. Sonny focus air."   †Isaiah 49:22
"The finer around, so rig yachts."   †Isaiah 66:20
"Right-hearted. Oar sync fusion."
"Right-hearted. Soon cars unify."

TEARFUL REJOICING AT THE SIGHT OF LOVED ONES!

"Right-hearted. A cry of unisons."
"Right-hearted. Far cosy unions."

**DURING THE MILLENNIUM THE SAGA FROM GENESIS
TO REVELATION REVEALING GOD'S PLAN THROUGH
THE AGES IS TAUGHT TO ALL**

"Thundery historians of grace." †Habakkuk 2:14
"Sage or rich thundery of saint."

**THE DIVINE INTERVENTION ON THE LAST DAY OF THE
PREVIOUS ERA IS A FAVORITE THEME**

"Orator says Chief thundering."
"Thundery of a right scenarios." †Psalm 45:4
"Fancy! Oh! Horse-riding stature." †Revelation 19:11

**SEXUAL PURITY WILL BECOME THE NORM WITHOUT THE
BLIGHT OF SOCIAL ENGINEERING TO ENCOURAGE PROMISCUITY**

"Era for enshrouding chastity."
"Urges far in honored chastity." †I Thessalonians 4:4

**IT WILL NOT BE UNCOMMON FOR ALL DAUGHTERS IN A
FAMILY TO REMAIN VIRGINAL UNTIL MARRIED**

"Heroine's grand chastity four."
"Honorary if nicest daughters." †Song of Solomon 4:12

**FOR THE YOUNG MEN, PURITY AND PROPER CONDUCT
BASED ON THE PRINCIPLES OF COURTING AND BETROTHAL**

"Fair dasher honesty courting."
"Ground hero finer as chastity." †I Timothy 5:2
"Enduring hero as for chastity."
"Or share of enduring chastity."

AND THEN MARRIAGE

"Synchronise to fair daughter." †Hebrews 13:4

**THE ENTIRE WORLD WILL RECEIVE THE KNOWLEDGE OF GOD
TO POSSESS THEIR VESSELS IN SANCTIFICATION AND HONOR**

"And chastity or hero refusing."
"And chastity or refusing hero."
"Grr! As honoured fine chastity."
"Honored, rare chastity fusing."
"Fair courting. Shared honesty."

**STATISTICS GATHERED THROUGHOUT SUBSEQUENT YEARS
WILL INDICATE A DRAMATIC DECREASE IN UNMARRIED
PREGNANCIES AND SEXUALLY TRANSMITTED DISEASES,
WHICH WILL EVENTUALLY BE ELIMINATED COMPLETELY**

"Honored ran chastity figures."
"Hero's fiery, astounding chart."
"Fiery hero charts. Astounding!!"
"Ha Ha! Fiery, strong reductions."
"Rare if charts young hedonist."

**CHILDREN WILL GROW UP LIKE FRUITFUL
PLANTS AND PRECIOUS STONES**

"Or nascent hardy if righteous."
"Or daughters to fancy shinier." †Psalm 144:12

**THEY WILL BE TAUGHT TO PLAY GENTLY WITH AND
SHARE THE CREATURES OF LOWER CREATION WHO
ARE NO LONGER AFRAID OF HUMANS**

"No fight. Ordinary shares cute." †Isaiah 11:6
"Right. Courtesy of and share in."

**THEY WILL BE TAUGHT GOOD STEWARDSHIP FROM THEIR
YOUTH UP ...IN THIS WAY THEY ARE PREPARED TO PROVIDE
FOR FAMILIES WHEN THEY COME OF AGE**

"Young radiate forth richness."
"The rich, fair youngster and so."
"Reasoned young rich as thrift." †Proverbs 27:23

THE ELDERLY ARE VIGOROUS AND AGILE

"Hoary and terrific toughness." †Isaiah 65:22

**THEY ARE SAFE WITH THEIR DOORS UNLOCKED, AND
NO LONGER NEED WORK UNTIL THEY DIE TO KEEP A
ROOF OVER THEIR HEADS AND FEED THEMSELVES**

"Hoary safe, considering Truth." †Ezekiel 28:26

**LONGEVITY WILL BECOME THE NORM TO THE EXTENT THAT
IF A PERSON DIES AT ONE HUNDRED YEARS OLD, THEY WILL
STILL BE CONSIDERED A CHILD**

"Fathers and historic younger." †Isaiah 65:20

**PEOPLE WILL NOT BE ELEVATED BASED ON PHYSICAL
ATTRACTIVENESS OR FALSE BRAVADO, BUT ON
DEMONSTRATION OF TRUE CHARACTER AND RIGHTEOUSNESS**

"Hardier chosen, not gutsy fair."
"Hardy of true right ascension." †Psalm 147:10

**THE PROVERBIAL ADAGE THAT "FAVOR IS
DECEITFUL AND BEAUTY IS VAIN" IS HONORED**

"Young fair star not cherished."
"Saucy honored finer straight." †Proverbs 31:30
"Thorough distance fair syren."
"Raunchier, dishy as forgotten."

**THE CABALS AND SECRET SOCIETIES WHICH PLAGUED
THE FORMER WORLD ARE NOT FOUND**

"Thorough refrain syndicates." †Proverbs 6:12-14

ENTERTAINMENT BASED ON DEATH AND VIOLENCE CEASES

"Adores straight funny heroic." †Proverbs 17:22
"Right! Funniest, sacred hooray."†Proverbs 15:13

**PEOPLE TRAVEL THE ROADS IN PEACE AND SAFETY,
DAY AND NIGHT– IN VEHICLES OR ON HORSEBACK**

"Sincerity and thoroughfares."
"Nifty car and righteous horse." †Zechariah 14:20
"Hurrah! considering to safety."

**THE STREETS AROUND THE WORLD BUSTLE WITH ACTIVITY
FROM VENDORS AND CRAFTSMEN ...THE CURSE INVOKED
WHEN ADAM SINNED IS BROKEN ...PEOPLE WORK IN THE
FIELDS OF THEIR NATURAL GIFTINGS AND LABOR IS JOYOUS**

"Stridency as in thoroughfare." †Psalm 144:13
†Jeremiah 31:12

**NATIONS CAN MANUFACTURE GOODS FOR THEMSELVES AND
TRADE WITH EQUITY – THERE IS NO MORE SLAVE OR CHILD
LABOR, HIJACKING OF OTHERS' LANDS, OR RAISING OF
POPPIES AND COCA FOR STREET DRUG USE**

"Right reason of each industry."
"So enthusing hardier factory."

**LIVESTOCK WILL BE PROPERLY RAISED AND PREPARED
FOR CONSUMPTION ...WORKING CONDITIONS ARE
MADE SAFE–OR SHUT DOWN**

"Ah! Industry, once safe or right."
"Ho! Or safe grain tech industry."
"Safe industry or hogtie ranch."
"Rigorous and finest hatchery."

**WAR IMPLEMENTS WILL HAVE TO BE QUICKLY CONVERTED
INTO FOOD PRODUCTION MACHINERY TO NOURISH THE
BOURGEONING POPULATION ...IT WILL BECOME DIFFICULT
TO FIND EVEN A SMALL FIREARM**

"Chief shortage or an industry."   †Isaiah 2:4
"Dear! Funny, historic shortage."   †Micah 4:3

**TECHNOLOGY WILL BE USED AS IT SHOULD BE,
WITHOUT SPYING OR INTENT OF CORRUPTION**

†Proverbs 3:30 *"This unerring of cathode rays."* †Psalm 37:32

PLANTS WILL ATTAIN THE ORIGINAL EDENIC QUALITIES

"Fancy! It hardier, or toughness."
"Father's rich nitrogenous day."   †Isaiah 35:1-2
"Hardier of to this sunny grace."

**WHAT A FIELD DAY FOR INVENTORS AS THEIR IDEAS AND
PATENTS TO BENEFIT MANKIND ARE NO LONGER SUPPRESSED**

"Fancy! The originators rushed."   † Proverbs 29:2
"Ho Ho! Genius's trendy aircraft."
"Adore genius's thrifty anchor."
"Hero's enthusing crafty radio."

**SOLAR POWER WILL BE USED EXTENSIVELY...NO MORE
CHEMICAL SPRAY-DARKENING OF THE ATMOSPHERE**

"Sunny of this red-hot carriage."

HYDROGEN WILL BE COMMONLY USED FOR ENERGY

"Hydrogen as a terrific hot sun."
"Fortunate his car is hydrogen."
"Is fortunate as rich hydrogen."
"Hydrogen or far enthusiastic."

**PEACE OFFICERS PATROL WHO HAVE
GREAT POWER BUT DO NOT ABUSE IT**

"Hoorah! Finest grand security."   †Isaiah 60:17
"Right! A safe, honored scrutiny."
"Red sash enforcing authority."
"Thorough scans identify rare."
"Fiery, straight scan honoured."
"Senior guards notify the arch."
"Honor Fiery guard. It chastens."

**THE FOURTH YEAR INTO THE MILLENNIUM MAY
BE SANCTIFIED TO PRAISE THE LORD WITHAL**

"Considering hast fourth-year."   †Leviticus 19:24
"It is fourth-year, grand chosen."

**THERE IS NO PROPHETIC WORD TO BE SPOKEN IN THAT
AGE – THOSE PURPORTING TO HAVE A WORD FROM
THE LORD WILL BE SILENCED**

"Soothsayer, and curt Fire nigh."
"Daring soothsayer turn - - Chief!!"
"And soothsayer incur Fighter."   †Ezekiel 13:9
"And soothsayer cringe if hurt."
"Soothsayer rig and fetch ruin."

**SORCERY OF ANY TYPE WILL NOT BE TOLERATED
AND BRINGS SEVERE PENALTIES**

"Hatred if anything sorcerous."   †Jeremiah 29:9
"Dearth if anything sorcerous."   †Zechariah 13:2

**THEREFORE, IT IS UNFORTUNATE THAT SOMEONE EVENTUALLY
ATTEMPTS TO SEDUCE THE YOUTH INTO WITCHCRAFT WITH
A DEVICE DESIGNED TO INVOKE DEMONS**

"Young faith and this sorcerer."   †I Timothy 2:22
"Younger or finish that sacred."   †Matthew 18:6, 10, 14
"Ha Ha! Nicest young order first."
"Toy as raunchier ghost-finder."
"A raunchier ghost-finder toys."

REBELLION IS AS THE SIN OF WITCHCRAFT AND
STUBBORNESS AS IDOLATRY ...THE POPULACE
HAS BEEN TAUGHT AND WARNED REPEATEDLY

"Hot or tragedy if raunchiness."
"So straight deny of raunchier." †I Peter 2:11
"Or sturdy reason hating Chief."
"So carries hating of Thundery."
"Naughty or finished creators." †Revelation 2:24
"Finished as tougher contrary."

ALL MUST KEEP THE FEAST OF TABERNACLES ON AN
ANNUAL BASIS ...THOSE NATIONS WHICH FAIL TO DO
SO WILL RECEIVE NO RAIN ...WHICH MEANS NO CROPS
...WHICH RESULTS IN HUNGER

"Is hungry if Orator chastened."
"If hunger, reason hydrostatic."
"Huge refrain on hydrostatics." †Zechariah 14:16-19

DURING THE THOUSAND YEARS OF PEACE, MILLIONS
HAVE COME TO KNOW THE LORD AND WILLINGLY SERVE
HIM, HAVING ACCEPTED HIS SACRIFICE FOR THEIR SINS
AND ENTERED INTO COVENANT WITH HIM BY VIRTUE
OF SPIRITUAL REBIRTH

...HOWEVER, A SIGNIFICANT NUMBER HAVE BOWED
THE KNEE ONLY BECAUSE THEY WERE FORCED TO BY
THE ROD OF IRON RULE

...THESE UNCIRMCUMCISED IN HEART WHO STEADFASTLY
RESIST THE GRACE OF GOD ARE RIPE FOR DECEPTION WHEN
SATAN IS LOOSED FROM THE BOTTOMLESS PIT FOR A SMALL
SEASON ...HE MARSHALS RECRUITS FROM THE NATIONS WHO
HELD POWER JUST BEFORE THE RETURN OF THE LORD JESUS
CHRIST – GOG AND MAGOG – A FORCE DESCRIBED IN NUMBER
LIKE THE SAND OF THE SEA

"Nifty, huge, sardonic, star hero."
"Ha Ha! if not studying. Sorcerer."†Revelation 20:1-3, 7

HE EMERGES WITH AN AXE TO GRIND...A GRUDGE
HE HAS NURSED FOR 1000 YEARS

"Theories undo this fragrancy."
"Out-herod shiniest fragrancy." †Revelation 20:8

HE PRESENTS NOT AS EVIL BUT AS AN ANGEL OF
LIGHT WHO HAS PEOPLE'S BEST INTEREST IN MIND

"Ha crafty! Oh, or sends intrigue." †II Corinthians 11:14
"Oh No! Crafty dasher intrigues."
"Hurray! Good! In the craftiness."
"Shh! Adores on crafty intrigue."

PERHAPS THE RALLYING CRY IS MADE TO REMEMBER
THE WICKED TOYMAKERS WHO WERE SLAIN FOR THEIR
REBELLION ...HE CONVINCES HIS FOLLOWERS THEY
HAVE RIGHTS THAT ARE NOT BEING HONORED ...HE
MAY TELL THEM THE GODHEAD IS A CONTROL FREAK
AND HAS ALWAYS BEEN UNFAIR

...HE IS DECEPTIVE ABOUT HIS RELEASE FROM THE PIT;
INSISTING HE ESCAPED BY SHEER WISDOM AND POWER ...
"AREN'T YOU TIRED OF BEING RULED AND CONSTRAINED
BY JESUS CHRIST AND HIS KINGS AND PRIESTS?" HE ASKS
...HIS RECRUITS AGREE... "LET US BREAK THEIR BANDS
ASUNDER, AND CAST AWAY THEIR CORDS FROM US!"

"Haunting of hardiest sorcery."
"Steady! Raunchier of on rights."
"Things of raunchier or steady."
"Steady or things of raunchier."
"Steady! Raunchier or on fights."

WHATEVER HIS SPIEL, WHEN HE IS FINISHED,
HE HAS MUSTERED A FORCE OF MILLIONS

"Hurrah! Good! Nifty resistance." †Psalm 2:1-3

CLANDESTINE PRODUCTION AND STOCKPILING OF
WEAPONS BEGINS ...WAR GAMES ARE REHEARSED, WITH
EMPHASIS ON NOT REPEATING THE MISTAKES MADE ON THE
DAY OF THE LORD ...THE COMMON USE OF AND ACCESS TO
HYDROGEN PERMIT CREATION OF FORMIDABLE WEAPONS

"Ready in thorough craftiness."
"Thorough readiness in crafty."
"Staunch as ordering hot fiery." †Ezekiel 38:9-16
"Staunchest or hoarding fiery."
"Hoard huge fiery constraints."
"Generous hoard in this crafty."

**THE EYES OF THE LORD SCAN THE EARTH
BEHOLDING THE GOOD AND THE EVIL ...**

"Hero on a farsighted scrutiny." †Proverbs 15:3 II
"Far scrutiny seeing hoard hot." †Chronicles 16:9

**WHEN SUFFICIENT MUNITIONS ARE SECURED, AND TROOPS
STRATEGICALLY PLACED, THE COMMAND IS GIVEN, AND
FORCES MOVE ACROSS THE BREADTH OF THE EARTH,
SURROUNDING THE CAMP OF THE SAINTS**

"Steady! Oh No! Craftier rushing." †Revelation 20:9
"Ahoy! Staunchest firing order."

**RIGHTEOUS WRATH INCINERATES THEM AS THE FIRE OF
GOD DESCENDS FROM HEAVEN WITH BLINDING SPEED**

"Right! Thundery of as scenario." †Ezekiel 38:18-19, 22
"Ugh! Fiery and orchestrations."
"Ugh! Oh Dear! Fiery constraints."
"Shh! Fiery rigour to Ascendant." †Revelation 20:9

**THEIR WEAPONS FAR SURPASSED 21ST CENTURY
TECHNOLOGY, BUT THEY FORGOT THE FACT THAT GOD
HIMSELF IS A CONSUMING FIRE ...THEY ARE EASILY DEFEATED**

"Ha ha! Discount stronger fiery." †Deuteronomy 4:24
"Constrained as through Fiery." †Hebrews 12:29
"Tough fire hydrant scenarios."
"Gosh! Fiery dasher truncation."

**THE LAKE WHICH BURNS WITH UNQUENCHABLE FIRE AND
BRIMSTONE CHURNS AND SEETHES WITH ANTICIPATION**

"Ho Ho! Tidy arresting furnaces..."
"Steady! Ho Ho! Stirring furnace!"

**HANDS IMPERVIOUS TO THE HEAT OF THE INFERNO CAST THE
DRAGON – THAT LIAR, DECEIVER, MURDERER, ACCUSER, AND
SLANDERER – SATAN – STRAIGHT IN!**

"Tougher, fiery, cast-iron hands..."
"Tougher iron hands cast fiery..."
"Handing fiery that sorcerous!" †Revelation 20:10
"Fiery constrain tough dasher."

THE FLAME IS OF A NATURE UNKNOWN ON EARTH;
INFLICTING EXCRUCIATING AGONY ON HIS FORM ...
HE BURNS, YET REMAINS INTACT FOR TORMENT

"Oh No! Fair, huge, star stridency!"
"Ugh! H-O-T reason fair stridency."

HE JOINS THE BEAST AND FALSE PROPHET WHO HAVE
ALREADY BEEN IN TORMENT FOR THE PAST THOUSAND
YEARS ...PERDITION IS HARDLY THE PARTY DEPICTED
IN SONGS AND POPULAR CULTURE

"Hating shared fiery contours."
"Or reach unsatisfying red-hot."
"Or unsatisfying reach red-hot."   †Revelation 20:10

GOD IS SANCTIFIED AND MAGNIFIED IN THE SIGHT OF
MANY NATIONS ...SIGNALING THE LAST RECORDED
INCIDENT OF INSURRECTION IN THE SCRIPTURES

"Righteous Ascendant horrify."   †Ezekiel 38:20, 23
"Fiery courage hand isn't short."   ┼Numbers 11:23
"Tidy far-reaching, so Hero stun."   †Ezekiel 39:21
"Farsighted stun. Nicer hooray."   †Isaiah 59:1

ONCE AGAIN, THE REMNANT PRINCIPLE IS AT WORK
...THESE WILL GO ON TO INHERIT THE NEW EARTH

"Fraction honest, hardier guys."   †Matthew 7:21

RELEVANT LONGEST WORDS/PHRASES USING SOME OF THE LETTERS

"transfigurations" "free association" "higher education" "reconfiguration"
"reconsideration" "string orchestra" "third-generation" "transfiguration"
"treasure-finding" "reinterrogation" "reintroductions" "reorganisations"
"configurations" "considerations" "function-theory" "ordinary shares"
"right ascension" "terra incognita" "heart-searching" "indoctrinators"

The wolf and the lamb shall feed together, and the lion shall eat straw
like the bullock: and dust shall be the serpent's meat. They shall not
hurt nor destroy in all my holy mountain, saith the LORD...Isaiah 65:25

But you shall be named the Priests of the LORD: men shall call you the
Ministers of our God: you shall eat the riches of the Gentiles, and in
their glory shall you boast yourselves... Isaiah 61:6

LAST JUDGMENT DAY

"Sadly at Judgment." †Matthew 8:12
"Dad get man justly." †Genesis 18:25
"Justly tag damned." †Matthew 13:41
"Dad: Man get justly." †Revelation 9:20
"My gladden at just." †Psalm 58:10

IT IS APPOINTED ONCE FOR MAN TO DIE...

There is one appointment all will keep: and that is a judicial hearing before a just and holy God. To the ecclesia, this is an occasion to look forward to. They are the spirits of just men made perfect, and God is able to present them to Himself faultless with exceeding joy. But even with this blessed assurance, it is through much tribulation that they enter the Kingdom of God. Those whose names are written in the Book of Life by virtue of repentance and spiritual rebirth through the New Covenant sacrifice of Jesus Christ have entered in at the Strait Gate, but they still have a strict mandate to travel the Narrow Path. If that be the case, is it any wonder the Apostle Peter queries in I Peter 4:18, "...if the righteous scarcely be saved, where shall the ungodly and the sinner appear?" The answer echoes through the word of the Lord found in Hebrews 10:31 "... It is a fearful thing to fall into the hands of the living God." It is terrifying to fall into His hands, rather than be led gently by them, because "...our God is a consuming fire."

TRIAL (NOT JUDGMENT) BY FIRE

The appearance of the New Testament believer before the Consuming Fire entails an accounting of the deeds done in the body, the words spoken, thoughts, motives, and very importantly – how they built on the Foundation which is Jesus Christ. A true New Testament believer is judging their own actions on a daily basis, repenting when necessary, and striving to give Jesus Christ the preeminence in their life. If one is diligent in this protocol, the personal accounting need not be a cause for concern.

The focus then shifts to how the Foundation was built upon. Speaking to the New Testament believers in I Corinthians 3:11-15, the Apostle Paul lists six types of material that can be used to build upon the Foundation of Jesus Christ, each consecutively decreasing in value. Gold, silver, and precious stones easily survive the fire, and the work abides. Wood is somewhat sturdy; but cannot survive trial by fire. Hay is much weaker than wood; it could nourish a pack animal; but is not something one would bring to present before a great and mighty King. Stubble (straw) has not much use except as stuffing or insulation. Works comparable to the last three materials will be burnt up in the testing of fire, but the individual himself will be saved.

LAY UP FOR YOURSELVES TREASURE IN HEAVEN

The author is convinced that the works which survive testing by fire have direct bearing on one's position in the eternal Kingdom of God, for he that is faithful over a few things is destined to be lord over many. This is the prize of the high calling in Christ Jesus which all New Testament believers should be striving for. Since many are called, but few are chosen, it is obvious that there will be many willing to acknowledge their need for a Savior and repent of their sins; but unwilling to follow hard after the Lord and unreservedly yield their all to Him. These may – as David alluded to in Psalm 84:10 – be relegated to lower level service positions, such as doorkeepers – still extremely blessed to be part of the Kingdom, but as not having achieved nearly what they could.

SINNERS IN THE HANDS OF AN ANGRY GOD

If all must come face to face with the Consuming Fire, what will the ungodly and sinners do? What will those, who have lived their earthly days in hatred toward God and those created in His image and likeness - do when account must be given for their actions? How will they explain the covetousness and greed which drove them to maim and murder? How will they justify the hard speeches spoken against the Lord and His Christ? What explanation will they have for attempting to silence and eradicate those who pledged to serve this One they now stand before?

And will all be judged with equal severity? While all sin is comprised of disobedience, rebellion, or moral failure (falling short of the perfect mark) based on Jesus' teachings in Luke 10:12-15, it does appear there are differing degrees of judgment, although how this manifests is not clear, as God's ways and thoughts are much higher than ours.

One thing is certain in this next topic: the Last Judgment appears to be most devastating for the haters of God, who manifested their virulent hatred of Him by inflicting pain on and destroying others created in His image and likeness. It appears that even after being raised for judgment at the close of the Millennium, sinful man will attempt to plead 'not guilty' and justify his actions when the charges are read against him. A marked hatred for the resurrected saints will still be manifest, for in the direction the tree falls, so it lies (Ecclesiastes 11:3) and, He that is unjust, let him be unjust still: and he which is filthy, let him be filthy still ...(Revelation 22:11.) Since every word is to be established in the mouth of two or three witnesses (Deuteronomy 17:6, II Corinthians 13:1) testimony will be presented both from the Everlasting Word, and from the saints. In the case of uncooperative defendants, their very thoughts will be manifested for all to see.

A PREVIEW OF THE HEAVENLY COURTROOM

The prophet Daniel paints a fascinating picture of the Judgment Day presiding judge and His courtroom ...He is robed in white, not black; His throne is fire, and mobile; fire proceeds forth from Him, and the room is packed for as far as the eye can see ... "I beheld till the thrones were cast down, and the Ancient of days did sit, whose garment was white as snow, and the hair of his head like the pure wool: his throne was like the fiery flame, and his wheels as burning fire. A fiery stream issued and came forth from before him: thousand thousands ministered unto him, and ten thousand times ten thousand stood before him: the judgment was set, and the books were opened."

Against this backdrop, imagine yourself present in the celestial courtroom. The *jet* is the fiery stream which issues forth from God. *Grand Gem* and *Truth Height Gem* indicate the Lord God, *gem* represents the saints. *Jeer* points to the derisory and mocking attitude those who have remained filthy possess. *Jutting* describes those who chose an unrepentant lifestyle of trespassing beyond acceptable limits in their dealings with their fellow man. *Jew* is the heavenly race composed of the spirits of just men made perfect out of every race, tribe and tongue on the earth (the spiritual seed of Abraham); it also represents the genealogical seed of Abraham, the descendants of Hebrews scattered around the world in the centuries since the dispersion. *Theta* is associated with death, and *argent* describes the shining white of the saint's garments. *Hat* depicts a crown, and the fiery *tetrahedron* appears to be a type of defendant restraint.

THE GREAT WHITE THRONE JUDGMENT

IT IS THE END OF THE THOUSAND YEARS OF PEACE UNDER THE LORD JESUS CHRIST ...THE OLD AND NEW TESTAMENT SAINTS, BELOVED OF GOD, MINISTER BEFORE THE ANCIENT OF DAYS AS HE PREPARES FOR FINAL JUDGMENT

"Hint: term age. Jew. Tender thought."

GOD HAS BEEN PATIENT AND MERCIFUL; NOW JUDGMENT TAKES PRECEDENCE

"Worn the edge thin. Mega jet Truth."
"The mega jet Truth wrote end nigh."   †Revelation 11:18

THE ANGELS WENT FORTH AT THE END OF THE AGE TO GATHER THE ELECT FROM THE EARTH; ANY NOT IN THAT NUMBER WILL STAND BEFORE THE WHITE THRONE

"Judgment. Went hither to gather."   †Mark 13:27
"Note judgment there with gather."   †Matthew 13:39
"Tag. Then the worthier judgment."
"Note right where that judgement."
"What ho! Met thundering. Greet jet."

THE REDEEMED OF THE AGES GLORY IN THE PRESENCE OF THE LORD ...THE FIERY STREAM ISSUING FROM HIM BODES NO HARM FOR HIS CHOSEN MINISTERS

"Jet not mug the new, right-hearted." †Daniel 7:10

THOSE BORN INTO CHRIST ARE THE SPIRITUAL SEED OF ABRAHAM ...THEY ARE THE CHILDREN OF THE LIVING GOD AND HE IS THEIR FATHER ...AND THE GENEAOLOGICAL SEED OF ABRAHAM HAVE BEEN GATHERED FROM THE FOUR WINDS AND GOD'S LAWS WRITTEN ON THEIR HEARTS... TOGETHER THESE TWO COMPRISE THE COMMONWEALTH OF ISRAEL AND THE FAMILY OF GOD

"Hint: Rate gem Jew; tender thought."   †Hosea 11:12
"Rating me the Jew; tender thought."   †Hebrews 8:10
"Treat me – Jew - nigh. Tender thought."
"Re: team thing. Jew, tender thought."   †Jeremiah 31:3

**THEY HAVE WASHED THEIR ROBES IN THE BLOOD OF
THE LAMB...GOD HAS FORGIVEN ALL THEIR SINS**

"Ah, Gent remit Jew. Tender thought." †Hebrews 10:16
†I John 1:7

HE HAS TRANSLATED THEM INTO HIS KINGDOM OF LIGHT

"Thought the emigrant Jew tender." †Ephesians 2:12-13
†Colossians 1:13

**HE HAS COMPLETED THE GOOD WORK BEGUN IN THEM ...
WORKS PURPOSED FOR THEM FROM ETERNITY PAST**

"He thought tender; grant Jew time."
"Jew in heart. End thought get term." †Philippians 1:6
"Them Jew, great in tender thought."

**THESE SET APART ONES HAVE BEEN THE OBJECTS OF
HATRED AND PERSECUTION IN THE WORLD – WHICH
HAS KNOWN NEITHER JESUS CHRIST, OR THE FATHER**

"It anger them thought Jew tender." †I John 3:13

**MANY HAVE SUFFERED MARTYRDOM, BUT THE WORD OF
GOD, WHICH IS SHARPER THAN ANY TWO-EDGE SWORD,
HAS SPOKEN LIFE AND RESURRECTED THEIR MORTAL BODIES**

"Men rig theta. Truth jot hewn edge."

**THE LORD HAS SEEN THE WRATH OF MAN AGAINST HIS
CHOSEN CHILDREN – AND DECLARING THAT TIME SHOULD
BE NO MORE, HAS TAKEN THEM TO HIMSELF**

"Thought tender Jew gem in threat." †Revelation 6:9
"Met Jew. Gather in. Tender thought." †Hebrews 11:36

**HE HAS GRANTED THEM CLEAN WHITE LINEN ROBES,
WHICH ARE THEIR RIGHTEOUSNESS IN HIS SIGHT
... ROYAL GARMENTS TO WEAR AS THEY REIGN**

"I garment the Jew. Tender thought." †Revelation 19:8
"I argent them. Jew. Tender thought." †Malachi 3:17
"He, Truth Jet gowned. Them reign at." †Revelation 3:4

**THEY CAN NOW LAUGH AT DEATH...THE SCRIPTURE HAS
BEEN FULFILLED WHICH ASKS, "WHERE IS THY STING?"**

"Me grin theta. Truth jot hewn edge." † I Corinthians 15:55

**AS JOHN WAS SHOWN IN HIS REVELATION OF THE
GLORY OF JESUS CHRIST, THEY WILL WEAR CROWNS
OF LIFE, JOY, AND RIGHTEOUSNESS**

"John de truth. We get that regimen."   †II Timothy 4:8
"John get de truth. We hat regiment."
"Right judgement to the new heart."   †James 1:12

**THEY STAND NOW TO MINISTER BEFORE HIM AS
EACH DEFENDANT IS CALLED …TIME IS NOT
EXPERIENCED AS IT IS IN THE EARTH REALM**

"The new – adoring the Truth-jet Gem. †Daniel 7:10

**WHEN THE JUDGMENT IS COMPLETE, THEY WILL
CONTINUE TO RULE AND REIGN ON THE NEW EARTH**

"Right judgement to the new earth."   †Revelation 20:4

THE ANCIENT OF DAYS IS SEATED

"The true, white-hot Grand Gem jet." †Daniel 7:9
"The True and Right Gem. Now jet."   †Daniel 7:10
"White hot, Grand Gem 'n' the true jet."
"The jet. Renowned age Truth Might."
"He – Truth-Might – now generated jet."

**GUILTY DEFENDANTS FACE A WRATHFUL GODHEAD IN
THE TRIUNE PERSON OF THE FATHER, THE LORD JESUS
CHRIST AND THE HOLY GHOST**

"Unhinged wrath, jet met together."
"Together tend huge warmth in jet."
"The Judge. Entering to the warmth."
"Three grant white-hot judgement."   †I John 5:7
"Renowned Three taught jet might."
"Now earth, the tighter judgement."
"Then huge modern water-tight jet."
"Nightmare jet wedge on the Truth."   †Hebrews 10:27
"Truth. Now the emerging death jet."

**THOSE WHO COMMITTED HORRIFIC CRIMES IN THE EARTH REALM
AND THOUGHT THERE WOULD BE NO CONSEQUENCES NOW FACE
BOTH THE CHARGES AND THE DEFENDER OF ALL WHO ARE OPPRESSED**

"The enduring wrath to the Gem jet."
"Hitherto target when judgement."
"Truth when the Gem joined target."
"Oh Dear Me! Jet when getting truth."
"Hating truth? Now the jet emerged."
"Ho! Wanted the truth? Jet emerging."
"Then, the Iron-jawed Gem get truth."   †II Corinthians 5:10
"There! Grant white-hot judgement."

**THE DEFENDANTS ARE IRRESISTABLY COMPELLED
BY THE FIERY STREAM AS THEY ARE SUMMONED**

"Greeted thou man-thing. Threw jet."
"Tethered thou man-thing. Jet grew."   †Revelation 20:12

**THERE IS NO ESCAPE FROM THE JUDGMENT
THEATER …THE COURTROOM AND DEFENDANT
RESTRAINT ARE LIKE NONE ON EARTH**

"Right! New, hot judgement theatre."
"The entering jam hot truth wedge."
"The Truth now degree tighten jam."
"Nightmare jet now edge the truth."
"Jet adhere. Now Truth Gem tighten."
"Nightmare jet wedge on the truth."
"New tetrahedron jet hug-me-tight."
"Red hug-me-tight. Jet now threaten."
"Generated the jet. Might hurt now."
"Oh! Water-tight, nether judgement."
"The hot treatment where judging."

**THE SENSE OF IMPENDING DOOM IS FELT
LONG BEFORE THE CHARGES ARE EVEN READ**

"Together. Wrath in the judgement."
"Then huge modern water-tight jet."
"Toughened wrath-might enter jet."
"Jet together thud new nightmare."
"Tend together jet in huge warmth."
"Huge jet tormented, threw hating."
"Thought that jet emerged winner."
"Grr! The neat, white-hot judgement."
"Judgment, than white-hot regret."   †Hebrews 12:16-17
"The true jam when getting red-hot."

THE SAINTS OF GOD ARE PRESENT IN THEIR
CAPACITY AS KINGS, PRIESTS, AND WITNESSES

"Gem note whether jutting hatred."
"The greater method when jutting."
"And The Gem throwing the true jet."
"Threw the thundering, mega jet to."
"'N' rather get white-hot judgement."

THOSE WHO LAUGHED AND JOKED UPON THE EARTH
ABOUT ENJOYING THE FLAMES AND REVELED IN MUSIC
GLORIFYING REBELLION AGAINST GOD ARE NOW HARD
PRESSED TO CONTINUE THE BRAVADO

"Thug that now entered might jeer."
"The thug jeering down the matter."   †Proverbs 14:9
"Might not jeer, went the daughter."
"Right! The thug wanted on mere jet."
"Wanted huge jet torment? Eh! Right!"

THEIR PRIDE AND HATRED OF GOD AND HIS KINGDOM
RESIDENTS INCITE THEM TO REVILE AND JUSTIFY
THEIR CRIMES, BUT THE FIERY STREAM KEEPS ORDER

"Thug regretted in the new hot jam."
"What? The thug jeered? Tormenting!"
"Thug grim when threatened to jet."
"Ho-hum! Regretted wanting the jet." †Proverbs 1:25-27
"Main thought regretted when jet."
"Rotten thug might jeer new death."
"Jeered not when mega truth tight."
"Need tougher warmth? Jet tighten."

THE MATTER IS BROUGHT UP OF THE HATRED OF THE
PEOPLE OF GOD THROUGHOUT THE CENTURIES

"White-hot jet. The rugged remnant."
"White-hot jet. The remnant grudge."
"There! The gem hatred jutting now."
"Hated truth gem; jeer. Now, tighten."
"The jet torturing when hated gem."
"Whether mean jutting get red-hot."
"Right! New, hotter hate judgement."
"Tighter judgement when to hater."
"New right judgement to the hater."

THEY HAVE BOLDLY SHED THE BLOOD
OF SAINTS, PROPHETS, AND INNOCENTS

	"Theme when the jutting garroted."	†Revelation 20:4
‡Papal Inquisitions	*"Merge when jutting to the hatred."*	†Matthew 24:9
‡Communist Purges	*"Them, and where jutting together."*	
‡Islamic Persecution	*"The hater; now tighter judgement."*	†Hebrews 11:36-37
	"Ahem! Jutting regretted when hot."	†Matthew 23:35

THE QUESTION IS RAISED ABOUT THE ANTEDILUVIAN
WORLD: THE REPLY IS THAT GOD JUDGED IT RIGHTEOUSLY

"The right judgement on the water."

"Right wet judgement on the hater."

THIS TIME, JUDGMENT IS BY FIRE

"The judgement on her water-tight." †Genesis 6:11-13

"Water-tight, then judgement hero." †Genesis 6:17

"Judge threaten new, hotter might."

"Now earth, the tighter judgement." †Isaiah 24:5-6

HIGH ON THE JUDGMENT AGENDA ARE THUGS;
PARTICULARLY THOSE WHO RAMPAGEDTHROUGHOUT
EARTH WREAKING HAVOC AND LEAVING DEATH
AND MISERY IN THEIR WAKE

"Thug jeered. Might threaten town."

"Thug threatening. Deem worth jet." †Habakkuk 2:12

"Jet me whether gun-toting hatred." †Psalm 55:23

"Jet tormented where thug hating."

RICHES PROFIT NOT IN THE DAY OF WRATH ...
THEIR PILLAGING AND LOOTING NOW
TESTIFY AGAINST THEM

"Jet tormented thug whether gain." †Jeremiah 22:13

"Now the thug regretted in the jam." †James 5:3

MANY TYPES OF EXCUSES ARE PLEADED BEFORE GOD
...SUCH AS MISTAKEN IDENTITY

"Jet threatened; I'm the wrong thug!"

PLEAS OF REFORMATION

"Jet not right-hearted, new me thug."

REFERRALS TO ROYALTY OR MILITARY RANK

"The renowned thug? Right! Jet tame."

**INSISTENCE ON NOT BEING AS WICKED AS OTHERS
WHO ARE PRESENT, OR YOUNG AGE**

"Jet the wrong! I am the tender thug."

PITY FOR THOSE OF ADVANCED AGE

"Eh! Torment whether aged jutting."
"Torment in jet whether thug aged."

**MANY ATTEMPT TO DENY THE IRREFUTABLE CHARGES,
OR PROTEST THAT THEIR SENTENCE IS TOO HARSH**

"Eh, jet grim! Now negated the truth."
"Nowhere that tighter judgement."
"Together that judgement whiner."

**FACED WITH A JUDGE WHO CANNOT BE TRICKED, FOOLED,
PERSUADED, OR BRIBED, THE TRUE NATURE OF THE
THUGS IS REVEALED –IN THREATS AND VIRULENT HATRED**

"I'm the grown!! Thug threatened jet."
"Me thug now threatened jet. Right!"
"Downright huge jet met threaten."
"Where the grand hot meet jutting."
"Thug demeaning. Threw hotter jet."
"Jet width or the thug enragement."
"Nightmare. Jet now tethered thug."
"Thug! Am the Renowned Jet. Tighter!"
"Thug. New mean tighter red-hot jet."

**THE JUDGMENT FOR THUGS IS HORRIFC AND SEVERE
REGARDLESS OF WHETHER THEY ARE STATE SANCTIONED ...**

"Jet rate the renowned thug might."
"Jet tear the renowned thug might."   ‡Mercenaries

OR GANG BANGERS

"Judgement whether rat in ghetto." ‡Gangs
"Jam, tethered whether gun-toting."

MURMURERS ARE CHECKED IMMEDIATELY

"Hot Jet when muttering gathered." †Jude 1:16
"God! The muttering when that jeer."
"Hot jet when the raging muttered."
"Jet when had together muttering."

CELESTIAL REBELS AND FILTHY DEMONIC ENTITIES JUDGED

"Then thug demon jeer water-tight."
"Now Truth Might jet the renegade." †Jude 1:6
"Rated whether the jutting gnome."

**REVILERS, MOCKERS AND SPEAKERS OF HARSH
SPEECHES AGAINST GOD ARE JUDGED**

"Now Might hated the turgent jeer."

THESE MOCKERS FIND THEMSELVES OUT-MOCKED

"Truth Height Gem not wanted jeer."
"Might not jeer Truth when at edge."
"Now, the turgent death might jeer."

WICKED MEN WHO SUPPRESSED THE TRUTH ARE JUDGED

"Jet them who degenerating truth." †Romans 1:18
"When demote Truth, gathering jet."
"Hinder truth? Now get the mega jet."
"Heed! Getting the new major truth." †Matthew 23:13
"The new merit on the jagged truth."

**JUDGMENT FOR THOSE WHO DELIBERATELY CAUSED
MISCARRIAGE OF JUSTICE**

"Judgement note thwarter height." †Isaiah 29:21
"Heighten judgement to thwarter." †Exodus 23:2
"Ugh! God jet the eminent thwarter."

JUDGMENT FOR THOSE WHO HAVE MOCKED GOD, REVILED HIS SON, AND BLASPHEMED HIS SPIRIT

"Threw judgement to Three-hating..." †Romans 1:30

JUDGMENT FOR SEXUAL IMMORALITY AND DISHONORABLE RELATIONSHIPS WHICH EXALT THEMSELVES AGAINST THE KNOWLEDGE OF GOD

"Tight judgement threaten whore."　†I Corinthians 6:9
"Judge whether the rotten mating."　†I Timothy 1:10

JUDGMENT FOR RAPISTS AND ABUSERS OF WOMEN

"Thug threatened women? Right! Jet!"
"Where that, the Judge tormenting."
"Right! We threaten hot judgement."

JUDGMENT FOR THOSE WHO MURDERED FOR SPORT OR HIRE

"Them the gun-toting jeered wrath."
"Tough hit man regretted when jet." †I Timothy 1:9
"Jet tormenting where death thug."

JUDGMENT FOR THOSE DESIGNING GENOCIDAL BIOLOGICAL AGENTS

"The new hate germ jutting. Red-hot!" †Romans 1:30

JUDGMENT FOR THOSE WHO CONSPIRED TO POISON OR SLAY OTHERS

"Jet rewarding thought-teeth men."

JUDGMENT FOR CRUEL RACIST ACTS

"Judgement whether rotting hate."
"Jet truth 'n' weighted hatemonger." †Romans 1:30
"Hatemongering. Jet wed the truth." †I John 3:15

JUDGMENT FOR PEOPLE WHO OUTRIGHT REFUSED TO REPENT

"Heathen whom regretted jutting." †Proverbs 29:1
"Mad jutting when there together." †Jeremiah 17:23

JUDGMENT FOR THOSE ALTERED AS
CYBORGS IN HOPE OF CHEATING DEATH

"Jet theme: The giant undergrowth." †Daniel 2:43
"Meet the jet hating undergrowth."
"Then huge jet terminated growth."
"Judgement hotter whether giant."
"Ugh! Jet tormented whether giant."

ALTHOUGH MANY BEING JUDGED VEHEMENTLY DENY
THE CHARGES AGAINST THEM, THE FIERY STREAM
WHICH ISSUES FORTH FROM THE THRONE CAUSES
THEIR THOUGHTS TO BE LITERALLY SPELLED OUT –
IN FRONT OF EVERYONE

"New hatred thought jet regiment."
"Now the hated truth jet emerging."
"I'm the jet and new thought regret."
"The truth emerging. Now hated jet." †Hebrews 4:12

"Generate jet - mind threw thought."
"Jet drew me threatening thought."
"Jet. Thought emerge handwritten!" †Mark 4:22

"Thought rated when jet regiment." †I Corinthians 4:5
"N' meet the thought-rewarding jet."
"Eh! Gem jet and thought rewritten."
"Eminent Jet wrath. Greed thought."
"When jet, regretted main thought."

REFUSING TO ANSWER TO THE CHARGES DOES
NOT PREVENT THE THOUGHTS FROM BEING
EXPOSED FOR ALL TO SEE

"Renowned thug jam teeth tighter."
"Jam. Regretted in the new thought."
"Jet there met wandering thought." †II Corinthians 10:5
"Jet red with thought enragement."
"Emergent hatred thought win jet."

EVEN IN JUDGMENT, THE HATRED OF THE
REBELLIOUS IS MANIFEST

"Eminent Jet thought hatred grew."

SO, MAN IS JUDGED ACCORDINGLY

"Jet then meet. Rewarding thought."

**SOPHISTRY, ARTICULATENESS, AND IMPASSIONED
ARGUMENTS WILL HAVE NO WEIGHT AT SENTENCING**

"The huge jaw not Might deterrent."

PROPER JUDGMENT IS METED OUT FOR THE OFFENSES

"Judge heart, then weight torment."   †Galatians 6:7
"Judge tighter torment when hate."

DIFFERING DEGREES OF JUDGMENT

"Threaten worth judgement eight."
"The raw, eighth, rotten judgement."
"Tenth, hot, rare judgement weight."
"What-ho! Enter tighter judgement."
"Tighter where on that judgement."

"Rat worth eighteenth judgement."
"Judge torment eighteenth wrath."
"Whinge, threat hotter judgement."
"Rat whinge the hotter judgement."

"Major thug greed. Then, twentieth."
"Together, hint the raw judgement."

**JUDGMENT FOR THOSE WHO TOOK THE MARK OF
THE BEAST IN THEIR RIGHT HAND OR FOREHEAD,
OR HIS NAME/NUMBER, OR WORSHIPPED HIS IMAGE**

"John urgent. Them get hatred wite." †Revelation 14:11

EVERY THOUGHT AND DEED IS TRIED BY FIRE

"Tonight jet entered huge warmth."
"Now the tighter heart judgement."
"Herewith. Grant to the judgement."
"Oh Dear Me! Tight when jet turgent."

THE JOKES TOLD DURING THE EARTHLY LIFE
ABOUT THIS DAY ARE NOW HOLLOW AND MOCKING

"Growth in the judgement theatre."
"Eh! Not the water judgement, right?"
"Right! Not the whate'er judgement."
"Whetting the rare, hot judgement?"
"Right! Hotter heat, new judgement."
"Me – the white-hot, grand, urgent jet."
"Judgement with the hotter range."
"Eh! Jet downright huge treatment."

THE FIERY STREAM FORCES THE GUILTY TO ADMIT
TO THE CHARGES WHICH ARE SUPPORTED BY
DAMNING EVIDENCE AND OBVIOUS TO ALL OTHERS

"Eh! Jet-might now generated truth."   †Job 20:27
"Nightmare jet now edge the truth."
"What ho! Jet emerge tending truth."
"I'm Truth engaged when jet hotter."
"Right! Hotter when augmented jet."

"Truth Gem now gathered in the jet."
"Gather, rent. White-hot judgement."
"Water-tight judgement 'n' hot here."
"Warm hot jet greeting the hunted."
"The warm jet. Tending the tougher."
"Jet together intend huge warmth."

"Than the worthier get judgement."
"Anew hotter the right judgement."
"Threw hotter, heating judgement."
"Anger with the hotter judgement."
"Tighter when a hotter judgement."
"There jet taught renowned might." †II Thessalonians 1:8-9

REGARDLESS OF THE FORMIDABLE COURTROOM SCENARIO,
THE TRIAL IS NOTHING COMPARED TO THE SENTENCING ...
FOR THE SECOND DEATH AWAITS ALL WHOSE NAMES ARE
NOT FOUND WRITTEN IN THE BOOK OF LIFE

"Jet terminated when get through."
"Get terminated when jet through."   †Revelation 20:15
"Right! Not weather the judgement."

RELEVANT LONGEST WORDS/PHRASES USING SOME OF THE LETTERS

"regeneration" "right-hearted" "unterminated" "hatemongering"
"degenerating" "degeneration" "interrogated" "heartrending"
"regurgitated" "remuneration" "ungerminated" "hang together"
"remunerating" "unintegrated" "unregimented"
"wetting agent" "Winter garden"

And many of them that sleep in the dust of the earth shall awake, some to everlasting life, and some to shame and everlasting contempt...Daniel 12:2

PAYDAY: THE WAGES OF SIN

Perhaps nothing is sadder and more heartrending than the thought of the flame, darkness, torment, and thirst which await the unrepentant and the haters of God. Suffering of this magnitude is made all the worse considering the duration is for eternity – an amount of time no finite mind is able to fathom. While some teach that those not entering the Kingdom will suffer and then be consumed, the Bible actually gives a much different view. Speaking of the punishment of the wicked, the Old Testament prophet Isaiah tells us... "And they shall go forth, and look upon the carcases of the men that have transgressed against me: for their worm shall not die, neither shall their fire be quenched; and they shall be an abhorring unto all flesh." This verse follows a description of the pattern of regular worship which will take place after the New Heavens and New Earth are created, so it is obvious the prophet is looking past the final judgment into the future beyond.

Jesus likewise described this scene of unspeakable agony as a place... "where their worm dieth not, and the fire is not quenched." He speaks of this punishment in direct relation to committing acts which offend. This word offend comes from the Greek word skandalizo from which we get our word scandalize. The implication is enticing someone to sin or go into apostasy. The idea is given of a bent sapling – a trap stick – something someone would trip over and fall. Since it takes time and deliberate planning to set a snare to trap or an obstacle to cause stumbling, the argument that God just arbitrarily sends people to hell is unsustainable. On the contrary, in light of God's patience, willingness to forgive, mercies which renew daily, unwillingness for any to perish, and personal sacrificial investment in sending His only Son to die for the sins of the world, there are many safeguards in place to help mankind steer clear of this horror. New Testament believers are entrusted with the sacred charge of warning the world of impending divine judgment and the coming Kingdom of God. But how much do churches today teach and preach on the fiery inferno known as the second death?

THE LAKE THAT BAKES ...AND HOW TO AVOID IT

In his first letter to the Corinthian church, the Apostle Paul lists ten unrighteous lifestyles which he warns will keep those who practice them out of the Kingdom of God.

Know ye not that the unrighteous shall not inherit the kingdom of God?

Be not deceived: neither fornicators, nor idolaters, nor adulterers, nor effeminate, nor abusers of themselves with mankind, Nor thieves, nor covetous, nor drunkards, nor revilers, nor extortioners, shall inherit the kingdom of God ...I Corinthians 6:9-10.   Speaking to the church at Ephesus, he again   stresses those excluded ..."For this ye know, that no whoremonger, nor unclean person, nor covetous man, who is an idolater, hath any inheritance in the kingdom of Christ and of God."

Let no man deceive you with vain words: for because of these things cometh the wrath of God upon the children of disobedience..." Ephesians 5:5-6.

He expounds further in Galatians 5:19-21..."Now the works of the flesh are manifest, which are these; Adultery, fornication, uncleanness, lasciviousness, idolatry, witchcraft, hatred, variance, emulations, wrath, strife, seditions, heresies, Envyings, murders, drunkenness, revellings, and such like: of the which I tell you before, as I have also told you in time past, that they which do such things shall not inherit the kingdom of God."

In his vision of the time of the Great Tribulation, the Apostle John recorded the following message to the earth's inhabitants, as spoken by an angel... "If any man worship the beast and his image, and receive his mark in his forehead, or in his hand,

The same shall drink of the wine of the wrath of God, which is poured out without mixture into the cup of his indignation; and he shall be tormented with fire and brimstone in the presence of the holy angels, and in the presence of the Lamb:

And the smoke of their torment ascendeth up for ever and ever: and they have no rest day nor night, who worship the beast and his image, and whosoever receiveth the mark of his name." Revelation 14: 9-11

Finally, in the last chapter of Revelation, we see who was not permitted into the Kingdom... "For without are dogs, and sorcerers, and whoremongers, and murderers, and idolaters, and whosoever loveth and maketh a lie ...Revelation 22:15. The verse previous to that one exhorts, "Blessed are they that do his commandments, that they may have right to the tree of life, and may enter in through the gates into the city..." Revelation 22:14. Avoiding the Lake of Fire is as simple as repenting of one's sins and faithfully keeping Jesus' commandments as revealed through the gospels and the exhortations of his disciples, and His commandments are not grievous. It is very important to note that twice Paul warns the churches to not allow anyone to deceive them about these things. This implies that there were false brethren who would practice these lifestyles and attempt to convince others that they could do likewise and still remain in unbroken fellowship with the Father and the Son. On the contrary, Paul says these practices invoke the wrath of God.

Two different phrases were anagrammed for this topic: "The Lake of Fire and Brimstone", and "Lake Burning with Fire and Brimstone." Both yield results which graphically illustrate the agony, misery, and regret experienced by those who consistently rejected every overture of the prompting of God, mocked and reviled Him, lived for the moment in the pleasures of the flesh, murdered, pursued a lifestyle of partying and drunkenness, or prepared occasions for others to stumble. *Termites* alludes to the agonizing boring and chewing of worms which cannot be killed. *Ark of halites* refers to the safe shelter which the salt of the earth (the saints) have found in Jesus. *Harlot* is the apostate church that will not preach the reality of this fiery horror for fear of losing their congregation and offending potential members. *Halo* refers to righteousness, *troika* means three, and *freethinkers* shun submission to the authority of God. *Kilo* is short for kiloton.

THE LAKE OF FIRE AND BRIMSTONE

IT'S NOT WHAT THE SONGS AND COMEDIANS HAVE DEPICTED

"Fool remark handiest benefit."   ‡Death Metal
"Hero-like rant of mad benefits."   song lyrics

BUT THEY DO NOT EXALT THE BENEFIT OF RIGHT STANDING WITH GOD

"If halo, not remarked benefits."

**OF COURSE, MANY WILL NOT BELIEVE THE TRUTH OF THE BIBLE
UNTIL THEY ARE ACTUALLY ON THE BRINK OF ETERNITY**

"Ahem! Benefiter?? Stinkard fool."   †II Timothy 3:3
"Shrieked of alarm, not benefit."
"Dreamier benefit? Thanks, fool!"
"Flash: not OK dreamier benefit."
"Trash on benefit of dreamlike."

THE REALITY WILL BE WORSE THAN THE WARNING

"Oh Man! Freak rotten disbelief!" †Luke 16:24
"Threaten of kind of miserable."

THE WAGES OF SIN IS DEATH ...DEATH PAYS QUITE A COMPREHENSIVE BENEFITS PACKAGE, TOO ...HATRED, IMMORALITY, IDOLATRY, AND LOVE OF DEATH QUALIFY ONE FOR THESE BENEFITS

"O! Benefits for man-like hatred."
"Or, man like benefits of hatred."
"Re formal benefit to skinhead."   †I John 3:15
"Hedonist freak moral benefit."
"Benefits there of amoral kind."
"Fine harlot? Some dark benefit."
"Benefiter on a darksome filth."   †Hebrews 13:4
"Dark finer, loathsome benefit."   †Proverbs 16:25
"Loath darksome, finer, benefit."   †Proverbs 5:3-5
"Or man-like hero's daft benefit."
"Benefiter on freak dismal hot."
"Death-mask on or lifer benefit."
"Ire; lorn of death-mask benefit."
"Borne no relief. Death-mask fit."

PRACTICES WHICH BIBLICALLY PLACE ONE IN JEOPARDY OF THE LAKE OF FIRE ...SUCH AS THIEVERY

"Heist. Bro knifed; torn a female."
"Heist. Knifed. Torn. Rob a female." †Psalm 10:3

NOW THE THIEF WILL BE ASSAULTED AND ROBBED

"Sneak thief frail or entombed."   †Exodus 20:13,15

THOSE WHO LIVE FOR PLEASURE

"Remarkable if often hedonist."   †Galatians 6:7

HABITUAL INTOXICATION

"Flake of smothered inebriant."   †Proverbs 20:1
"Sin foam at hot, feeble drinker."
"OK, barflies of eminent hatred."

ALL TYPES OF SEXUAL IMMORALITY ...THEIR DEEDS DISPLAYED AGAIN AND AGAIN FOR ALL TO SEE

"Lo! Stamina of bed freethinker."
"Stamina of bed; therefore kiln."   †I Corinthians 6:18

PRODUCERS AND PURVEYORS OF PORNOGRAPHY

"Before then, 'tis naked; or a film." †Matthew 5:28

SEDUCERS LEAVING BROKEN HOMES IN THEIR WAKE

"Thine sort–a deb-like man, offer."
"Thine sort like a man, offer bed."   †Proverbs 6:25-26
"Erst in hot-like, a man breed off."
"Famed broken a life. Tost her in!"

EFFEMINATENESS

"Effeminate kind, or a brothels."
"Dark or this noble effeminate."   †Jude 1:7
"Effeminate blinders hook rat."
"Fine trembler if Satan hooked."

THE WARNING IS TO FLEE FORNICATION!!

"Shirk bold, ornate effeminate."
                   †Leviticus 18:22

PERPETRATORS OF INCEST

"There is man of inbreed at folk."
"Interbred amok of in self-hate."   †Leviticus 20:17, 19-20
"He interbreed at folk; am of sin."

PEDOPHILES

"Hint: freak bona fide molester."
"To freak: abhors in defilement."   †Mark 9:42
"Knife brain death of molester."

IDOLATRY

"I'm of Satan; forbid kneel there."
"Rebel kind thereof; omits a fan."   †Deuteronomy 5:8-9

ALL LIARS

"Red-hot lake tame fib of sinner." †Proverbs 26:28
"Nitre host doff. Bemire a ankle."
"A bemired; sin rot the ankle off."
"A Nitre host fib ankle freedom."

ABORTIONISTS AND THOSE CHOOSING THEIR TRADE AS A PREFERRED METHOD OF BIRTH CONTROL

"OK abort = feminine self-hatred." †Romans 3:14-16
"Hot defamers broke infantile."
"Fold to feminine heartbreaks."

YOUTH WHO HATE THEIR PARENTS – CAUSING THEIR INCARCERATION OR DEATHS

"Bleakest hatred of fine minor."   †Matthew 10:21

MURDERERS OF PARENTS AND FAMILY MEMBERS

"Beheld retro a man foist knife."   †I Timothy 1:9
"A man foist. Therefor kin bleed."
"Knife bolder there; aim aft son."

... SECRET SOCIETIES WHICH VILIFY THE LORD JESUS CHRIST AT THE HIGHEST LEVELS

"A Mason fit. Be old freethinker." †John 10:1
"Freethinker defamation slob."

THOSE WHO TRAFFIC IN THE SOULS OF MEN VIA MIND-CONTROL TECHNOLOGIES

"Beheld oft is a tinkerer of man."   †Revelation 18:13

THOSE WHO USED THEIR MUSICAL TALENTS TO COMMIT OFFENCE – THE ENTICEMENT FOR OTHERS TO SIN

"Hot refinements of a bard-like."   †Isaiah 23:16
"The In sort. A famed before kiln."

THE LUCIFERIANS WHO HATE THOSE WHO LOVE JESUS CHRIST AND WORK TO FORMULATE POLICES WHICH WILL BE SELECTIVELY ENFORCED AGAINST THE PEOPLE OF GOD

"Feeblish rant of Edomite rank." †Revelation 2:9
"Defer half-broken estimation."
"Snakier. Offendable. Merit hot."

**THOSE WHO INCITED THE DEATH OF OTHERS BY
BEING MOUTHPIECES OF SATAN AND SPEWING
HATRED VIA MEDIA AND PUBLIC VENUES SUFFER
THE VORACIOUS MOUTH OF THE WORM**

"Man-like of fine or best hatred." †Proverbs 10:31
"Bore of finest man-like hatred."

**THOSE WHO HAVE UNDERGONE TRANS-HUMAN
MODIFICATIONS WITH THE STATED GOAL OF CHEATING
DEATH AND BECOMING A SUPERIOR RACE ON THE EARTH**

"Lot befit a freakish drone men."
"A freakish lot men bend to fire." †Daniel 2:41-43

**THOSE WHO LED A DOUBLE LIFE, PRETENDING TO LOVE THE
LORD, WHEN ALL ALONG THEY DESPISED HIM AND HIS GOODNESS**

"Then a mike blare to offend sir." †Matthew 15:8
"Hotter sin! Faked a belief norm."

**BREAKING OF THE GREAT COMMANDMENT TO LOVE THY NEIGHBOR
AS THYSELF ...MAN REWARDS AND HONORS SUCH ACTIONS, BUT THE
HONORS BESTOWED IN HELL ARE OF A MUCH DIFFERENT NATURE ...**

**MERCENARIES AND OTHERS WHO INCINERATED AND MAIMED WITH
IMPUNITY NOW FACE INCINERATION AND MAIMING, BUT THEIR
NEWLY CRAFTED BODIES CONTINUALLY REGENERATE TO EXPERIENCE
THE AGONY FRESH EACH TIME ...THEY ARE FORBIDDEN TO KNEEL
AND BEG FOR MERCY, EVEN AS THEY MOCKED THOSE WHO
FORMERLY COWERED IN FEAR BEFORE THEM**

"I the bad men sort like an offer." ‡Mercenaries
"I the sort. Blame inked an offer."
"Reeks beforehand of militant."
"Here, forbad knees of militant."
"Titan of mil sneer. Behead fork."
"Sneer. Fork behead. I faint; molt."
"Aft fork behead, sneer no limit."
"Dark benefit of manliest hero."
"Drat! Benefits of man-like hero." †Jeremiah 48:44

**THOSE WHO WORSHIPPED SATAN IN EXCHANGE
FOR HIS FALSE PROMISE OF RULING WITH HIM
DISCOVER WHAT A LIAR HE IS**

"Rank? Fine falsehood embitter." †Revelation 20:10
"Half-broken or famed entities."
"Merit rank benefit falsehood."
"Fib rated freakish. Molten eon."

**THOSE WHO MADE A NAME FOR THEMSELVES IN TERMS OF
BLOODSHED AND VIOLENCE UPON THE EARTH WITH
NO ACCOUNTABILITY GNASH THEIR TEETH IN REGRET**

"Rethink free bloodstain fame." †Genesis 4:10

**FOR THOSE WHO SPREAD THEIR CRIMES OVER
A WIDE GEOGRAPHICAL AREA AND WERE NEVER
BROUGHT TO JUSTICE, THE AGONY THEIR
VICTIMS EXPERIENCED IS AN ONGOING REALITY**

"Note shirt. A famed biker felon." ‡Violent Biker Gangs
"A demon flake fiber. Eh! Sit, torn."
"A femoral be knifed. Eh! Sit, torn."
"A knife bled femora. Eh! Sit torn."
"No!! A forked hitter be in flames!"
"At finale, embed fork. Is he torn?"
"Informs a fake bleed. Then I rot."

**THOSE WHO CONSIDERED THEMSELVES LOFTY, ELITE,
AND WORTHY OF EXTERMINATING OTHERS VIA POVERTY
AND GENOCIDE RECEIVE THE ULTIMATE REALITY CHECK**

"He rank, so be of inflated merit." †James 2:6
"Harken! Be so inflated of merit?" †Job 21:14-15
"Bask here on inflated of merit!"
"Ashen broke of inflated merit."
"This rank = feeble deformation."
"Hearken! Sob of inflated merit."
"He's broken of a inflated merit." †James 5:3
"Instil brokenhearted of fame."
"Darksome threat if fine noble."

**THOSE WHO MANUFACTURED AND MARKETED
PHARMACEUTICALS WHICH LABORATORY TRIALS
SHOWED HAD DANGEROUS AND FATAL SIDE
EFFECTS WISH FOR DEATH, BUT CANNOT DIE**

"I marketed stiffen honorable." †Exodus 20:13
"Oh no! Re if lab, infest. Marketed."
"Lab: Ooh! Stiffener in. Marketed."
"Market if infested. A hole born."
"Market if infested. Lo, no rehab."

**AFTER ALL, THE LOSS OF HUMAN LIFE WAS CONSIDERED
A NECESSARY COMPONENT IN GENERATING A RETURN
ON THE RESEARCH & DEVELOPMENT AND ADVERTISING**

"Lab: Hereof finis ton. Marketed."
"If lab marketed, inferno ethos."
"Lab marketed? Shoe fit. Inferno."
"Inferno those if lab marketed!"
"Market and foolish benefiter." †I Timothy 6:10

**BLESSED AND HOLY IS HE THAT HATH PART IN THE FIRST
RESURRECTION: ON SUCH THE SECOND DEATH HATH NO
POWER, BUT THEY SHALL BE PRIESTS OF GOD AND OF
CHRIST, AND SHALL REIGN WITH HIM A THOUSAND YEARS**

"Ark of halites modern benefit." †Colossians 1:13
"Mend or benefit. Ark of halites."
"Bet Ark of halites freedom inn." † John 8:36
"Halo benefit of Kinder Master."

**BUT POPULAR CULTURE TEACHES YOUTH THEY WILL
BE BLESSED TO MEET UP WITH THEIR FRIENDS IN HELL:
THERE ALLEGEDLY, THEY WILL PARTY, PARTY, PARTY…**

"Oafish talker: Teen mob finder."
"Oafish talker: Teen friend mob."
"Oafish talker: Mob. Dinner. Fete."

**NOTHING COULD BE FURTHER FROM THE TRUTH THAN
THE NOTION THAT HELL IS A PLAYGROUND
…BETTER TO GET THE TRUTH FROM AN ORACLE OF GOD**

"Oafish talker modern teen fib."
"Aha! Bet demon infer frostlike…"
"Ah! A frostlike, modern benefit???"

"Fake demon fib. Liars enter hot."
"Tho mentor, liar's fake. Be fiend."
"Fib. Need Ark of halites mentor." †Psalm 119:9

**EVERY YOUNG PERSON SHOULD KNOW THEY HAVE TO
SPEND ETERNITY SOMEWHERE; THEIR ONLY SAFEGUARD
AGAINST HELL IS TO HIDE THE WORD OF GOD IN THEIR
HEARTS SO THEY WON'T SIN AGAINST HIM**

"Oft Ark of halites been remind."
"Ark of halites: Oft inner embed." †Psalm 119:11

HELL IS REAL

"Be informed. Oh! A fire net stalk."†Luke 12:5

**ALTHOUGH IT IS ON FIRE, THERE IS DARKNESS AND THE
PLACE IS A VAST EXPANSE ...THEY WILL NOT FIND ANY
OF THEIR FRIENDS AND THERE IS TOO MUCH EXCRUCIATING
AGONY FOR CELEBRATION OF ANY TYPE**

"Fake liars! Hot. No met befriend."

**YOUNG WOMEN WHO MODEL THEMSELVES AFTER THE
ICONS OF POPULAR CULTURE IN AN ATTEMPT TO ALLURE
BY DESIRES OF THE FLESH – MUST BE WARNED...**

"Inform teen deb. Soak hilt fear."   †Isaiah 3:16-24

**YOUTH AND YOUNG ADULTS WHO HAVE BOUGHT INTO THE
POPULAR CULTURE PARADIGM THAT PROMISCUITY IS
DESIRABLE AND TO BE CONSIDERED AS A NORMAL WAY OF
LIFE –SHOULD BE AWARE THEY ARE SINNING AGAINST
THEIR OWN FLESH AND URGENTLY WARNED**

"Inform bed teen. Soak hilt fear."   †I Corinthians 6:18

**MOST CHURCHES TODAY WILL NOT SPEAK ABOUT THE LAKE
OF FIRE FOR FEAR OF DRIVING AWAY THEIR CONGREGATION,
OR DISCOURAGING NEW MEMBERSHIP ...BUT JESUS SAID
WHOEVER WAS ASHAMED OF HIM AND HIS WORDS WOULD
FIND THEMSELVES THE OBJECT OF HIS EMBARRASSMENT
WHEN HE RETURNS IN GLORY WITH THE HOLY ANGELS**

"Harlot is fake – men toned brief."
"Harlot is fake – none imbed fret." †John 12:43
"Harlot is fake – infer not embed."

HOLY GRAMS   PART III   THE FUTURE

212

"Harlot is fake – not briefed men." †John 10:12-13

**HE WHO THE SON SETS FREE IS FREE INDEED, BUT
THOSE DECEIVED BY THE LUKEWARM LAODICEAN
CHURCH WILL FIND THEMSELVES ENSLAVED AGAIN**

"Harlot is fake. It bond freemen."   †Romans 6:1-2
"Solar hit fake. Men bend to fire."   †John 8:34
"Solar hit fake. Fine red entomb."   †Romans 6:23

**TRUE SALT OF THE EARTH NEW TESTAMENT BELIEVERS
WILL NOT HESITATE TO WARN OF JUDGMENT TO COME…
THEY WILL CRY ALOUD, AND SPARE NOT… AND THE
SAVING GOSPEL HAS BEEN PREACHED FOR MANY YEARS**

"Ark of halites briefed men ton."   †II Timothy 4:1-3

**THOSE WHO WALLOWED IN FILTH DURING THEIR LIFE
GET TO CONTINUE THE PRACTICE IN ETERNITY, BUT
THEY CAN'T CHOOSE WHICH KIND OF FILTH**

"I am berserk! One fated on filth." †Revelation 22:11
"Freakier as entombed on filth."
"Freakish if alert on entombed."
"I am berserk! Fated on filth eon."
"Aforementioned filth breaks."

**THE RICH MEN OF THE EARTH WHO CONTROL THE
FOREIGN POLICIES OF NATIONS AND FINANCE WARS
ON BOTH SIDES ARE TORMENTED FOR THE MISERY
AND DEATH THEIR SCHEMES CAUSED**

"So he banker of inflated merit."   †James 5:1

THEY HEAP UP GOLD AND SILVER FOR THE LAST DAYS

"He ores. Bank of inflated merit." †James 5:3

**THEY HAVE NO USE OR HONOR FOR THE LORD JESUS
CHRIST …GOD IS NOT IN ALL THEIR THOUGHTS, AND
THEY DO NOT PRAY TO HIM OR BOW IN WORSHIP**

"Inflated of merit abhor knees."
"Or inflated of merit: Knees?? Bah!" †Job 21:15

**THEY HAVE ACCUMULATED SO MUCH, ALL THEY CAN
THINK TO DO IS TEAR DOWN THEIR BARNS AND BUILD**

BIGGER ONES ...THEY DO NOT WANT TO HELP THE
POOR OF THIS WORLD WHOM THEY DESPISE

"Inflated of merit: Oh! Seek barn."†Luke 12:18

BUT THEY WILL SEE TO IT THAT CRONY
TEAM PLAYERS ARE WELL REWARDED

"So he banker fattened oil firm." †Luke 6:32

THERE IS MUCH TO DO TO MOLD THE WORLD
CLOSER TO THEIR DESIRED PLAN, SUCH AS
MANIPULATING NATIONAL CURRENCIES

"So he banker deflate to infirm."
"So he banker inform it deflate."
"Deflation if he banker term so."   †Proverbs 20:23

WHEN THE CITIZENS OF COUNTRIES COMPLAIN OF
THEIR NATIONAL COFFERS BEING LOOTED, IT
MEANS NOTHING TO THE RICH MEN OF THE WORLD

"So he banker defiant. Lift more."†Exodus 20:15

WITH THEIR UNLIMITED SUPPLY OF FUNDS,
THEY ARE ABLE TO COMPROMISE GOVERNMENTS

"So he banker infiltrated of me."

ONCE THE GOVERNMENT IS INFILTRATED, THE FOREIGN
POLICY CAN BE DIRECTED ...DECISIONS OF HUGE IMPORT
ARE MADE ...NOT BY VOTE OF CONGRESS, BUT PERHAPS
OVER A TOAST BY WEALTHY FINANCIERS ON PRIVATE JETS

"So he banker. Loft men ratified."

AS THE PREPARATIONS FOR WAR BEGIN; THE SAME
FINANCIERS WILL BANKROLL THE PROPAGANDA NEEDED
TO RALLY PUBLIC SUPPORT FOR THE IMPENDING CARNAGE

"Banker shoe tirade. Film often." †Exodus 20:16

SOON, YOUNG PEOPLE BEGIN RECEIVING DRAFT NOTICES

"He banker, so milt draftee info."

NO EXPENSE IS SPARED FOR PROPAGANDA TO DO ITS JOB
AND CONVINCE THESE YOUTH THEY ARE FIGHTING TO
PROTECT THEIR COUNTRY AND FREEDOM ...THEY MUST
NEVER KNOW THEY ARE GOING FORTH AS A PRIVATE
SECURITY DETAIL TO LINE THE COFFERS OF THE BANKERS

"He banker, so mil offer tainted."

WITH FEWER AND FEWER EMPLOYMENT OPTIONS, OFF THEY WILL
GO – UNINFORMED, MISINFORMED, BUT UNIFORMED – IN THE
SERVICE OF THE MULTI-NATIONAL BANKERS...HOWEVER, THE
BANKERS COULD CARE LESS HOW MANY MAKE IT BACK HOME

"He banker, so enfilade. Oft trim."

WHILE MOST INDUSTRIES BEG FOR BAILOUTS,
THE ENGINE OF THE MILITARY-INDUSTRIAL
COMPLEX HUMS ALONG SMOOTHLY, FUELED BY
HUGE CONTRACTS FOR WAR MACHINERY

"He banker, so foment airlifted."
"He banker, so oft airlifted men."

HALFWAY AROUND THE WORLD,
THE BANKERS WILL IS EXECUTED

"He banker, so oft left meridian."
"He banker, so tot flamed in fire."

BUT THERE IS A HIGHER WILL THAT WILL BE DONE...

"He Son, break. Inform title fade."   †Proverbs 11:4

YOUR GOLD AND SILVER IS CANKERED; AND THE RUST
OF THEM SHALL BE A WITNESS AGAINST YOU, AND
SHALL EAT YOUR FLESH AS IT WERE FIRE...YE HAVE
HEAPED TREASURE TOGETHER FOR THE LAST DAYS

"Totaled fine bank firm he ores."

THOU FOOL, THIS NIGHT THY SOUL SHALL BE
REQUIRED OF THEE: THEN WHOSE SHALL THOSE
THINGS BE, WHICH THOU HAST PROVIDED?

"Be shaken or lot infirm. Defeat."
"Hearse knob. Torment if failed."   †Luke 12:20
"A knobs here! Torment if failed."

"Dark noblemen fortifies hate."
"I offer atheist noblemen dark..."
"Fire of atheist dark noblemen."
"OK. Fair if noblemen shattered."
"Dark noblemen fate: Hoist fire!"

**SOME FEEL JUDGMENT FOR DEEDS DONE IN THE BODY IS OF
LITTLE CONSEQUENCE IF THE BODY NO LONGER EXISTS ...
FOR THIS REASON, THEY MAY OPT FOR CREMATION**

**BUT THE REUNITING OF AN INDIVIDUAL'S BODY IS NOTHING
FOR THE GOD WHO CAN COUNT EVERY GRAIN OF SAND ON
THE EARTH AND NUMBER AND CALL THE NAME OF EVERY
CELESTIAL ORB IN THE VAST UNIVERSE**

"I, a boned flesh troika, ferment."   †Thessalonians 5:23

†Genesis 3:19

**BUT JUST AS THE PROPHET EZEKIEL SAW, AT THE LORD'S
COMMAND BODIES REMATERIALIZE – BONE, SINEW, AND
SKIN ...ABJECT FEAR WILL TAKE HOLD UPON THE WICKED
AS THEY REALIZE THE MOMENT OF RECKONING HAS ARRIVED**

"Hast kilo fear. Met Bone Finder."
"Hast kilo fear. Bone Mender fit."   †Ezekiel 37:1-9
"Hast kilo fear. Mend bone; refit."
"Hast kilo fear. Refit boned men."
"Fear soak hilt. Noted men fiber."
"Fear soak hilt. Me tendon fiber."
"Fear soak hilt. Note mend fiber."

**THE DEEDS OF A LIFETIME BEAR WITNESS TO WHY
THEIR NAMES ARE NOT FOUND IN THE BOOK OF LIFE ...
SCREAMS, PLEADING, AND CURSING ARE HEARD AS
THEY ARE CAST ALIVE INTO THE BURNING LAKE**

"A shriek aloft. Bonfire tend me!"
"Talk of ashier...ember intend of."   †Revelation 20:15
"Oh, a fire talks. Infer entombed."

THE ATMOSPHERE OF THE IMMENSE FIERY LAKE

"Brethren! Most fain a dike; floe!"
"Rekindle. Oh, bereft a moist fan!"   †Luke 16:24
"Freakish latrine of entombed."

THE HORRIBLE DESTRUCTION AND REGENERATION
OF THE BODY OF DEATH FOR ETERNAL PUNISHMENT

"Terminator of feeblish naked."
"A bonfire flaked me. Oh! It stern."
"The sin rot. A flake bone firmed."
"I - stern hot- bake; firmed a felon."

THEIR WORM WILL NOT DIE

"Termites bore in half of naked."   †Mark 9:44,46,48

SIGHTS AND SOUNDS OF THE HELLISH ARENA

"A bear-like doff men; tie thorns."
"Sit then. Or a flambeed foe rink."
"A flambe doer insert hot knife."
"No rest. Bore a flamed knife; hit."
"Fat shrieker if notable demon."
"Shriek to an offendable merit."
"I'm offendable streaker in hot."
"Met inferno bed. Afloat. Shriek!!"

THE HOPELESSNESS AND SHAME IS EVERYWHERE

"Bleakest informer of in death."   †Matthew 24:51
"A bleak, smoother indifferent."
"Forth or fiendlike abasement."
"Bad afternoon. I'm the serflike."
"OK offendable. Thirstier amen."
"If abhorrent, defilement soak."

THE FEELINGS OF THOSE DOOMED TO REMAIN

"Liken of abhorrent defeatism."
"Heartbroken if lamented if so."
"A thorn site bide. Men folk fear."
"Kinda feeble from a eon thirst."

THE BOLDEST AND BRAVEST MEN WHO STRODE ACROSS
THE EARTH VANQUISHING WHIMPER LIKE TERRIFIED
BABIES AS THEY ARE TRAPPED IN THE SIDES OF THE PIT

"Lionheart freaks if entombed."   †Isaiah 13:7

THE LAKE OCCUPANTS WANT TO DIE, BUT THEY CAN'T

"Determine as if to half-broken."
"Half-broken, defiant, tiresome."
"Terminates die of half-broken."   †Revelation 20:10
"No fine of terrible death mask."
"O dear! Firm sin fee. Hot blanket."

SUFFERERS WILL RECALL THE TESTIMONY AND MINISTRY OF PARENTS, FAMILY, AND OTHERS, AND THEIR HEARTFELT PLEAS TO TURN FROM SIN TO THE TRUE AND LIVING GOD THROUGH JESUS CHRIST

"Saint of Ma kneeled of rebirth."   †Ecclesiastes 12:1
"Ma sat; info. Led rethink before..."   †Proverbs 1:8

IN THIS UNEARTHLY DIMENSION, WHERE THE LINE BETWEEN REAL-TIME HORROR AND THE FANTASY OF ESCAPE IS BLURRED, CRUEL MOCKERY ALWAYS BRINGS THE CRUSHING WEIGHT OF REALITY BACK

"A fake firemen. One bold thirst."

THE MEEK, WHO HAVE INHERITED THE EARTH, VIEW CARCASSES OF THE TRANSGRESSORS

"Bold fame freakish retention..."
"In front of hardiest, able meek..."   †Isaiah 66:24
"Rethink free of able saintdom."
"A rebel think of saint freedom."

THIS DESTINATION IS NOT RECOMMENDED

"If red-hot sinner, bleak fame to."
"Hot of red. It bake, flame sinner."
"Bake of red-hot metal if sinner."
"Thorniest bleak of fine dream."

RELEVANT LONGEST WORDS/PHRASES USING SOME OF THE LETTERS

"self-determination" "three-dimensional" "half-interested"
"transformation" "aforementioned" "determinations"
"rematerialised" "renationalised" "fraternisation"
"abnormalities" "administrator" "demonstration"
"deterioration"

LAKE BURNING WITH FIRE AND BRIMSTONE

THIS IS A PLACE FOR REBELS

"Infernal break down bright mutinies."
"Nefarious rabblement kind writhing." †Isaiah 57:4
"Untoward shrieking, if in rabblement."

THE LAODICEAN CHURCH MUST BE ZEALOUS AND REPENT

"Inferior lukewarmth stabbing in end." †Revelation 3:16

NAGGING THIRST THAT CANNOT BE QUENCHED

"Innumerable break down if thirsting." †Luke 16:24

**THE HORROR OF THE NEVER-ENDING ROUTINE OF THE
FLESH BEING TORMENTED, TORTURED, AND DESTROYED,
THEN REBUILDING ITSELF ONLY TO BE DESTROYED AGAIN
CREATES A STATE OF INSANE TERROR**

"Filthier, numbing, nastier break down."
"Humbling in niftiest; rare break down."
"Mantra: bio renew. Skin build frighten."

**THE WORM IS DESIGNATED FOR THE
OFFENDER AND DOES NOT DIE**

"Hearken! File it: bandit's burning worm."
"Bandit's afire. Burning. Kneel. Worm hit." †Mark 9:48
"Worm likes thine fear, burning bandit."
"Bandit's ilk fate herein; worm, burning."

**HERE DRUNKARDS SUFFER FOR THEIR SELFISHNESS, WASTED
LIFE, AND PAIN THEIR ACTIONS INFLICTED ON OTHERS**

"Swankier inebriant fumbling. Red-hot."
"Inebriate warm. Thinking of blunders." †I Corinthians 6:10
"Fist lurking behind beer wino mantra."
"Now fat, rumbling inebriant shrieked."

THEY ARE SURROUNDED BY THE HORROR OF DARKNESS

"Darkening, or swift humble inebriant."

"Worst darkening humble if inebriant."
"Dark now frighten sublime inebriant."
"Drink grief inn. This worm unbeatable."
"This worm unbeatable. Infer drinking."

WHAT SEEMED LIKE FREEDOM WAS A DEADLY SNARE

"Dank brew of inebriant lush. Meriting."
"Inebriant lush meriting. Knew bad for."   †I Corinthians 3:17
"Inebriant lush drank of web. Meriting."

**BECAUSE THEY DELIBERATELY DEFILED
THEIR TEMPLE, GOD DESTROYS THEM**

"Is rightful, Eminent break down brain."
"Inebriant 'n' undrinkable. Fights worm."
"Inebriant burned in lake. Fights worm."

**THEY NEVER IMAGINED THIS DREADFUL ANGUISH
WHEN THEY WENT INTO THEIR DRUNKEN
RAGES, TERRORIZING THEIR FAMILY**

"Filth rains down. A imbiber enter gunk."
"Wrathful inebriant broken, demising."

**HE THAT IS FILTHY, LET HIM BE FILTHY STILL...
RAPISTS ARE NOW THE VICTIMS -- FOR ETERNITY**

"Brute brag inner filth – I know maidens."
"I'm known brute; ideas earn, bring filth."
"Demon grab brute. Ask? I win inner filth."   †Revelation 22:11

**A WILD AND TWISTED CELEBRATION OF PAIN AND
TORMENT FOR RAPISTS AND MOLESTERS THAT
INCREASES TO BRUTAL VIOLENCE**

"Womanise-kind brute; bright feral inn."

**HERE, THE MACHO MAN IS MET BY A SAVAGE ENTITY
WITH THE FURY OF AN ENRAGED RELATIVE; BENT ON
DESTROYING HIM AS HE BEATS HIM TO A PULP AND
HURLS HIM INTO FLAMING THORNS**

"Brute gnarl fibre thin; said women kin."
"Then brute fling womanise-kind - briar."

HERE IS THE DESTINATION OF PERSONS WHO FOR
MONEY, OR OUT OF FEAR OR HATEFULNESS REPORTED
THE WHEREABOUTS OF NEW TESTAMENT SAINTS
DURING THE GREAT TRIBULATION ...SUBSEQUENTLY,
THEIR NAME IS BLOTTED OUT OF THE BOOK OF LIFE ...
DEFAULT JUDGMENT IS THE LAKE OF FIRE

"Saint informer. Blank due. Be writhing."
"Rinse ink. Writhing of damnable brute."
"A blab tied. Writhing informer sunken." †Matthew 10:21-22
"A unkindest babel. Informer writhing."

THOSE WHO FOISTED RELIGIOUS OR POLITICAL IDEOLOGIES
UPON POPULATIONS WHICH DEMANDED IDOLATRY
(LOVE FOR THE STATE OR AN IDOL) ARE SURROUNDED
BY WRATH AND HATRED

"Now debunking if aberrant Hitlerism." ‡State-sponsored
"Writhing ailments debunker of brain." religions and
"Writhing debunker of manliest brain." ideologies
"If debunker, now thirsting lamebrain."
"Win debunking of aberrant Hitlerism."
"Roman win burnished kiln gift rebate."

THOSE WHO TORTURED AND MURDERED OTHERS ARE
DISMEMBERED AND RENDERED HELPLESS TO ESCAPE
FROM THEIR TORTURERS

"Thug rear 'n' limbs infinite break down."

THOSE WHO BULLIED OTHERS BY EITHER PERSONAL OR
MILITARY MEANS ARE NOW BULLIED BY WRATHFUL
TORMENTORS AND THE UNDYING WORM ...THEY WILL
WISH IT WAS A DREAM THEY COULD WAKE UP FROM

"Sinful browbeater thinking in dream."
"Sinful browbeater kind in nightmare."
"Browbeater mad in thinking self-ruin."
"Inhuman-kind finger slit browbeater."

THOSE WHO TRAPPED PEOPLE BEFORE KILLING THEM
NOW EXPERIENCE CONFINEMENT WHICH PREVENTS
THEM FROM ESCAPING MAULING FANGS

"Inner tomb. Aware. Wanna biter more."

FAMILIES WHO INBRED TO KEEP THE RICHES OF THE
WORLD IN THE CLUTCHES OF THE RULING CLASSES FIND
THEY HAVE GAINED THE ENTIRE WORLD AT THE EXPENSE
OF THEIR SOUL ...FOR RICHES PROFIT NOT IN THE DAY
OF WRATH, BUT RIGHTEOUSNESS DELIVERS FROM DEATH

"Worm thankful, brainiest inbreeding."

THEY COULD HAVE REACHED OUT TO HELP MULTITUDES ON
THE BRINK OF PERIL AND DEATH; INSTEAD THEY WITHHELD
THE GOOD THEY COULD HAVE DONE ... NOW THEY MUST
BEAR THE CONSEQUENCES OF THE REWARD OF THE
HARDNESS OF THEIR HEART

"Skinflint? Bear-baiter worm unhinged."
"If thirsting, innumerable breakdown."

EUGENICISTS WHO CAMPAIGNED LOUDLY FOR A WOMAN'S
RIGHT TO KILL HER CHILD IN UTERO FACE TORMENTS
THAT MAKE THEM REGRET EVERY WORD SPOKEN AND
EVERY LIFE ABORTED

"Break down rattling feminine hubris."
"Humbling. Diatribes freak not winner."
"Wrinkled of stabbing in harm uterine."
"Know fling hinted uterine barbarism."

THOSE WHO USED THEIR KNOWLEDGE OF THE SCIENCES
TO CREATE EVIL INVENTIONS FOR THE PURPOSE OF
HARMING AND CONTROLLING PEOPLE HAVE ETERNITY
TO PONDER THEIR CHOICES

"I'm the brains knowing refined brutal."   †Revelation 18:13
"I am brightest. Winner of undrinkable."
"I'm the undrinkable if brain wrongest."   ‡Mind control
"Thinking defamers brain win trouble."   Manchurian
"Finest bright brain now undreamlike."   candidates
"Break down in fluent, mightier brains."
"Humbling, rare break down. It isn't fine."
"Is rightful, Eminent break down brain."

THEY EXPANDED THEIR KNOWLEDGE BASE FOR THE
PURPOSE OF MAKING LIFE HELLISH FOR OTHERS; NOW
THEY WILL EXPERIENCE EXCRUCIATING PAIN AS THEIR
SKULL AND BRAIN ARE FORCIBLY SHRUNKEN

"Right! Awful skinnier entombed brain."

THOSE WHO USED LIFE-EXTENSION TECHNOLOGIES
FOR THE PURPOSE OF CHEATING DEATH AND
CONTINUING THEIR MISSION TO DOMINATE THE
WORLD FIND IT WAS ALL FOR NOUGHT

"Shabbier terminating of unwrinkled." †Daniel 2:43

INDIVIDUALS OR AGENCIES WHO KIDNAPPED CHILDREN,
THEN FARMED THEM OUT TO PEDOPHILES, MURDER,
OR ORGAN HARVESTING GET THEIR ETERNAL REWARD
...THEIR NAMES ARE NOT IN THE BOOK OF LIFE ...THEY
WILL BEG, EVEN AS THE PARENTS BEGGED FOR THEIR
CHILDREN AND THEIR VICTIMS PLEADED FOR MERCY

"Grislier death ebb infant. Mourn, wink."
"Knife sin or damnable brute writhing."
"Inking find err. This worm unbeatable."
"Skin on fire. Damnable brute writhing." †Timothy 1:9-10
"A writhing, subnormal benefiter kind."
"Beg. Undrinkable. Wrath Inn mortifies."
"I am undrinkable. Now biter frightens."

THE HEAVENLY EVENT LOG HAS TRACKED ALL ACTIVITY
DESIGNED TO FOMENT RACISM AND HATE ...THESE TWO
PRACTICES DO NOT YIELD THE NINE FRUITS OF THE SPIRIT
BUT RATHER REPRESENT THE CHAFF (HUSKS) WHICH
WILLBE DRIVEN AWAY TO BE CONSUMED BY FIRE...
BARBERING REFERS TO SHAVING OF THE HEAD

"Renowned militant husk if barbering."
"Renowned militant bring fake hubris." †I John 3:15
"Renowned militant hubris grief bank."

BOLSTERED BY LIQUID COURAGE, AN ASSAULT IS CARRIED
OUT ON AN INDIVIDUAL OF DIFFERENT CULTURE AND FAITH

"Keg furbish renowned militant brain." †Proverbs 20:1
"Renowned militant knife rabbi; shrug."
"Renowned militant break; fibrin gush."

A LIE IS QUICKLY CRAFTED TO COVER
THE DEEDS OF THE PERPETRATORS

"Breaking! Renowned militant rush fib." †Exodus 20:16

BECAUSE OF GOD'S MERCY, THE VICTIM SURVIVES
THE ATTACK AND IDENTIFIES HIS ASSAILANT

"Rabbi finger renowned militant husk."
"Rabbi: 'Renowned militant husk fringe'."†Lamentations 3:22

**EVERY THOUGHT, MOTIVE, AND ACTION ASSOCIATED
WITH THE EVENT HAS BEEN CAREFULLY RECORDED
BY UNSEEN EYES, EARS, AND HANDS**

"Brutal skinhead worriment. Be fining."
"Inform brutal skinhead been writing."
"Writing brutal skinhead men bonfire." †II Corinthians 5:10

**HE WILL RECEIVE FIERY INDIGNATION AND WRATH
BECAUSE HE DID NOT LOVE HIS NEIGHBOR AS
HIMSELF AND HATED OTHERS WITHOUT CAUSE ...
BY DEFAULT HE IS A MURDERER**

"Skinhead wrongful embitter in brain."

**NOW A RESIDENT IN THE BURNING LAKE, HE
REGRETS HE HEEDED THE HATEFUL RHETORIC
OF THE ORIGINAL MURDERER, SATAN**

"Brain now debunking filthier master."
"Worm Inn. Bet brutal skinhead in grief."
"Worm: benefit in brutal skinhead ring."
"Worm grin in brutal skinhead benefit."

**THE MAN OF SIN – THE SON OF PERDITION – IS BROUGHT
FORTH BY NEFARIOUS MEANS TO ASSUME LEADERSHIP
OF THE ENTIRE WORLD ...A SHORT-LIVED REIGN WHICH
WILL TERMINATE WHEN HE IS CAST INTO THE FIERY
LAKE AT THE RETURN OF THE LORD JESUS CHRIST**

"I am the weird, infernal, stubborn king." †Revelation 13:5
"Sinful brain birthed worm-eaten king."
"Worm-eaten, sinful king a inbred birth."
"Bad rebirth in worm-eaten, sinful king."
"Hint: worm-eaten, sinful king debar rib." ‡Laboratory created
"A worm-eaten, sinful king bred in birth." humans and cloning
"Worm-eaten, sinful king beard in birth."
"Worm-eaten, sinful king birth bind era."
"Win damnable king; finish be torturer."
"King win damnable; be thrust inferior."
"Damnable king win bonfire, rue, thirst."

ETERNAL TORMENT FOR THOSE WHO TOOK HIS MARK...

"Burnt beg. I see mark in; filth rain down."   †Revelation 14:9-10

AND THE KINGS OF THE EARTH WHO GAVE THEIR POWER TO HIM

"I, Kaiser men burnt. Beg. Filth rain down."
"Sin aim, rain filth down. Burnt, reek, beg."
"Am burnt! Beg 'ere I sink! Filth rain down."   †Revelation 17:12-13

THE WAGES OF SIN IS DEATH ...WAGES ARE PAID
FOR WHAT ONE WORKED FOR

"Mankind labourer writhing benefits."
"Undrinkable benefits or am writhing."
"Brains break down. Trim genuine filth."

THE HORROR OF THE VAST DARK EXPANSE WITH NO END IN
SIGHT COUPLED WITH THE TORMENT OF THE FLAME CREATES
A PSYCHOLOGICAL NIGHTMARE ... AND THE CHARACTERS
OF THE NIGHTMARE ARE REAL

"Inane break down. Fumbling thirstier."
"Now bat-like fright undermines brain."
"Mind-blowing than infuriate berserk."   †Isaiah 24:17
"Win blind. Brains make out frightener."
"Snakebite filth now murdering brain."

THE SAINTS OBSERVE SOLEMNLY ACROSS THE GREAT GULF
AT THE PUNISHED ...THOSE SUFFERING CAN SEE THEM BUT
CANNOT GET TO THEM ...THE SIGHT OF THE DAMNED GROWS
FAINT AS THEY UNDERGO DESTRUCTION BEFORE BEING
RENEWED TO CONTINUE TORMENT

"Humbling. Identifiers. Know aberrant."   †Isaiah 66:24
"Numbering saint, filthier break down."   †Luke 16:26
"I'm the break down ...fine saint blurring."

THE SAINTS SING PRAISES TO GOD FOR HIS MERCY IN THEIR
LIVES, DRAWING THEM WITH CORDS OF LOVE, LEADING THEM
TO REPENTANCE, DELIVERING THEM FROM DARKNESS AND
WASHING THEIR SINS AWAY WITH THE BLOOD OF THE LAMB
SO THEY COULD AVOID THIS HORRIBLE FATE

"Famed Stunner in bright rainbow-like." †Revelation 4:3
"Stunner inhibited from lawbreaking."   †Colossians 1:13
"Sing! Rainbow-like Truth befriend man."

RELEVANT LONGEST WORDS/PHRASES USING SOME OF THE LETTERS

"three-dimensional" "dimension-walking" "finite-dimensional"
"drinking fountain" "third-generation" "transfiguration"
"untransmogrified" "self-determination" "registration number"
"blank endorsement" "image intensifier" "magistrate-briber"
"foreign minister" "indetermination" "infra dignitatem"
"irrationalities" "internationalised" "unstraightforward"
"internationalise" "non-transferrable" "nitrogen mustard"
"redistributable" "straight-forward" "defragmentation"

Marvel not at this: for the hour is coming, in the which all that are in the graves shall hear his voice, And shall come forth; they that have done good, unto the resurrection of life; and they that have done evil, unto the resurrection of damnation ...John 5:29-30

And whosoever was not found written in the book of life was cast into the lake of fire ...Revelation 20:15

JUBILEE ...THE EVERLASTING KINGDOM

"Jubilant gem like God in the verse."   †Psalm 119:54
"Jubilant, meek, Sovereign delight."   †Psalm 149:4
"Jubilant evoke mightier legends."   †Habakkuk 3:3
"Saint gem thrive like noble judge."   †Revelation 20:4
"Insight over judgement likeable."   †Psalm 67:1-4
"Blokes thrive in agile judgement."   †Psalm 67:5

"Kindest elite marveling huge job."   †Matthew 25:21,23
"Jobs might need angel-like virtue."
"I'm diligent, Keen. Huge jobs travel?"
"Might like d'elegant universe job!"

"The Skilled Gem. Big rejuvenation."   †Isaiah 65:17 †Isaiah 49:13
"Even jumbo granite-like delights!"   †Psalm 98:8   †Isaiah 44:23
"The jubilant, dovelike gems reign."   †Revelation 5:10
"I'm liked! Join huge gentlest brave."   †Hebrews 12:1
"OK! Amen! Believer just delighting!"   †Hebrews 12:22
"Keen is jubilant; delight over gem!"   †Psalm 147:11
"I, Keen delights over jubilant gem."   †Isaiah 62:5
"Eh! Jubilant, kinglier gems devote."   †Psalm 37:4
"Seek delighting over jubilant me."   †John 14:23
"Evoke in jubilant! Delights merge!!"   †John 17 :21-24

CREATION OF A NEW UNIVERSE

WITH THE LAST JUDGMENT COMPLETED, AND THE LAST ENEMY
(DEATH) DESTROYED, THE EARTH IS PREPARED FOR THE ENDURING
KINGDOM: THE HERITAGE OF THE REDEEMED OF THE AGES

"Win of a secure veneration."
"Now if a secure veneration..."
"Now innovate if era secure."   †Isaiah 65:17

THIS CROWNING ACHIEVEMENT HAS BEEN RESERVED FOR
THOSE WHO HAVE DEMONSTRATED THEIR LOVE FOR GOD
THROUGH THE COVENANT SACRIFICE OF AND COMPLETE
DEVOTION TO THE LORD JESUS CHRIST

"Innovate Ace now sure-fire."
"New. A nice reason of virtue."
"Reason now ace fine virtue."
"Veracious won neater, fine."   †Psalm 111:7-8

THEY BELIEVED AND ACTED ON THE WORDS OF GOD,
AND THEY EARNESTLY CONTENDED FOR THE FAITH
WHICH WAS ONCE DELIVERED TO THE SAINTS

"Favour. Wise or ante-nicene." †Jude 1:3

FOR THIS, THEY ARE GREATLY BELOVED OF THE LORD

"Nice reason new: favourite." † John 14:23
"Ace favourite ones winner." †Matthew 25:34

BECAUSE WAR AND VIOLENCE WERE A REALITY ONCE
AGAIN AT THE END OF THE MILLENNIUM, THE EARTH
WILL NOW BE RE-CREATED, AND ALL TRACES OF THE
FORMER THINGS THAT DEFILED WILL CEASE TO EXIST

"Owe favour as internecine."

PERHAPS SOMEONE IN THE KINGDOM COMMUNITY
COMMUNES WITH THE CREATOR-KING TO GET THE
INSIDE SCOOP ABOUT THIS EXCITING, IMPENDING EVENT

"A secure of on an interview."
"A interview of as renounce."

"Saviour inference to a new."
"A new recourse if innovate."

THE NEW EARTH IS PROMISED TO BE VASTLY SUPERIOR TO THE OLD, EVEN SURPASSING THE CHANGES OF THE EARLIER RENOVATION ...THERE WILL BE SUBSTANTIALLY GREATER INCREASE OF ALL TYPES OF RESOURCES COMPARED TO WHAT IS CURRENTLY AVAILABLE

"Few. Or announce varieties."
"A new resource if innovate." †I Corinthians 2:9
"Resource if innovate anew."

THE EARTH WILL BE BEAUTIFUL AND ESTABLISHED IN TRUTH

"New, fine, veracious, ornate."
"New, veracious of an entire."

IT WILL CONSTANTLY REJUVENATE ITSELF

"Not in vain! Eco refuse wear."

THE FEAR OF FORMER NATURAL DISASTERS SUCH AS EARTHQUAKES, FLOODS, AND VOLCANOES WILL DISAPPEAR

"Now ease if uncertain over."
"Nice virtue on now safe era." †Isaiah 11:9
"Nice virtue on now are safe."

AS AT THE BEGINNING OF THE MILLENNIUM, EARTH DWELLERS MUST CLEAR THE CONSTRUCTION ZONE

"Wire unforeseen vacation."
"Now if a sentence: Au-revoir!"
"Safe courier. Innovate new."
"Finest ace on new au-revoir."
"Au-revoir! Now ace fine nest."
"Au-revoir! Sweet, fine canon."
"Au-revoir! Now if neat scene."
"Senior evacuate of winner."
"Fine or so evacuate winner."
"Now senior evacuate finer."
"Senior infer now evacuate."
"Rise of winner on evacuate."
"Finer rise now on evacuate."
"Evacuate fine or now risen."

"Or finer ones win evacuate."

WITH THE EARTH CLEARED, THE NEW CREATION BEGINS

"Now innovate if are secure."
"If secure, a Owner innovate."
"Now secure. Innovate. A fire."

COMPLETE BREAKDOWN AND RE-CREATION OF THE EARTH

"Suave Owner incinerate of."   †Peter 3:12
"Now favour see incinerate."
"Veneration now cause fire."
"Woe! Surface in veneration."
"Owe fire in a sure covenant."   †Micah 1:4
"Vain sweetie or on furnace."
"I owe furnaces veneration."
"Favour. Now cease in entire."
"'N' now erase nice favourite."

COMPLETE BREAKDOWN AND RE-CREATION OF THE ATMOSPHERE, RESULTING IN AIR THAT IS FRAGRANT AND REJUVENATING TO BREATHE

"Now fire even aeronautics."
"Now if aeronautics, veneer."
"Now finer eve aeronautics."
"Now ever fine aeronautics."
"Innovate new of secure air."
"If now, even air nectareous."

COMPLETE RE-DESIGN AND RE-CREATION OF THE AQUIFERS

"Fountain receives on wear."

THE SPRINGS OF WATER APPEAR TO BE RECREATED TO SENSE THE PRESENCE OF APPROACHING PEOPLE, AND THE SPLASH OF THE FOUNTAINS RISING FROM THEM POSSESSES A MUSICAL QUALITY IN PRAISE TO GOD, DELIGHTFUL TO THE EARS

"Now fountain receives ear."
"New nice, favourite on ears."

**THE NEW EARTH FEATURES AN EXPANDED LANDMASS
IN PLACE OF AREAS FORMERLY COVERED
WITH SALT SEAS AND OCEANS**

"If Veneration, now use care."
"One incur, refit. No sea wave."
"Cut. Refine iron. No sea wave."   †Job 38:8-11
"I Refiner, count. No sea wave."
"Count, rein fire. No sea wave."
"Irenic fortune. No sea wave."
"Run!! Recite info. No sea wave!!" †Revelation 21:1
"Nicer, true info – no sea wave!"
"Nice finer tour. No sea wave!"
"Nicer unite, for no sea wave!"
"I recount finer. No sea wave!"

**LOWER CREATION IS COMPLETELY RESTORED AS IN
THE FIFTH AND SIXTH DAYS**

"Now Ace verifies on nature."
"Envies of now in a creature."   †Romans 8:19-21
"Creature win on of a envies!"

**WHEN RE-CREATION IS COMPLETE, THE LORD ONCE
AGAIN ESTABLISHES THE EARTH, THAT IT CANNOT
BE MOVED, VERIFYING THE VERSE THAT
"THE EARTH ABIDETH FOREVER..."**

"Now Suave enforce inertia."   †Psalm 104:5

**THE LORD HIMSELF EXTENDS THE INVITATION TO TOUR
AND VIEW THE NEW DOMAINS... "HOW BEAUTIFUL UPON
THE MOUNTAINS ARE THE FEET OF HIM THAT BRINGETH
GOOD TIDINGS, THAT PUBLISHETH PEACE; THAT BRINGETH
GOOD TIDINGS OF GOOD, THAT PUBLISHETH SALVATION;
THAT SAITH UNTO ZION, THY GOD REIGNETH!" ...BEHOLD
UPON THE MOUNTAINS THE FEET OF HIM THAT BRINGETH
GOOD TIDINGS, THAT PUBLISHETH PEACE! O JUDAH, KEEP
THY SOLEMN FEASTS, PERFORM THY VOWS: FOR THE WICKED
SHALL NO MORE PASS THROUGH THEE; HE IS UTTERLY CUT OFF.**

"Veracious feet in an Owner."
"Now earn in veracious feet."   †Isaiah 52:7
"Fair toes. Announce review."   †Nahum 1:15
"Fair toes announce viewer."
"Or announce: I've sweet, fair."

THE MESSAGE IS PICKED UP AND BROADCAST TO THE
VARIOUS SAFEKEEPING LOCATIONS

"Owner enunciative, or safe."
"A tower announce, verifies."
"Announce as if to reviewer."
"It announce safe or review."
"Or it announce viewer safe."
"Cause review in afternoon."
"Cause viewer in afternoon."
"Now I can. A serene of virtue."
"Secure in a afternoon view."

ANGELIC SERVANTS OF THE MOST HIGH GOD ACT
AS TOUR GUIDES, POINTING OUT NEW FEATURES

"Voice on a winner features."
"Continue on safe, rare view."
"Wave on fine, true scenario."

FLORA AND FAUNA LEAP AND WAVE AT THE PRESENCE
OF THE LORD, BLESSED IN THEIR NEW ENVIRONMENTS

"Nature wave of nice Senior…"
"if as encounter on a review."
"Secure in on a new favorite."

PERHAPS THERE IS GREAT INCREASE AND VARIETY AMONG
ALL THINGS GREEN AND FRUIT-BEARING, INCREASED BY
MULTIPLES OF THE NUMBER REPRESENTING PERFECTION

"Anon favour nicer sweetie."
"Now ace on a fruitier seven."
"Now increase via fourteen."
"Variance of sweeter union."

THIS NEW EARTH DIFFERS FROM THE OLD, WHICH STAGGERED
UNDER THE CURSE AND THE WEIGHT OF MAN'S SIN …
THE NEW EARTH WILL ABIDE BEFORE THE LORD FOREVER

"Were of ruin. Ace innovates." †Isaiah 24:20
"Fine Innovate so cure wear."
"Rescue on wear if innovate."
"Innovate of insecure wear."
"Win innovate of secure era."

"Fine as continue over wear."   †Isaiah 66:22
"Now fine, creative or an use."

**THERE WILL BE NO NEED TO MAR THE SURFACE OF THE
EARTH MINING FOR PRECIOUS METALS ...SOURCES WILL
BE EXPOSED AND ABUNDANT...FOR GIFTS FOR THE KING
AND FOR THE BEAUTY OF THE BEHOLDERS**

"Now vein if nectareous era."
"Now feature vein scenario."   †Psalm 112:3
"Revenue or I fascinate now."

**ESTABLISHED IN TRUTH, THESE VEINS OF PRECIOUS
GEMS AND METALS WILL SELF REPLENISH**

"New of tenacious, rare vein."
"Now tenacious even if rare!"
"Renew of in neat veracious."   †Ecclesiastes 1:4

**HEALING AND REJUVENATING PROPERTIES WILL ABOUND
IN THE LEAVES OF THE TREE OF LIFE ...JUICES, INFUSIONS,
TINCTURES AND POULTICES MADE FROM THEM ARE
FOR THE HEALING OF THE NATIONS**

"Innovate earn of wise cure."
"Innovate. Now see fair cure." †Revelation 22:2
"If innovate, cure now erase."
"Veneration of wine as cure."
"Wave on our fine nectaries."

**A STUNNING CELESTIAL SKY OF SUCH SPARKLING BEAUTY
THAT THE FORMER NIGHT SKIES CANNOT BE RECALLED**

"If Ace, universe ornate now."

**PERHAPS ROADS WILL BE NATURALLY EMBEDDED
IN THE EARTH'S SURFACE WITH DIFFERENT LEVELS
FOR VEHICLES AND PEDESTRIANS**

"Now to fair, sincere avenue."
"Now I craft. One avenue rise."
"Wit reason of nicer avenue."
"Avenue of wiser container."
"Now safe avenue criterion."
"Innovate. Now use if career."

**WOULD MAJOR THOROUGHWAYS HAVE DIMENSIONAL
EXITS LEADING TO THE GLORIOUS NEW JERUSALEM?**

"Or so win avenue interface."

**CONVERSATION REVOLVES AROUND THE
BREATHTAKING CHANGES**

"In sweet favour on nice era."
"Win of avenue or nectaries."
"Nice, new, neater of Saviour."

**ADMIRATION OF AND APPRECIATION FOR THE NEW
CREATION IS UNANIMOUS ...AS GOD KEEPS HIS PROMISE
THAT THE MEEK SHALL INHERIT THE EARTH**

"On a finer, nectareous view!"
"Newer, nice as on favourite."
"On a new, sincere favourite."
"See favour. Now retain nice."
"Winners ace favourite eon!"   †Revelation 21:1
"Sure! On a new, nice favorite!"
"On our sweet, fine variance."
"Favour in a nicer, sweet one."
"Favour nice ease on winter!"
"Ensure of win on a creative!"

**A GREAT CELEBRATION COMMENCES FOR THE DEDICATION
OF THE NEW HEAVENS AND EARTH, AND THE DESCENDING
OF THE NEW JERUSALEM OUT OF HEAVEN, SPARKLING WITH
RADIANCE AS A BEJEWELED BRIDE ADORNED FOR HER HUSBAND**

"Now ace festive, rare union."   †Revelation 21:2
"Or a wire announce festive."
"Or cause veneration if new."

**WITH ALL THINGS SUBDUED, REVERENCE AND REJOICING
AT THE ENTRANCE OF THE KING OF KINGS; AND THE
SON NOW SUBJECTS HIMSELF TO HIM THAT PUT ALL
THINGS UNDER HIM, THAT GOD MAY BE ALL IN ALL**

"Enter now Ace Fine Saviour."   †I Corinthians 15:25
"A Fine, Veracious now enter."   †I Corinthians 15:28
"Virtuoso! An Ace! Newer, fine."

A TOAST TO THE ENDURING KINGDOM ...
<u>WORLD WITHOUT END</u>

"Action! Favour serene wine."
"Over a fine, nectarous wine."
"Favourite wine. An encores."   †John 2:10

AND ARE THESE THE WORDS THE GUEST OF
HONOR PROPOSES AS HE LIFTS HIS CUP...

"Fine, Suave Owner reaction?"
"I innovate!! Now carefree us!"
"Now tune a carefree vision!!"   †Revelation 21:3-4
"A carefree vision tune now!!"   †Jeremiah 31:13-14

RELEVANT LONGEST WORDS/PHRASES USING SOME OF THE LETTERS

"interconversion" "nectariferous" "conservatoire" "functionaries"
"fusion reactor" "fire insurance" "intensive care" "interference"
"conservation" "conversation" "interviewers" "interviewees"
"transference" "inter-surface" "air-to-surface" "centenarians"
"canonisation"

And I saw a new heaven and a new earth: for the first heaven and the first earth were passed away; and there was no more sea...And I John saw the holy city, new Jerusalem, coming down from God out of heaven, prepared as a bride adorned for her husband ...

And I heard a great voice out of heaven saying, Behold, the tabernacle of God is with men, and he will dwell with them, and they shall be his people, and God himself shall be with them, and be their God. Revelation 21: 1-3

EPILOGUE

Holy Grams is written to the church of the last days as a wakeup call. This summons entails repentance, a love of truth, and a love for the appearing of the Lord Jesus Christ. It is a warning to turn away from carnality and conformation to the present perishing world and earnestly contend for the faith once delivered to the saints – the "ante-nicene" faith referenced in the anagrams. It is the exhortation of the Lord as recorded in Jeremiah 6:16 ...Stand by the ways and see and ask for the ancient paths, Where the good way is, and walk in it; And you will find rest for your souls."

Reading this book should spark renewed faith in the veracity of the word of God as recorded in the books of the Bible, for there is nothing hidden that will not be brought to light. The Lord Jesus Christ once alluded to the fact that the very rocks were able to shout praises to Him. If rocks can cry out, should we be surprised that words can rearrange themselves to reveal the magnificence of God and the truth of His recorded word? For everything – regardless of who or what it is - will confess that Jesus is Lord to the glory of the Father.

By the Spirit of God, it is known that the time is short. The ominous portend of a period of intense suffering looms like storm clouds gathering in the distance. Stop laboring for the trinkets of this world, and labor rather for the souls of people. Jesus compared his Kingdom to a field containing priceless buried treasure, and a pearl so exquisite it is worth giving up everything to possess it. This Kingdom is composed of the souls of men and women, boys and girls, and they will be a huge portion of your enduring Treasure, in a glorious world without end.

Fear not those things prophesied to come upon the earth, nor the wrath of man against you as one purchased by the blood of Jesus Christ. Rather, memorize the Word and study to show yourself approved, a workman who is not ashamed, rightly dividing the word of the Truth, so that in meekness you can answer anyone who enquires about your faith, as they witness your life modeling the teachings of Jesus Christ. Ask the Father to make your love perfect – for perfect love casts out fear. Petition the Father in the name of Jesus for the infilling of the Holy Ghost. Obey the scriptures and seek God for the infilling of His spirit. This book was written by one filled with the Holy Ghost, and He has promised to lead and guide His own into all truth. May God be merciful to you and keep you in His love.

INDEX OF SCRIPTURE REFERENCES

Part I The Past
GENESIS CREATION AND FALL OF MAN

Genesis 3:7 ...And the eyes of them both were opened, and they knew that they were naked; and they sewed fig leaves together, and made themselves aprons.

Genesis 3:8...And they heard the voice of the Lord God walking in the garden in the cool of the day: and Adam and his wife hid themselves from the presence of the Lord God amongst the trees of the garden.

Isaiah 9:6-7 ...For unto us a child is born, unto us a son is given: and the government shall be upon his shoulder: and his name shall be called Wonderful, Counseller, The mighty God, The everlasting Father, The Prince of Peace.

Colossians 2:14 ...Blotting out the handwriting of ordinances that was against us, which was contrary to us, and took it out of the way, nailing it to his cross...

Luke 10:18-19 ...And he said unto them, I beheld Satan as lightning fall from heaven. Behold, I give unto you power to tread on serpents and scorpions, and over all the power of the enemy: and nothing shall by any means hurt you.

Hebrews 9:22 ...And almost all things are by the law purged with blood; and without shedding of blood is no remission.

CAIN'S VEGETABLE OFFERING ABEL'S ANIMAL SACRIFICE
I John 3:12 ...Not as Cain, who was of that wicked one, and slew his brother. And wherefore slew he him? Because his own works were evil, and his brother's righteous.

Hebrews 9:22 ...And almost all things are by the law purged with blood; and without shedding of blood is no remission.

VEGETABLES: REJECTION FLOCK SACRIFICE: ACCEPTED

Hebrews 9:22 ...And almost all things are by the law purged with blood; and without shedding of blood is no remission.

I John 3:12 ...Not as Cain, who was of that wicked one, and slew his brother. And wherefore slew he him? Because his own works were evil, and his brother's righteous.

THE EARTH WAS CORRUPT AND FILLED WITH VIOLENCE
James 5:1-6 ...Go to now, ye rich men, weep and howl for your miseries that shall come upon you. Your riches are corrupted, and your garments are motheaten. Your gold and silver is cankered; and the rust of them shall be a witness against you, and shall eat your flesh as it were fire. Ye have heaped treasure together for the last days. Behold, the hire of the labourers who have reaped down your fields, which is of you kept back by fraud, crieth: and the cries of them which have reaped are entered into the ears of the Lord of sabaoth. Ye have lived in pleasure on the earth, and been wanton; ye have nourished your hearts, as in a day of slaughter. Ye have condemned and killed the just; and he doth not resist you.

James 5:4 ...Behold, the hire of the labourers who have reaped down your fields, which is of you kept back by fraud, crieth: and the cries of them which have reaped are entered into the ears of the Lord of sabaoth.

Rev 13: 14-15 ...And deceiveth them that dwell on the earth by the means of those miracles which he had power to do in the sight of the beast; saying to them that dwell on the earth, that they should make an image to the beast, which had the wound by a sword, and did live. And he had power to give life unto the image of the beast, that the image of the beast should both speak, and cause that as many as would not worship the image of the beast should be killed.

Romans 1:30 ...Backbiters, haters of God, despiteful, proud, boasters, inventors of evil things, disobedient to parents

Romans 1:30 ...Backbiters, haters of God, despiteful, proud, boasters, inventors of evil things, disobedient to parents

II Peter 2:5 ...And spared not the old world, but saved Noah the eighth person, a preacher of righteousness, bringing in the flood upon the world of the ungodly;

Jude 1:6 ...And the angels which kept not their first estate, but left their own habitation, he hath reserved in everlasting chains under darkness unto the judgment of the great day.

NOAHS FLOOD – ANTEDILUVIAN ERA

Psalm 18:2 ...The Lord is my rock, and my fortress, and my deliverer; my God, my strength, in whom I will trust; my buckler, and the horn of my salvation, and my high tower.

Luke 1:69 ...And hath raised up an horn of salvation for us in the house of his servant David;

Genesis 6:21 ...And take thou unto thee of all food that is eaten, and thou shalt gather it to thee; and it shall be for food for thee, and for them.

Revelation 2:24 ...But unto you I say, and unto the rest in Thyatira, as many as have not this doctrine, and which have not known the depths of Satan, as they speak; I will put upon you none other burden.

Deuteronomy 32:17 ...They sacrificed unto devils, not to God; to gods whom they knew not, to new gods that came newly up, whom your fathers feared not.

Revelation 21:8 ...But the fearful, and unbelieving, and the abominable, and murderers, and whoremongers, and sorcerers, and idolaters, and all liars, shall have their part in the lake which burneth with fire and brimstone: which is the second death.

Psalm 82:5 ...They know not, neither will they understand; they walk on in darkness: all the foundations of the earth are out of course.

Romans 3:15 ...Their feet are swift to shed blood

Romans 1:30 ...Backbiters, haters of God, despiteful, proud, boasters, inventors of evil things, disobedient to parents

Proverbs 4:17 ...For they eat the bread of wickedness, and drink the wine of violence.

Psalm 52:1 ...Why boastest thou thyself in mischief, O mighty man? the goodness of God endureth continually.

Revelation 9:21 ...Neither repented they of their murders, nor of their sorceries(Grk. pharmakeia), nor of their fornication, nor of their thefts.

Habakkuk 2:15 ...Woe unto him that giveth his neighbour drink, that puttest thy bottle to him, and makest him drunken also, that thou mayest look on their nakedness!

Psalm 10:7 ...His mouth is full of cursing and deceit and fraud: under his tongue is mischief and vanity.

Genesis 6:4 ...There were giants in the earth in those days; and also after that, when the sons of God came in unto the daughters of men, and they bare children to them, the same became mighty men which were of old, men of renown.

Jude 1:6-7 ...And the angels which kept not their first estate, but left their own habitation, he hath reserved in everlasting chains under darkness unto the judgment of the great day. Even as Sodom and Gomorrha, and the cities about them in like manner, giving themselves over to fornication, and going after strange flesh, are set forth for an example, suffering the vengeance of eternal fire.

Isaiah 51:13 ...And forgettest the Lord thy maker, that hath stretched forth the heavens, and laid the foundations of the earth...

Revelation 11:18 ...And the nations were angry, and thy wrath is come, and the time of the dead, that they should be judged, and that thou shouldest give reward unto thy servants the prophets, and to the saints, and them that fear thy name, small and great; and shouldest destroy them which destroy the earth.

Genesis 7:1 ...And the Lord said unto Noah, Come thou and all thy house into the ark; for thee have I seen righteous before me in this generation.

Genesis 6:8 ...But Noah found grace in the eyes of the Lord.

Genesis 6:18 ...But with thee will I establish my covenant; and thou shalt come into the ark, thou, and thy sons, and thy wife, and thy sons' wives with thee.

Genesis 6:9 ...These are the generations of Noah: Noah was a just man and perfect in his generations, and Noah walked with God.

Genesis 8:15-19 ...And God spake unto Noah, saying, Go forth of the ark, thou, and thy wife, and thy sons, and thy sons' wives with thee. Bring forth with thee every living thing that is with thee, of all flesh, both of fowl, and of cattle, and of every creeping thing that creepeth upon the earth; that they may breed abundantly in the earth, and be fruitful, and multiply upon the earth.

And Noah went forth, and his sons, and his wife, and his sons' wives with him: Every beast, every creeping thing, and every fowl, and whatsoever creepeth upon the earth, after their kinds, went forth out of the ark.

Genesis 8:20-21 ...And Noah builded an altar unto the Lord; and took of every clean beast, and of every clean fowl, and offered burnt offerings on the altar. And the Lord smelled a sweet savour; and the Lord said in his heart, I will not again curse the ground any more for man's sake; for the imagination of man's heart is evil from his youth; neither will I again smite any more every thing living, as I have done.

Genesis 9:8-17 ...And God spake unto Noah, and to his sons with him, saying, And I, behold, I establish my covenant with you, and with your seed after you; And with every living creature that is with you, of the fowl, of the cattle, and of every beast of the earth with you; from all that go out of the ark, to every beast of the earth. And I will establish my covenant with you, neither shall all flesh be cut off any more by the waters of a flood; neither shall there any more be a flood to destroy the earth. And God said, This is the token of the covenant which I make between me and you and every living creature that is with you, for perpetual generations: I do set my bow in the cloud, and it shall be for a token of a covenant between me and the earth.

And it shall come to pass, when I bring a cloud over the earth, that the bow shall be seen in the cloud: And I will remember my covenant, which is between me and you and every living creature of all flesh; and the waters shall no more become a flood to destroy all flesh. And the bow shall be in the cloud; and I will look upon it, that I may remember the everlasting covenant between God and every living creature of all flesh that is upon the earth. And God said unto Noah, This is the token of the covenant, which I have established between me and all flesh that is upon the earth.

BUILDS CITY, TOWER - ONE LANGUAGE
Genesis 11:7 ...Go to, let us go down, and there confound their language, that they may not understand one another's speech.

TWELVE TRIBES – SONS OF JACOB
Genesis 37:3 ...Now Israel loved Joseph more than all his children, because he was the son of his old age: and he made him a coat of many colours.

Genesis 37:7 ...For, behold, we were binding sheaves in the field, and, lo, my sheaf arose, and also stood upright; and, behold, your sheaves stood round about, and made obeisance to my sheaf.

Genesis 37:9 ...And he dreamed yet another dream, and told it his brethren, and said, Behold, I have dreamed a dream more; and, behold, the sun and the moon and the eleven stars made obeisance to me.

Genesis 37:18 ...And when they saw him afar off, even before he came near unto them, they conspired against him to slay him.

Genesis 37:19 ...And they said one to another, Behold, this dreamer cometh.

Genesis 37:20 ...Come now therefore, and let us slay him, and cast him into some pit, and we will say, Some evil beast hath devoured him: and we shall see what will become of his dreams.

Genesis 37:21 ...And Reuben heard it, and he delivered him out of their hands; and said, Let us not kill him.

Genesis 37:22 ...And Reuben said unto them, Shed no blood, but cast him into this pit that is in the wilderness, and lay no hand upon him; that he might rid him out of their hands, to deliver him to his father again.

Genesis 37:23-24 ...And it came to pass, when Joseph was come unto his brethren, that they stript Joseph out of his coat, his coat of many colours that was on him; And they took him, and cast him into a pit: and the pit was empty, there was no water in it.

Genesis 37:27 ...Come, and let us sell him to the Ishmeelites, and let not our hand be upon him; for he is our brother and our flesh.

Genesis 37:28 ...Then there passed by Midianites merchantmen; and they drew and lifted up Joseph out of the pit, and sold Joseph to the Ishmeelites for twenty pieces of silver: and they brought Joseph into Egypt.

Genesis 37:32 ...And they sent the coat of many colours, and they brought it to their father; and said, This have we found: know now whether it be thy son's coat or no.

Genesis 37:33 ...And he knew it, and said, It is my son's coat; an evil beast hath devoured him; Joseph is without doubt rent in pieces.

Genesis 39:4 ...And Joseph found grace in his sight, and he served him: and he made him overseer over his house, and all that he had he put into his hand.

Genesis 39:5-6 ...And it came to pass from the time that he had made him overseer in his house, and over all that he had, that the LORD blessed the Egyptian's house for Joseph's sake; and the blessing of the LORD was upon all that he had in the house, and in the field. And he left all that he had in Joseph's hand; and he knew not ought he had, save the bread which he did eat. And Joseph was a goodly person, and well favoured.

Genesis 39:7 ...And it came to pass after these things, that his master's wife cast her eyes upon Joseph; and she said, Lie with me.

Genesis 39:8-9...But he refused, and said unto his master's wife, Behold, my master wotteth not what is with me in the house, and he hath committed all that he hath to my hand; There is none greater in this house than I; neither hath he kept back any thing from me but thee, because thou art his wife: how then can I do this great wickedness, and sin against God?

Genesis 39:10 ...And it came to pass, as she spake to Joseph day by day, that he hearkened not unto her, to lie by her, or to be with her.

Genesis 39:12 ...And she caught him by his garment, saying, Lie with me: and he left his garment in her hand, and fled, and got him out.

Genesis 39:14-15 ...That she called unto the men of her house, and spake unto them, saying, See, he hath brought in an Hebrew unto us to mock us; he came in unto me to lie with me, and I cried with a loud voice: And it came to pass, when he heard that I lifted up my voice and cried, that he left his garment with me, and fled, and got him out.

Genesis 39:19 ...And it came to pass, when his master heard the words of his wife, which she spake unto him, saying, After this manner did thy servant to me; that his wrath was kindled.

Genesis 39:20 ...And Joseph's master took him, and put him into the prison, a place where the king's prisoners were bound: and he was there in the prison.

Genesis 39:21-23 ...But the LORD was with Joseph, and shewed him mercy, and gave him favour in the sight of the keeper of the prison. And the keeper of the prison committed to Joseph's hand all the prisoners that were in the prison; and whatsoever they did there, he was the doer of it. The keeper of the prison looked not to any thing that was under his hand; because the LORD was with him, and that which he did, the LORD made it to prosper.

Genesis 40:1-3 ...And it came to pass after these things, that the butler of the king of Egypt and his baker had offended their lord the king of Egypt. And Pharaoh was wroth against two of his officers, against the chief of the butlers, and against the chief of the bakers. And he put them in ward in the house of the captain of the guard, into the prison, the place where Joseph was bound.

Genesis 40:9-13 ...And the chief butler told his dream to Joseph, and said to him, In my dream, behold, a vine was before me; And in the vine were three branches: and it was as though it budded, and her blossoms shot forth; and the clusters thereof brought forth ripe grapes: And Pharaoh's cup was in my hand: and I took the grapes, and pressed them into Pharaoh's cup, and I gave the cup into Pharaoh's hand. And Joseph said unto him, This is the interpretation of it: The three branches are three days: Yet within three days shall Pharaoh lift up thine head, and restore thee unto thy place: and thou shalt deliver Pharaoh's cup into his hand, after the former manner when thou wast his butler.

Genesis 40:16-19 ...When the chief baker saw that the interpretation was good, he said unto Joseph, I also was in my dream, and, behold, I had three white baskets on my head: And in the uppermost basket there was of all manner of bakemeats for Pharaoh; and the birds did eat them out of the basket upon my head. And Joseph answered and said, This is the interpretation thereof: The three baskets are three days: Yet within three days shall Pharaoh lift up thy head from off thee, and shall hang thee on a tree; and the birds shall eat thy flesh from off thee.

Genesis 41:12-13 ...And there was there with us a young man, an Hebrew, servant to the captain of the guard; and we told him, and he interpreted to us our dreams; to each man according to his dream he did interpret. And it came to pass, as he interpreted to us, so it was; me he restored unto mine office, and him he hanged.

Genesis 41:25-32 ...And Joseph said unto Pharaoh, The dream of Pharaoh is one: God hath shewed Pharaoh what he is about to do. The seven good kine are seven years; and the seven good ears are seven years: the dream is one. And the seven thin and ill favoured kine that came up after them are seven years; and the seven empty ears blasted with the east wind shall be seven years of famine. This is the thing which I have spoken unto Pharaoh: What God is about to do he sheweth unto Pharaoh. Behold, there come seven years of great plenty throughout all the land of Egypt: And there shall arise after them seven years of famine; and all the plenty shall be forgotten in the land of Egypt; and the famine shall consume the land; And the plenty shall not be known in the land by reason of that famine following; for it shall be very grievous. And for that the dream was doubled unto Pharaoh twice; it is because the thing is established by God, and God will shortly bring it to pass.

Genesis 41:32-33 ...And for that the dream was doubled unto Pharaoh twice; it is because the thing is established by God, and God will shortly bring it to pass. Now therefore let Pharaoh look out a man discreet and wise, and set him over the land of Egypt.

Genesis 41:33-35 ...Now therefore let Pharaoh look out a man discreet and wise, and set him over the land of Egypt. Let Pharaoh do this, and let him appoint officers over the land, and take up the fifth part of the land of Egypt in the seven plenteous years. And let them gather all the food of those good years that come, and lay up corn under the hand of Pharaoh, and let them keep food in the cities.

Genesis 41:39 ...And Pharaoh said unto Joseph, Forasmuch as God hath shewed thee all this, there is none so discreet and wise as thou art:

Genesis 41:40-41 ...Thou shalt be over my house, and according unto thy word shall all my people be ruled: only in the throne will I be greater than thou.
And Pharaoh said unto Joseph, See, I have set thee over all the land of Egypt.

Genesis 41:48-49 ...And he gathered up all the food of the seven years, which were in the land of Egypt, and laid up the food in the cities: the food of the field, which was round about every city, laid he up in the same. And Joseph gathered corn as the sand of the sea, very much, until he left numbering; for it was without number.

Genesis 42:1-2 ...Now when Jacob saw that there was corn in Egypt, Jacob said unto his sons, Why do ye look one upon another? And he said, Behold, I have heard that there is corn in Egypt: get you down thither, and buy for us from thence; that we may live, and not die.

Genesis 42:6 ...And Joseph was the governor over the land, and he it was that sold to all the people of the land: and Joseph's brethren came, and bowed down themselves before him with their faces to the earth.

Genesis 42:10-13 ...And they said unto him, Nay, my lord, but to buy food are thy servants come. We are all one man's sons; we are true men, thy servants are no spies. And he said unto them, Nay, but to see the nakedness of the land ye are come. And they said, Thy servants are twelve brethren, the sons of one man in the land of Canaan; and, behold, the youngest is this day with our father, and one is not.

Genesis 42:21 ...And they said one to another, We are verily guilty concerning our brother, in that we saw the anguish of his soul, when he besought us, and we would not hear; therefore is this distress come upon us.

Genesis 42:22 ...And Reuben answered them, saying, Spake I not unto you, saying, Do not sin against the child; and ye would not hear? therefore, behold, also his blood is required.

Genesis 42:24 ...And he turned himself about from them, and wept; and returned to them again, and communed with them, and took from them Simeon, and bound him before their eyes.

Genesis 43:14 ...And God Almighty give you mercy before the man, that he may send away your other brother, and Benjamin. If I be bereaved of my children, I am bereaved.

Genesis 43:16 ...And when Joseph saw Benjamin with them, he said to the ruler of his house, Bring these men home, and slay, and make ready; for these men shall dine with me at noon.

Genesis 43:30 ...And Joseph made haste; for his bowels did yearn upon his brother: and he sought where to weep; and he entered into his chamber, and wept there.

Genesis 43:34 ...And he took and sent messes unto them from before him: but Benjamin's mess was five times so much as any of theirs. And they drank, and were merry with him.

Genesis 44:2 ...And put my cup, the silver cup, in the sack's mouth of the youngest, and his corn money. And he did according to the word that Joseph had spoken.
Genesis 44:6 ...And he overtook them, and he spake unto them these same words.

Genesis 44:8-9 ...Behold, the money, which we found in our sacks' mouths, we brought again unto thee out of the land of Canaan: how then should we steal out of thy lord's house silver or gold? With whomsoever of thy servants it be found, both let him die, and we also will be my lord's bondmen.

Genesis 44:12 ...And he searched, and began at the eldest, and left at the youngest: and the cup was found in Benjamin's sack.

Genesis 44:14 ...And Judah and his brethren came to Joseph's house; for he was yet there: and they fell before him on the ground.

Genesis 44:15 ...And Joseph said unto them, What deed is this that ye have done? wot ye not that such a man as I can certainly divine?

Genesis 44:16 ...And Judah said, What shall we say unto my lord? what shall we speak? or how shall we clear ourselves? God hath found out the iniquity of thy servants: behold, we are my lord's servants, both we, and he also with whom the cup is found.

Genesis 44:17 ...And he said, God forbid that I should do so: but the man in whose hand the cup is found, he shall be my servant; and as for you, get you up in peace unto your father.

Genesis 44:18 ...Then Judah came near unto him, and said, Oh my lord, let thy servant, I pray thee, speak a word in my lord's ears, and let not thine anger burn against thy servant: for thou art even as Pharaoh.

Genesis 44:33 ...Now therefore, I pray thee, let thy servant abide instead of the lad a bondman to my lord; and let the lad go up with his brethren.

Genesis 45:1 ...Then Joseph could not refrain himself before all them that stood by him; and he cried, Cause every man to go out from me. And there stood no man with him, while Joseph made himself known unto his brethren.

Genesis 45:2 ...And he wept aloud: and the Egyptians and the house of Pharaoh heard.

Genesis 45:3 ...And Joseph said unto his brethren, I am Joseph; doth my father yet live? And his brethren could not answer him; for they were troubled at his presence.

Genesis 45:14-15 ...And he fell upon his brother Benjamin's neck, and wept; and Benjamin wept upon his neck. Moreover he kissed all his brethren, and wept upon them: and after that his brethren talked with him.

Genesis 45:17-20 ...And Pharaoh said unto Joseph, Say unto thy brethren, This do ye; lade your beasts, and go, get you unto the land of Canaan; And take your father and your households, and come unto me: and I will give you the good of the land of Egypt, and ye shall eat the fat of the land. Now thou art commanded, this do ye; take you wagons out of the land of Egypt for your little ones, and for your wives, and bring your father, and come. Also regard not your stuff; for the good of all the land of Egypt is yours.

Genesis 46:5-6 ...And Jacob rose up from Beersheba: and the sons of Israel carried Jacob their father, and their little ones, and their wives, in the wagons which Pharaoh had sent to carry him. 6And they took their cattle, and their goods, which they had gotten in the land of Canaan, and came into Egypt, Jacob, and all his seed with him:

Genesis 47:6 ...The land of Egypt is before thee; in the best of the land make thy father and brethren to dwell; in the land of Goshen let them dwell: and if thou knowest any men of activity among them, then make them rulers over my cattle.

SAMSON AND DELILAH
Judges 13:1 ...And the children of Israel did evil again in the sight of the LORD; and the LORD delivered them into the hand of the Philistines forty years.

Judges 13:5 ...For, lo, thou shalt conceive, and bear a son; and no rasor shall come on his head: for the child shall be a Nazarite unto God from the womb: and he shall begin to deliver Israel out of the hand of the Philistines.

Judges 13:24-25 ...And the woman bare a son, and called his name Samson: and the child grew, and the LORD blessed him. And the Spirit of the LORD began to move him at times in the camp of Dan between Zorah and Eshtaol.

Judges 14:1-3 ...And Samson went down to Timnath, and saw a woman in Timnath of the daughters of the Philistines. And he came up, and told his father and his mother, and said, I have seen a woman in Timnath of the daughters of the Philistines: now therefore get her for me to wife. Then his father and his mother said unto him, Is there never a woman among the daughters of thy brethren, or among all my people, that thou goest to take a wife of the uncircumcised Philistines? And Samson said unto his father, Get her for me; for she pleaseth me well.

Judges 14:5 ...Then went Samson down, and his father and his mother, to Timnath, and came to the vineyards of Timnath: and, behold, a young lion roared against him.

Judges 14:6 ...And the Spirit of the LORD came mightily upon him, and he rent him as he would have rent a kid, and he had nothing in his hand: but he told not his father or his mother what he had done.

Judges 14:8 ... And after a time he returned to take her, and he turned aside to see the carcase of the lion: and, behold, there was a swarm of bees and honey in the carcase of the lion.

Judges 14:19 ...And the Spirit of the LORD came upon him, and he went down to Ashkelon, and slew thirty men of them, and took their spoil, and gave change of garments unto them which expounded the riddle. And his anger was kindled, and he went up to his father's house.

Judges 14:20 ...But Samson's wife was given to his companion, whom he had used as his friend.

Judges 15:4 ...And Samson went and caught three hundred foxes, and took firebrands, and turned tail to tail, and put a firebrand in the midst between two tails.

Judges 15:5 ...And when he had set the brands on fire, he let them go into the standing corn of the Philistines, and burnt up both the shocks, and also the standing corn, with the vineyards and olives.

Judges 15:8 ...And he smote them hip and thigh with a great slaughter: and he went down and dwelt in the top of the rock Etam.

Judges 15:14 ...And when he came unto Lehi, the Philistines shouted against him: and the Spirit of the LORD came mightily upon him, and the cords that were upon his arms became as flax that was burnt with fire, and his bands loosed from off his hands.

Judges 15:15 ...And he found a new jawbone of an ass, and put forth his hand, and took it, and slew a thousand men therewith.

Judges 16:1 ...Then went Samson to Gaza, and saw there an harlot, and went in unto her.

Judges 16:3 ...And Samson lay till midnight, and arose at midnight, and took the doors of the gate of the city, and the two posts, and went away with them, bar and all, and put them upon his shoulders, and carried them up to the top of an hill that is before

Hebron.

Judges 16:4 ...And it came to pass afterward, that he loved a woman in the valley of Sorek, whose name was Delilah.

Judges 16:5 ...And the lords of the Philistines came up unto her, and said unto her, Entice him, and see wherein his great strength lieth, and by what means we may prevail against him, that we may bind him to afflict him: and we will give thee every one of us eleven hundred pieces of silver.

Judges 16:16 ...And it came to pass, when she pressed him daily with her words, and urged him, so that his soul was vexed unto death;

Judges 16:18 ...And when Delilah saw that he had told her all his heart, she sent and called for the lords of the Philistines, saying, Come up this once, for he hath shewed me all his heart. Then the lords of the Philistines came up unto her, and brought money in their hand.

Judges 16:19 ...And she made him sleep upon her knees; and she called for a man, and she caused him to shave off the seven locks of his head; and she began to afflict him, and his strength went from him.

Judges 16:21 ...But the Philistines took him, and put out his eyes, and brought him down to Gaza, and bound him with fetters of brass; and he did grind in the prison house.

Judges 16:23 ...Then the lords of the Philistines gathered them together for to offer a great sacrifice unto Dagon their god, and to rejoice: for they said, Our god hath delivered Samson our enemy into our hand.

Judges 16:25 ...And it came to pass, when their hearts were merry, that they said, Call for Samson, that he may make us sport. And they called for Samson out of the prison house; and he made them sport: and they set him between the pillars.

Judges 16:28 ...And Samson called unto the LORD, and said, O Lord GOD, remember me, I pray thee, and strengthen me, I pray thee, only this once, O God, that I may be at once avenged of the Philistines for my two eyes.

Judges 16:27 Now the house was full of men and women; and all the lords of the Philistines were there; and there were upon the roof about three thousand men and women, that beheld while Samson made sport.

Judges 16:30 And Samson said, Let me die with the Philistines. And he bowed himself with all his might; and the house fell upon the lords, and upon all the people that were therein. So the dead which he slew at his death were more than they which he slew in his life.

Judges 16:31 Then his brethren and all the house of his father came down, and took him, and brought him up, and buried him between Zorah and Eshtaol in the buryingplace of Manoah his father. And he judged Israel twenty years.

Part II The Present
SHAPING THE POST-CHRISTIAN ERA
II Corinthians 6:14 ...Be ye not unequally yoked together with unbelievers: for what fellowship hath righteousness with unrighteousness? and what communion hath light with darkness?

Ezekiel 3:18 ...When I say unto the wicked, Thou shalt surely die; and thou givest him not warning, nor speakest to warn the wicked from his wicked way, to save his life; the same wicked man shall die in his iniquity; but his blood will I require at thine hand.

Amos 5:10 ...They hate him that rebuketh in the gate, and they abhor him that speaketh uprightly.

ACHIEVING THE AMERICAN DREAM
I Timothy 6:10 ...For the love of money is the root of all evil: which while some coveted after, they have erred from the faith, and pierced themselves through with many sorrows.

Proverbs 27:15 ... A continual dropping in a very rainy day and a contentious woman are alike.

Proverbs 30:15 ...The horseleach hath two daughters, crying, Give, give. There are three things that are never satisfied, yea, four things say not, It is enough...

I Timothy 6:9 ...But they that will be rich fall into temptation and a snare, and into many foolish and hurtful lusts, which drown men in destruction and perdition.

Proverbs 22:16 ...He that oppresseth the poor to increase his riches, and he that giveth to the rich, shall surely come to want.

Proverbs 13:11 ...Wealth gotten by vanity shall be diminished: but he that gathereth by labour shall increase.

Proverbs 12:11 ...He that tilleth his land shall be satisfied with bread: but he that followeth vain persons is void of understanding.

I Corinthians 15:33 ...Be not deceived: evil communications corrupt good manners.

Proverbs 22:24 ...Make no friendship with an angry man; and with a furious man thou shalt not go:

Revelation 9:21 ...Neither repented they of their murders, nor of their sorceries, nor of their fornication, nor of their thefts.

Proverbs 13:4 ...The soul of the sluggard desireth, and hath nothing: but the soul of the diligent shall be made fat.

Deuteronomy 28:29,33 ...And thou shalt grope at noonday, as the blind gropeth in darkness, and thou shalt not prosper in thy ways: and thou shalt be only oppressed and spoiled evermore, and no man shall save thee... The fruit of thy land, and all thy labours, shall a nation which thou knowest not eat up; and thou shalt be only oppressed and crushed alway...

James 2:2-4 ... For if a man comes into your assembly with a gold ring and dressed in fine clothes, and there also comes in a poor man in dirty clothes, and you pay special attention to the one who is wearing the fine clothes, and say, "You sit here in a good place," and you say to the poor man, "You stand over there, or sit down by my footstool," have you not made distinctions among yourselves, and become judges with evil motives?

Isaiah 58:7 ...Is it not to deal thy bread to the hungry, and that thou bring the poor that are cast out to thy house? when thou seest the naked, that thou cover him; and that thou hide not thyself from thine own flesh?

Romans 1:30 ...Backbiters, haters of God, despiteful, proud, boasters, inventors of evil things, disobedient to parents

Revelation 9:21 ...Neither repented they of their murders, nor of their sorceries (Grk. pharmakeia), nor of their fornication, nor of their thefts.

Romans 1:30 ...Backbiters, haters of God, despiteful, proud, boasters, inventors of evil things, disobedient to parents

Revelation 9:21 ...Neither repented they of their murders, nor of their sorceries (Grk. pharmakeia), nor of their fornication, nor of their thefts.

Philippians 4:19 ...But my God shall supply all your need according to his riches in glory by Christ Jesus.

Matthew 6:33 ...But seek ye first the kingdom of God, and his righteousness; and all these things shall be added unto you.

I Timothy 6:7 ...For we brought nothing into this world, and it is certain we can carry nothing out.

Luke 12:20 ...But God said unto him, Thou fool, this night thy soul shall be required of thee: then whose shall those things be, which thou hast provided?

TELEVISION PROGRAMMING

Proverbs 4:23 ...Keep thy heart with all diligence; for out of it are the issues of life.

Ephesians 5:16-17 ...Redeeming the time, because the days are evil. Wherefore be ye not unwise, but understanding what the will of the Lord is.

Proverbs 22:6 ...Train up a child in the way he should go: and when he is old, he will not depart from it.

Matthew 19:5 ...And said, For this cause shall a man leave father and mother, and shall cleave to his wife: and they twain shall be one flesh...

Romans 1:24 ...Wherefore God also gave them up to uncleanness through the lusts of their own hearts, to dishonour their own bodies between themselves

I Corinthians 6:9 ...Know ye not that the unrighteous shall not inherit the kingdom of God? Be not deceived: neither fornicators, nor idolaters, nor adulterers, nor effeminate, nor abusers of themselves with mankind...

Matthew 5:28 ...But I say unto you, That whosoever looketh on a woman to lust after her hath committed adultery with her already in his heart.

I Kings 14:23 ...For they also built them high places, and images, and groves, on every high hill, and under every green tree.

Romans 1:24 ...Wherefore God also gave them up to uncleanness through the lusts of their own hearts, to dishonour their own bodies between themselves...

I Timothy 1:10 ...For whoremongers, for them that defile themselves with mankind, for menstealers, for liars, for perjured persons, and if there be any other thing that is contrary to sound doctrine;

Proverbs 13:2 ...A man shall eat good by the fruit of his mouth: but the soul of the transgressors shall eat violence.

Psalm 14:3 ...They are all gone aside, they are all together become filthy: there is none that doeth good, no, not one.

Proverbs 4:17 ...They eat the bread of wickedness and drink the wine of violence.

Isaiah 23:16 ...Take an harp, go about the city, thou harlot that hast been forgotten; make sweet melody, sing many songs, that thou mayest be remembered...

James 4:4 ... Ye adulterers and adulteresses, know ye not that the friendship of the world is enmity with God? whosoever therefore will be a friend of the world is the enemy of God.

Isaiah 40:6-7 ...The voice said, Cry. And he said, What shall I cry? All flesh is grass, and all the goodliness thereof is as the flower of the field: The grass withereth, the flower fadeth: because the spirit of the LORD bloweth upon it: surely the people is grass.

Luke 16:21 ...And desiring to be fed with the crumbs which fell from the rich man's table: moreover the dogs came and licked his sores.

Micah 2:1-2 ...Woe to them that devise iniquity, and work evil upon their beds! when the morning is light, they practise it, because it is in the power of their hand. And they covet fields, and take them by violence; and houses, and take them away: so they oppress a man and his house, even a man and his heritage.

Proverbs 11:22 ...As a jewel of gold in a swine's snout, so is a fair woman which is without discretion

Ecclesiastes 10:20 ... Curse not the king, no not in thy thought; and curse not the rich in thy bedchamber: for a bird of the air shall carry the voice, and that which hath wings shall tell the matter.

APOSTASY...FALSE PROPHETS AND BRETHREN
Matthew 6:5 ... And when thou prayest, thou shalt not be as the hypocrites are: for they love to pray standing in the synagogues and in the corners of the streets, that they may be seen of men. Verily I say unto you, They have their reward.

I Peter 2:18 ... For when they speak great swelling words of vanity, they allure through the lusts of the flesh, through much wantonness, those that were clean escaped from them who live in error.

Jude 1:16 ... These are murmurers, complainers, walking after their own lusts; and their mouth speaketh great swelling words, having men's persons in admiration because of advantage.

Matthew 23:4 ... For they bind heavy burdens and grievous to be borne, and lay them on men's shoulders; but they themselves will not move them with one of their fingers.

I Peter 5:2 ... Feed the flock of God which is among you, taking the oversight thereof, not by constraint, but willingly; not for filthy lucre, but of a ready mind;

James 2:15-16 ... If a brother or sister be naked, and destitute of daily food, And one of you say unto them, Depart in peace, be ye warmed and filled; notwithstanding ye give them not those things which are needful to the body; what doth it profit?

I Timothy 6:5 ... Perverse disputings of men of corrupt minds, and destitute of the truth, supposing that gain is godliness: from such withdraw thyself.

Matthew 8:20 ... And Jesus saith unto him, The foxes have holes, and the birds of the air have nests; but the Son of man hath not where to lay his head.

II Timothy 3:12 ... Yea, and all that will live godly in Christ Jesus shall suffer persecution.

I Thessalonians 5:3 ... For when they shall say, Peace and safety; then sudden destruction cometh upon them, as travail upon a woman with child; and they shall not escape.

Jeremiah 5:31 ... The prophets prophesy falsely, and the priests bear rule by their means; and my people love to have it so: and what will ye do in the end thereof?

Jeremiah 23:2 ... Therefore thus saith the LORD God of Israel against the pastors that feed my people; Ye have scattered my flock, and driven them away, and have not visited them: behold, I will visit upon you the evil of your doings, saith the LORD.

Ezekiel 34:6 ... My sheep wandered through all the mountains, and upon every high hill: yea, my flock was scattered upon all the face of the earth, and none did search or seek after them.

Matthew 23:27 ... Woe unto you, scribes and Pharisees, hypocrites! for ye are like unto whited sepulchres, which indeed appear beautiful outward, but are within full of dead men's bones, and of all uncleanness.

I Peter 2:2 ... And many shall follow their pernicious ways; by reason of whom the way of truth shall be evil spoken of.

Titus 2:15 ... These things speak, and exhort, and rebuke with all authority. Let no man despise thee.
II Peter 2:10 ... But chiefly them that walk after the flesh in the lust of uncleanness, and despise government. Presumptuous are they, selfwilled, they are not afraid to speak evil of dignities.

II Timothy 4:14-15 ... Alexander the coppersmith did me much evil: the Lord reward him according to his works: Of whom be thou ware also; for he hath greatly withstood our words.

Hebrews 12:8 ... But if ye be without chastisement, whereof all are partakers, then are ye bastards, and not sons.

II Peter 2:3 ... And through covetousness shall they with feigned words make merchandise of you: whose judgment now of a long time lingereth not, and their damnation slumbereth not.

INNOCENT BLOOD ON THE HANDS OF EVANGELICALS
II Corinthians 4:2 ...But have renounced the hidden things of dishonesty, not walking in craftiness, nor handling the word of God deceitfully; but by manifestation of the truth commending ourselves to every man's conscience in the sight of God.

Romans 1:30 ... Backbiters, haters of God, despiteful, proud, boasters, inventors of evil things, disobedient to parents...

I Timothy 4:1 ...Now the Spirit explicitly says that in later times some will depart from the faith, paying attention to deceitful spirits and the teachings of demons...

II Timothy 3:13 ... But evil men and seducers shall wax worse and worse, deceiving, and being deceived.

Jeremiah 22:17 ... But thine eyes and thine heart are not but for thy covetousness, and for to shed innocent blood, and for oppression, and for violence, to do it.

Proverbs 29:25 ... The fear of man bringeth a snare: but whoso putteth his trust in the LORD shall be safe.

II Peter 2:2 ... And many shall follow their pernicious ways; by reason of whom the way of truth shall be evil spoken of.

Matthew 23:27 ... Woe unto you, scribes and Pharisees, hypocrites! for ye are like unto whited sepulchres, which indeed appear beautiful outward, but are within full of dead men's bones, and of all uncleanness.

I Corinthians 6:9 ... Know ye not that the unrighteous shall not inherit the kingdom of God? Be not deceived: neither fornicators, nor idolaters, nor adulterers, nor effeminate, nor abusers of themselves with mankind...

II Timothy 3:5 ... Having a form of godliness, but denying the power thereof: from such turn away.

Jude 1:16 ...These are murmurers, complainers, walking after their own lusts; and their mouth speaketh great swelling words, having men's persons in admiration because of advantage.

Romans 3:15 ...Their feet are swift to shed blood...

Galatians 5:14 ...For all the law is fulfilled in one word, even in this; Thou shalt love thy neighbour as thyself.

Acts 8:10-11 ... To whom they all gave heed, from the least to the greatest, saying, This man is the great power of God. And to him they had regard, because that of long time he had bewitched them with sorceries.

Matthew 24:12 ... And because iniquity shall abound, the love of many shall wax cold.

Luke 14:11 ... For whosoever exalteth himself shall be abased; and he that humbleth himself shall be exalted.

II Timothy 3:13 ... But evil men and seducers shall wax worse and worse, deceiving, and being deceived.

II Peter 2:2 ... And many shall follow their pernicious ways; by reason of whom the way of truth shall be evil spoken of.

Amos 5:23 ...Take thou away from me the noise of thy songs; for I will not hear the melody of thy viols.

Isaiah 5:14 ... Therefore hell hath enlarged herself, and opened her mouth without measure: and their glory, and their multitude, and their pomp, and he that rejoiceth, shall descend into it.

Revelation 3:16 ... So then because thou art lukewarm, and neither cold nor hot, I will spue thee out of my mouth.

Matthew 24:12 ...And because iniquity shall abound, the love of many shall wax cold.

Matthew 3:12 ... Whose fan is in his hand, and he will throughly purge his floor, and gather his wheat into the garner; but he will burn up the chaff with unquenchable fire.

Matthew 22:11-13 ... And when the king came in to see the guests, he saw there a man which had not on a wedding garment: And he saith unto him, Friend, how camest thou in hither not having a wedding garment? And he was speechless. Then said the king to the servants, Bind him hand and foot, and take him away, and cast him into outer darkness; there shall be weeping and gnashing of teeth.

Hebrews 10:30 ... For we know him that hath said, Vengeance belongeth unto me, I will recompense, saith the Lord. And again, The Lord shall judge his people.

Revelation 20: 1-3 ... And I saw an angel come down from heaven, having the key of the bottomless pit and a great chain in his hand. And he laid hold on the dragon, that old serpent, which is the Devil, and Satan, and bound him a thousand years...

Daniel 5:27 ...TEKEL; Thou art weighed in the balances, and art found wanting.

Matthew 24:48-51 ... But suppose that servant is wicked and says to himself, 'My master is staying away a long time,' and he then begins to beat his fellow servants and to eat and drink with drunkards. The master of that servant will come on a day when he does not expect him and at an hour he is not aware of. He will cut him to pieces and assign him a place with the hypocrites, where there will be weeping and gnashing of teeth.

Matthew 13:41-42 ... "The Son of Man will send forth His angels, and they will gather out of His kingdom all stumbling blocks, and those who commit lawlessness, and will throw them into the furnace of fire; in that place there will be weeping and gnashing of teeth.

I John 5:21 ...Little children, keep yourselves from idols. Amen.

Psalm 125:3 ... For the rod of the wicked shall not rest upon the lot of the righteous; lest the righteous put forth their hands unto iniquity.

Psalm 37:32 ... The wicked watcheth the righteous, and seeketh to slay him.

MERGER OF CHURCH AND STATE
Revelation 2:4 ...Nevertheless I have somewhat against thee, because thou hast left thy first love.

II Corinthians 6:14 ... Be ye not unequally yoked together with unbelievers: for what fellowship hath righteousness with unrighteousness? and what communion hath light with darkness?

I Timothy 6:10 ... For the love of money is the root of all evil: which while some coveted after, they have erred from the faith, and pierced themselves through with many sorrows.

Matthew 7:6 ... Give not that which is holy unto the dogs, neither cast ye your pearls before swine, lest they trample them under their feet, and turn again and rend you.

I Peter 2:18 ... For when they speak great swelling words of vanity, they allure through the lusts of the flesh, through much wantonness, those that were clean escaped from them who live in error.

Hebrews 5:14 ... But strong meat belongeth to them that are of full age, even those who by reason of use have their senses exercised to discern both good and evil.

II Timothy 4:3 ... For the time will come when they will not endure sound doctrine; but after their own lusts shall they heap to themselves teachers, having itching ears;

Romans 3:15 ... Their feet are swift to shed blood...

Matthew 26:52 ... Then said Jesus unto him, Put up again thy sword into his place: for all they that take the sword shall perish with the sword.

Revelation 13:10 ... He that leadeth into captivity shall go into captivity: he that killeth with the sword must be killed with the sword. Here is the patience and the faith of the saints.

Revelation 13:7 ... And it was given unto him to make war with the saints, and to overcome them: and power was given him over all kindreds, and tongues, and nations.

I John 4:1 ... Beloved, believe not every spirit, but try the spirits whether they are of God: because many false prophets are gone out into the world.

I John 5:21 ...Little children, keep yourselves from idols. Amen.
John 3:20 ... For every one that doeth evil hateth the light, neither cometh to the light, lest his deeds should be reproved.

I John 4:20 ... If a man say, I love God, and hateth his brother, he is a liar: for he that loveth not his brother whom he hath seen, how can he love God whom he hath not seen?

I John 4:18 ... There is no fear in love; but perfect love casteth out fear: because fear hath torment. He that feareth is not made perfect in love.

Jeremiah 17:5 ... Thus saith the LORD; Cursed be the man that trusteth in man, and maketh flesh his arm, and whose heart departeth from the LORD.

James 3:15 ... This wisdom descendeth not from above, but is earthly, sensual, devilish.

Proverbs 1:10-16 ... My son, if sinners entice thee, consent thou not. If they say, Come with us, let us lay wait for blood, let us lurk privily for the innocent without cause: Let us swallow them up alive as the grave; and whole, as those that go down into the pit: We shall find all precious substance, we shall fill our houses with spoil: Cast in thy lot among us; let us all have one purse: My son, walk not thou in the way with them; refrain thy foot from their path: For their feet run to evil, and make haste to shed blood.

James 4:1 ... From whence come wars and fightings among you? come they not hence, even of your lusts that war in your members?

Matthew 5:8 ... Blessed are the pure in heart: for they shall see God.

Titus 2:15 ...These things speak, and exhort, and rebuke with all authority. Let no man despise thee.

Psalm 7:17 ... I will praise the LORD according to his righteousness: and will sing praise to the name of the LORD most high.

Isaiah 50:7 ... For the Lord GOD will help me; therefore shall I not be confounded: therefore have I set my face like a flint, and I know that I shall not be ashamed.

Luke 15:7 ... I say unto you, that likewise joy shall be in heaven over one sinner that repenteth, more than over ninety and nine just persons, which need no repentance.

Luke 15:10 ... Likewise, I say unto you, there is joy in the presence of the angels of God over one sinner that repenteth.

Psalm 37:32 ... The wicked watcheth the righteous, and seeketh to slay him.

Revelation 12:11 ... And they overcame him by the blood of the Lamb, and by the word of their testimony; and they loved not their lives unto the death.

Revelation 13:16 ... And he causeth all, both small and great, rich and poor, free and bond, to receive a mark in their right hand, or in their foreheads..

Matthew 24:22 ... And except those days should be shortened, there should no flesh be saved: but for the elect's sake those days shall be shortened.

Luke 17:24 ... For as the lightning, that lighteneth out of the one part under heaven, shineth unto the other part under heaven; so shall also the Son of man be in his day.

Luke 16:28 ... For I have five brethren; that he may testify unto them, lest they also come into this place of torment.

Revelation 22:15 ... For without are dogs, and sorcerers, and whoremongers, and murderers, and idolaters, and whosoever loveth and maketh a lie.

Isaiah 5:14 ... Therefore hell hath enlarged herself, and opened her mouth without measure: and their glory, and their multitude, and their pomp, and he that rejoiceth, shall descend into it.

Revelation 14:11 ... And the smoke of their torment ascendeth up for ever and ever: and they have no rest day nor night, who worship the beast and his image, and whosoever receiveth the mark of his name.

CLERGY RESPONSE TEAMS
I Peter 5:2 ...Feed the flock of God which is among you, taking the oversight thereof, not by constraint, but willingly; not for filthy lucre, but of a ready mind;

II Peter 2:15 ... Which have forsaken the right way, and are gone astray, following the way of Balaam the son of Bosor, who loved the wages of unrighteousness;

I Timothy 6:10 ... For the love of money is the root of all evil: which while some coveted after, they have erred from the faith, and pierced themselves through with many sorrows.

I Timothy 4:1-2 ... Now the Spirit speaketh expressly, that in the latter times some shall depart from the faith, giving heed to seducing spirits, and doctrines of devils; Speaking lies in hypocrisy; having their conscience seared with a hot iron;

Matthew 7:6 ... Give not that which is holy unto the dogs, neither cast ye your pearls before swine, lest they trample them under their feet, and turn again and rend you.

II Corinthians 6:14 ... Be ye not unequally yoked together with unbelievers: for what fellowship hath righteousness with unrighteousness? and what communion hath light with darkness?

Romans 13:1-5 ... Let every soul be subject unto the higher powers. For there is no power but of God: the powers that be are ordained of God. Whosoever therefore resisteth the power, resisteth the ordinance of God: and they that resist shall receive to themselves damnation. For rulers are not a terror to good works, but to the evil. Wilt thou then not be afraid of the power? do that which is good, and thou shalt have praise of the same: For he is the minister of God to thee for good. But if thou do that which is evil, be afraid; for he beareth not the sword in vain: for he is the minister of God, a revenger to execute wrath upon him that doeth evil. Wherefore ye must needs be subject, not only for wrath, but also for conscience sake.

Matthew 24:9-10 ... Then shall they deliver you up to be afflicted, and shall kill you: and ye shall be hated of all nations for my name's sake. And then shall many be offended, and shall betray one another, and shall hate one another.
Mark 13:11 ... But when they shall lead you, and deliver you up, take no thought beforehand what ye shall speak, neither do ye premeditate: but whatsoever shall be given you in that hour, that speak ye: for it is not ye that speak, but the Holy Ghost.

Luke 21:12 ... But before all these, they shall lay their hands on you, and persecute you, delivering you up to the synagogues, and into prisons, being brought before kings and rulers for my name's sake.

John 16:2 ... They shall put you out of the synagogues: yea, the time cometh, that whosoever killeth you will think that he doeth God service.

Proverbs 27:12 ... A prudent man foreseeth the evil, and hideth himself; but the simple pass on, and are punished.

Psalm 108:12 ... Give us help from trouble: for vain is the help of man.

Psalm 140:4-5 ... Keep me, O Lord, from the hands of the wicked; preserve me from the violent man; who have purposed to overthrow my goings. The proud have hid a snare for me, and cords; they have spread a net by the wayside; they have set gins for me. Selah.

Psalm 141:3 ... Set a watch, O LORD, before my mouth; keep the door of my lips.

Psalm 107:20 ... He sent his word, and healed them, and delivered them from their destructions.

I Peter 2:24 ... Who his own self bare our sins in his own body on the tree, that we, being dead to sins, should live unto righteousness: by whose stripes ye were healed.

James 5:14-16 ... Is any sick among you? let him call for the elders of the church; and let them pray over him, anointing him with oil in the name of the Lord: And the prayer of faith shall save the sick, and the Lord shall raise him up; and if he have committed sins, they shall be forgiven him. Confess your faults one to another, and pray one for another, that ye may be healed.

I Thessalonians 5:3 ...For when they shall say, Peace and safety; then sudden destruction cometh upon them, as travail upon a woman with child; and they shall not escape.

I Peter 4:1 ... Forasmuch then as Christ hath suffered for us in the flesh, arm yourselves likewise with the same mind: for he that hath suffered in the flesh hath ceased from sin;

Ephesians 5:19 ... Speaking to yourselves in psalms and hymns and spiritual songs, singing and making melody in your heart to the Lord;

Jeremiah 29:13 ... And ye shall seek me, and find me, when ye shall search for me with all your heart.

Mark 13:20 ... And except that the Lord had shortened those days, no flesh should be saved: but for the elect's sake, whom he hath chosen, he hath shortened the days.

I Thessalonians 4:16-17 ... For the Lord himself shall descend from heaven with a shout, with the voice of the archangel, and with the trump of God: and the dead in Christ shall rise first: Then we which are alive and remain shall be caught up together with them in the clouds, to meet the Lord in the air: and so shall we ever be with the Lord.

I Corinthians 15:50-54 ... Now I say this, brethren, that flesh and blood cannot inherit the kingdom of God; nor does the perishable inherit the imperishable. Behold, I tell you a mystery; we will not all sleep, but we will all be changed, in a moment, in the twinkling of an eye, at the last trumpet; for the trumpet will sound, and the dead will be raised imperishable, and we will be changed. For this perishable must put on the imperishable, and this mortal must put on immortality. But when this perishable will have put on the imperishable, and this mortal will have put on immortality, then will come about the saying that is written, "Death is swallowed up in victory.

Part III The Future
LET GOD ARISE
I John 5:19 ... And we know that we are of God, and the whole world lieth in wickedness.

Revelation 20:2-3 ... And he laid hold on the dragon, that old serpent, which is the Devil, and Satan, and bound him a thousand years, And cast him into the bottomless pit, and shut him up, and set a seal upon him, that he should deceive the nations no more, till the thousand years should be fulfilled: and after that he must be loosed a little season.

Revelation 12:3-4 ... And there appeared another wonder in heaven; and behold a great red dragon, having seven heads and ten horns, and seven crowns upon his heads. And his tail drew the third part of the stars of heaven, and did cast them to the earth: and the dragon stood before the woman which was ready to be delivered, for to devour her child as soon as it was born.

Revelation 13:10, 14:12 ... He that leadeth into captivity shall go into captivity: he that killeth with the sword must be killed with the sword. Here is the patience and the faith of the saints... Here is the patience of the saints: here are they that keep the commandments of God, and the faith of Jesus.

John 8:44 ... Ye are of your father the devil, and the lusts of your father ye will do. He was a murderer from the beginning, and abode not in the truth, because there is no truth in him. When he speaketh a lie, he speaketh of his own: for he is a liar, and the father of it.

Revelation 21:8 ... But the fearful, and unbelieving, and the abominable, and murderers, and whoremongers, and sorcerers, and idolaters, and all liars, shall have their part in the lake which burneth with fire and brimstone: which is the second death.

Revelation 16:11 ... And blasphemed the God of heaven because of their pains and their sores, and repented not of their deeds.

Isaiah 13:11-12 ... And I will punish the world for their evil, and the wicked for their iniquity; and I will cause the arrogancy of the proud to cease, and will lay low the haughtiness of the terrible. I will make a man more precious than fine gold; even a man than the golden wedge of Ophir.

Isaiah 24:21 ... And it shall come to pass in that day, that the LORD shall punish the host of the high ones that are on high, and the kings of the earth upon the earth.

Revelation 20:1-2 ... And I saw an angel come down from heaven, having the key of the bottomless pit and a great chain in his hand. And he laid hold on the dragon, that old serpent, which is the Devil, and Satan, and bound him a thousand years...

Revelation 20:3 ... And cast him into the bottomless pit, and shut him up, and set a seal upon him, that he should deceive the nations no more, till the thousand years should be fulfilled: and after that he must be loosed a little season.

Revelation 19:17 ... And I saw an angel standing in the sun; and he cried with a loud voice, saying to all the fowls that fly in the midst of heaven, Come and gather yourselves together unto the supper of the great God...

Isaiah 63:1 ... Who is this that cometh from Edom, with dyed garments from Bozrah? this that is glorious in his apparel, travelling in the greatness of his strength? I that speak in righteousness, mighty to save.

Isaiah 29:6 ... Thou shalt be visited of the LORD of hosts with thunder, and with earthquake, and great noise, with storm and tempest, and the flame of devouring fire.

Isaiah 51:15 ... But I am the LORD thy God, that divided the sea, whose waves roared: The LORD of hosts is his name.

Job 40:11-12 ... Cast abroad the rage of thy wrath: and behold every one that is proud, and abase him. Look on every one that is proud, and bring him low; and tread down the wicked in their place.

Habakkuk 2:14 ... For the earth shall be filled with the knowledge of the glory of the LORD, as the waters cover the sea.

I Timothy 2:12 ... If we suffer, we shall also reign with him: if we deny him, he also will deny us:

Revelation 1:5-6 And from Jesus Christ, who is the faithful witness, and the first begotten of the dead, and the prince of the kings of the earth. Unto him that loved us, and washed us from our sins in his own blood, And hath made us kings and priests unto God and his Father; to him be glory and dominion for ever and ever. Amen.

Hebrews 4:9-11 ... There remaineth therefore a rest to the people of God. For he that is entered into his rest, he also hath ceased from his own works, as God did from his. Let us labour therefore to enter into that rest, lest any man fall after the same example of unbelief.

Mark 2:27-28 ... And he said unto them, The sabbath was made for man, and not man for the sabbath: Therefore the Son of man is Lord also of the sabbath.

MENE MENE TEKEL UPHARSIN

Isaiah 46:10 ... Declaring the end from the beginning, and from ancient times the things that are not yet done, saying, My counsel shall stand, and I will do all my pleasure:

Ezekiel 34:1-6 ... And the word of the LORD came unto me, saying, Son of man, prophesy against the shepherds of Israel, prophesy, and say unto them, Thus saith the Lord GOD unto the shepherds; Woe be to the shepherds of Israel that do feed themselves! should not the shepherds feed the flocks? Ye eat the fat, and ye clothe you with the wool, ye kill them that are fed: but ye feed not the flock. The diseased have ye not strengthened, neither have ye healed that which was sick, neither have ye bound up that which was broken, neither have **ye** brought again that which was driven away, neither have ye sought that which was lost; but with force and with cruelty have ye ruled them. And they were scattered, because there is no shepherd: and they became meat to all the beasts of the field, when they were scattered. My sheep wandered through all the mountains, and upon every high hill: yea, my flock was scattered upon all the face of the earth, and none did search or seek after them.

Revelation 7:14 ... And I said unto him, Sir, thou knowest. And he said to me, These are they which came out of great tribulation, and have washed their robes, and made them white in the blood of the Lamb.

Psalm 50:5 ... Gather my saints together unto me; those that have made a covenant with me by sacrifice.

Revelation 7:3 ... Saying, Hurt not the earth, neither the sea, nor the trees, till we have sealed the servants of our God in their foreheads.

Revelation 11:3-6 ... And I will give power unto my two witnesses, and they shall prophesy a thousand two hundred and threescore days, clothed in sackcloth. These are the two olive trees, and the two candlesticks standing before the God of the earth. And if any man will hurt them, fire proceedeth out of their mouth, and devoureth their enemies: and if any man will hurt them, he must in this manner be killed. These have power to shut heaven, that it rain not in the days of their prophecy: and have power over waters to turn them to blood, and to smite the earth with all plagues, as often as they will.

I Corinthians 15:52 ... In a moment, in the twinkling of an eye, at the last trump: for the trumpet shall sound, and the dead shall be raised incorruptible, and we shall be changed.

I Corinthians 15:53 ... For this corruptible must put on incorruption, and this mortal must put on immortality.

Revelation 15:3-4 ... And they sing the song of Moses the servant of God, and the song of the Lamb, saying, Great and marvellous are thy works, Lord God Almighty; just and true are thy ways, thou King of saints. Who shall not fear thee, O Lord, and glorify thy name? for thou only art holy: for all nations shall come and worship before thee; for thy judgments are made manifest.

Revelation 7:15 ... Therefore are they before the throne of God, and serve him day and night in his temple: and he that sitteth on the throne shall dwell among them.

Romans 8:7 ... Because the carnal mind is enmity against God: for it is not subject to the law of God, neither indeed can be.

II Thessalonians 2:4 ... Who opposeth and exalteth himself above all that is called God, or that is worshipped; so that he as God sitteth in the temple of God, shewing himself that he is God.

Job 21:15 ... What is the Almighty, that we should serve him? and what profit should we have, if we pray unto him?

Revelation 9:20-21 ... And the rest of the men which were not killed by these plagues yet repented not of the works of their hands, that they should not worship devils, and idols of gold, and silver, and brass, and stone, and of wood: which neither can see, nor hear, nor walk: Neither repented they of their murders, nor of their sorceries, nor of their fornication, nor of their thefts.

Revelation 16:9-11 ... And men were scorched with great heat, and blasphemed the name of God, which hath power over these plagues: and they repented not to give him glory. And the fifth angel poured out his vial upon the seat of the beast; and his kingdom was full of darkness; and they gnawed their tongues for pain, And blasphemed the God of heaven because of their pains and their sores, and repented not of their deeds.

Revelation 6:15 ... And the kings of the earth, and the great men, and the rich men, and the chief captains, and the mighty men, and every bondman, and every free man, hid themselves in the dens and in the rocks of the mountains;

Proverbs 21:30 ... There is no wisdom nor understanding nor counsel against the LORD.

Job 28:24 ... For he looketh to the ends of the earth, and seeth under the whole heaven;

Revelation 16:1 ... And I heard a great voice out of the temple saying to the seven angels, Go your ways, and pour out the vials of the wrath of God upon the earth.

Isaiah 59:17 ... For he put on righteousness as a breastplate, and an helmet of salvation upon his head; and he put on the garments of vengeance for clothing, and was clad with zeal as a cloke.

Ephesians 6:11-13 ... Put on the whole armour of God, that ye may be able to stand against the wiles of the devil. For we wrestle not against flesh and blood, but against principalities, against powers, against the rulers of the darkness of this world, against spiritual wickedness in high places. Wherefore take unto you the whole armour of God, that ye may be able to withstand in the evil day, and having done all, to stand.

Ephesians 6:17 ... And take the helmet of salvation, and the sword of the Spirit, which is the word of God:

Revelation 14:18 ... And another angel came out from the altar, which had power over fire; and cried with a loud cry to him that had the sharp sickle, saying, Thrust in thy sharp sickle, and gather the clusters of the vine of the earth; for her grapes are fully ripe.

Daniel 2:41-43 ... And whereas thou sawest the feet and toes, part of potters' clay, and part of iron, the kingdom shall be divided; but there shall be in it of the strength of the iron, forasmuch as thou sawest the iron mixed with miry clay. And as the toes of the feet were part of iron, and part of clay, so the kingdom shall be partly strong, and partly broken. And whereas thou sawest iron mixed with miry clay, they shall mingle themselves with the seed of men: but they shall not cleave one to another, even as iron is not mixed with clay.

Psalm 46:9-10 ... He maketh wars to cease unto the end of the earth; he breaketh the bow, and cutteth the spear in sunder; he burneth the chariot in the fire. Be still, and know that I am God: I will be exalted among the heathen, I will be exalted in the earth.

Revelation 6:14 ... And the heaven departed as a scroll when it is rolled together; and every mountain and island were moved out of their places.

Revelation 6:17 ... For the great day of his wrath is come; and who shall be able to stand?

Psalm 33:6 ... By the word of the LORD were the heavens made; and all the host of them by the breath of his mouth.

Psalm 110:6 ...He shall judge among the heathen, he shall fill the places with the dead bodies; he shall wound the heads over many countries.

Revelation 16:21 ... And there fell upon men a great hail out of heaven, every stone about the weight of a talent: and men blasphemed God because of the plague of the hail; for the plague thereof was exceeding great.

Philippians 2:10 ... That at the name of Jesus every knee should bow, of things in heaven, and things in earth, and things under the earth;

Colossians 2:9 ... For in him dwelleth all the fulness of the Godhead bodily.

Ephesians 1:21-22 ... Far above all principality, and power, and might, and dominion, and every name that is named, not only in this world, but also in that which is to come: And hath put all things under his feet, and gave him to be the head over all things to the church...

Daniel 7:14 ... And there was given him dominion, and glory, and a kingdom, that all people, nations, and languages, should serve him: his dominion is an everlasting dominion, which shall not pass away, and his kingdom that which shall not be destroyed.

Revelation 11:15 ... And the seventh angel sounded; and there were great voices in heaven, saying, The kingdoms of this world are become the kingdoms of our Lord, and of his Christ; and he shall reign for ever and ever.

Psalm 102:15 ... So the heathen shall fear the name of the LORD, and all the kings of the earth thy glory.

Philippians 2:10 That at the name of Jesus every knee should bow, of things in heaven, and things in earth, and things under the earth;

WHEN THE TIMES OF THE GENTILES ARE FULFILLED
Proverbs 21:24 ...Proud and haughty scorner is his name, who dealeth in proud wrath.

Isaiah 2:11 ...The lofty looks of man shall be humbled, and the haughtiness of men shall be bowed down, and the LORD alone shall be exalted in that day.

Psalm 9:17 ...The wicked shall be turned into hell, and all the nations that forget God.

THE LATE GREAT USA

Mark 7:8-9 ... For laying aside the commandment of God, ye hold the tradition of men, as the washing of pots and cups: and many other such like things ye do. And he said unto them, Full well ye reject the commandment of God, that ye may keep your own tradition.

I Timothy 6:20-21 ...O Timothy, keep that which is committed to thy trust, avoiding profane and vain babblings, and oppositions of science falsely so called: Which some professing have erred concerning the faith. Grace be with thee. Amen.

Deuteronomy 5:8-9 ... Thou shalt not make thee any graven image, or any likeness of any thing that is in heaven above, or that is in the earth beneath, or that is in the waters beneath the earth: Thou shalt not bow down thyself unto them, nor serve them: for I the LORD thy God am a jealous God, visiting the iniquity of the fathers upon the children unto the third and fourth generation of them that hate me...

Ezekiel 27:3-9, 25-34 ... And say unto Tyrus, O thou that art situate at the entry of the sea, which art a merchant of the people for many isles, Thus saith the Lord GOD; O Tyrus, thou hast said, I am of perfect beauty. Thy borders are in the midst of the seas, thy builders have perfected thy beauty. They have made all thy ship boards of fir trees of Senir: they have taken cedars from Lebanon to make masts for thee. Of the oaks of Bashan have they made thine oars; the company of the Ashurites have made thy benches of ivory, brought out of the isles of Chittim. Fine linen with broidered work from Egypt was that which thou spreadest forth to be thy sail; blue and purple from the isles of Elishah was that which covered thee. The inhabitants of Zidon and Arvad were thy mariners: thy wise men, O Tyrus, that were in thee, were thy pilots. The ancients of Gebal and the wise men thereof were in thee thy calkers: all the ships of the sea with their mariners were in thee to occupy thy merchandise.

The ships of Tarshish did sing of thee in thy market: and thou wast replenished, and made very glorious in the midst of the seas. Thy rowers have brought thee into great waters: the east wind hath broken thee in the midst of the seas. Thy riches, and thy fairs, thy merchandise, thy mariners, and thy pilots, thy calkers, and the occupiers of thy merchandise, and all thy men of war, that are in thee, and in all thy company which is in the midst of thee, shall fall into the midst of the seas in the day of thy ruin. The suburbs shall shake at the sound of the cry of thy pilots. And all that handle the oar, the mariners, and all the pilots of the sea, shall come down from their ships, they shall stand upon the land; And shall cause their voice to be heard against thee, and shall cry bitterly, and shall cast up dust upon their heads, they shall wallow themselves in the ashes: And they shall make themselves utterly bald for thee, and gird them with sackcloth, and they shall weep for thee with bitterness of heart and bitter wailing. And in their wailing they shall take up a lamentation for thee, and lament over thee, saying, What city is like Tyrus, like the destroyed in the midst of the sea? When thy wares went forth out of the seas, thou filledst many people; thou didst enrich the kings of the earth with the multitude of thy riches and of thy merchandise. In the time when thou shalt be broken by the seas in the depths of the waters thy merchandise and all thy company in the midst of thee shall fall.

Romans 1:28 ... And even as they did not like to retain God in their knowledge, God gave them over to a reprobate mind, to do those things which are not convenient;

Exodus 23:1 ... Thou shalt not raise a false report: put not thine hand with the wicked to be an unrighteous witness.

Habakkuk 2:5 ... Yea also, because he transgresseth by wine, he is a proud man, neither keepeth at home, who enlargeth his desire as hell, and is as death, and cannot be satisfied, but gathereth unto him all nations, and heapeth unto him all people...

Hebrews 4:13 ... Neither is there any creature that is not manifest in his sight: but all things are naked and opened unto the eyes of him with whom we have to do.

Ecclesiastes 11:9 ... Rejoice, O young man, in thy youth; and let thy heart cheer thee in the days of thy youth, and walk in the ways of thine heart, and in the sight of thine eyes: but know thou, that for all these things God will bring thee into judgment.

Romans 1:30 ... Backbiters, haters of God, despiteful, proud, boasters, inventors of evil things, disobedient to parents...

Psalm 10:3-4 ... For the wicked boasteth of his heart's desire, and blesseth the covetous, whom the LORD abhorreth. The wicked, through the pride of his countenance, will not seek after God: God is not in all his thoughts.

I Timothy 1:9-11 ... Knowing this, that the law is not made for a righteous man, but for the lawless and disobedient, for the ungodly and for sinners, for unholy and profane, for murderers of fathers and murderers of mothers, for manslayers, For whoremongers, for them that defile themselves with mankind, for menstealers, for liars, for perjured persons, and if there be any other thing that is contrary to sound doctrine; According to the glorious gospel of the blessed God, which was committed to my trust.

Isaiah 40:6 ... The voice said, Cry. And he said, What shall I cry? All flesh is grass, and all the goodliness thereof is as the flower of the field:

II Corinthians 10:5 ... Casting down imaginations, and every high thing that exalteth itself against the knowledge of God, and bringing into captivity every thought to the obedience of Christ;

Ecclesiastes 7:5 ... It is better to hear the rebuke of the wise, than for a man to hear the song of fools.

Matthew 5:28 ... But I say unto you, That whosoever looketh on a woman to lust after her hath committed adultery with her already in his heart.

Proverbs 26:28 ... A lying tongue hateth those that are afflicted by it; and a flattering mouth worketh ruin.

Proverbs 6:19 ... A false witness that speaketh lies, and he that soweth discord among brethren.

Romans 1:30 ... Backbiters, haters of God, despiteful, proud, boasters, inventors of evil things, disobedient

Mark 13:13 ... And ye shall be hated of all men for my name's sake: but he that shall endure unto the end, the same shall be saved.

Matthew 16:3 ...And in the morning, It will be foul weather to day: for the sky is red and lowring. O ye hypocrites, ye can discern the face of the sky; but can ye not discern the signs of the times?

Jeremiah 17:5 ... Thus saith the LORD; Cursed be the man that trusteth in man, and maketh flesh his arm, and whose heart departeth from the LORD.

Revelation 16:12 ... And the sixth angel poured out his vial upon the great river Euphrates; and the water thereof was dried up, that the way of the kings of the east might be prepared.

Daniel 11:44 ... But tidings out of the east and out of the north shall trouble him: therefore he shall go forth with great fury to destroy, and utterly to make away many.

Revelation 11:15 ... And the seventh angel sounded; and there were great voices in heaven, saying, The kingdoms of this world are become the kingdoms of our Lord, and of his Christ; and he shall reign for ever and ever.

Revelation 18:21-23 ... And a mighty angel took up a stone like a great millstone, and cast it into the sea, saying, Thus with violence shall that great city Babylon be thrown down, and shall be found no more at all. And the voice of harpers, and musicians, and of pipers, and trumpeters, shall be heard no more at all in thee; and no craftsman, of whatsoever craft he be, shall be found any more in thee; and the sound of a millstone shall be heard no more at all in thee; And the light of a candle shall shine no more at all in thee; and the voice of the bridegroom and of the bride shall be heard no more at all in thee: for thy merchants were the great men of the earth; for by thy sorceries were all nations deceived.

Jeremiah 30:23-24 ... Behold, the whirlwind of the LORD goeth forth with fury, a continuing whirlwind: it shall fall with pain upon the head of the wicked.
The fierce anger of the LORD shall not return, until he have done it, and until he have performed the intents of his heart: in the latter days ye shall consider it.

Jeremiah 51:47 ... Therefore, behold, the days come, that I will do judgment upon the graven images of Babylon: and her whole land shall be confounded, and all her slain shall fall in the midst of her.

Isaiah 2:18 ... And the idols he shall utterly abolish.

Revelation 18:21 ... And a mighty angel took up a stone like a great millstone, and cast it into the sea, saying, Thus with violence shall that great city Babylon be thrown down, and shall be found no more at all.

Revelation 19:17-18 ... And I saw an angel standing in the sun; and he cried with a loud voice, saying to all the fowls that fly in the midst of heaven, Come and gather yourselves together unto the supper of the great God; That ye may eat the flesh of kings, and the flesh of captains, and the flesh of mighty men, and the flesh of horses, and of them that sit on them, and the flesh of all men, both free and bond, both small and great.

Psalm 9:19 ... Arise, O LORD; let not man prevail: let the heathen be judged in thy sight.

Isaiah 47:1-3 ... Come down, and sit in the dust, O virgin daughter of Babylon, sit on the ground: there is no throne, O daughter of the Chaldeans: for thou shalt no more be called tender and delicate. ake the millstones, and grind meal: uncover thy locks, make bare the leg, uncover the thigh, pass over the rivers. Thy nakedness shall be uncovered, yea, thy shame shall be seen: I will take vengeance, and I will not meet thee as a man.

Exodus 20:4 ... Thou shalt not make unto thee any graven image, or any likeness of any thing that is in heaven above, or that is in the earth beneath, or that is in the water under the earth:

Isaiah 24:21-22 ... And it shall come to pass in that day, that the LORD shall punish the host of the high ones that are on high, and the kings of the earth upon the earth. And they shall be gathered together, as prisoners are gathered in the pit, and shall be shut up in the prison, and after many days shall they be visited.

Proverbs 6:12-19 ... A naughty person, a wicked man, walketh with a froward mouth. He winketh with his eyes, he speaketh with his feet, he teacheth with his fingers; Frowardness is in his heart, he deviseth mischief continually; he soweth discord. Therefore shall his calamity come suddenly; suddenly shall he be broken without remedy. These six things doth the LORD hate: yea, seven are an abomination unto him: A proud look, a lying tongue, and hands that shed innocent blood, An heart that deviseth wicked imaginations, feet that be swift in running to mischief, A false witness that speaketh lies, and he that soweth discord among brethren.

Psalm 68:30 ... Rebuke the company of spearmen, the multitude of the bulls, with the calves of the people, till every one submit himself with pieces of silver: scatter thou the people that delight in war.

Isaiah 59:3-4, 7-8 For your hands are defiled with blood, and your fingers with iniquity; your lips have spoken lies, your tongue hath muttered perverseness. None calleth for justice, nor any pleadeth for truth: they trust in vanity, and speak lies; they conceive mischief, and bring forth iniquity... Their feet run to evil, and they make haste to shed innocent blood: their thoughts are thoughts of iniquity; wasting and destruction are in their paths. The way of peace they know not; and there is no judgment in their goings: they have made them crooked paths: whosoever goeth therein shall not know peace.

Isaiah 10:13-14 ... For he saith, By the strength of my hand I have done it, and by my wisdom; for I am prudent: and I have removed the bounds of the people, and have robbed their treasures, and I have put down the inhabitants like a valiant man: And my hand hath found as a nest the riches of the people: and as one gathereth eggs that are left, have I gathered all the earth; and there was none that moved the wing, or opened the mouth, or peeped.

Revelation 11:18 ... And the nations were angry, and thy wrath is come, and the time of the dead, that they should be judged, and that thou shouldest give reward unto thy servants the prophets, and to the saints, and them that fear thy name, small and great; and shouldest destroy them which destroy the earth.

Psalm 52:3 ... Thou lovest evil more than good; and lying rather than to speak righteousness. Selah.

Revelation 22:15 ... For without are dogs, and sorcerers, and whoremongers, and murderers, and idolaters, and whosoever loveth and maketh a lie.

Proverbs 26:28 ... A lying tongue hateth those that are afflicted by it; and a flattering mouth worketh ruin.

Isaiah 14:6 ... He who smote the people in wrath with a continual stroke, he that ruled the nations in anger, is persecuted, and none hindereth.

Revelation 9:21 ... Neither repented they of their murders, nor of their sorceries, nor of their fornication, nor of their thefts.

Revelation 18:24 ... And in her was found the blood of prophets and of saints and of all who have been slain on the earth.

Habakkuk 2:14 ... For the earth shall be filled with the knowledge of the glory of the LORD, as the waters cover the sea.

Genesis 15:18 ... In the same day the LORD made a covenant with Abram, saying, Unto thy seed have I given this land, from the river of Egypt unto the great river, the river Euphrates...

Hebrews 8:10 ... For this is the covenant that I will make with the house of Israel after those days, saith the Lord; I will put my laws into their mind, and write them in their hearts: and I will be to them a God, and they shall be to me a people...

Isaiah 14:7 ... The whole earth is at rest, and is quiet: they break forth into singing.

Psalm 34:8 ... O taste and see that the LORD is good: blessed is the man that trusteth in him.

Revelation 20:6 ... Blessed and holy is he that hath part in the first resurrection: on such the second death hath no power, but they shall be priests of God and of Christ, and shall reign with him a thousand years.

John 6:45 ... It is written in the prophets, And they shall be all taught of God. Every man therefore that hath heard, and hath learned of the Father, cometh unto me.

John 14:6 ... Jesus saith unto him, I am the way, the truth, and the life: no man cometh unto the Father, but by me.

Isaiah 2:2-3 ... And it shall come to pass in the last days, that the mountain of the LORD'S house shall be established in the top of the mountains, and shall be exalted above the hills; and all nations shall flow unto it. And many people shall go and say, Come ye, and let us go up to the mountain of the LORD, to the house of the God of Jacob; and he will teach us of his ways, and we will walk in his paths: for out of Zion shall go forth the law, and the word of the LORD from Jerusalem.

Revelation 20:7-8 ... And when the thousand years are expired, Satan shall be loosed out of his prison, And shall go out to deceive the nations which are in the four quarters of the earth, Gog and Magog, to gather them together to battle: the number of whom is as the sand of the sea.

Revelation 20:9 ... And they went up on the breadth of the earth, and compassed the camp of the saints about, and the beloved city: and fire came down from God out of heaven, and devoured them.

Revelation 21:1-4 ... And I saw a new heaven and a new earth: for the first heaven and the first earth were passed away; and there was no more sea. And I John saw the holy city, new Jerusalem, coming down from God out of heaven, prepared as a bride adorned for her husband. And I heard a great voice out of heaven saying, Behold, the tabernacle of God is with men, and he will dwell with them, and they shall be his people, and God himself shall be with them, and be their God. And God shall wipe away all tears from their eyes; and there shall be no more death, neither sorrow, nor crying, neither shall there be any more pain: for the former things are passed away.

JUSTICE EXECUTED FOR THE ORPHAN AND WIDOW
-Feux de Joie Theme-

Daniel 7:22 ... Until the Ancient of days came, and judgment was given to the saints of the most High; and the time came that the saints possessed the kingdom.

Ezekiel 37:14 ... And shall put my spirit in you, and ye shall live, and I shall place you in your own land: then shall ye know that I the LORD have spoken it, and performed it, saith the LORD.

Psalm 2:2-3 ... The kings of the earth set themselves, and the rulers take counsel together, against the LORD, and against his anointed, saying, Let us break their bands asunder, and cast away their cords from us.

Joel 3:2 ... I will also gather all nations, and will bring them down into the valley of Jehoshaphat, and will plead with them there for my people and for my heritage Israel, whom they have scattered among the nations, and parted my land.

Jeremiah 25:30-33 ... Therefore prophesy thou against them all these words, and say unto them, The LORD shall roar from on high, and utter his voice from his holy habitation; he shall mightily roar upon his habitation; he shall give a shout, as they that tread the grapes, against all the inhabitants of the earth...A noise shall come even to the ends of the earth; for the LORD hath a controversy with the nations, he will plead with all flesh; he will give them that are wicked to the sword, saith the LORD. Thus saith the LORD of hosts, Behold, evil shall go forth from nation to nation, and a great whirlwind shall be raised up from the coasts of the earth. And the slain of the LORD shall be at that day from one end of the earth even unto the other end of the earth: they shall not be lamented, neither gathered, nor buried; they shall be dung upon the ground.

Jeremiah 25:27-29 ... Therefore thou shalt say unto them, Thus saith the LORD of hosts, the God of Israel; Drink ye, and be drunken, and spue, and fall, and rise no more, because of the sword which I will send among you. And it shall be, if they refuse to take the cup at thine hand to drink, then shalt thou say unto them, Thus saith the LORD of hosts; Ye shall certainly drink. For, lo, I begin to bring evil on the city which is called by my name, and should ye be utterly unpunished? Ye shall not be unpunished: for I will call for a sword upon all the inhabitants of the earth, saith the LORD of hosts.

Jeremiah 25:32 ... Thus saith the LORD of hosts, Behold, evil shall go forth from nation to nation, and a great whirlwind shall be raised up from the coasts of the earth.

Isaiah 51:11 ... Therefore the redeemed of the LORD shall return, and come with singing unto Zion; and everlasting joy shall be upon their head: they shall obtain gladness and joy; and sorrow and mourning shall flee away.

Isaiah 33:22-24 ... For the LORD is our judge, the LORD is our lawgiver, the LORD is our king; he will save us. Thy tacklings are loosed; they could not well strengthen their mast, they could not spread the sail: then is the prey of a great spoil divided; the lame take the prey. And the inhabitant shall not say, I am sick: the people that dwell therein shall be forgiven their iniquity.

Zechariah 13:8-9 ... And it shall come to pass, that in all the land, saith the LORD, two parts therein shall be cut off and die; but the third shall be left therein. And I will bring the third part through the fire, and will refine them as silver is refined, and will try them as gold is tried: they shall call on my name, and I will hear them: I will say, It is my people: and they shall say, The LORD is my God.

Revelation 6:15 ... And the kings of the earth, and the great men, and the rich men, and the chief captains, and the mighty men, and every bondman, and every free man, hid themselves in the dens and in the rocks of the mountains...

Isaiah 2:19 ... And they shall go into the holes of the rocks, and into the caves of the earth, for fear of the LORD, and for the glory of his majesty, when he ariseth to shake terribly the earth.

Psalm 9:16 ... The LORD is known by the judgment which he executeth: the wicked is snared in the work of his own hands. Higgaion. Selah.

Acts 10:34-35 ... Then Peter opened his mouth, and said, Of a truth I perceive that God is no respecter of persons: But in every nation he that feareth him, and worketh righteousness, is accepted with him.

Psalm 58:10 ... The righteous shall rejoice when he seeth the vengeance: he shall wash his feet in the blood of the wicked.

Revelation 7:9,13-14 ... After this I beheld, and, lo, a great multitude, which no man could number, of all nations, and kindreds, and people, and tongues, stood before the throne, and before the Lamb, clothed with white robes, and palms in their hands; And one of the elders answered, saying unto me, What are these which are arrayed in white robes? and whence came they? And I said unto him, Sir, thou knowest. And he said to me, These are they which came out of great tribulation, and have washed their robes, and made them white in the blood of the Lamb.

II Chronicles 20:21-22 ... And when he had consulted with the people, he appointed singers unto the LORD, and that should praise the beauty of holiness, as they went out before the army, and to say, Praise the LORD; for his mercy endureth for ever. And when they began to sing and to praise, the LORD set ambushments against the children of Ammon, Moab, and mount Seir, which were come against Judah; and they were smitten.

Psalm 83:1-5 ... Keep not thou silence, O God: hold not thy peace, and be not still, O God. For, lo, thine enemies make a tumult: and they that hate thee have lifted up the head. They have taken crafty counsel against thy people, and consulted against thy hidden ones. They have said, Come, and let us cut them off from being a nation; that the name of Israel may be no more in remembrance. For they have consulted together with one consent: they are confederate against thee:

Isaiah 35:1-10 ... The wilderness and the solitary place shall be glad for them; and the desert shall rejoice, and blossom as the rose. It shall blossom abundantly, and rejoice even with joy and singing: the glory of Lebanon shall be given unto it, the excellency of Carmel and Sharon, they shall see the glory of the LORD, and the excellency of our God. Strengthen ye the weak hands, and confirm the feeble knees. Say to them that are of a fearful heart, Be strong, fear not: behold, your God will come with vengeance, even God with a recompence; he will come and save you. Then the eyes of the blind shall be opened, and the ears of the deaf shall be unstopped. Then shall the lame man leap as an hart, and the tongue of the dumb sing: for in the wilderness shall waters break out, and streams in the desert. And the parched ground shall become a pool, and the thirsty land springs of water: in the habitation of dragons, where each lay, shall be grass with reeds and rushes. And an highway shall be there, and a way, and it shall be called The way of holiness; the unclean shall not pass over it; but it shall be for those: the wayfaring men, though fools, shall not err therein. No lion shall be there, nor any ravenous beast shall go up thereon, it shall not be found there; but the redeemed shall walk there: And the ransomed of the LORD shall return, and come to Zion with songs and everlasting joy upon their heads: they shall obtain joy and gladness, and sorrow and sighing shall flee away.

Joel 2:31 ... The sun shall be turned into darkness, and the moon into blood, before the great and the terrible day of the LORD come.

Revelation 19:14 ... And the armies which were in heaven followed him upon white horses, clothed in fine linen, white and clean.

Leviticus 26:34-35 38-39,43 ... Then shall the land enjoy her sabbaths, as long as it lieth desolate, and ye bein your enemies' land; even then shall the land rest, and enjoy her sabbaths. As long as it lieth desolate it shall rest; because it did not rest in your sabbaths, when ye dwelt upon it. ..And ye shall perish among the heathen, and the land of your enemies shall eat you up. And they that are left of you shall pine away in their iniquity in your enemies' lands; and also in the iniquities of their fathers shall they pine away with them... The land also shall be left of them, and shall enjoy her sabbaths, while she lieth desolate without them: and they shall accept of the punishment of their iniquity: because, even because they despised my judgments, and because their soul abhorred my statutes.

Jeremiah 50:7,33 ... All that found them have devoured them: and their adversaries said, We offend not, because they have sinned against the LORD, the habitation of justice, even the LORD, the hope of their fathers... Thus saith the LORD of hosts; The children of Israel and the children of Judah were oppressed together: and all that took them captives held them fast; they refused to let them go.

Isaiah 59:17 ... For he put on righteousness as a breastplate, and an helmet of salvation upon his head; and he put on the garments of vengeance for clothing, and was clad with zeal as a cloke.

Revelation 16:15 ... Behold, I come as a thief. Blessed is he that watcheth, and keepeth his garments, lest he walk naked, and they see his shame.

Joel 3:2 ... I will also gather all nations, and will bring them down into the valley of Jehoshaphat, and will plead with them there for my people and for my heritage Israel, whom they have scattered among the nations, and parted my land.

Psalm 50:3 ... Our God shall come, and shall not keep silence: a fire shall devour before him, and it shall be very tempestuous round about him.

Psalm 2:2-3 ... The kings of the earth set themselves, and the rulers take counsel together, against the LORD, and against his anointed, saying, Let us break their bands asunder, and cast away their cords from us.

Psalm 2:4-5 ... He that sitteth in the heavens shall laugh: the Lord shall have them in derision. Then shall he speak unto them in his wrath, and vex them in his sore displeasure.

Revelation 16:12 ... And the sixth angel poured out his vial upon the great river Euphrates; and the water thereof was dried up, that the way of the kings of the east might be prepared.

Psalm 46:9 ... He maketh wars to cease unto the end of the earth; he breaketh the bow, and cutteth the spear in sunder; he burneth the chariot in the fire.

Jude 1:14-15 ... And Enoch also, the seventh from Adam, prophesied of these, saying,

Behold, the Lord cometh with ten thousands of his saints, To execute judgment upon all, and to convince all that are ungodly among them of all their ungodly deeds which they have ungodly committed, and of all their hard speeches which ungodly sinners have spoken against him.

Deuteronomy 32:41-43 ... If I whet my glittering sword, and mine hand take hold on judgment; I will render vengeance to mine enemies, and will reward them that hate me. I will make mine arrows drunk with blood, and my sword shall devour flesh; and that with the blood of the slain and of the captives, from the beginning of revenges upon the enemy. Rejoice, O ye nations, with his people: for he will avenge the blood of his servants, and will render vengeance to his adversaries, and will be merciful unto his land, and to his people.

Revelation 11:15 ... And the seventh angel sounded; and there were great voices in heaven, saying, The kingdoms of this world are become the kingdoms of our Lord, and of his Christ; and he shall reign for ever and ever.

Daniel 7:13-14 ... I saw in the night visions, and, behold, one like the Son of man came with the clouds of heaven, and came to the Ancient of days, and they brought him near before him... And there was given him dominion, and glory, and a kingdom, that all people, nations, and languages, should serve him: his dominion is an everlasting dominion, which shall not pass away, and his kingdom that which shall not be destroyed.

Revelation 19:12 ... His eyes were as a flame of fire, and on his head were many crowns; and he had a name written, that no man knew, but he himself.

JUSTICE EXECUTED FOR THE ORPHAN AND WIDOW
-The Judicious Expert Theme-

Psalm 13:1 ... How long, LORD? Will you forget me forever? How long will you hide your face from me?

Revelation 6:10 ... And they cried with a loud voice, saying, How long, O Lord, holy and true, dost thou not judge and avenge our blood on them that dwell on the earth?

Revelation 19:11 ...And I saw heaven opened, and behold a white horse; and he that sat upon him was called Faithful and True, and in righteousness he doth judge and make war.

Revelation 19:12 ...His eyes were as a flame of fire, and on his head were many crowns; and he had a name written, that no man knew, but he himself.

Revelation 19:15 ...And out of his mouth goeth a sharp sword, that with it he should smite the nations: and he shall rule them with a rod of iron: and he treadeth the winepress of the fierceness and wrath of Almighty God.

Revelation 19:14 ...And the armies which were in heaven followed him upon white horses, clothed in fine linen, white and clean.

Jude 1:14-15 ...And Enoch also, the seventh from Adam, prophesied of these, saying,

Behold, the Lord cometh with ten thousands of his saints, 15To execute judgment upon all, and to convince all that are ungodly among them of all their ungodly deeds which they have ungodly committed, and of all their hard speeches which ungodly sinners have spoken against him.

Psalm 50:3 ... Our God shall come, and shall not keep silence: a fire shall devour before him, and it shall be very tempestuous round about him.

Isaiah 46:10 ... Declaring the end from the beginning, and from ancient times the things that are not yet done, saying, My counsel shall stand, and I will do all my pleasure...

Jeremiah 25:31-32 ... A noise shall come even to the ends of the earth; for the LORD hath a controversy with the nations, he will plead with all flesh; he will give them that are wicked to the sword, saith the LORD. Thus saith the LORD of hosts, Behold, evil shall go forth from nation to nation, and a great whirlwind shall be raised up from the coasts of the earth.

Ezekiel 34:6 ... My sheep wandered through all the mountains, and upon every high hill: yea, my flock was scattered upon all the face of the earth, and none did search or seek after them.

Psalm 50:5 ... Gather my saints together unto me; those that have made a covenant with me by sacrifice.

Isaiah 26:20 ... Come, my people, enter thou into thy chambers, and shut thy doors about thee: hide thyself as it were for a little moment, until the indignation be overpast.

Psalm 91:8 ... Only with thine eyes shalt thou behold and see the reward of the wicked.

Isaiah 24:17 ...Fear, and the pit, and the snare, are upon thee, O inhabitant of the earth.

Isaiah 34:6-8 ... The sword of the LORD is filled with blood, it is made fat with fatness, and with the blood of lambs and goats, with the fat of the kidneys of rams: for the LORD hath a sacrifice in Bozrah, and a great slaughter in the land of Idumea. And the unicorns shall come down with them, and the bullocks with the bulls; and their land shall be soaked with blood, and their dust made fat with fatness. For it is the day of the LORD'S vengeance, and the year of recompences for the controversy of Zion.

Habakkuk 2:5 ... Yea also, because he transgresseth by wine, he is a proud man, neither keepeth at home, who enlargeth his desire as hell, and is as death, and cannot be satisfied, but gathereth unto him all nations, and heapeth unto him all people:

Jeremiah 50:7 ... All that found them have devoured them: and their adversaries said, We offend not, because they have sinned against the LORD, the habitation of justice, even the LORD, the hope of their fathers.

Deuteronomy 28:37 ... And thou shalt become an astonishment, a proverb, and a byword, among all nations whither the LORD shall lead thee.

Jeremiah 24:9 ... And I will deliver them to be removed into all the kingdoms of the earth for their hurt, to be a reproach and a proverb, a taunt and a curse, in all places whither I shall drive them.

Proverbs 26:27 ... Whoso diggeth a pit shall fall therein: and he that rolleth a stone, it will return upon him.

Revelation 13:6 ... And he opened his mouth in blasphemy against God, to blaspheme his name, and his tabernacle, and them that dwell in heaven.

Isaiah 63:3 ... I have trodden the winepress alone; and of the people there was none with me: for I will tread them in mine anger, and trample them in my fury; and their blood shall be sprinkled upon my garments, and I will stain all my raiment.

Revelation 14:14-20 ... And I looked, and behold a white cloud, and upon the cloud one sat like unto the Son of man, having on his head a golden crown, and in his hand a sharp sickle. And another angel came out of the temple, crying with a loud voice to him that sat on the cloud, Thrust in thy sickle, and reap: for the time is come for thee to reap; for the harvest of the earth is ripe. And he that sat on the cloud thrust in his sickle on the earth; and the earth was reaped. And another angel came out of the temple which is in heaven, he also having a sharp sickle. And another angel came out from the altar, which had power over fire; and cried with a loud cry to him that had the sharp sickle, saying, Thrust in thy sharp sickle, and gather the clusters of the vine of the earth; for her grapes are fully ripe. And the angel thrust in his sickle into the earth, and gathered the vine of the earth, and cast it into the great winepress of the wrath of God. And the winepress was trodden without the city, and blood came out of the winepress, even unto the horse bridles, by the space of a thousand and six hundred furlongs.

Joel 3:12-14 ... Let the heathen be wakened, and come up to the valley of Jehoshaphat: for there will I sit to judge all the heathen round about.

Proverbs 28:28 ... When the wicked rise, men hide themselves: but when they perish, the righteous increase.

Psalm 37:17 ... For the arms of the wicked shall be broken: but the LORD upholdeth the righteous.

Psalm 3:7 ... Arise, O LORD; save me, O my God: for thou hast smitten all mine enemies upon the cheek bone; thou hast broken the teeth of the ungodly.

Zechariah 14:9 ... And the LORD shall be king over all the earth: in that day shall there be one LORD, and his name one.

Psalm 146:7 ... Which executeth judgment for the oppressed: which giveth food to the hungry. The LORD looseth the prisoners...

Psalm 144:11-15 ... Rid me, and deliver me from the hand of strange children, whose mouth speaketh vanity, and their right hand is a right hand of falsehood: That our sons may be as plants grown up in their youth; that our daughters may be as corner stones, polished afterthe similitude of a palace: That our garners may be full, affording all manner of store: that our sheep may bring forth thousands and ten thousands in our streets: That our oxen may be strong to labour; that there be no breaking in, nor going out; that there be no complaining in our streets. Happy is that people, that is in such a case: yea, happy is that people, whose God is the LORD.

Revelation 21:2 ... And I John saw the holy city, new Jerusalem, coming down from God out of heaven, prepared as a bride adorned for her husband.

Revelation 19:8 ... And to her was granted that she should be arrayed in fine linen, clean and white: for the fine linen is the righteousness of saints.

JUSTICE EXECUTED FOR THE ORPHAN AND WIDOW
-The Iron-jawed Theme-
Matthew 25:21 ...His lord said unto him, Well done, thou good and faithful servant: thou hast been faithful over a few things, I will make thee ruler over many things: enter thou into the joy of thy lord.

Hebrews 11:6 ...But without faith it is impossible to please him: for he that cometh to God must believe that he is, and that he is a rewarder of them that diligently seek him.

Song of Solomon 2:3,10 ...As the apple tree among the trees of the wood, so is my beloved among the sons. I sat down under his shadow with great delight, and his fruit was sweet to my taste.... My beloved spake, and said unto me, Rise up, my love, my fair one, and come away.

Deuteronomy 33:2-3 ...And he said, The LORD came from Sinai, and rose up from Seir unto them; he shined forth from mount Paran, and he came with ten thousands of saints: from his right hand went a fiery law for them...Yea, he loved the people; all his saints are in thy hand: and they sat down at thy feet; every one shall receive of thy words.

Ephesians 5:32 ...This is a great mystery: but I speak concerning Christ and the church.

II Thessalonians 1:8 ...In flaming fire taking vengeance on them that know not God, and that obey not the gospel of our Lord Jesus Christ.

Psalm 110:5 ...The LORD at thy right hand shall strike through kings in the day of his wrath.He shall judge among the heathen, he shall fill the places with the dead bodies; he shall wound the heads over many countries.

Isaiah 26:21 ...For, behold, the LORD cometh out of his place to punish the inhabitants of the earth for their iniquity: the earth also shall disclose her blood, and shall no more cover her slain.

Isaiah 48:3 ...I have declared the former things from the beginning; and they went forth out of my mouth, and I shewed them; I did them suddenly, and they came to pass.

Isaiah 55:11 ...So shall my word be that goeth forth out of my mouth: it shall not return unto me void, but it shall accomplish that which I please, and it shall prosper in the thing whereto I sent it.

Isaiah 46:10 ...Declaring the end from the beginning, and from ancient times the things that are not yet done, saying, My counsel shall stand, and I will do all my pleasure...

Isaiah 2:17 ...And the loftiness of man shall be bowed down, and the haughtiness of men shall be made low: and the LORD alone shall be exalted in that day.

Psalm 147:6 ...The Lord lifteth up the meek: he casteth the wicked down to the ground.

Amos 5:26 ...But ye have borne the tabernacle of your Moloch and Chiun your images, the star of your god, which ye made to yourselves.

Isaiah 2:17 ...And the loftiness of man shall be bowed down, and the haughtiness of men shall be made low: and the LORD alone shall be exalted in that day.

Zechariah 13:8 ...And it shall come to pass, that in all the land, saith the LORD, two parts therein shall be cut off and die; but the third shall be left therein.

Joel 3:2 ...I will also gather all nations, and will bring them down into the valley of Jehoshaphat, and will plead with them there for my people and for my heritage Israel, whom they have scattered among the nations, and parted my land.

Deuteronomy 7:10 ...And repayeth them that hate him to their face, to destroy them: he will not be slack to him that hateth him, he will repay him to his face.
Psalm 24:8 ...Who is this King of glory? The LORD strong and mighty, the LORD mighty in battle.

Isaiah 30:30 ...And the LORD shall cause his glorious voice to be heard, and shall shew the lighting down of his arm, with the indignation of his anger, and with the flame of a devouring fire, with scattering, and tempest, and hailstones.

Psalm 104:3 ...Who layeth the beams of his chambers in the waters: who maketh the clouds his chariot: who walketh upon the wings of the wind:

Isaiah 66:15-16 ...Look, the LORD will come with fire--his chariots are like the whirlwind--to execute his anger with fury and his rebuke with flames of fire. For by fire and by his sword will the LORD plead with all flesh: and the slain of the LORD shall be many.

Malachi 4:1 ...For, behold, the day cometh, that shall burn as an oven; and all the proud, yea, and all that do wickedly, shall be stubble: and the day that cometh shall burn them up, saith the LORD of hosts, that it shall leave them neither root nor branch.

Revelation 19:11 ...And I saw heaven opened, and behold a white horse; and he that sat upon him was called Faithful and True, and in righteousness he doth judge and make war.

Psalm 46:9-10 ...He maketh wars to cease unto the end of the earth; he breaketh the bow, and cutteth the spear in sunder; he burneth the chariot in the fire. Be still, and know that I am God: I will be exalted among the heathen, I will be exalted in the earth.

Proverbs 21:30 ...There is no wisdom nor understanding nor counsel against the LORD.

Nahum 1:3 ...The LORD is slow to anger, and great in power, and will not at all acquit the wicked: the LORD hath his way in the whirlwind and in the storm, and the clouds are the dust of his feet.

Isaiah 30:30 ...And the LORD shall cause his glorious voice to be heard, and shall shew the lighting down of his arm, with the indignation of his anger, and with the flame of a devouring fire, with scattering, and tempest, and hailstones.

Deuteronomy 32:41 ...If I whet my glittering sword, and mine hand take hold on judgment; I will render vengeance to mine enemies, and will reward them that hate me.

Zechariah 9:14 ...And the LORD shall be seen over them, and his arrow shall go forth as the lightning: and the Lord GOD shall blow the trumpet, and shall go with whirlwinds of the south.

Amos 2:14 ... Therefore the flight shall perish from the swift, and the strong shall not strengthen his force, neither shall the mighty deliver himself...

Psalm 139:11-12 ...If I say, Surely the darkness shall cover me; even the night shall be light about me. Yea, the darkness hideth not from thee; but the night shineth as the day: the darkness and the light are both alike to thee.

Job 34:22 ...There is no darkness or deep shadow where the workers of iniquity can hide.

Jeremiah 23:24 ...Can any hide himself in secret places that I shall not see him? saith the LORD. Do not I fill heaven and earth? saith the LORD.
Habakkuk 3:12-15 ...Thou didst march through the land in indignation, thou didst thresh the heathen in anger. Thou wentest forth for the salvation of thy people, even for salvation with thine anointed; thou woundedst the head out of the house of the wicked, by discovering the foundation unto the neck. Selah. Thou didst strike through with his staves the head of his villages: they came out as a whirlwind to scatter me: their rejoicing was as to devour the poor secretly. Thou didst walk through the sea with thine horses, through the heap of great waters.

Zephaniah 1:15 ...That day is a day of wrath, a day of trouble and distress, a day of wasteness and desolation, a day of darkness and gloominess, a day of clouds and thick darkness...

Psalm 91:8 ...Only with thine eyes shalt thou behold and see the reward of the wicked.

Isaiah 26:20 ...Come, my people, enter thou into thy chambers, and shut thy doors about thee: hide thyself as it were for a little moment, until the indignation be overpast.

Ephesians 1:5, 11 ...Having predestinated us unto the adoption of children by Jesus Christ to himself, according to the good pleasure of his will ...In whom also we have obtained an inheritance, being predestinated according to the purpose of him who worketh all things after the counsel of his own will:

Isaiah 33:15-16 ...He that walketh righteously, and speaketh uprightly; he that despiseth the gain of oppressions, that shaketh his hands from holding of bribes, that stoppeth his ears from hearing of blood, and shutteth his eyes from seeing evil...

Genesis 18:25 ...That be far from thee to do after this manner, to slay the righteous with the wicked: and that the righteous should be as the wicked, that be far from thee: Shall not the Judge of all the earth do right?

Psalm 33:16 ...There is no king saved by the multitude of an host: a mighty man is not delivered by much strength.

Psalm 68:30 ...Rebuke the company of spearmen, the multitude of the bulls, with the calves of the people, till every one submit himself with pieces of silver: scatter thou the people that delight in war.

Hosea 7:3 ...They make the king glad with their wickedness, and the princes with their lies.

Psalm 110:5-6 ...The Lord at thy right hand shall strike through kings in the day of his wrath ...He shall judge among the heathen, he shall fill the places with the dead bodies; he shall wound the heads over many countries.

Psalm 76:12 ...He shall cut off the spirit of princes: he is terrible to the kings of the earth.

Proverbs 28:28 ...When the wicked rise, men hide themselves: but when they perish, the righteous increase.

Proverbs 29:16 ...When the wicked are multiplied, transgression increaseth: but the righteous shall see their fall.

Acts 17:26 ...And hath made of one blood all nations of men for to dwell on all the face of the earth, and hath determined the times before appointed, and the bounds of their habitation;

I John 3:15 ...Whosoever hateth his brother is a murderer: and ye know that no murderer hath eternal life abiding in him.

Revelation 2:9 ...I know thy works, and tribulation, and poverty, (but thou art rich) and I know the blasphemy of them which say they are Jews, and are not, but are the synagogue of Satan.

Revelation 3:9 …Behold, I will make them of the synagogue of Satan, which say they are Jews, and are not, but do lie; behold, I will make them to come and worship before thy feet, and to know that I have loved thee.

Ezekiel 28:25-26 …Thus saith the Lord GOD; When I shall have gathered the house of Israel from the people among whom they are scattered, and shall be sanctified in them in the sight of the heathen, then shall they dwell in their land that I have given to my servant Jacob. And they shall dwell safely therein, and shall build houses, and plant vineyards; yea, they shall dwell with confidence, when I have executed judgments upon all those that despise them round about them; and they shall know that I am the LORD their God.

Jeremiah 31:12 …Therefore they shall come and sing in the height of Zion, and shall flow together to the goodness of the LORD, for wheat, and for wine, and for oil, and for the young of the flock and of the herd: and their soul shall be as a watered garden; and they shall not sorrow any more at all.

Jeremiah 31:8-11 …Behold, I will bring them from the north country, and gather them from the coasts of the earth, and with them the blind and the lame, the woman with child and her that travaileth with child together: a great company shall return thither. They shall come with weeping, and with supplications will I lead them: I will cause them to walk by the rivers of waters in a straight way, wherein they shall not stumble: for I am a father to Israel, and Ephraim is my firstborn. Hear the word of the LORD, O ye nations, and declare it in the isles afar off, and say, He that scattered Israel will gather him, and keep him, as a shepherd doth his flock. For the LORD hath redeemed Jacob, and ransomed him from the hand of him that was stronger than he.

Jeremiah 30:18 …Thus saith the LORD; Behold, I will bring again the captivity of Jacob's tents, and have mercy on his dwellingplaces; and the city shall be builded upon her own heap, and the palace shall remain after the manner thereof.

Isaiah 60:3 …And the Gentiles shall come to thy light, and kings to the brightness of thy rising.

Revelation 19:11 …And I saw heaven opened, and behold a white horse; and he that sat upon him was called Faithful and True, and in righteousness he doth judge and make war.

Revelation 19:7-9 …Let us be glad and rejoice, and give honour to him: for the marriage of the Lamb is come, and his wife hath made herself ready. And to her was granted that she should be arrayed in fine linen, clean and white: for the fine linen is the righteousness of saints. And he saith unto me, Write, Blessed are they which are called unto the marriage supper of the Lamb. And he saith unto me, These are the true sayings of God.

Romans 11:33 …O the depth of the riches both of the wisdom and knowledge of God! how unsearchable are his judgments, and his ways past finding out!

Isaiah 34:5 ...For my sword shall be bathed in heaven: behold, it shall come down upon Idumea, and upon the people of my curse, to judgment.

Jeremiah 25:29-33 ...For, lo, I begin to bring evil on the city which is called by my name, and should ye be utterly unpunished? Ye shall not be unpunished: for I will call for a sword upon all the inhabitants of the earth, saith the LORD of hosts. Therefore prophesy thou against them all these words, and say unto them, The LORD shall roar from on high, and utter his voice from his holy habitation; he shall mightily roar upon his habitation; he shall give a shout, as they that tread the grapes, against all the inhabitants of the earth. A noise shall come even to the ends of the earth; for the LORD hath a controversy with the nations, he will plead with all flesh; he will give them that are wicked to the sword, saith the LORD. Thus saith the LORD of hosts, Behold, evil shall go forth from nation to nation, and a great whirlwind shall be raised up from the coasts of the earth. And the slain of the LORD shall be at that day from one end of the earth even unto the other end of the earth: they shall not be lamented, neither gathered, nor buried; they shall be dung upon the ground.

Psalm 2:9 ...Thou shalt break them with a rod of iron; thou shalt dash them in pieces like a potter's vessel.

Revelation 2:27 ...And he shall rule them with a rod of iron; as the vessels of a potter shall they be broken to shivers: even as I received of my Father.

Malachi 3:5 ...Then I will draw near to you for judgment; and I will be a swift witness against the sorcerers and against the adulterers and against those who swear falsely, and against those who oppress the wage earner in his wages, the widow and the orphan, and those who turn aside the alien and do not fear Me," says the LORD of hosts.

Ephesians 2:18-22 ...For through him we both have access by one Spirit unto the Father. Now therefore ye are no more strangers and foreigners, but fellowcitizens with the saints, and of the household of God; And are built upon the foundation of the apostles and prophets, Jesus Christ himself being the chief corner stone; In whom all the building fitly framed together groweth unto an holy temple in the Lord: In whom ye also are builded together for an habitation of God through the Spirit.

John 6:45 ...It is written in the prophets, And they shall be all taught of God. Every man therefore that hath heard, and hath learned of the Father, cometh unto me...

I Timothy 2:15 ...Study to shew thyself approved unto God, a workman that needeth not to be ashamed, rightly dividing the word of truth.

II Timothy 3:16-17 ...All scripture is given by inspiration of God, and is profitable for doctrine, for reproof, for correction, for instruction in righteousness, That the man of God may be perfect, throughly furnished unto all good works.

Jeremiah 16:19 ...O LORD, my strength, and my fortress, and my refuge in the day of affliction, the Gentiles shall come unto thee from the ends of the earth, and shall say, Surely our fathers have inherited lies, vanity, and things wherein there is no profit.

Isaiah 52:13,15 ...Behold, my servant shall deal prudently, he shall be exalted and extolled, and be very high...So shall he sprinkle many nations; the kings shall shut their mouths at him: for that which had not been told them shall they see; and that which they had not heard shall they consider.

Romans 14:11 ...For it is written, As I live, saith the Lord, every knee shall bow to me, and every tongue shall confess to God.

Philippians 2:10 ...That at the name of Jesus every knee should bow, of things in heaven, and things in earth, and things under the earth...

JUSTICE EXECUTED FOR THE ORPHAN AND WIDOW
-The Winepress of Wrath-
Isaiah 63:2 ...Wherefore art thou red in thine apparel, and thy garments like him that treadeth in the winefat?

Revelation 14:19 ...And the angel thrust in his sickle into the earth, and gathered the vine of the earth, and cast it into the great winepress of the wrath of God.

Isaiah 63:4,6 ...For the day of vengeance is in mine heart, and the year of my redeemed is come...And I will tread down the people in mine anger, and make them drunk in my fury, and I will bring down their strength to the earth.

Ezekiel 35:6 ...Therefore, as I live, saith the Lord GOD, I will prepare thee unto blood, and blood shall pursue thee: sith thou hast not hated blood, even blood shall pursue thee.

Revelation 19:15 ...And out of his mouth goeth a sharp sword, that with it he should smite the nations: and he shall rule them with a rod of iron: and he treadeth the winepress of the fierceness and wrath of Almighty God.

JUSTICE EXECUTED FOR THE ORPHAN AND WIDOW
-Fourteen-
Revelation 14:14 ...And I looked, and behold a white cloud, and upon the cloud one sat like unto the Son of man, having on his head a golden crown, and in his hand a sharp sickle.

Isaiah 2:11 ... The lofty looks of man shall be humbled, and the haughtiness of men shall be bowed down, and the LORD alone shall be exalted in that day.

Isaiah 2:17-18 ... And the loftiness of man shall be bowed down, and the haughtiness of men shall be made low: and the LORD alone shall be exalted in that day. And the idols he shall utterly abolish.

Habakkuk 2:14 ...For the earth shall be filled with the knowledge of the glory of the LORD, as the waters cover the sea.

Revelation 19:15 ...And out of his mouth goeth a sharp sword, that with it he should smite the nations: and he shall rule them with a rod of iron: and he treadeth the winepress of the fierceness and wrath of Almighty God.

JUSTICE EXECUTED FOR THE ORPHAN AND WIDOW
-Adjudication-

Psalm 140:12 ... I know that the LORD will maintain the cause of the afflicted, and the right of the poor.

Isaiah 9:6 ... For unto us a child is born, unto us a son is given: and the government shall be upon his shoulder: and his name shall be called Wonderful, Counseller, The mighty God, The everlasting Father, The Prince of Peace.

Psalm 35:10 ... All my bones shall say, LORD, who is like unto thee, which deliverest the poor from him that is too strong for him, yea, the poor and the needy from him that spoileth him?

Proverbs 13:22 ... A good man leaveth an inheritance to his children's children: and the wealth of the sinner is laid up for the just.

Matthew 19:30 ... But many that are first shall be last; and the last shall be first.

JUSTICE EXECUTED FOR THE ORPHAN AND WIDOW
-The White-hot Jauntier Chief-

Matthew 24:36 ...But of that day and hour knoweth no man, no, not the angels of heaven, but my Father only.

I Thessalonians 4:16 ...For the Lord himself shall descend from heaven with a shout, with the voice of the archangel, and with the trump of God: and the dead in Christ shall rise first: Then we which are alive and remain shall be caught up together with them in the clouds, to meet the Lord in the air: and so shall we ever be with the Lord.

I Corinthians 15:52 ...In a moment, in the twinkling of an eye, at the last trump: for the trumpet shall sound, and the dead shall be raised incorruptible, and we shall be changed.

Isaiah 26:20-21 ...Come, my people, enter thou into thy chambers, and shut thy doors about thee: hide thyself as it were for a little moment, until the indignation be overpast. For, behold, the LORD cometh out of his place to punish the inhabitants of the earth for their iniquity: the earth also shall disclose her blood, and shall no more cover her slain.

Luke 21:24 ...And they shall fall by the edge of the sword, and shall be led away captive into all nations: and Jerusalem shall be trodden down of the Gentiles, until the times of the Gentiles be fulfilled.

Joel 3:14 ...Multitudes, multitudes in the valley of decision: for the day of the LORD is near in the valley of decision.

Psalm 46:9 ...He maketh wars to cease unto the end of the earth; he breaketh the bow, and cutteth the spear in sunder; he burneth the chariot in the fire.

Joel 2:11 ...And the LORD shall utter his voice before his army: for his camp is very great: for he is strong that executeth his word: for the day of the LORD is great and very terrible; and who can abide it?

Isaiah 30:30 ...And the LORD shall cause his glorious voice to be heard, and shall shew the lighting down of his arm, with the indignation of his anger, and with the flame of a devouring fire, with scattering, and tempest, and hailstones.

Psalm 29:5 ...The voice of the LORD breaketh the cedars; yea, the LORD breaketh the cedars of Lebanon.

Isaiah 34:16 ...Seek ye out of the book of the LORD, and read: no one of these shall fail, none shall want her mate: for my mouth it hath commanded, and his spirit it hath gathered them.

Isaiah 14:8 ...Yea, the fir trees rejoice at thee, and the cedars of Lebanon, saying, Since thou art laid down, no feller is come up against us.

JUSTICE EXECUTED FOR THE ORPHAN AND WIDOW
-Rejoice-
Obadiah 1:15-21 ...For the day of the LORD is near upon all the heathen: as thou hast done, it shall be done unto thee: thy reward shall return upon thine own head. For as ye have drunk upon my holy mountain, so shall all the heathen drink continually, yea, they shall drink, and they shall swallow down, and they shall be as though they had not been. But upon mount Zion shall be deliverance, and there shall be holiness; and the house of Jacob shall possess their possessions. And the house of Jacob shall be a fire, and the house of Joseph a flame, and the house of Esau for stubble, and they shall kindle in them, and devour them; and there shall not be any remaining of the house of Esau; for the LORD hath spoken it. And they of the south shall possess the mount of Esau; and they of the plain the Philistines: and they shall possess the fields of Ephraim, and the fields of Samaria: and Benjamin shall possess Gilead. And the captivity of this host of the children of Israel shall possess that of the Canaanites, even unto Zarephath; and the captivity of Jerusalem, which is in Sepharad, shall possess the cities of the south. And saviours shall come up on mount Zion to judge the mount of Esau; and the kingdom shall be the LORD'S.

Psalm 83:4 ... They have said, Come, and let us cut them off from being a nation; that the name of Israel may be no more in remembrance.

Proverbs 22:16 ...He that oppresseth the poor to increase his riches, and he that giveth to the rich, shall surely come to want.

Psalm 12:5 ...For the oppression of the poor, for the sighing of the needy, now will I arise, saith the LORD; I will set him in safety from him that puffeth at him.

Revelation 19:16 ...And he hath on his vesture and on his thigh a name written, KING OF KINGS, AND LORD OF LORDS.

Psalm 110:1 ...A Psalm of David. The LORD said unto my Lord, Sit thou at my right hand, until I make thine enemies thy footstool.

Psalm 68:1 ...To the chief Musician, A Psalm or Song of David. Let God arise, let his enemies be scattered: let them also that hate him flee before him.

Isaiah 66:15-16 ...For, behold, the LORD will come with fire, and with his chariots like a whirlwind, to render his anger with fury, and his rebuke with flames of fire. For by fire and by his sword will the LORD plead with all flesh: and the slain of the LORD shall be many.

Isaiah 34:5 ...For my sword shall be bathed in heaven: behold, it shall come down upon Idumea, and upon the people of my curse, to judgment.

Isaiah 63:1-3 ...Who is this that cometh from Edom, with dyed garments from Bozrah? this that is glorious in his apparel, travelling in the greatness of his strength? I that speak in righteousness, mighty to save. Wherefore art thou red in thine apparel, and thy garments like him that treadeth in the winefat? I have trodden the winepress alone; and of the people there was none with me: for I will tread them in mine anger, and trample them in my fury; and their blood shall be sprinkled upon my garments, and I will stain all my raiment.

Proverbs 13:22 ...A good man leaveth an inheritance to his children's children: and the wealth of the sinner is laid up for the just.

Isaiah 35:1-2 ...The wilderness and the solitary place shall be glad for them; and the desert shall rejoice, and blossom as the rose. It shall blossom abundantly, and rejoice even with joy and singing: the glory of Lebanon shall be given unto it, the excellency of Carmel and Sharon, they shall see the glory of the LORD, and the excellency of our God.

Genesis 15:18 ...In the same day the LORD made a covenant with Abram, saying, Unto thy seed have I given this land, from the river of Egypt unto the great river, the river Euphrates:

Luke 9:23 ...And he said to them all, If any man will come after me, let him deny himself, and take up his cross daily, and follow me.

Mark 10:14 ...But when Jesus saw it, he was much displeased, and said unto them, Suffer the little children to come unto me, and forbid them not: for of such is the kingdom of God.

Isaiah 60:16 ...Thou shalt also suck the milk of the Gentiles, and shalt suck the breast of kings: and thou shalt know that I the LORD am thy Saviour and thy Redeemer, the mighty One of Jacob.

Psalm 104:16 ...The trees of the LORD are full of sap; the cedars of Lebanon, which he hath planted;

Micah 4:3 ...And he shall judge among many people, and rebuke strong nations afar off; and they shall beat their swords into plowshares, and their spears into pruninghooks: nation shall not lift up a sword against nation, neither shall they learn war any more.

Hebrews 2:17 ... Therefore in all things he had to be made like unto his brethren, that he might be a merciful and faithful high priest in things pertaining to God, to make reconciliation for the sins of the people.

Proverbs 28:28 ...When the wicked rise, men hide themselves: but when they perish, the righteous increase.

Ezekiel 11:17 ...Therefore say, Thus saith the Lord GOD; I will even gather you from the people, and assemble you out of the countries where ye have been scattered, and I will give you the land of Israel.

Micah 4:4 ...But they shall sit every man under his vine and under his fig tree; and none shall make them afraid: for the mouth of the LORD of hosts hath spoken it.

Jeremiah 31:13 ...Then shall the virgin rejoice in the dance, both young men and old together: for I will turn their mourning into joy, and will comfort them, and make them rejoice from their sorrow.

JUSTICE EXECUTED FOR THE ORPHAN AND WIDOW
-Conjecture-
Revelation 3:9 ..Behold, I will make them of the synagogue of Satan, which say they are Jews, and are not, but do lie; behold, I will make them to come and worship before thy feet, and to know that I have loved thee.

Revelation 2:9 ...I know thy works, and tribulation, and poverty, (but thou art rich) and I know the blasphemy of them which say they are Jews, and are not, but are the synagogue of Satan.

JUSTICE EXECUTED FOR THE ORPHAN AND WIDOW
- ECSTATIC-
Jeremiah 31:13-14 ...Then shall the virgin rejoice in the dance, both young men and old together: for I will turn their mourning into joy, and will comfort them, and make them rejoice from their sorrow. And I will satiate the soul of the priests with fatness, and my people shall be satisfied with my goodness, saith the LORD.

Revelation 19:17-18 ...And I saw an angel standing in the sun; and he cried with a loud voice, saying to all the fowls that fly in the midst of heaven, Come and gather yourselves together unto the supper of the great God; That ye may eat the flesh of kings, and the flesh of captains, and the flesh of mighty men, and the flesh of horses, and of them that sit on them, and the flesh of all men, both free and bond, both small and great.

JUSTICE EXECUTED FOR THE ORPHAN AND WIDOW
-Hadj Crescendi-
Isaiah 65:1 ...I am sought of them that asked not for me; I am found of them that sought me not: I said, Behold me, behold me, unto a nation that was not called by my name.

Isaiah 45:22 ...Look unto me, and be ye saved, all the ends of the earth: for I am God, and there is none else.

Daniel 2:34-35 ...Thou sawest till that a stone was cut out without hands, which smote the image upon his feet that were of iron and clay, and brake them to pieces. Then was the iron, the clay, the brass, the silver, and the gold, broken to pieces together, and became like the chaff of the summer threshingfloors; and the wind carried them away, that no place was found for them: and the stone that smote the image became a great mountain, and filled the whole earth.

Quran 78:33 ...And full-breasted companions of equal age

Jeremiah 16:19 ...O LORD, my strength, and my fortress, and my refuge in the day of affliction, the Gentiles shall come unto thee from the ends of the earth, and shall say, Surely our fathers have inherited lies, vanity, and things wherein there is no profit.

Isaiah 53:5 ...But he was wounded for our transgressions, he was bruised for our iniquities: the chastisement of our peace was upon him; and with his stripes we are healed.

Mark 9:24 ...And straightway the father of the child cried out, and said with tears, Lord, I believe; help thou mine unbelief.

Isaiah 11:10 ...And in that day there shall be a root of Jesse, which shall stand for an ensign of the people; to it shall the Gentiles seek: and his rest shall be glorious.

Genesis 2:21 ...And the LORD God caused a deep sleep to fall upon Adam, and he slept: and he took one of his ribs, and closed up the flesh instead thereof;

Psalm 139:14 ...I will praise thee; for I am fearfully and wonderfully made: marvellous are thy works; and that my soul knoweth right well.
John 12:32 ...And I, if I be lifted up from the earth, will draw all men unto me.

Genesis 9:7 ...And you, be ye fruitful, and multiply; bring forth abundantly in the earth, and multiply therein.

Luke 8:39 ...Return to thine own house, and shew how great things God hath done unto thee. And he went his way, and published throughout the whole city how great things Jesus had done unto him.

RENOVATION OF THE HEAVENS AND EARTH
Isaiah 24:6 ...Therefore hath the curse devoured the earth, and they that dwell therein are desolate: therefore the inhabitants of the earth are burned, and few men left.

Isaiah 24:20 ...The earth shall reel to and fro like a drunkard, and shall be removed like a cottage; and the transgression thereof shall be heavy upon it; and it shall fall, and not rise again.

Genesis 7:11 ...In the six hundredth year of Noah's life, in the second month, the seventeenth day of the month, the same day were all the fountains of the great deep broken up, and the windows of heaven were opened.

II Peter 3:7 ...But the heavens and the earth, which are now, by the same word are kept in store, reserved unto fire against the day of judgment and perdition of ungodly men.

Psalm 102:25-26 ...Of old hast thou laid the foundation of the earth: and the heavens are the work of thy hands. They shall perish, but thou shalt endure: yea, all of them shall wax old like a garment; as a vesture shalt thou change them, and they shall be changed:

Deuteronomy 32:40 ...For I lift up my hand to heaven, and say, I live for ever. Genesis 1:1 ...In the beginning God created the heaven and the earth.

I John 5:7 ...For there are three that bear record in heaven, the Father, the Word, and the Holy Ghost: and these three are one.

Luke 3:21-22 ... Now when all the people were baptized, it came to pass, that Jesus also being baptized, and praying, the heaven was opened, And the Holy Ghost descended in a bodily shape like a dove upon him, and a voice came from heaven, which said, Thou art my beloved Son; in thee I am well pleased.

I Timothy 3:16 ...And without controversy great is the mystery of godliness: God was manifest in the flesh, justified in the Spirit, seen of angels, preached unto the Gentiles, believed on in the world, received up into glory.

Genesis 1:1 ... In the beginning God created the heaven and the earth.

Isaiah 9:6 ... For unto us a child is born, unto us a son is given: and the government shall be upon his shoulder: and his name shall be called Wonderful, Counsellor, The mighty God, The everlasting Father, The Prince of Peace.

John 1:1-4 ...In the beginning was the Word, and the Word was with God, and the Word was God. The same was in the beginning with God. All things were made by him; and without him was not any thing made that was made. In him was life; and the life was the light of men....

John 1:14 ...And the Word was made flesh, and dwelt among us, (and we beheld his glory, the glory as of the only begotten of the Father,) full of grace and truth.

Genesis 1:2 ...And the earth was without form, and void; and darkness was upon the face of the deep. And the Spirit of God moved upon the face of the waters.

Romans 8:22-23 ...For we know that the whole creation groaneth and travaileth in pain together until now. And not only they, but ourselves also, which have the firstfruits of the Spirit, even we ourselves groan within ourselves, waiting for the adoption, to wit, the redemption of our body.

Romans 8:20 ...For the creature was made subject to vanity, not willingly, but by reason of him who hath subjected the same in hope...

Psalm 104:31 ...The glory of the LORD shall endure for ever: the LORD shall rejoice in his works.

Matthew 5:5 ...Blessed are the meek: for they shall inherit the earth.

Psalm 126:2 ...Then was our mouth filled with laughter, and our tongue with singing: then said they among the heathen, The LORD hath done great things for them.

Isaiah 30:29 ...Ye shall have a song, as in the night when a holy solemnity is kept; and gladness of heart, as when one goeth with a pipe to come into the mountain of the LORD, to the mighty One of Israel.

Psalm 61:4 ...I will abide in thy tabernacle for ever: I will trust in the covert of thy wings. Selah.

II Peter 3:10,12 ...But the day of the Lord will come as a thief in the night; in the which the heavens shall pass away with a great noise, and the elements shall melt with fervent heat, the earth also and the works that are therein shall be burned up...Looking for and hasting unto the coming of the day of God, wherein the heavens being on fire shall be dissolved, and the elements shall melt with fervent heat?

Isaiah 40:4 ...Every valley shall be exalted, and every mountain and hill shall be made low: and the crooked shall be made straight, and the rough places plain:

Isaiah 30:26 ...Moreover the light of the moon shall be as the light of the sun, and the light of the sun shall be sevenfold, as the light of seven days, in the day that the LORD bindeth up the breach of his people, and healeth the stroke of their wound.

I Corinthians 2:9 ...But as it is written, Eye hath not seen, nor ear heard, neither have entered into the heart of man, the things which God hath prepared for them that love him.

Isaiah 35:1 ...The wilderness and the solitary place shall be glad for them; and the desert shall rejoice, and blossom as the rose.

Revelation 15:4 ...Who shall not fear thee, O Lord, and glorify thy name? for thou only art holy: for all nations shall come and worship before thee; for thy judgments are made manifest.

Isaiah 49:13 ...Sing, O heavens; and be joyful, O earth; and break forth into singing, O mountains: for the LORD hath comforted his people, and will have mercy upon his afflicted.

Isaiah 44:23 ...Sing, O ye heavens; for the LORD hath done it: shout, ye lower parts of the earth: break forth into singing, ye mountains, O forest, and every tree therein: for the LORD hath redeemed Jacob, and glorified himself in Israel.

I Chronicles 16:28-30 ...Give unto the LORD, ye kindreds of the people, give unto the LORD glory and strength. Give unto the LORD the glory due unto his name: bring an offering, and come before him: worship the LORD in the beauty of holiness. Fear before him, all the earth: the world also shall be stable, that it be not moved.

Revelation 19:12 ...His eyes were as a flame of fire, and on his head were many crowns; and he had a name written, that no man knew, but he himself.

Mark 2:27-28 ...And he said unto them, The sabbath was made for man, and not man for the sabbath: Therefore the Son of man is Lord also of the sabbath.

Matthew 8:11 ...And I say unto you, That many shall come from the east and west, and shall sit down with Abraham, and Isaac, and Jacob, in the kingdom of heaven.

Revelation 22:1 ...And he shewed me a pure river of water of life, clear as crystal, proceeding out of the throne of God and of the Lamb.

Revelation 22:10 ...And he saith unto me, Seal not the sayings of the prophecy of this book: for the time is at hand.

ON THE THRESHOLD OF GLORY

Romans 8:22-23 ...For we know that the whole creation groaneth and travaileth in pain together until now. And not only they, but ourselves also, which have the firstfruits of the Spirit, even we ourselves groan within ourselves, waiting for the adoption, to wit, the redemption of our body.

Revelation 3:11 ...Behold, I come quickly: hold that fast which thou hast, that no man take thy crown.

John 16:13 ...Howbeit when he, the Spirit of truth, is come, he will guide you into all truth: for he shall not speak of himself; but whatsoever he shall hear, that shall he speak: and he will shew you things to come.

Luke 24:49 ...And, behold, I send the promise of my Father upon you: but tarry ye in the city of Jerusalem, until ye be endued with power from on high.

Romans 8:30 ...Moreover whom he did predestinate, them he also called: and whom he called, them he also justified: and whom he justified, them he also glorified.

Revelation 3:5 ...He that overcometh, the same shall be clothed in white raiment; and I will not blot out his name out of the book of life, but I will confess his name before my Father, and before his angels.

John 10:27-28 ...My sheep hear my voice, and I know them, and they follow me: And I give unto them eternal life; and they shall never perish, neither shall any man pluck them out of my hand.

Psalm 145:10-11 ...All thy works shall praise thee, O LORD; and thy saints shall bless thee. They shall speak of the glory of thy kingdom, and talk of thy power;

Job 23:10 ...But he knoweth the way that I take: when he hath tried me, I shall come forth as gold.

Daniel 7:9 ... I beheld till the thrones were cast down, and the Ancient of days did sit, whose garment was white as snow, and the hair of his head like the pure wool: his throne was like the fiery flame, and his wheels as burning fire.

Isaiah 6:1-3 ...In the year of King Uzziah's death I saw the Lord sitting on a throne, lofty and exalted, with the train of His robe filling the temple. Seraphim stood above Him, each having six wings: with two he covered his face, and with two he covered his feet, and with two he flew. And one called out to another and said, "Holy, Holy, Holy, is the LORD of hosts, The whole earth is full of His glory."

I Corinthians 15:53-54 ...For this corruptible must put on incorruption, and this mortal must put on immortality. So when this corruptible shall have put on incorruption, and this mortal shall have put on immortality, then shall be brought to pass the saying that is written, Death is swallowed up in victory.

Psalm 106:48 ...Blessed be the LORD God of Israel from everlasting to everlasting: and let all the people say, Amen. Praise ye the LORD.

Isaiah 43:10 ...Ye are my witnesses, saith the LORD, and my servant whom I have chosen: that ye may know and believe me, and understand that I am he: before me there was no God formed, neither shall there be after me.

I John 3:2 ...Beloved, now are we the sons of God, and it doth not yet appear what we shall be: but we know that, when he shall appear, we shall be like him; for we shall see him as he is.

Matthew 22:30 ...For in the resurrection they neither marry, nor are given in marriage, but are as the angels of God in heaven.

THOUSAND YEAR REIGN OF CHRIST

Habakkuk 2:14 ...For the earth shall be filled with the knowledge of the glory of the LORD, as the waters cover the sea.

Daniel 12:3 ...And they that be wise shall shine as the brightness of the firmament; and they that turn many to righteousness as the stars for ever and ever.

Revelation 7:3 ...Saying, Hurt not the earth, neither the sea, nor the trees, till we have sealed the servants of our God in their foreheads.

Isaiah 11:9 ...They shall not hurt nor destroy in all my holy mountain: for the earth shall be full of the knowledge of the LORD, as the waters cover the sea.

John 6:45 ...It is written in the prophets, And they shall be all taught of God. Every man therefore that hath heard, and hath learned of the Father, cometh unto me.

Revelation 19:15 ...And out of his mouth goeth a sharp sword, that with it he should smite the nations: and he shall rule them with a rod of iron: and he treadeth the winepress of the fierceness and wrath of Almighty God.

Job 34:24-28 ...He shall break in pieces mighty men without number, and set others in their stead. Therefore he knoweth their works, and he overturneth them in the night, so that they are destroyed. He striketh them as wicked men in the open sight of others; Because they turned back from him, and would not consider any of his ways: So that they cause the cry of the poor to come unto him, and he heareth the cry of the afflicted.

Habakkuk 2:20 ...But the LORD is in his holy temple: let all the earth keep silence before him.

Matthew 3:12 ...Whose fan is in his hand, and he will throughly purge his floor, and gather his wheat into the garner; but he will burn up the chaff with unquenchable fire.

Psalm 37:1-2 ...A Psalm of David. Fret not thyself because of evildoers, neither be thou envious against the workers of iniquity. For they shall soon be cut down like the grass, and wither as the green herb.

John 15:8 ...Herein is my Father glorified, that ye bear much fruit; so shall ye be my disciples.

Ephesians 1:4 ...According as he hath chosen us in him before the foundation of the world, that we should be holy and without blame before him in love:

Psalm 145:7 ...They shall abundantly utter the memory of thy great goodness, and shall sing of thy righteousness.

Revelation 15:4 ...Who shall not fear thee, O Lord, and glorify thy name? for thou only art holy: for all nations shall come and worship before thee; for thy judgments are made manifest.

Psalm 149:1-4 ...Praise ye the LORD. Sing unto the LORD a new song, and his praise in the congregation of saints. Let Israel rejoice in him that made him: let the children of Zion be joyful in their King. Let them praise his name in the dance: let them sing praises unto him with the timbrel and harp. For the LORD taketh pleasure in his people: he will beautify the meek with salvation.

Jeremiah 31:4 ...Again I will build thee, and thou shalt be built, O virgin of Israel: thou shalt again be adorned with thy tabrets, and shalt go forth in the dances of them that make merry.

Psalm 150 ...Praise ye the LORD. Praise God in his sanctuary: praise him in the firmament of his power. Praise him for his mighty acts: praise him according to his excellent greatness. Praise him with the sound of the trumpet: praise him with the psaltery and harp. Praise him with the timbrel and dance: praise him with stringed instruments and organs. Praise him upon the loud cymbals: praise him upon the high sounding cymbals. Let every thing that hath breath praise the LORD. Praise ye the LORD.

Psalm 45:7-8 ...Thou lovest righteousness, and hatest wickedness: therefore God, thy God, hath anointed thee with the oil of gladness above thy fellows. All thy garments smell of myrrh, and aloes, and cassia, out of the ivory palaces, whereby they have made thee glad.

Psalm 45:8 ... All thy garments smell of myrrh, and aloes, and cassia, out of the ivory palaces, whereby they have made thee glad.

I John 3:2 ...Beloved, now are we the sons of God, and it doth not yet appear what we shall be: but we know that, when he shall appear, we shall be like him; for we shall see him as he is.

I Corinthians 15:53-54 ...For this corruptible must put on incorruption, and this mortal must put on immortality. So when this corruptible shall have put on incorruption, and this mortal shall have put on immortality, then shall be brought to pass the saying that is written, Death is swallowed up in victory.

Luke 20:35-36 ...But they which shall be accounted worthy to obtain that world, and the resurrection from the dead, neither marry, nor are given in marriage: Neither can they die any more: for they are equal unto the angels; and are the children of God, being the children of the resurrection.

John 14:2 ...In my Father's house are many mansions: if it were not so, I would have told you. I go to prepare a place for you.

Psalm 37:4 ...Delight thyself also in the LORD; and he shall give thee the desires of thine heart.
Revelation 20:4 ...And I saw thrones, and they sat upon them, and judgment was given unto them: and I saw the souls of them that were beheaded for the witness of Jesus, and for the word of God, and which had not worshipped the beast, neither his image, neither had received his mark upon their foreheads, or in their hands; and they lived and reigned with Christ a thousand years.

Romans 11:29 ...For the gifts and calling of God are without repentance.

Mark 14:25 ...Verily I say unto you, I will drink no more of the fruit of the vine, until that day that I drink it new in the kingdom of God.

Hebrews 12: 1-2 ...Wherefore seeing we also are compassed about with so great a cloud of witnesses, let us lay aside every weight, and the sin which doth so easily beset us, and let us run with patience the race that is set before us, Looking unto Jesus the author and finisher of our faith; who for the joy that was set before him endured the cross, despising the shame, and is set down at the right hand of the throne of God.

Genesis 13:16 ...And I will make thy seed as the dust of the earth: so that if a man can number the dust of the earth, then shall thy seed also be numbered.

Galatians 3:26-29 ... For ye are all the children of God by faith in Christ Jesus. For as many of you as have been baptized into Christ have put on Christ. There is neither Jew nor Greek, there is neither bond nor free, there is neither male nor female: for ye are all one in Christ Jesus. And if ye be Christ's, then are ye Abraham's seed, and heirs according to the promise.

Genesis 15:5 ...And he brought him forth abroad, and said, Look now toward heaven, and tell the stars, if thou be able to number them: and he said unto him, So shall thy seed be.

Habakkuk 2:14 ...For the earth shall be filled with the knowledge of the glory of the LORD, as the waters cover the sea.

II Timothy 2:15 ...Study to shew thyself approved unto God, a workman that needeth not to be ashamed, rightly dividing the word of truth.

Daniel 12:3 ...And they that be wise shall shine as the brightness of the firmament; and they that turn many to righteousness as the stars for ever and ever.

Psalm 112:3,9 ...Wealth and riches shall be in his house: and his righteousness endureth for ever...He hath dispersed, he hath given to the poor; his righteousness endureth for ever; his horn shall be exalted with honour.

I John 3:2 ...Beloved, now are we the sons of God, and it doth not yet appear what we shall be: but we know that, when he shall appear, we shall be like him; for we shall see him as he is.

Ephesians 1:4 ...According as he hath chosen us in him before the foundation of the world, that we should be holy and without blame before him in love:

Revelation 1:6 ...And hath made us kings and priests unto God and his Father; to him be glory and dominion for ever and ever. Amen.

Isaiah 49:22 ...Thus saith the Lord GOD, Behold, I will lift up mine hand to the Gentiles, and set up my standard to the people: and they shall bring thy sons in their arms, and thy daughters shall be carried upon their shoulders.

Isaiah 66:20 ...And they shall bring all your brethren for an offering unto the LORD out of all nations upon horses, and in chariots, and in litters, and upon mules, and upon swift beasts, to my holy mountain Jerusalem, saith the LORD, as the children of Israel bring an offering in a clean vessel into the house of the LORD.

Habakkuk 2:14 ...For the earth shall be filled with the knowledge of the glory of the LORD, as the waters cover the sea.

Psalm 45:4 ...And in thy majesty ride prosperously because of truth and meekness and righteousness; and thy right hand shall teach thee terrible things.

Revelation 19:11 ...And I saw heaven opened, and behold a white horse; and he that sat upon him was called Faithful and True, and in righteousness he doth judge and make war.

I Thessalonians 4:4 ...That every one of you should know how to possess his vessel in sanctification and honour;

Song of Solomon 4:12 ...A garden inclosed is my sister, my spouse; a spring shut up, a fountain sealed.

I Timothy 5:2 ...The elder women as mothers; the younger as sisters, with all purity.

Hebrews 13:4 ...Marriage is honourable in all, and the bed undefiled: but whoremongers and adulterers God will judge.

Psalm 144:12 ...That our sons may be as plants grown up in their youth; that our daughters may be as corner stones, polished after the similitude of a palace...

Isaiah 11:6 ...The wolf also shall dwell with the lamb, and the leopard shall lie down with the kid; and the calf and the young lion and the fatling together; and a little child shall lead them.

Proverbs 27:23 ...Be thou diligent to know the state of thy flocks, and look well to thy herds.

Isaiah 65:22 ...They shall not build, and another inhabit; they shall not plant, and another eat: for as the days of a tree are the days of my people, and mine elect shall long enjoy the work of their hands.

Ezekiel 28:26 ...And they shall dwell safely therein, and shall build houses, and plant vineyards; yea, they shall dwell with confidence, when I have executed judgments upon all those that despise them round about them; and they shall know that I am the LORD their God.

Isaiah 65:20 ...There shall be no more thence an infant of days, nor an old man that hath not filled his days: for the child shall die an hundred years old; but the sinner being an hundred years old shall be accursed.

Psalm 147:10 ...He delighteth not in the strength of the horse: he taketh not pleasure in the legs of a man.

Proverbs 31:30 ...Favour is deceitful, and beauty is vain: but a woman that feareth the LORD, she shall be praised.

Proverbs 6:12-14 ...A naughty person, a wicked man, walketh with a froward mouth. He winketh with his eyes, he speaketh with his feet, he teacheth with his fingers; Frowardness is in his heart, he deviseth mischief continually; he soweth discord.

Proverbs 17:22 ...A merry heart doeth good like a medicine: but a broken spirit drieth the bones.

Proverbs 15:13 ...A merry heart maketh a cheerful countenance: but by sorrow of the heart the spirit is broken.

Zechariah 14:20 ...In that day shall there be upon the bells of the horses, HOLINESS UNTO THE LORD; and the pots in the LORD'S house shall be like the bowls before the altar.

Psalm 144:13 ...That our garners may be full, affording all manner of store: that our sheep may bring forth thousands and ten thousands in our streets:

Jeremiah 31:12 ...Therefore they shall come and sing in the height of Zion, and shall flow together to the goodness of the LORD, for wheat, and for wine, and for oil, and for the young of the flock and of the herd: and their soul shall be as a watered garden; and they shall not sorrow any more at all.

Isaiah 2:4 ...And he shall judge among the nations, and shall rebuke many people: and they shall beat their swords into plowshares, and their spears into pruninghooks: nation shall not lift up sword against nation, neither shall they learn war any more.

Micah 4:3 ...And he shall judge among many people, and rebuke strong nations afar off; and they shall beat their swords into plowshares, and their spears into pruninghooks: nation shall not lift up a sword against nation, neither shall they learn war any more.

Psalm 37:32 ...The wicked watcheth the righteous, and seeketh to slay him.

Proverbs 3:30 ...Strive not with a man without cause, if he have done thee no harm.

Isaiah 35:1-2 ... The wilderness and the solitary place shall be glad for them; and the desert shall rejoice, and blossom as the rose.

Proverbs 29:2 ...When the righteous are in authority, the people rejoice: but when the wicked beareth rule, the people mourn.

Isaiah 60:17 ...For brass I will bring gold, and for iron I will bring silver, and for wood brass, and for stones iron: I will also make thy officers peace, and thine exactors righteousness.

Leviticus 19:24 ...But in the fourth year all the fruit thereof shall be holy to praise the LORD withal.

Ezekiel 13:9 ...And mine hand shall be upon the prophets that see vanity, and that divine lies: they shall not be in the assembly of my people, neither shall they be written in the writing of the house of Israel, neither shall they enter into the land of Israel; and ye shall know that I am the Lord GOD.

Jeremiah 29:9 ...For they prophesy falsely unto you in my name: I have not sent them, saith the LORD.

Zechariah 13:2 ...And it shall come to pass in that day, saith the LORD of hosts, that I will cut off the names of the idols out of the land, and they shall no more be remembered: and also I will cause the prophets and the unclean spirit to pass out of the land.

I Timothy 2:22 ...Flee also youthful lusts: but follow righteousness, faith, charity, peace, with them that call on the Lord out of a pure heart.

Matthew 18:6, 10, 14 ...But whoso shall offend one of these little ones which believe in me, it were better for him that a millstone were hanged about his neck, and that he were drowned in the depth of the sea....Take heed that ye despise not one of these little ones; for I say unto you, That in heaven their angels do always behold the face of my Father which is in heaven...Even so it is not the will of your Father which is in heaven, that one of these little ones should perish.

I Peter 2:11 ...Dearly beloved, I beseech you as strangers and pilgrims, abstain from fleshly lusts, which war against the soul...

Revelation 2:24 ...But unto you I say, and unto the rest in Thyatira, as many as have not this doctrine, and which have not known the depths of Satan, as they speak; I will put upon you none other burden.

Zechariah 14:16-19 ...And it shall come to pass, that every one that is left of all the nations which came against Jerusalem shall even go up from year to year to worship the King, the LORD of hosts, and to keep the feast of tabernacles.

And it shall be, that whoso will not come up of all the families of the earth unto Jerusalem to worship the King, the LORD of hosts, even upon them shall be no rain. And if the family of Egypt go not up, and come not, that have no rain; there shall be the plague, wherewith the LORD will smite the heathen that come not up to keep the feast of tabernacles. This shall be the punishment of Egypt, and the punishment of all nations that come not up to keep the feast of tabernacles.

Revelation 20:1-3, 7 ...And I saw an angel come down from heaven, having the key of the bottomless pit and a great chain in his hand. And he laid hold on the dragon, that old serpent, which is the Devil, and Satan, and bound him a thousand years, And cast him into the bottomless pit, and shut him up, and set a seal upon him, that he should deceive the nations no more, till the thousand years should be fulfilled: and after that he must be loosed a little season...And when the thousand years are expired, Satan shall be loosed out of his prison...

Revelation 20:8 ...And shall go out to deceive the nations which are in the four quarters of the earth, Gog and Magog, to gather them together to battle: the number of whom is as the sand of the sea.

II Corinthians 11:14 ...And no marvel; for Satan himself is transformed into an angel of light.

Psalm 2:1-3 ...Why do the heathen rage, and the people imagine a vain thing? The kings of the earth set themselves, and the rulers take counsel together, against the LORD, and against his anointed, saying, Let us break their bands asunder, and cast away their cords from us.

Ezekiel 38:9-16 ...Thou shalt ascend and come like a storm, thou shalt be like a cloud to cover the land, thou, and all thy bands, and many people with thee. Thus saith the Lord GOD; It shall also come to pass, that at the same time shall things come into thy mind, and thou shalt think an evil thought: And thou shalt say, I will go up to the land of unwalled villages; I will go to them that are at rest, that dwell safely, all of them dwelling without walls, and having neither bars nor gates, To take a spoil, and to take a prey; to turn thine hand upon the desolate places that are now inhabited, and upon the people that are gathered out of the nations, which have gotten cattle and goods, that dwell in the midst of the land. Sheba, and Dedan, and the merchants of Tarshish, with all the young lions thereof, shall say unto thee, Art thou come to take a spoil? hast thou gathered thy company to take a prey? to carry away silver and gold, to take away cattle and goods, to take a great spoil?

Therefore, son of man, prophesy and say unto Gog, Thus saith the Lord GOD; In that day when my people of Israel dwelleth safely, shalt thou not know it? And thou shalt come from thy place out of the north parts, thou, and many people with thee, all of them riding upon horses, a great company, and a mighty army: And thou shalt come up against my people of Israel, as a cloud to cover the land; it shall be in the latter days, and I will bring thee against my land, that the heathen may know me, when I shall be sanctified in thee, O Gog, before their eyes.

Proverbs 15:3 ...The eyes of the LORD are in every place, beholding the evil and the good.

II Chronicles 16:9 ...For the eyes of the LORD run to and fro throughout the whole earth, to shew himself strong in the behalf of them whose heart is perfect toward him...

Revelation 20:9 ...And they went up on the breadth of the earth, and compassed the camp of the saints about, and the beloved city: and fire came down from God out of heaven, and devoured them.

Ezekiel 38:18-19, 22 ...And it shall come to pass at the same time when Gog shall come against the land of Israel, saith the Lord GOD, that my fury shall come up in my face. For in my jealousy and in the fire of my wrath have I spoken, Surely in that day there shall be a great shaking in the land of Israel; And I will plead against him with pestilence and with blood; and I will rain upon him, and upon his bands, and upon the many people that are with him, an overflowing rain, and great hailstones, fire, and brimstone.

Revelation 20:9 ...And they went up on the breadth of the earth, and compassed the camp of the saints about, and the beloved city: and fire came down from God out of heaven, and devoured them.

Deuteronomy 4:24 ...For the LORD thy God is a consuming fire, even a jealous God.

Hebrews 12:29 ...For our God is a consuming fire.

Revelation 20:10 ...And the devil that deceived them was cast into the lake of fire and brimstone, where the beast and the false prophet are, and shall be tormented day and night for ever and ever.

Revelation 20:10 ...nd the devil that deceived them was cast into the lake of fire and brimstone, where the beast and the false prophet are, and shall be tormented day and night for ever and ever.

Ezekiel 38:20, 23 ...So that the fishes of the sea, and the fowls of the heaven, and the beasts of the field, and all creeping things that creep upon the earth, and all the men that are upon the face of the earth, shall shake at my presence, and the mountains shall be thrown down, and the steep places shall fall, and every wall shall fall to the ground ...Thus will I magnify myself, and sanctify myself; and I will be known in the eyes of many nations, and they shall know that I am the LORD.

Numbers 11:23 ...And the LORD said unto Moses, Is the LORD'S hand waxed short? thou shalt see now whether my word shall come to pass unto thee or not.

Ezekiel 39:21 ...And I will set my glory among the heathen, and all the heathen shall see my judgment that I have executed, and my hand that I have laid upon them.

Isaiah 59:1 ...Behold, the LORD'S hand is not shortened, that it cannot save; neither his ear heavy, that it cannot hear...

Matthew 7:21 ...Not every one that saith unto me, Lord, Lord, shall enter into the kingdom of heaven; but he that doeth the will of my Father which is in heaven.

LAST JUDGMENT DAY
Matthew 8:12 ...But the children of the kingdom shall be cast out into outer darkness: there shall be weeping and gnashing of teeth.

Genesis 18:25 ...That be far from thee to do after this manner, to slay the righteous with the wicked: and that the righteous should be as the wicked, that be far from thee: Shall not the Judge of all the earth do right?

Matthew 13:41 ...The Son of man shall send forth his angels, and they shall gather out of his kingdom all things that offend, and them which do iniquity...

Revelation 9:20 ...And the rest of the men which were not killed by these plagues yet repented not of the works of their hands, that they should not worship devils, and idols of gold, and silver, and brass, and stone, and of wood: which neither can see, nor hear, nor walk:

Psalm 58:10 ...The righteous shall rejoice when he seeth the vengeance: he shall wash his feet in the blood of the wicked.

THE GREAT WHITE THRONE JUDGMENT
Revelation 11:18 ...And the nations were angry, and thy wrath is come, and the time of the dead, that they should be judged, and that thou shouldest give reward unto thy servants the prophets, and to the saints, and them that fear thy name, small and great; and shouldest destroy them which destroy the earth.

Mark 13:27 ...And then shall he send his angels, and shall gather together his elect from the four winds, from the uttermost part of the earth to the uttermost part of heaven.

Matthew 13:39 ...The enemy that sowed them is the devil; the harvest is the end of the world; and the reapers are the angels.

Daniel 7:10 ...A fiery stream issued and came forth from before him: thousand thousands ministered unto him, and ten thousand times ten thousand stood before him: the judgment was set, and the books were opened.

Hosea 11:12 ...Ephraim compasseth me about with lies, and the house of Israel with deceit: but Judah yet ruleth with God, and is faithful with the saints.

Hebrews 8:10 ...For this is the covenant that I will make with the house of Israel after those days, saith the Lord; I will put my laws into their mind, and write them in their hearts: and I will be to them a God, and they shall be to me a people...

Jeremiah 31:3 ...The LORD hath appeared of old unto me, saying, Yea, I have loved thee with an everlasting love: therefore with lovingkindness have I drawn thee.

Hebrews 10:16 ...This is the covenant that I will make with them after those days, saith the Lord, I will put my laws into their hearts, and in their minds will I write them;

I John 1:7 ...But if we walk in the light, as he is in the light, we have fellowship one with another, and the blood of Jesus Christ his Son cleanseth us from all sin.

Ephesians 2:12-13 ...that at that time ye were without Christ, being aliens from the commonwealth of Israel, and strangers from the covenants of promise, having no hope, and without God in the world: But now in Christ Jesus ye who sometimes were far off are made nigh by the blood of Christ.

Colossians 1:13 ...Who hath delivered us from the power of darkness, and hath translated us into the kingdom of his dear Son...

Proverbs 2:2 ...So that thou incline thine ear unto wisdom, and apply thine heart to understanding...

Philippians 1:6 ...Being confident of this very thing, that he which hath begun a good work in you will perform it until the day of Jesus Christ...

I John 3:13 ...Marvel not, my brethren, if the world hate you.

Revelation 6:9 ...And when he had opened the fifth seal, I saw under the altar the souls of them that were slain for the word of God, and for the testimony which they held...

Hebrews 11:36 ...And others had trial of cruel mockings and scourgings, yea, moreover of bonds and imprisonment...

Revelation 19:8 ...And to her was granted that she should be arrayed in fine linen, clean and white: for the fine linen is the righteousness of saints.

Malachi 3:17 ...And they shall be mine, saith the LORD of hosts, in that day when I make up my jewels; and I will spare them, as a man spareth his own son that serveth him.

Revelation 3:4 ...Thou hast a few names even in Sardis which have not defiled their garments; and they shall walk with me in white: for they are worthy.

I Corinthians 15:55 ...O death, where is thy sting? O grave, where is thy victory?

II Timothy 4:8 ...Henceforth there is laid up for me a crown of righteousness, which the Lord, the righteous judge, shall give me at that day: and not to me only, but unto all them also that love his appearing.

James 1:12 ...Blessed is the man that endureth temptation: for when he is tried, he shall receive the crown of life, which the Lord hath promised to them that love him.

Daniel 7:10 ...A fiery stream issued and came forth from before him: thousand thousands ministered unto him, and ten thousand times ten thousand stood before him: the judgment was set, and the books were opened.

Revelation 20:4 ...And I saw thrones, and they sat upon them, and judgment was given unto them: and I saw the souls of them that were beheaded for the witness of Jesus, and for the word of God, and which had not worshipped the beast, neither his image, neither had received his mark upon their foreheads, or in their hands; and they lived and reigned with Christ a thousand years.

Daniel 7:9 ...I beheld till the thrones were cast down, and the Ancient of days did sit, whose garment was white as snow, and the hair of his head like the pure wool: his throne was like the fiery flame, and his wheels as burning fire.
Daniel 7:10 ...A fiery stream issued and came forth from before him: thousand thousands ministered unto him, and ten thousand times ten thousand stood before him: the judgment was set, and the books were opened.

I John 5:7 ...For there are three that bear record in heaven, the Father, the Word, and the Holy Ghost: and these three are one.

Hebrews 10:27 ...But a certain fearful looking for of judgment and fiery indignation, which shall devour the adversaries.

II Corinthians 5:10 ...For we must all appear before the judgment seat of Christ; that every one may receive the things done in his body, according to that he hath done, whether it be good or bad.

Revelation 20:12 ...And I saw the dead, small and great, stand before God; and the books were opened: and another book was opened, which is the book of life: and the dead were judged out of those things which were written in the books, according to their works.

Hebrews 12:16-17 ...Lest there be any fornicator, or profane person, as Esau, who for one morsel of meat sold his birthright. For ye know how that afterward, when he would have inherited the blessing, he was rejected: for he found no place of repentance, though he sought it carefully with tears.

Proverbs 14:9 ...Fools make a mock at sin: but among the righteous there is favour.

Proverbs 1:25-27 ...But ye have set at nought all my counsel, and would none of my reproof: I also will laugh at your calamity; I will mock when your fear cometh; When your fear cometh as desolation, and your destruction cometh as a whirlwind; when distress and anguish cometh upon you.

Revelation 20:4 ...And I saw thrones, and they sat upon them, and judgment was given unto them: and I saw the souls of them that were beheaded for the witness of Jesus, and for the word of God, and which had not worshipped the beast, neither his image, neither had received his mark upon their foreheads, or in their hands; and they lived and reigned with Christ a thousand years.

Matthew 24:9 ...Then shall they deliver you up to be afflicted, and shall kill you: and ye shall be hated of all nations for my name's sake.

Hebrews 11:36-37 ...And others had trial of cruel mockings and scourgings, yea, moreover of bonds and imprisonment: They were stoned, they were sawn asunder, were tempted, were slain with the sword: they wandered about in sheepskins and goatskins; being destitute, afflicted, tormented;

Matthew 23:35 ...That upon you may come all the righteous blood shed upon the earth, from the blood of righteous Abel unto the blood of Zacharias son of Barachias, whom ye slew between the temple and the altar.

Genesis 6:11-13 ...The earth also was corrupt before God, and the earth was filled with violence. And God looked upon the earth, and, behold, it was corrupt; for all flesh had corrupted his way upon the earth. And God said unto Noah, The end of all flesh is come before me; for the earth is filled with violence through them; and, behold, I will destroy them with the earth.

Genesis 6:17 ...And, behold, I, even I, do bring a flood of waters upon the earth, to destroy all flesh, wherein is the breath of life, from under heaven; and every thing that is in the earth shall die.
Isaiah 24:5-6 ...The earth also is defiled under the inhabitants thereof; because they have transgressed the laws, changed the ordinance, broken the everlasting covenant. Therefore hath the curse devoured the earth, and they that dwell therein are desolate: therefore the inhabitants of the earth are burned, and few men left.

Habakkuk 2:12 ...Woe to him that buildeth a town with blood, and stablisheth a city by iniquity!

Psalm 55:23 ...But thou, O God, shalt bring them down into the pit of destruction: bloody and deceitful men shall not live out half their days; but I will trust in thee.

Jeremiah 22:13 ...Woe unto him that buildeth his house by unrighteousness, and his chambers by wrong; that useth his neighbour's service without wages, and giveth him not for his work;

James 5:3 ...Your gold and silver is cankered; and the rust of them shall be a witness against you, and shall eat your flesh as it were fire. Ye have heaped treasure together for the last days.

Jude 1:16 ...These are murmurers, complainers, walking after their own lusts; and their mouth speaketh great swelling words, having men's persons in admiration because of advantage.

Isaiah 24:21 ...And it shall come to pass in that day, that the LORD shall punish the host of the high ones that are on high, and the kings of the earth upon the earth.

Jude 1:6 ...And the angels which kept not their first estate, but left their own habitation, he hath reserved in everlasting chains under darkness unto the judgment of the great day.

Romans 1:18 ...For the wrath of God is revealed from heaven against all ungodliness and unrighteousness of men, who hold the truth in unrighteousness...

Matthew 23:13 ...But woe unto you, scribes and Pharisees, hypocrites! for ye shut up the kingdom of heaven against men: for ye neither go in yourselves, neither suffer ye them that are entering to go in.

Isaiah 29:21 ...That make a man an offender for a word, and lay a snare for him that reproveth in the gate, and turn aside the just for a thing of nought.

Exodus 23:2 ...Thou shalt not follow a multitude to do evil; neither shalt thou speak in a cause to decline after many to wrest judgment...

Romans 1:30 ...Backbiters, haters of God, despiteful, proud, boasters, inventors of evil things, disobedient to parents...

I Corinthians 6:9 ...Know ye not that the unrighteous shall not inherit the kingdom of God? Be not deceived: neither fornicators, nor idolaters, nor adulterers, nor effeminate, nor abusers of themselves with mankind...

I Timothy 1:10 ...For whoremongers, for them that defile themselves with mankind, for menstealers, for liars, for perjured persons, and if there be any other thing that is contrary to sound doctrine...

I Timothy 1:9 ...Knowing this, that the law is not made for a righteous man, but for the lawless and disobedient, for the ungodly and for sinners, for unholy and profane, for murderers of fathers and murderers of mothers, for manslayers...

Romans 1:30 ...Backbiters, haters of God, despiteful, proud, boasters, inventors of evil things, disobedient to parents...

Romans 1:30 ...Backbiters, haters of God, despiteful, proud, boasters, inventors of evil things, disobedient to parents...

I John 3:15 ...Whosoever hateth his brother is a murderer: and ye know that no murderer hath eternal life abiding in him.

Proverbs 29:1 ...He, that being often reproved hardeneth his neck, shall suddenly be destroyed, and that without remedy.

Jeremiah 17:23 ...But they obeyed not, neither inclined their ear, but made their neck stiff, that they might not hear, nor receive instruction.

Daniel 2:43 ...And whereas thou sawest iron mixed with miry clay, they shall mingle themselves with the seed of men: but they shall not cleave one to another, even as iron is not mixed with clay.

Hebrews 4:12 ...For the word of God is quick, and powerful, and sharper than any twoedged sword, piercing even to the dividing asunder of soul and spirit, and of the joints and marrow, and is a discerner of the thoughts and intents of the heart.

Mark 4:22 ...For there is nothing hid, which shall not be manifested; neither was any thing kept secret, but that it should come abroad.

I Corinthians 4:5 ...Therefore judge nothing before the time, until the Lord come, who both will bring to light the hidden things of darkness, and will make manifest the counsels of the hearts: and then shall every man have praise of God.

II Corinthians 10:5 ...Casting down imaginations, and every high thing that exalteth itself against the knowledge of God, and bringing into captivity every thought to the obedience of Christ...

Galatians 6:7 ...Be not deceived; God is not mocked: for whatsoever a man soweth, that shall he also reap.

Revelation 14:11 ...And the smoke of their torment ascendeth up for ever and ever: and they have no rest day nor night, who worship the beast and his image, and whosoever receiveth the mark of his name.

Job 20:27 ...The heaven shall reveal his iniquity; and the earth shall rise up against him.

II Thessalonians 1:8-9 ...In flaming fire taking vengeance on them that know not God, and that obey not the gospel of our Lord Jesus Christ: Who shall be punished with everlasting destruction from the presence of the Lord, and from the glory of his power...

Revelation 20:15 ...And whosoever was not found written in the book of life was cast into the lake of fire.

THE LAKE OF FIRE AND BRIMSTONE
II Timothy 3:3 ...Without natural affection, trucebreakers, false accusers, incontinent, fierce, despisers of those that are good...

Luke 16:24 ...And he cried and said, Father Abraham, have mercy on me, and send Lazarus, that he may dip the tip of his finger in water, and cool my tongue; for I am tormented in this flame.

I John 3:15 ...Whosoever hateth his brother is a murderer: and ye know that no murderer hath eternal life abiding in him.

Hebrews 13:4 ...Marriage is honourable in all, and the bed undefiled: but whoremongers and adulterers God will judge.

Proverbs 16:25 ...There is a way that seemeth right unto a man, but the end thereof are the ways of death.

Proverbs 5:3-5 ...For the lips of a strange woman drop as an honeycomb, and her mouth is smoother than oil: But her end is bitter as wormwood, sharp as a twoedged sword. Her feet go down to death; her steps take hold on hell.

Exodus 20:13,15 ...Thou shalt not kill. Thou shalt not steal.

Galatians 6:7 ...Be not deceived; God is not mocked: for whatsoever a man soweth, that shall he also reap.

Psalm 10:3 ...For the wicked boasteth of his heart's desire, and blesseth the covetous, whom the LORD abhorreth.

Proverbs 20:1 ...Wine is a mocker, strong drink is raging: and whosoever is deceived thereby is not wise.

I Corinthians 6:18 ...Flee fornication. Every sin that a man doeth is without the body; but he that committeth fornication sinneth against his own body.

Matthew 5:28 ...But I say unto you, That whosoever looketh on a woman to lust after her hath committed adultery with her already in his heart.
Proverbs 6:25-26 ...Lust not after her beauty in thine heart; neither let her take thee with her eyelids. For by means of a whorish woman a man is brought to a piece of bread: and the adulteress will hunt for the precious life.

Jude 1:7 ...Even as Sodom and Gomorrha, and the cities about them in like manner, giving themselves over to fornication, and going after strange flesh, are set forth for an example, suffering the vengeance of eternal fire.

Leviticus 18:22 ...Thou shalt not lie with mankind, as with womankind: it is abomination.

Leviticus 20:17, 19, 20 ...And if a man shall take his sister, his father's daughter, or his mother's daughter, and see her nakedness, and she see his nakedness; it is a wicked thing; and they shall be cut off in the sight of their people: he hath uncovered his sister's nakedness; he shall bear his iniquity...And thou shalt not uncover the nakedness of thy mother's sister, nor of thy father's sister: for he uncovereth his near kin: they shall bear their iniquity...And if a man shall lie with his uncle's wife, he hath uncovered his uncle's nakedness: they shall bear their sin; they shall die childless.

Mark 9:42 ...And whosoever shall offend one of these little ones that believe in me, it is better for him that a millstone were hanged about his neck, and he were cast into the sea.

Deuteronomy 5:8-9 ...Thou shalt not make thee any graven image, or any likeness of any thing that is in heaven above, or that is in the earth beneath, or that is in the waters beneath the earth: Thou shalt not bow down thyself unto them, nor serve them: for I the LORD thy God am a jealous God, visiting the iniquity of the fathers upon the children unto the third and fourth generation of them that hate me...

Proverbs 26:28 ...A lying tongue hateth those that are afflicted by it; and a flattering mouth worketh ruin.

Romans 3:14-16 ...Whose mouth is full of cursing and bitterness. Their feet are swift to shed blood: Destruction and misery are in their ways...

Matthew 10:21 ...And the brother shall deliver up the brother to death, and the father the child: and the children shall rise up against their parents, and cause them to be put to death.

I Timothy 1:9 ...Knowing this, that the law is not made for a righteous man, but for the lawless and disobedient, for the ungodly and for sinners, for unholy and profane, for murderers of fathers and murderers of mothers, for manslayers...

John 10:1 ...Verily, verily, I say unto you, He that entereth not by the door into the sheepfold, but climbeth up some other way, the same is a thief and a robber.

Revelation 18:13 ...And cinnamon, and odours, and ointments, and frankincense, and wine, and oil, and fine flour, and wheat, and beasts, and sheep, and horses, and chariots, and slaves, and souls of men.

Isaiah 23:16 ...Take an harp, go about the city, thou harlot that hast been forgotten; make sweet melody, sing many songs, that thou mayest be remembered.

Revelation 2:9 ...I know thy works, and tribulation, and poverty, (but thou art rich) and I know the blasphemy of them which say they are Jews, and are not, but are the synagogue of Satan.

Proverbs 10:31 ...The mouth of the just bringeth forth wisdom: but the froward tongue shall be cut out.

Daniel 2:41-43 ...And whereas thou sawest the feet and toes, part of potters' clay, and part of iron, the kingdom shall be divided; but there shall be in it of the strength of the iron, forasmuch as thou sawest the iron mixed with miry clay. And as the toes of the feet were part of iron, and part of clay, so the kingdom shall be partly strong, and partly broken. And whereas thou sawest iron mixed with miry clay, they shall mingle themselves with the seed of men: but they shall not cleave one to another, even as iron is not mixed with clay.

Matthew 15:8 ...This people draweth nigh unto me with their mouth, and honoureth me with their lips; but their heart is far from me.

Jeremiah 48:44 ...He that fleeth from the fear shall fall into the pit; and he that getteth up out of the pit shall be taken in the snare...

Revelation 20:10 ... And the devil that deceived them was cast into the lake of fire and brimstone, where the beast and the false prophet are, and shall be tormented day and night for ever and ever.

Genesis 4:10 ... And he said, What hast thou done? the voice of thy brother's blood crieth unto me from the ground.

James 2:6 ...But ye have despised the poor. Do not rich men oppress you, and draw you before the judgment seats?

Job 21:14-15 ...Therefore they say unto God, Depart from us; for we desire not the knowledge of thy ways. What is the Almighty, that we should serve him? and what profit should we have, if we pray unto him?

James 5:3 ...Your gold and silver is cankered; and the rust of them shall be a witness against you, and shall eat your flesh as it were fire. Ye have heaped treasure together for the last days.

Exodus 20:13 ...Thou shalt not kill.

I Timothy 6:10 ...For the love of money is the root of all evil: which while some coveted after, they have erred from the faith, and pierced themselves through with many sorrows.

Colossians 1:13 ...Who hath delivered us from the power of darkness, and hath translated us into the kingdom of his dear Son...

John 8:36 ...If the Son therefore shall make you free, ye shall be free indeed.

Psalm 119:9 ...BETH. Wherewithal shall a young man cleanse his way? by taking heed thereto according to thy word.

Psalm 119:11 ...Thy word have I hid in mine heart, that I might not sin against thee.

Luke 12:5 ...But I will forewarn you whom ye shall fear: Fear him, which after he hath killed hath power to cast into hell; yea, I say unto you, Fear him.

Isaiah 3:16-24 ...Moreover the LORD saith, Because the daughters of Zion are haughty, and walk with stretched forth necks and wanton eyes, walking and mincing as they go, and making a tinkling with their feet: Therefore the Lord will smite with a scab the crown of the head of the daughters of Zion, and the LORD will discover their secret parts. In that day the Lord will take away the bravery of their tinkling ornaments about their feet, and their cauls, and their round tires like the moon, The chains, and the bracelets, and the mufflers, The bonnets, and the ornaments of the legs, and the headbands, and the tablets, and the earrings, The rings, and nose jewels, The changeable suits of apparel, and the mantles, and the wimples, and the crisping pins, The glasses, and the fine linen, and the hoods, and the vails. And it shall come to pass, that instead of sweet smell there shall be stink; and instead of a girdle a rent; and instead of well set hair baldness; and instead of a stomacher a girding of sackcloth; and burning instead of beauty.

I Corinthians 6:18 ...Flee fornication. Every sin that a man doeth is without the body; but he that committeth fornication sinneth against his own body.

John 12:43 ...For they loved the praise of men more than the praise of God.

John 10:12-13 ....But he that is an hireling, and not the shepherd, whose own the sheep are not, seeth the wolf coming, and leaveth the sheep, and fleeth: and the wolf catcheth them, and scattereth the sheep. The hireling fleeth, because he is an hireling, and careth not for the sheep.

Romans 6:1-2 ...What shall we say then? Shall we continue in sin, that grace may abound? God forbid. How shall we, that are dead to sin, live any longer therein?

John 8:34 ...Jesus answered them, Verily, verily, I say unto you, Whosoever committeth sin is the servant of sin.

Romans 6:23 ...For the wages of sin is death; but the gift of God is eternal life through Jesus Christ our Lord.

II Timothy 4:1-3 ...I charge thee therefore before God, and the Lord Jesus Christ, who shall judge the quick and the dead at his appearing and his kingdom; Preach the word; be instant in season, out of season; reprove, rebuke, exhort with all longsuffering and doctrine. For the time will come when they will not endure sound doctrine; but after their own lusts shall they heap to themselves teachers, having itching ears...

Revelation 22:11 ...He that is unjust, let him be unjust still: and he which is filthy, let him be filthy still: and he that is righteous, let him be righteous still: and he that is holy, let him be holy still.

James 5:1 ...Go to now, ye rich men, weep and howl for your miseries that shall come upon you.

James 5:3 ...Your gold and silver is cankered; and the rust of them shall be a witness against you, and shall eat your flesh as it were fire. Ye have heaped treasure together for the last days.

Job 21:15 ...What is the Almighty, that we should serve him? and what profit should we have, if we pray unto him?

Luke 12:18 ...And he said, This will I do: I will pull down my barns, and build greater; and there will I bestow all my fruits and my goods.
Luke 6:32 ...For if ye love them which love you, what thank have ye? for sinners also love those that love them.

Proverbs 20:23 ...Divers weights are an abomination unto the LORD; and a false balance is not good.

Exodus 20:15 ...Thou shalt not steal.

Exodus 20:16 ...Thou shalt not bear false witness against thy neighbour.

Proverbs 11:4 ...Riches profit not in the day of wrath: but righteousness delivereth from death.

Luke 12:20 ...But God said unto him, Thou fool, this night thy soul shall be required of thee: then whose shall those things be, which thou hast provided?

I Thessalonians 5:23 ...And the very God of peace sanctify you wholly; and I pray God your whole spirit and soul and body be preserved blameless unto the coming of our Lord Jesus Christ.

Genesis 3:19 ...In the sweat of thy face shalt thou eat bread, till thou return unto the ground; for out of it wast thou taken: for dust thou art, and unto dust shalt thou return.

Ezekiel 37:1-9 ...The hand of the LORD was upon me, and carried me out in the spirit of the LORD, and set me down in the midst of the valley which was full of bones, And caused me to pass by them round about: and, behold, there were very many in the open valley; and, lo, they were very dry. And he said unto me, Son of man, can these bones live? And I answered, O Lord GOD, thou knowest. 4Again he said unto me, Prophesy upon these bones, and say unto them, O ye dry bones, hear the word of the LORD. Thus saith the Lord GOD unto these bones; Behold, I will cause breath to enter into you, and ye shall live: And I will lay sinews upon you, and will bring up flesh upon you, and cover you with skin, and put breath in you, and ye shall live; and ye shall know that I am the LORD.

So I prophesied as I was commanded: and as I prophesied, there was a noise, and behold a shaking, and the bones came together, bone to his bone. And when I beheld, lo, the sinews and the flesh came up upon them, and the skin covered them above: but there was no breath in them. Then said he unto me, Prophesy unto the wind, prophesy, son of man, and say to the wind, Thus saith the Lord GOD; Come from the four winds, O breath, and breathe upon these slain, that they may live.

Revelation 20:15 ...And whosoever was not found written in the book of life was cast into the lake of fire.

Luke 16:24 ...And he cried and said, Father Abraham, have mercy on me, and send Lazarus, that he may dip the tip of his finger in water, and cool my tongue; for I am tormented in this flame.

Mark 9:44,46,48 ...Where their worm dieth not, and the fire is not quenched...Where their worm dieth not, and the fire is not quenched...Where their worm dieth not, and the fire is not quenched.

Mark 9:44,46,48 ...Where their worm dieth not, and the fire is not quenched...Where their worm dieth not, and the fire is not quenched...Where their worm dieth not, and the fire is not quenched.

Matthew 24:51 ...And shall cut him asunder, and appoint him his portion with the hypocrites: there shall be weeping and gnashing of teeth.

Isaiah 13:7 ...Therefore shall all hands be faint, and every man's heart shall melt...

Revelation 20:10 ...And the devil that deceived them was cast into the lake of fire and brimstone, where the beast and the false prophet are, and shall be tormented day and night for ever and ever.

Ecclesiastes 12:1 ...Remember now thy Creator in the days of thy youth, while the evil days come not, nor the years draw nigh, when thou shalt say, I have no pleasure in them;

Proverbs 1:8 ...My son, hear the instruction of thy father, and forsake not the law of thy mother...

Isaiah 66:24 ...And they shall go forth, and look upon the carcases of the men that have transgressed against me: for their worm shall not die, neither shall their fire be quenched; and they shall be an abhorring unto all flesh.

LAKE BURNING WITH FIRE AND BRIMSTONE
Isaiah 57:4 ...Against whom do ye sport yourselves? against whom make ye a wide mouth, and draw out the tongue? are ye not children of transgression, a seed of falsehood...

Revelation 3:16 ...So then because thou art lukewarm, and neither cold nor hot, I will spue thee out of my mouth.

Luke 16:24 ...And he cried and said, Father Abraham, have mercy on me, and send Lazarus, that he may dip the tip of his finger in water, and cool my tongue; for I am tormented in this flame.

Mark 9:48 ...Where their worm dieth not, and the fire is not quenched.

I Corinthians 6:10 ...Nor thieves, nor covetous, nor drunkards, nor revilers, nor extortioners, shall inherit the kingdom of God.

I Corinthians 3:17 ...If any man defile the temple of God, him shall God destroy; for the temple of God is holy, which temple ye are.

Revelation 22:11 ...He that is unjust, let him be unjust still: and he which is filthy, let him be filthy still: and he that is righteous, let him be righteous still: and he that is holy, let him be holy still.

Matthew 10:21-22 ...And the brother shall deliver up the brother to death, and the father the child: and the children shall rise up against their parents, and cause them to be put to death. And ye shall be hated of all men for my name's sake: but he that endureth to the end shall be saved.

Revelation 18:13 ...And cinnamon, and odours, and ointments, and frankincense, and wine, and oil, and fine flour, and wheat, and beasts, and sheep, and horses, and chariots, and slaves, and souls of men.

Daniel 2:43 ...And whereas thou sawest iron mixed with miry clay, they shall mingle themselves with the seed of men: but they shall not cleave one to another, even as iron is not mixed with clay.

I Timothy 1:9-10 ...Knowing this, that the law is not made for a righteous man, but for the lawless and disobedient, for the ungodly and for sinners, for unholy and profane, for murderers of fathers and murderers of mothers, for manslayers, For whoremongers, for them that defile themselves with mankind, for menstealers, for liars, for perjured persons, and if there be any other thing that is contrary to sound doctrine...

I John 3:15 ...Whosoever hateth his brother is a murderer: and ye know that no murderer hath eternal life abiding in him.

Proverbs 20:1 ...Wine is a mocker, strong drink is raging: and whosoever is deceived thereby is not wise.

Exodus 20:16 ...Thou shalt not bear false witness against thy neighbour.

Lamentations 3:22 ...It is of the LORD'S mercies that we are not consumed, because his compassions fail not.

II Corinthians 5:10 ...For we must all appear before the judgment seat of Christ; that every one may receive the things done in his body, according to that he hath done, whether it be good or bad.

Revelation 13:5 ...And there was given unto him a mouth speaking great things and blasphemies; and power was given unto him to continue forty and two months.

Revelation 14:9-10 ...And the third angel followed them, saying with a loud voice, If any man worship the beast and his image, and receive his mark in his forehead, or in his hand, The same shall drink of the wine of the wrath of God, which is poured out without mixture into the cup of his indignation; and he shall be tormented with fire and brimstone in the presence of the holy angels, and in the presence of the Lamb...

Revelation 17:12-13 ...And the ten horns which thou sawest are ten kings, which have received no kingdom as yet; but receive power as kings one hour with the beast. These have one mind, and shall give their power and strength unto the beast.

Isaiah 24:17 ...Fear, and the pit, and the snare, are upon thee, O inhabitant of the earth.

Luke 16:26 ...And beside all this, between us and you there is a great gulf fixed: so that they which would pass from hence to you cannot; neither can they pass to us, that would come from thence.

Isaiah 66:24 ...And they shall go forth, and look upon the carcases of the men that have transgressed against me: for their worm shall not die, neither shall their fire be quenched; and they shall be an abhorring unto all flesh.

Revelation 4:3 ...And he that sat was to look upon like a jasper and a sardine stone: and there was a rainbow round about the throne, in sight like unto an emerald.

Colossians 1:13 ...Who hath delivered us from the power of darkness, and hath translated us into the kingdom of his dear Son...

JUBILEE...THE EVERLASTING KINGDOM
Psalm 119:54 ...Thy statutes have been my songs in the house of my pilgrimage.

Psalm 149:4 ...For the LORD taketh pleasure in his people: he will beautify the meek with salvation.

Habakkuk 3:3 ...God came from Teman, and the Holy One from mount Paran. Selah. His glory covered the heavens, and the earth was full of his praise.

Revelation 20:4 ...And I saw thrones, and they sat upon them, and judgment was given unto them: and I saw the souls of them that were beheaded for the witness of Jesus, and for the word of God, and which had not worshipped the beast, neither his image, neither had received his mark upon their foreheads, or in their hands; and they lived and reigned with Christ a thousand years.

Psalm 67:1-4 ...To the chief Musician on Neginoth, A Psalm or Song. God be merciful unto us, and bless us; and cause his face to shine upon us; Selah. That thy way may be known upon earth, thy saving health among all nations. Let the people praise thee, O God; let all the people praise thee. O let the nations be glad and sing for joy: for thou shalt judge the people righteously, and govern the nations upon earth. Selah.

Psalm 67:5 ...Let the people praise thee, O God; let all the people praise thee.

Matthew 25:21,23 ...His lord said unto him, Well done, thou good and faithful servant: thou hast been faithful over a few things, I will make thee ruler over many things: enter thou into the joy of thy lord...His lord said unto him, Well done, good and faithful servant; thou hast been faithful over a few things, I will make thee ruler over many things: enter thou into the joy of thy lord.

Isaiah 65:17 ...For, behold, I create new heavens and a new earth: and the former shall not be remembered, nor come into mind.

Isaiah 49:13 ...Sing, O heavens; and be joyful, O earth; and break forth into singing, O mountains: for the LORD hath comforted his people, and will have mercy upon his afflicted.

Psalm 98:8 ...Let the floods clap their hands: let the hills be joyful together

Isaiah 44:23 ...Sing, O ye heavens; for the LORD hath done it: shout, ye lower parts of the earth: break forth into singing, ye mountains, O forest, and every tree therein: for the LORD hath redeemed Jacob, and glorified himself in Israel.

Revelation 5:10 ...And hast made us unto our God kings and priests: and we shall reign on the earth.

Hebrews 12:1 ...Wherefore seeing we also are compassed about with so great a cloud of witnesses, let us lay aside every weight, and the sin which doth so easily beset us, and let us run with patience the race that is set before us...

Hebrews 12:22 ...But ye are come unto mount Sion, and unto the city of the living God, the heavenly Jerusalem, and to an innumerable company of angels...

Psalm 147:11 ...The LORD taketh pleasure in them that fear him, in those that hope in his mercy.

Isaiah 62:5 ...For as a young man marrieth a virgin, so shall thy sons marry thee: and as the bridegroom rejoiceth over the bride, so shall thy God rejoice over thee.

Psalm 37:4 ...Delight thyself also in the LORD; and he shall give thee the desires of thine heart.

John 14:23 ...Jesus answered and said unto him, If a man love me, he will keep my words: and my Father will love him, and we will come unto him, and make our abode with him.
John 17 :21-24 ...That they all may be one; as thou, Father, art in me, and I in thee, that they also may be one in us: that the world may believe that thou hast sent me. And the glory which thou gavest me I have given them; that they may be one, even as we are one: I in them, and thou in me, that they may be made perfect in one; and that the world may know that thou hast sent me, and hast loved them, as thou hast loved me. Father, I will that they also, whom thou hast given me, be with me where I am; that they may behold my glory, which thou hast given me: for thou lovedst me before the foundation of the world.

CREATION OF A NEW UNIVERSE
Isaiah 65:17 ...For, behold, I create new heavens and a new earth: and the former shall not be remembered, nor come into mind.

Psalm 111:7-8 ...The works of his hands are verity and judgment; all his commandments are sure. They stand fast for ever and ever, and are done in truth and uprightness.

Jude 1:3 ...Beloved, when I gave all diligence to write unto you of the common salvation, it was needful for me to write unto you, and exhort you that ye should earnestly contend for the faith which was once delivered unto the saints.

John 14:23 ...Jesus answered and said unto him, If a man love me, he will keep my words: and my Father will love him, and we will come unto him, and make our abode with him.

Matthew 25:34 ...Then shall the King say unto them on his right hand, Come, ye blessed of my Father, inherit the kingdom prepared for you from the foundation of the world...

I Corinthians 2:9 ...But as it is written, Eye hath not seen, nor ear heard, neither have entered into the heart of man, the things which God hath prepared for them that love him.

Isaiah 11:9 ...They shall not hurt nor destroy in all my holy mountain: for the earth shall be full of the knowledge of the LORD, as the waters cover the sea.

I Peter 3:12 ...Looking for and hasting unto the coming of the day of God, wherein the heavens being on fire shall be dissolved, and the elements shall melt with fervent heat?

Micah 1:4 ...And the mountains shall be molten under him, and the valleys shall be cleft, as wax before the fire, and as the waters that are poured down a steep place.

Job 38:8-11 ...Or who shut up the sea with doors, when it brake forth, as if it had issued out of the womb? When I made the cloud the garment thereof, and thick darkness a swaddlingband for it, And brake up for it my decreed place, and set bars and doors, And said, Hitherto shalt thou come, but no further: and here shall thy proud waves be stayed?

Revelation 21:1 ...And I saw a new heaven and a new earth: for the first heaven and the first earth were passed away; and there was no more sea.

Romans 8:19-21 ...For the earnest expectation of the creature waiteth for the manifestation of the sons of God. For the creature was made subject to vanity, not willingly, but by reason of him who hath subjected the same in hope, Because the creature itself also shall be delivered from the bondage of corruption into the glorious liberty of the children of God.

Psalm 104:5 ...Who laid the foundations of the earth, that it should not be removed for ever.

Isaiah 52:7 ...How beautiful upon the mountains are the feet of him that bringeth good tidings, that publisheth peace; that bringeth good tidings of good, that publisheth salvation; that saith unto Zion, Thy God reigneth!

Nahum 1:15 ...Behold upon the mountains the feet of him that bringeth good tidings, that publisheth peace! O Judah, keep thy solemn feasts, perform thy vows: for the wicked shall no more pass through thee; he is utterly cut off.

Isaiah 24:20 ...The earth shall reel to and fro like a drunkard, and shall be removed like a cottage; and the transgression thereof shall be heavy upon it; and it shall fall, and not rise again.

Isaiah 66:22 ...For as the new heavens and the new earth, which I will make, shall remain before me, saith the LORD, so shall your seed and your name remain.

Psalm 112:3...Wealth and riches shall be in his house: and his righteousness endureth for ever.

Ecclesiastes 1:4 ...One generation passeth away, and another generation cometh: but the earth abideth for ever.

Revelation 22:2 ...In the midst of the street of it, and on either side of the river, was there the tree of life, which bare twelve manner of fruits, and yielded her fruit every month: and the leaves of the tree were for the healing of the nations.

Revelation 21:1 ...And I saw a new heaven and a new earth: for the first heaven and the first earth were passed away; and there was no more sea.

Revelation 21:2 ...And I John saw the holy city, new Jerusalem, coming down from God out of heaven, prepared as a bride adorned for her husband.

I Corinthians 15:25 ...For he must reign, till he hath put all enemies under his feet.

I Corinthians 15:28 ... And when all things shall be subdued unto him, then shall the Son also himself be subject unto him that put all things under him, that God may be all.

John 2:10 ...And saith unto him, Every man at the beginning doth set forth good wine; and when men have well drunk, then that which is worse: but thou hast kept the good wine until now.

Revelation 21:3-4 ...And I heard a great voice out of heaven saying, Behold, the tabernacle of God is with men, and he will dwell with them, and they shall be his people, and God himself shall be with them, and be their God. And God shall wipe away all tears from their eyes; and there shall be no more death, neither sorrow, nor crying, neither shall there be any more pain: for the former things are passed away.

Jeremiah 31:13-14 ...Then shall the virgin rejoice in the dance, both young men and old together: for I will turn their mourning into joy, and will comfort them, and make them rejoice from their sorrow. And I will satiate the soul of the priests with fatness, and my people shall be satisfied with my goodness, saith the LORD.

NOTES

www.ingramcontent.com/pod-product-compliance
Lightning Source LLC
LaVergne TN
LVHW081332060426
835513LV00014B/1257